EASTBOURNE 1851-1951

A SOCIAL HISTORY

BY

CLIVE GRIGGS

Grosvenor House
Publishing Limited

All rights reserved
Copyright © Clive Griggs, 2016

The right of Clive Griggs to be identified as the author of this
work has been asserted in accordance with Section 78
of the Copyright, Designs and Patents Act 1988

The book cover picture is copyright to Clive Griggs

This book is published by
Grosvenor House Publishing Ltd
28-30 High Street, Guildford, Surrey, GU1 3EL.
www.grosvenorhousepublishing.co.uk

This book is sold subject to the conditions that it shall not, by way of
trade or otherwise, be lent, resold, hired out or otherwise circulated
without the author's or publisher's prior consent in any form of binding or
cover other than that in which it is published and
without a similar condition including this condition being imposed
on the subsequent purchaser.

A CIP record for this book
is available from the British Library

ISBN 978-1-78623-728-6

To Sheila

Previous Books:-

The Trades Union Congress and the Struggle for Education 1868-1925 (1983)

Private Education in Britain (1985)

Education – The Wasted Years 1973-86 (1988)
Co-Editor with Max Morris

George Meek – Labouring Man: Protege of H.G. Wells (1996) with Bill Coxall

The TUC and Education Reform 1926-1970 (2002)

CONTENTS

Acknowledgements	ix
Abbreviations	xi
Precface	xiii
Introduction - Challenges to a Conservative Establishment	xv

Part 1 The 1850s to the early 20th Century — 1

Chapter 1 – Early Rural Disputes in Eastbourne and the surrounding area	3
Chapter 2 – Growth of the Town and Politics of Principal Landowners	11
Chapter 3 – Religious Institutions and Social Class	44
Chapter 4 – Schooling in the Eastbourne Area during the 19th Century	61

Part 2 The Edwardian Years — 103

Chapter 5 – Challenging the Powers that Be	105
Chapter 6 – Socialist Groups – Late 19th Century	136
Chapter 7 – Edwardian Days - 1901-1914	153
Chapter 8 – The 1914-1918 War	219

Part 3 – The Inter-War Years — 245

Chapter 9 – The Coal Industry and the 1926 General Strike	247
Chapter 10 – Competing Political Pressure Groups, 1930s	282
Chapter 11 – Conflicting Political Ideas – Left and Right	345
Chapter 12 - Hope for Peace – Prepare for War	386

Part 4 – Early Post-War Years 1945-1951   409

Chapter 13 - The War and Immediate Aftermath   411
Chapter 14 – Early Political and Social Progress   454

Appendices   501

Appendix 1 - Results of Parliamentary Elections – Eastbourne 1885-1951   501
Appendix 2 – Alphabetical List of Councillors and Aldermen (1945)   503
Appendix 3 – Results of Labour Candidates standing in Eastbourne Borough Elections 1913-1938   505
Appendix 4 – Eastbourne Trade Union and 'Labour' Organisations 1872-1930   507
Appendix 5 – Terms of Agreement for Reinstatement of Eastbourne Corporation Bus Staff – 1926   513

Bibliography   515

Index   523

ACKNOWLEDGEMENTS

I am grateful for the help afforded me from many people over a period of several years and I thank them all most sincerely. They include:-

Trevor Alston, Peggy Attlee, Francis Beckett, Dave Brinson, Roger Brown, Phillip Bye, Len Caine, Bill Coxall, Katy Cullen, Sheila Harper, Rosalind Hodge, Eileen Hollingdale, Trevor Hopper, Michael Partridge, Clive Ragsdale, Eve Riddington, Simon Russell, John Surtees, Hannah Williamson and Percy Wood. My thanks to Ian Whilde for proof reading the MS; Gordon Beckman, Sandy Medway and Paul Weisman for providing their computer skills when I most needed them.

I am also particularly grateful to the many librarians who have provided help in the search for much of the original material which has provided the major source for this book. They include staff from the following libraries:

Eastbourne Town Hall, East Sussex Records Office, Lewes; Manchester Art Gallery; Lambeth Palace; Queenwood
Library, University of Brighton.

Above all a special thanks to the Librarians in the Reference Section of Eastbourne Central Library who have located information I needed and regularly helped to master the ageing microfiche machines.

ABBREVIATIONS

ARP	Air Raid Precautions
ARW	Air Raid Wardens
ATS	Auxiliary Territorial Service (Women's Branch – British Army)
BBU	British Bible Union
BEF	British Expeditionary Force
BFSS	British and Foreign School Society
BMA	British Medical Association
BSP	British Socialist Party
BUF	British Union of Fascists
CORB	Children's Overseas Reception Board
CP	Communist Party of GB
CTA	Council Tenants Association
CUA	Conservative & Unionist Association
EBC	Eastbourne Borough Council
E. Chron.	*Eastbourne Chronicle*
EDTC	Eastbourne & District Trades Council
E. Gaz.	*Eastbourne Gazette*
E.Her.	*Eastbourne Herald*
ETULP	Eastbourne Trade Union & Labour Party
ILP	Independent Labour Party
LBSCR	London Brighton & South Coast Railway
LCC	London County Council
LRC	Labour Representation Committee
NCA	National Clerks Association
NCU	National Citizens' Union
NSPCK	National Society for Promoting the Education of the Poor in the Principles of the Church of England

RFC	Royal Flying Corps
SAC	School Attendance Committee
SDF	Social Democratic Federation
SEFSS	South East Federation of Socialist Societies
WEA	Workers Education Association

TRADES UNIONS:

AWU	Agricultural Workers Union
ASHP&D	Amalgamated Society of House Painters & Decorators
ASLEF & Firemen	Associated Society of Locomotive Engineers
ASRS	Amalgamated Society of Railway Servants
ATTI	Association of Teachers in Technical Institutions
AUBTW	Amalgamated Union of Building Trade Workers
AUOBC	Amal. Union Operatives, Bakers & Confectioners
BU	Boilermakers Union
BTOU	Building Trades Operative Union
DWU	Domestic Workers Union
MFGB	Miners Federation of G.B.
NCA	National Clerks Assoc.
NFWT	National Federation of Women Teachers
NUG&MWU	National Union of General & Municipal Workers Union
NUT	National Union of Teachers
NUR	National Union of Railwaymen
NUT	National Union of Teachers
NUVB	National Union of Vehicle Builders
RCA	Railway Clerks Association
TA	Typographical Assoc.
TGWU	Transport & General Workers Union
TUC	**Trades Union Congress**

PREFACE

There are numerous histories concerning Eastbourne. Some such as John Surtees's *'Eastbourne ; A History*, provide a wealth of detailed information from the mid-eighteenth century to the present day, whilst John Stevens's, short *History of Eastbourne* giving a brief overall account from Roman times to the 1960s, is probably the best place to begin for newcomers to the town. Among others there are wonderful detailed studies of particular aspects of the town's history; *Eastbourne's Historic Street Furniture* (1984), Graham Neville's (1982) *Religion and Society in Eastbourne 1735-1920*, Surtees's (1992)) *Barracks, Workhouse and Hospital; St Mary's – Eastbourne 1794-1900*, and Milton's (1995) *Origins of Eastbourne's Street Names*. All but the first are publications of the Eastbourne Local History Society. I have used all of these studies and others which appear in the bibliography.

They have all helped to build up a picture of the social and political forces at work in the town which were always more complex and controversial than a brief glance at the town's development might suggest. To go beyond what might be considered a familiar picture of a comfortable prosperous town it is important to examine the contents of the local newspapers where a range of reports draw attention to the complex pattern of life in different parts of the town. The *Eastbourne Chronicle, Gazette* and *Herald* provide a wealth of detailed information covering many of the of happenings relating to both local and national events, when the latter affected the life of the the town. For the most part these reports were far more objective than that to be found in national newspapers with only an occasional lapse when strong editorial views appeared, such as the disputes about a proposed National Government during the 1930s.

INTRODUCTION

Eastbourne – Challenges to a Conservative Establishment

For many people, Eastbourne will be regarded as both a conservative and Conservative town in much the same way as Bournemouth or Cheltenham. As with most generalisations there is some truth in this if one considers parliamentary representation alone. Conservative candidates were returned to Parliament for the period under consideration in every General Election except in the year of the Liberal landslide of 1906 when H.S. Beaumont broke the pattern. Even when governments stood under other titles, such as Coalition in 1918, R. Gwynne won the seat standing as a well known member of the Conservative Party. The two National Governments of 1931 and 1935 were also in reality Conservative; a fact reflected from E. Marjorybanks win by more than 25,000 votes over A.J Marshall who was standing for Labour, whilst in both the by-election and General Election of 1935, Charles Taylor, the Conservative candidate, was returned unopposed on both occasions.

However, such stark facts hide a far more complex picture of political views within the town and its immediate surroundings. It is not possible to gauge accurately the ideas of the majority of the population for a variety of reasons. During the 100 year period being examined it needs to be remembered that for much of the time the majority of adults were not enfranchised. For more than the first sixty years women were excluded from voting in Parliamentary elections. The 1832 Franchise Act had given the vote to little more than about 1 in 25 of the population; mainly middle class males. The 1867 Act enfranchised the urban working class males whilst that of 1884 expanded voting to most rural working class males. Women had to wait until 1918 for the vote and even then it was restricted to those over 30. It would be another ten years before they were on equal footing with men in this respect. It was almost impossible for working class people to consider standing for Parliament. There was a property qualification which was not abolished until 1858 and MPs did not receive a salary until 1911. Moreover, it was not until 1872 that the secret ballot was introduced which meant that in a small community a degree of intimidation prevailed for those whose livelihood depended upon an employer who might be openly supporting a political party opposed to that favoured by one of his employees. Even more so if the employee lived in a tied cottage. Social pressure in small communities remained a considerable force for conformity in all kinds of attitudes and activities. It was not until the 1948 Representation of the People Act that plural voting was abolished; a system which had allowed a minority of people to have a second vote if they held land or property in another constituency. University graduates had also been entitled to an extra vote. In 1969 the vote was granted to those over 18 years of age. As for the hereditary House of Lords, it remained as a conservative force throughout the years; hardly surprising given its membership.

It can be misleading to look for named organisations to record the level of resentment felt by ordinary people to what they might consider unduly harsh treatment and some-times individuals would try to resist policies forced upon them by officials of the State. One such example was the occasional defiance by individuals of the rules and regulations imposed upon them in organisations such as workhouses or the power exercised by landowners and landlords against some families who had little means to recourse.

For much of the time the Liberal Party was considered to be more sympathetic to the interests of the working classes in Britain. Among the few working class men who were elected to the House of Commons nearly all were leaders of emerging and expanding trade unions. They stood as candidates for the Liberal Party. (v. Chap. 3) Not all members or supporters of the Liberal Party approved of this situation but there were those who realised that these men were backed by substantial sections of the labour movement and increasingly as the nineteenth century came to a close, it became apparent that there were those within the trade union world who wished to establish a political party of their own. The leadership believed it was better to have them within the Liberal Party than as rivals in a competing political party; a situation which would nevertheless steadily emerge towards the end of the 19th century.

The term labour movement is usually used to cover a wide range of organisations; trade unions, the

Co-operative movement and various socialist organisations which came into being during the last quarter of the nineteenth century. Skilled workers had formed trade unions by the middle of that century often following bitter disputes with employers but there were also welfare and educational functions undertaken by many at a time when elementary education was neither well resourced nor compulsory, whilst secondary schooling, which usually required fees, was well beyond the reach of the majority of the population. Hence the buildings established by some trade unions as places for members to meet on both social occasions and at other times to discuss relevant political issues when the need arose. Guest speakers were often invited to talk on issues relevant to trade unionists both in the town and elsewhere. Many such places provided a library room containing newspapers and books as a means of further education in the broadest sense of the word. The trade union club in Seaside, Eastbourne, is a good example of such a building.

Rochdale in 1844 witnessed the opening of the first shop of the Cooperative Movement which was not just a matter of members sharing in the profits of the Society but just as important at the time, the need to provide unadulterated food for customers. (1) Whilst the principles of the Movement were widely discussed in the country it was not until 1887, after several earlier failed attempts, that the Brighton Equitable Co-operative Society was established. There were general rules for guidance within the movement, individual societies could have 'specials' and it is significant that Brighton chose to include 'the right of married women to be members'. (2)

One of the driving forces behind the Brighton Society was George Holyoake (1817-1906) who had known Robert Owen. He was born in Birmingham and was at one time a lecturer at the Mechanics Institute in that city. In response to a question raised by one of the audience at a lecture he was giving at the Cheltenham Institute, he was convicted of blasphemy; gaining the dubious distinction of being the last person in the country to face such a charge. As a result he suffered six months imprisonment for expressing his views and would later coin the term 'secularism'. He was editor of *The Oracle* and *The Movement* journals, wrote several histories of the Co-operative movement and served as President of the Brighton Co-operative for two spells during 1888-91 and 1895-1906. He devoted most of his life campaigning to spread co-operative principles.

Another key figure in Brighton who was an enthusiastic supporter of co-operatives was Dr William King (1786-1865). His father was a clergyman but after attending Westminster school, Oxford and Cambridge Universities, he trained as a doctor at St Bartholomew's Hospital in London before studying surgery in France. He settled in Brighton in 1821 and became concerned at the plight of the poor. He met with Elizabeth Fry, the campaigner who sought to improve the terrible conditions in the country's prisons and Lady Byron, widow of the poet. They were all influenced by Robert Owen's ideas of co-operatives and worked to develop such enterprises in Brighton, although like some others, they did not agree with all of Owen's ideas. King had reservations as to how far the environment was responsible in forming a person's character and Lady Byron, as a devout Christian, did not approve of his atheism. In

1828 King edited the first copy of *The Co-operator*, a monthly journal which ran for two years in which he explained the requirements needed to establish successful co-operative organisations. His writings were based upon the bitter experiences of those who tried to set up businesses attempting to follow Owen's ideas during the early nineteenth century, all of which failed. He explained the reasons for their failures and what was needed if they were to stand any chance of success when competing against shops and other businesses run as private enterprises. These early experiments, however short-lived, have given a measure of credence to the claim that Brighton was a town with some of the first co-operatives in the country even if they did not last as long as the successful shop in Rochdale.

Workhouses – the Victorian Solution to Poverty

Life for most people was hard and lacked security. For those unable to earn a sufficient income, the Speenhamland system of 1795 provided a minimum payment to supplement low wages and support large families by means of Parish Relief. In reality the origins of this system went back to Elizabethan times. It had helped to sustain the rural poor in particular but came under great strain as the thousands of servicemen who had fought against the French for more than 20 years, (with a brief interlude between 1802-1803), upon returning home to be demobilised, were unemployed and therefore sought Parish Relief. The local parishes could not cope and the Commission of Enquiry set up in 1832 with Edwin Chadwick as Secretary reported two years later, the result of which was the Poor Law Act of

1834. (3) Union Workhouses were established throughout the country and the poor seeking financial help could now only receive such assistance by entering the Workhouse. The intention was to ensure that the conditions of the inmates should be poorer than those of the meanest labourer. In that aim they were entirely successful. The system of Union Workhouses established for those seeking financial help meant that the families entering were split up within the institution; husbands, wives, and their children all in separate dormitories. When they were allowed out of the building to attend church or for some of the children to go to school their poverty was displayed for all to see through the grey uniform they wore.

Eastbourne's workhouse was situated on Church Street past St Marys Church, the opposite side of the road on the way out of town. It had been built in the last decade of the 18th century as a cavalry barracks. (4) As John Surtees has stated, in terms of basic food, hygiene and medical care, many inmates were physically better off than some of the poorest residents in the community who would rather go hungry and suffer the cold in Winter than enter the Workhouse. At the same time the whole system denied all dignity to the inmates, provided a heartless regime which devalued and degraded their individual humanity. At times it provided an opportunity for overseers to wield often arbitrary power over those in no position to defend themselves. The diet was monotonous; bread and gruel for breakfast and supper, bread and cheese for lunch. Misbehaviour by an inmate could be punished by their being restricted to only bread and water.

In 1835 some of the inmates at the Eastbourne Workhouse took action against the enforced separation of husbands and wives:

> '...a great disturbance in the Eastbourne Workhouse.
>
> The married persons in the house appear to have conspired to prevent the separation of man and wife. All the married women took advantage of the occasion of cleaning out the men's apartments and went to their husband's and they all resolutely refused to be again separated...The conduct of the parties has been most desperate: fortunately it happened to be the Board day, and the Guardians have (by force) succeeded in getting two of the worst characters (men) into the blackhole, some have been prevailed upon to be again separated, but the house still continues in great confusion. The Governor is protected for the night by the constables and head boroughs...(5)

In fact the local Guardians in the town did not approve of the families of inmates being separated but had to follow the general rules which arose from a fear, one might almost say an obsession, among some of the most prosperous and powerful in the country, that a major social and economic problem was the increasing numbers of pauper children in the country. From the workhouses some orphan children were sent to work in the textile mills of Lancashire enduring long hours and sometimes having to sleep under the looms. Others were sent abroad. George Meek's two younger brothers were sent to Eastbourne Workhouse by their mother who had fallen upon hard times. She sailed to New York to join her husband, Joe, a plasterer by trade, who had emigrated in 1872, leaving George behind with her grandparents. She was widowed when her husband died in a fire in the Brooklyn Theatre in which about 350 people lost their lives. She returned to England with two other sons, went to live with a cabman, and when her financial circumstances deteriorated, sent the two children to the Eastbourne Workhouse. From there they were sent to Melton Mowbray to learn a trade and then to Canada. They were only two of the children of poor means sent abroad as part of a movement which had started in 1618 when a group of orphaned and destitute children were sent to Richmond, Virginia, to reduce the demands upon rates in towns and people colonies with inhabitants from Britain. This child migration would continue until 1967 when the last group were sent to Australia. (6)

Within a short time of the workhouses opening, between the years 1837-1839, Charles Dickens wrote *Oliver Twist*, as an indictment of this aspect of the social system of Victorian Britain, to be followed by *Bleak House* (1852-53) and *Little Dorrit* (1855-57), respectively critiques of the Chancery Court and Debtors' Prisons. Dickens was not really political in most of his writings but he was scathing about the hierarchical structure of Victorian Society and believed that the system allowed an aristocratic minority to live a life of luxury through their exploitation of low paid working people, many of whom lived in wretched conditions. Feeding the poor cheaply was a continuing problem throughout these years and it does seem somewhat ironic that the Chief Cook to Queen Victoria should produce a book in 1852 entitled *A Plain Cookery Book for the Working Class* in which chapter 4 dealt with 'Economical and Substantial Soup for Distribution to the Poor'. Dickens saw the two-party political system as a means by which those in Parliament used their position to maintain a social order which benefited them and those in similar privileged positions.

What follows is an attempt to record aspects of life in Eastbourne and the immediate surrounding area which were as significant a part of town life as the splendid houses and buildings provided for the more prosperous inhabitants on the estates developed by the Dukes of Devonshire and the Gilberts. After all more people lived in the areas around Seaside than in the Meads. Their circumstances were considerably different in most aspects of their lives. At the same time they were probably more typical of the experiences of the majority of the country's population.

This study does not restrict itself only to Eastbourne town, which was inevitably influenced by developments within the surrounding area and indeed by events taking place throughout the whole country from time to time. For example the construction of the railway line linking the town to a growing railway network or the widespread support of many people for the 1926 General Strike in the town which ended with a rally at the Recreation Ground. One difference which might surprise some people thinking of the town in stereotypical terms was to find that most members of the town council spent considerable time discussing with trade unionists how best to resolve the situation with the strikers to enable them to return to work. This approach thereby avoided the hostile attitude which prevailed in some industrial areas.

The heavy bombing during World War 2 of a seaside town which was neither a military base nor involved with the manufacture of armaments led to the need to rethink of it as an ideal place to receive children and mothers from the London area which was suffering from the continued attention of the German air force. It soon became necessary not only to organise the re-evacuation of London children well away from the town but also to send the town's own children and mothers further afield. Yet like many other places there were sometimes aspects of policy by the most influential members within the town, which if not unique, were rather selfish, in terms of elementary school provision, when compared to almost every other town in the country. For example, during the 19th century the combined action of most religious groups and the dominant Conservative Party worked to prevent school boards being developed within the town; a policy undertaken by no more than 3 or 4 other urban areas in the whole country which led to the underfunding of local elementary schools before 1902.

What follows is not a complete and exhaustive covering of every element of Eastbourne life but rather an attempt to examine some of the major social and political developments within the town. It will doubtless come as a surprise to some to learn that during the 1926 Miners' Strike a fund was raised from public donations to the tune of £2,530 to support the families of miners; £1,000 of it being sent to the Lord Mayor's fund for general assistance in Wales. Rhymney was 'adopted' by Eastbourne and regular financial assistance sent to relieve distress in that town.

During the years covered by this study Eastbourne gained an increasing measure of civic and political independence. Under the Local Government Act of 1858 a local board for the parish of the town was elected the following year. The Local Board petitioned for incorporation under the 1882 Municipal Corporation Act and a Charter was granted to establish the Borough of Eastbourne the following year. County Borough status was gained in 1911 with an extension of the boundaries to take in a part of Willingdon.

References - Introduction

1) Burnett, J. (1968) *Plenty and Want; A Social History of Diet from 1815 to the Present Day.* p.245.
2) Richardson, W. [1985] *The People's Business; A History of Brighton Co-operative Society* p.50
3) v. Checkland, S.G. & E.O.A. (1971) *The Poor Law Report of 1834.*
4) For a detailed study of the history of Eastbourne's workhouse v. Surtees, J. (1992) *The Story of St Mary's Eastbourne 1794-1990*
5) Quoted in Surtees, J. *ibid.,* pp.20-21
6) v. Bean, P. & Melville, J. (1990) *Lost Children of the Empire.*

Part 1
The 1850s to the early 20th Century

CHAPTER 1

EARLY RURAL DISPUTES IN EASTBOURNE AND THE SURROUNDING AREA

Early disputes among agricultural workers

Sussex was primarily an agricultural county with little industrial development once the iron, timber and glass making industries of the Weald had declined during the eighteenth century. Production scattered across several areas of the County and into Kent had fed demand arising from coastal fishing boats, naval vessels in time of war and general building of timber framed constructions throughout the area. (1) Gradually however the larger deposits of coal and iron ore in the North of the country meant that southern counties could no longer compete with these 'new' areas of manufacturing and went into decline. In the first half of the nineteenth century the population almost doubled although there were considerable variations in the rate of growth, the most rapid being in the urban parishes near the coast, especially Brighton and to a lesser extent Hastings. Eastbourne, and other coastal towns such as Seaford and Worthing grew and visitors were attracted to them both as places in which to live and visit as the idea of sea bathing being good for health gained in popularity.

The building of railways to coastal resorts speeded up the increase in population in these coastal areas. For villages near to Eastbourne, such as East Dean, Folkington, Hankham, Jevington, Pevensey, Westham, Willingdon and Wilmington almost the only source of employment for men during the first half of the 19th century was to be found in various forms of agriculture. Without any regular means of local transport villages were more self-sufficient with bakers, butchers, general stores and dressmaking shops to cater for the needs of the inhabitants Walking was the main means of journeys between these villages. This was true for those working any distance from home, for some children to attend a school in a larger village, (often depending upon the demands for them to work) and for social occasions. In general people accepted that for many needs a walk of two or three miles was inevitable. Directories of the second half of the nineteenth century such as Gowlands, listing 'private occupants', shops and other residents, illustrate the steady decline in the rural population. Farming methods changed, migration to towns and overseas continued as people sought an alternative way of life with promises of a higher standard of living. Village shops closed and many elementary village schools had followed suit by the inter-war period. It needs to be borne in mind that the decline in village populations was not always a nineteenth century phenomenon for earlier factors such as the Plague in the 14th century had devastated communities to a level from which some never recovered. e.g. Alciston. (2)

Riots in Sussex – The Peasants Revolt 1381

Yet it would be wrong to assume that agricultural workers in the County were inevitably docile. There was a history of action in pursuit of what they regarded as fair treatment. It is probable that some took part in the Peasants' Revolt of 1381 for whilst most of them came from Essex and Kent, areas of East Sussex were also involved; 'All England south and east of a line drawn from York to Bristol had risen'. (3) There were riots on the Continent too and whilst 'all' is doubtless an exaggeration, this revolt was the best organised given the limited means of communication at the time. A sparsity of written evidence specifically confirming that the Eastbourne area was involved should not imply no action was taken. Many were illiterate and this was not a period of the recordings of events by agricultural workers. The Plague of 1348 is estimated to have reduced the population by about one third which gave those working on the land and many others an opportunity afforded by the shortage of labour to ask for increased payment of wages. Some land owners faced with harvest time, much to their annoyance, were forced to pay higher rates. The prime cause of the revolt was the introduction of a series of poll taxes between 1377-80, especially the last of one shilling a head, three times that of earlier increases, to finance war with France. Conflicts arose between the peasants, the tax collectors and justices trying to enforce compliance. (4) The revolt was exceptional in its intensity, length and broad appeal. It was joined by many people from the towns. An increasing criticism of those associated with the Church was also an underlying source of discontentment; an attitude made apparent in Geoffrey Chaucer's (c1333-1400) *Canterbury Tales*, on which he was working during the late 1380s.

Jack Cade Rebellion of 1450

There is no evidence to suggest anything like a similar measure of support for the rebellion of Jack Cade in 1450. All that can be said for certain is that he was hunted down, wounded about 14 miles north of Eastbourne and died on his way to London. He was hung, drawn and quartered. A monument marks his death on the outskirts of Heathfield not far from the *Jack Cade* public house, with a harsh declaration concerning his fate: 'Thus be success of all rebels, and this fortune chanceth ever to traitors.' Shakespeare in *Henry VI Part 2 Act 1V* deals with him just as unsympathetically.

Captain Swing

During the years leading up to 1830 there was discontent among many working people in rural areas who worked on the land. Much of the South East was given over to cereal production which meant there were times when labour was in considerable demand and times when there was less work to do on farms. Hence those employed regularly with an element of security did not receive high wages whilst casual workers might be better paid when employed but received no income when their services were no longer required. By contrast, in the North and Midlands, industry and mining were competing for labour just as fishing fleets were in coastal areas, so that farmers had to offer higher rates of pay to compete with these other occupations. London was always an exception, able to attract staff for certain occupations by offering higher rates of pay although conditions for the large number of unskilled who lived in squalid conditions were very poor. Prices for wheat had fallen since the boom times of the Napoleonic wars. (5)

Unemployment rose, parish relief became overburdened, wages were forced down, and the introduction of steam-driven threshing machines on some farms reduced demand for labour even further. Rural communities in the South East were becoming desperate. Whereas in past years some farm workers had boarded in the farmer's house receiving meals rather than being rewarded only by wages, farmers began to find it cheaper to end this practice and hire workers by the hour. If the weather was inclement and work could not be undertaken the farmer did not have to pay, but this also meant hired labour received no pay. There were farmers who resisted the introduction of machinery and in particular resented the enforced payment of the tithe, one tenth of their income to the established church. Faced with deteriorating circumstances some rural workers began to take action. In general this took one of three forms at night; threshing machines were destroyed, hayricks were burned and threatening letters sent to farmers and landowners. These became known as the Captain Swing riots, the name often left at the scene of destruction.

Brede was the original centre of riots in Sussex but they were soon widespread from Crowborough in the north to Worthing on the south coast. Areas nearer to Eastbourne which experienced Captain Swing riots included Lewes, Ringmer and Robertsbridge.

In Eastbourne Davies Gilbert mentioned the 'firing of his hayricks on his Sussex estates in the Autumn of 1830,' (6) believed to be attributed 'to the oppression of the unemployed.') One very early attempt at organisation in a rural area was the Alfriston Club in 1792 when farm labourers sought 'to compel their masters to augment their wages'. Another case was due to 'the formation of a Labourers' Union at Rye, Eastbourne and Winchelsea' (8) This would have been quite unusual because several earlier attempts to organise trade unions among agricultural workers in the country had failed and it would be more than forty years on before the first successful such union was established by Joseph Arch and Thomas Parker in Warwickshire in 1872. Even then it was strongly resisted by farmers and landowners who evicted workers and their family from tied cottages if they joined the union. (9) Indeed in June 1782 'Farmer Garrett of Tadmarton in North Oxfordshire...... flogged a middle-aged labourer (Isaac Bodfish) in his employ because he had joined the Union. (10)

The Captain Swing riots which peaked in 1830 led to many rumours as to both who Swing was and the rioters. Talk of suspicious strangers in public houses was familiar but in reality, as the court records show, for the three major offences for which people were convicted, the vast majority were agricultural labourers, although their leaders were often craftsmen who accounted for 142 out of 1000 prisoners whose occupations were recorded from 19 counties. It is interesting to see how often shoemakers were found to be among the more radical thinkers in the community. George Meek when he was twelve years of age and living in Willingdon related how 'a friendly shoemaker- a strong Radical and atheist, who lent me books – told me the Liberals were the friends of the poor working people. I became an ardent Liberal.' (11)

Of those who wrote threatening letters four were labourers, one an attorney's clerk and two were school masters. (The prison and judicial records show that of nearly 2000 persons tried in 13 counties, a quarter were transported to Australian colonies including three married men sent to Tasmania who left their wives in England 'on the Parish' rates. (12) The vast majority of participants did not have criminal records although convictions were found among some 'for typically rural offences – poaching, trespass, bastardy, cutting fences'. (13) Most were working people within the local community who were acting for the right to work and earn a living wage. To give some idea of the extent of the riots in Sussex there are references to 63 different places in the County in the 'Index of Places' which appear at the end of Hobsbawm and Rude's major study of the riots. Incidents are recorded 13 times in Battle and on 6 occasions in Lewes.

The East Sussex Special Assizes opened at Lewes on 20th December 1830, and from then until the Easter sessions of 1831, 52 men and women were tried by five separate courts in both parts of the county; here the toll was one execution (for arson), 16 jail sentences, 17 sentenced to transportation and 18 acquittals. (14) Transportation to Australia meant a 12,000 mile sea voyage which took on average 120 days with the almost certain fate that they would never be able to return to their home in England. Whilst the food was deemed to be adequate on board, discipline was harsh; they could be put in irons or flogged. Whilst most escaped this fate it became a regular feature of life for the most trivial of offences if they were unfortunate enough to be sent on arrival to 'the penal hells of Port Arthur in Tasmania and Northfolk Island off the coast of New South Wales.' Transportation was used as a punishment instead of the death penalty!

References – Chapter 1

(1) Leslie, K. & Short, B. pp.62-63
(2) c. Vigar, J. *The Lost Villages of Sussex*
(3) Morton, A.L. & Tate, G. *A Peoples' History of England*, p.112
(4) Morgan, K.O. [Ed] *The Oxford History of Britain*, pp.206-207
(5) Hobsbawm, E. & Rude, G. *Captain Swing*, p.10
(6) Todd, A.C. *Beyond the Blaze*, p.258
(7) Hobsbawm, E. & Rude, G. *op.cit.* p.54
(8) ibid. p.244
(9) Horn, P. *Joseph Arch 1826-1919; The Farmworkers' Leader.* A photograph of a family being evicted because the father was a trade unionist can be seen facing p.42.
(10) Horn, P. *ibid.* pp. 59-60
(11) Meek, G. *George Meek – Bath Chair-Man by himself* p.34
(12) Hobsbawm, E. & Rude, G., *op.cit.* pp.209-211
(13) ibid.
(14) ibid. p.244

CHAPTER 2

GROWTH OF THE TOWN AND POLITICS OF THE PRINCIPAL LANDOWNERS

The main areas of settlement, Sea Houses, Old Town, Meads and Coastguard Cottages gradually merged as the population, which was 1,760 in 1801, almost doubled to 3,433 within 50 years. Over the next 30 years it had increased more than six-fold to reach 22,014 in 1881. This entitled it to County Borough status, which was granted in 1883. The rapid growth during the second half of the 19th century resulted from two developments which reciprocated the success of each other. One was the extension of the L.B.S.C.R. line which progressed in stages. It reached Polegate in 1849 but travellers then required a horse-drawn vehicle to reach Eastbourne. In 1862 a single line track provided a link to the town, until finally in 1868, the town was fully connected to the railway system. A replacement station was now needed to cope with the increased traffic and the large impressive Victorian Station was completed in 1886. (1) The railway stimulated trade for some albeit at the expense of others. The stage coaches ceased to operate and coastal shipping of bulk goods, especially coal, went into decline. Freight trains were faster and more flexible. They could carry coal from the North of England, detach several wagons at different marshalling yards en route before carrying on to their final destination in the South, be it Eastbourne, Brighton or Hastings. By comparison, coastal shipping was slower and more likely to be affected adversely by poor weather resulting in delay and less reliability. The railway was able to bring a greater variety of goods and provide a wider range of items for sale in shops.

The second event was the planned development of the town. There were three principal landowners; the rectoral glebe of 178 acres, the Gilbert Estate of 956 acres and by far the largest, the Cavendishes with 3,526 acres. (2) The last two estates were both partly the result of 'advantageous marriages'. Davies Giddy from Cornwall was a distinguished mathematician but he was not wealthy when he married Mary Anne Gilbert of Eastbourne in 1807 and inherited her estates. He took the name of Gilbert on the death of her uncle in 1816. Lady Elizabeth Compton Peters, an only child of the Earl of Northampton, married Lord George Augustus Cavendish, younger son of the 4th Duke of Devonshire in February 1782. By this means her Sussex estates came to the Cavendishes. It was her grandchild, William the second Earl of Burlington who would become the 7th Duke of Devonshire. Land speculation also added to their extensive holdings. (3) These together with other properties they owned meant that the family were amongst the biggest landowners in the country.

The Gilbert estates were mainly north of the railway station. The Cavendishes stretched from the Downs in the West along the coast to the Langney area in the East, including much of the hinterland. The strategic position of their holdings provided them with the opportunity to plan the major part of the town; including the seafront whose development they were able to control. Almost all towns develop with housing in districts which reflect the differences in the income and wealth of the occupants. For Eastbourne planned development was built purposely with social distinctions clearly in mind.

As George Wallis, the agent for the Devonshires explained:

> ...there would be the extension of good large houses in one direction; and there would be the extension of smaller houses in another direction; and they are not mixed up. We have what we call our artisan town; we have our high class villa town; and we have our terrace houses; and they are all quite separate...(4)

The entertainment and shopping area which included the Devonshire Park Theatre and Sea Water Swimming Baths, the Winter Gardens and Terminus Road, formed a triangular wedge dividing the Meads area from the Seaside Road area to the East and as the town expanded in that direction so the terraced houses became smaller, the density of housing greater and streets narrower, reflecting the lower incomes of the residents. Hence the planning of the town in zones accepted that the higher income groups would need skilled building workers, tradesmen and women to serve in shops, laundries and work as domestic servants but ensured that as far as possible, any given association would be formal and largely restricted to that of master and servant. Given the town's layout, any other form of contact was more likely to be by accident rather than design.

The geography of the town only served to reinforce the planning policy of Eastbourne by its principal landowners and it is worth quoting Cannadine at length to illustrate this effect:

> To the south-west, ascending the wooded, undulating slopes towards Beachy Head, and basking in the reflected glory of proximity to Compton Place, were to be found those opulent houses, costing between ten thousand pounds, which belonged to Eastbourne's wealthiest inhabitants – those rentiers, retired professionals and local big businessmen who made up the town's elite. The cliffs and western parades protected them from the beach, and the grounds of Eastbourne College and the Parks and Baths Company effectively insulated them from the noise and bustle of the central entertainments area. That in turn was located between the railway station and the shore, and included the promenades, the bandstand, the pier, hotels and winter gardens. Finally, beyond the pier, on relatively low-lying ground, were located those few service industries – laundries, builders' yards and so on – and the artisan quarter itself, which consisted of houses of less than £500, built by speculative builders. Here was to be found a considerable working-class population of servants, builders, labourers and artisans. Yet as contemporaries noted, these communities were "all quite separate". The central area was rigidly defined. Its western extremity, the Grand Hotel, marked the transition to high-class residential housing. And the eastern end, the massive Queen's Hotel served to block any possible encroachment of working-class housing. (5)

Weather also provided an additional influence on the zoning of towns in many parts of the country and not just in Eastbourne. At a time when coal was the major source of heating hundreds of chimneys from homes, hotels and many other businesses were pouring smoke out into the atmosphere. Given that the prevailing winds in Britain were from the south-west, pollution moved in that direction most of the time taking fumes from the western to eastern areas of towns and cities. At the very least it is possible to suggest that it reinforced the differences in social housing in the development of so much of 19th century urban Britain. There are doubtless exceptions to this general observation but cities and towns as diverse as London, (Kensington and the East End), Brighton (Hove and Kemp Town) and Eastbourne (Meads and Langney) provide some evidence for this view.

Differences in wealth and income permeated every aspect of life in Victorian Britain forming the background to the stories of many novelists of the time; Charles Dickens (1867-1870), Elizabeth Gaskell (1810-1865) and John Galsworthy (1867-1933). In the first half of the 19th century, wealth, (preferably linked to an aristocratic background) and possession of land, were considered to be the most desirable social position in which to be and this comes through clearly in the novels of Jane Austen (1775-1817) such as *Sense and Sensibility* (1811) and particularly in *Pride and Prejudice* (1813).

This situation was steadily challenged by those who gained their wealth from industry and trade as the century progressed, much to the dismay of some of the former who found their power in decline in spite of inherited titles to which they clung, often providing them with a seat in the House of Lords, providing they were male! The middle classes formed a comparatively small but growing proportion of the population, earning respect from their professions in general but tinged with a certain degree of mistrust if they were involved with legal matters, if only because the lay person was unable to understand the practices they undertook. Skilled workers, the 'aristocracy of labour', who had served a lengthy apprenticeship of five or seven years, were better paid and less likely to be unemployed than the large army of 'unskilled' workers who performed many of the manual jobs; railway construction, working on building sites, in the mines and on the land. Among women who worked in 1841 about half were in domestic service and during the last decade of the 19th century there were more servants in the country than there were coal miners as the middle classes also began to employ non-residential domestic servants. The lives of the 'respectable' aspiring middle classes were successfully satirised by the Grossmith brothers in their book *The Diary of a Nobody* (1892). During times of economic downturn thousands of working people emigrated to North America, Australia, New Zealand and South Africa in the hope of a better life.

Apart from the 178 acres of rectoral Glebe lands the two major land owners in Eastbourne were the Gilbert and Devonshire families. The Gilberts had other holdings in the county and a further 2895 acres in Cornwall but by far the largest landowners were the Devonshires, who owned the strategic coastal stretch which would enable them to plan so much of the town. The Devonshires' land holdings were acquired according to David Cannadine through 'advantageous marriages and land speculation'. (6) In earlier years the Gilbert and Cavendish family represented different political views; Carew Davies Gilbert was President of the local Conservative Association whilst Edward Cavendish was President of the Liberals. To some extent these were almost honourable positions for Cavendish certainly did not hold strong political views. By the 1890s the 8th Duke, Spencer Compton Cavendish (1833-1908) was an active member of the Conservative Party.

Davies (Giddy) Gilbert (1767-1839)

Davies Giddy was born in Cornwall in 1767. His father, Edward was educated at Truro School, Christ Church College, Oxford and after considerable indecision as to a future career he became a curate at St Erth, eight years later marrying Catherine Davies. (7) Profiting from certain investments he moved to Penzance and sent Davies to the Corporation Grammar School. When Catherine inherited a substantial house in St Erth they returned and the boy's education was continued at home by his father, who worked to instil in him a form of morality which was to underly certain aspects of his behaviour for the remainder of his life. For those people he knew in poor circumstances he was kind and helpful as was evident from his personal dealings with those in his employ and living nearby in Cornwall. By contrast, for the large numbers who were unemployed following the end of the Napoleonic wars when thousands of discharged servicemen returned to the country or those who suffered a similar fate from widespread fluctuations in trade, especially the textile industries, he showed little compassion.

When 17 years of age he was sent to the Mathematical Academy of Benjamin Donne at Bristol before going to Pembroke College Oxford, only to find his father decided to share his room whilst he was attending Christchurch to study for his MA; an action which for all its good intentions prevented Giddy from sharing in the life of an undergraduate. He studied a wide variety of subjects including astronomy, chemistry, natural history and in particular, mathematics. He was an outstanding scholar but these were years when a large proportion of the teaching staff were both incompetent and idle; Giddy was not alone among the serious scholars in being highly critical of the teaching of certain members of staff. His marked ability in maths brought him into contact with leading scientists of the time including James Watt, Richard Trevithick working on steam engines and Humphrey Davy, also from Cornwall who would design the miners' safety lamp. As an undergraduate he was introduced to Sir Joseph Banks, President of the Royal Society, who had been with the navigator James Cook on his voyages to Australia and New Zealand. His attendance at the lectures of leading scientists of the day and his own studies led to the fulfilment of an early ambition; to be elected to membership of the Royal Society. He achieved this in 1792 while still only 25 years of age. His calculations on the Catenary curve in relation to the design of the chains for suspension bridges were the subject of a paper in the *Philosophical Transactions* and were used for the Menai Bridge. It was therefore as a leading intellectual that he first became known before turning his attention to the political scene. (8)

Like many of his generation he had first welcomed the French Revolution of 1789. Whilst an undergraduate at Oxford he had met Tom Paine (1737-1809), author of *The Rights of Man*, who was by then fifty years of age. Paine had been an Excise Officer in Lewes several years earlier before being dismissed for writing a pamphlet in support of higher wages. Gilbert's enthusiasm for the new ideas emanating from revolutionary France were still evident in 1792 by his wearing of the red, white and blue cockade on his return to Oxford but these sympathies were about to undergo a considerable change. When only 24 years of age he was made Sheriff of Cornwall. Whilst not doubting his intellectual ability the appointment to such offices depended primarily upon social background and acceptance of the political views of the most dominant groups in the area. Shortly afterwards he was informed that 300 hungry tin miners were marching on Looe to seize a shipment of corn. He had no hesitation in calling out the militia guard in the town. On this occasion he also promised each miner one shilling to buy grain. Three weeks later faced with a similar situation he dealt with the matter in a different manner; no money was offered and a round of grapeshot fired to persuade them to return home. (9) He was MP for Heston 1804-1806 and for Bodmin 1806-1832; both elections taking place before the 1832 Reform Act when fewer than one in fifty males had the vote. Once Pitt had declared war on France, Giddy found Paine's views on equal rights for women and opposition to slavery not only revolutionary but unpatriotic.

In 1803 he was approached about becoming MP for Heston. The price was £5,000 to be paid by Major Nicholson and himself to Sir Christopher Hawkins who then obtained the signatures of the mayor, four aldermen and five freemen. Within two years he was persuaded to stand down in favour of Sir John Shelley who could afford to pay more to Sir Christopher! By way of compensation he was promised another seat when it became vacant. Bodmin became available and in November 1806 he was back in Parliament and would remain in that seat for the next 27 years.

Politically he moved sharply to the right. Alongside a belief that people should be contented with the place in Society to which they had been born, he also thought they should be encouraged to help themselves, an idea which would be strongly associated later with Samuel Smiles (1812-1904). Alongside many among the upper classes he was frightened of the masses of poor people who might turn against the wealthier members of society. He was completely against the use of the Poor Law to deal with the widespread unemployment following the Napoleonic Wars: 'Inevitably the judgement was made that the industrious worked to provide for the idle and shifty, and this was on the whole the opinion of Gilbert. 'He was one of those who subscribed to the view that the poorest in intellect and character would always be the poorest in possessions, and that nothing should be done to alter the picture of the rich man at his castle and the poor man at his gate, for had not God so ordered their estate?' (10) He was one of many Tories opposed to the spread of education. When Samuel Whitbread, the Liberal-Whig leader introduced a Bill in 1807 to the House of Commons to establish parish schools throughout the country Davies Giddy spoke out against such a proposal:

> However specious in theory the project might be of giving education to the labouring classes of the poor,

it would, in effect, be found to be prejudicial to their morals and happiness; it would teach them to despise their lot in life, instead of making them good servants in agriculture, and other laborious employments to which their rank in society had destined them; instead of teaching them subordination, it would render them factious and refractory, as was evident in the manufacturing counties; it would enable them to read seditious pamphlets, vicious books and publications against Christianity; it would render them insolent to their superiors; and, in a few years, the result would be, that the legislature would find it necessary to direct the strong arm of power towards them. (11)

The Poor Law was under massive strain and Gilbert wanted to see it abolished but without some form of payment to the thousands of unemployed the harsh economic reality would have been 'nothing less than the severe remedy of throwing the unemployed on the labour market to fend for themselves, whilst the families were protected from the extremities of starvation by the parish. Fending for themselves meant looking for work where none existed. (12) Given these general views it will be no surprise to learn that Gilbert opposed the 1832 Reform Act which proposed extending the franchise to about one in twenty-five middle class males and getting rid of the corruption resulting from numerous 'rotten boroughs'.

At the end of his Parliamentary career he boasted he had been returned to the House of Commons nine times without opposition; once for Helston, eight times for Bodmin. This was true but as only a few men were eligible to vote and payments, in reality bribes, were required, this was not much of an achievement. Having initially opposed the 1832 Reform Act he later provided a measure of support when he considered it might be a barrier against 'the friends of anarchy and confusion'. (13) In his journal he quoted a newspaper report which read. 'Mr Gilbert, throughout his parliamentary life, voted, without a single exception that I can trace, for every measure now deemed corrupt and infamous, and against every measure esteemed pure and pragmatic.'(14)

His appointment to various learned societies was a result of his proven knowledge and skills; his Parliamentary career a matter of patronage. When it comes to the former, even in his membership of the Royal Society, patronage also played some part although in this regard that was true of most institutions in these years. It was his traditional views which made his resignation as President almost inevitable. As with many societies there was bickering between factions each pushing for their own point of view, sometimes plotting to influence the way the Society should develop. From May 1829 all new fellows had to pay in addition to the £10 admission fee a composition payment of £40 with older members encouraged to convert their £4 fee to a similar amount. Charles Babbage (1791-1871), the mathematician and inventor of the mechanical computer, commented that 'the amount of the subscription is too large', accordingly, 'membership still depended on wealth and social prestige, conformity to a constitution which was antiquated and no longer met the needs of the time.' (15) Gilbert thought he should have the right to appoint his successor and wished for the Duke of Sussex, one of the King's brothers, to succeed him. The members believed the new President should be elected.

Scientists wanted the Society to be restricted to those for whom science was a full-time occupation rather than including interested amateurs. Gilbert resisted these suggestions believing that the past ways of patronage should be followed. In reality too many social changes had taken place for his ideas to be accepted any more. 'For Gilbert the only rights were those which were earned by the exercise of ability in service of man and society. And if one asked how that ability could be recognised, there was only one answer; through property.' (16) His views were illustrated well by his family motto: 'Die rather than change'.

Mary Ann Gilbert (1776-1845)

He married Mary Ann Gilbert in 1808 at Northian, Sussex. She was the second largest landowner in Eastbourne. He took her uncle's name, Gilbert, eight years later in order to inherit her estates. He was generally regarded as reactionary in his political views; by contrast she was progressive and compassionate towards the lower income groups. She set up a pilot scheme of allotments on waste land at Beachy Head which she had inherited from her father and owned jointly with her husband. In this scheme 'she employed 27 paupers... who drained marshland and brought wasteland under cultivation. The paupers also produced a healthy crop of potatoes from the newly cultivated land and, seeing the possibilities, were keen to rent the land from Mrs Gilbert.' (17) Her scheme of land reclamation was designed to enable 200 paupers to rent land from her on which they produced potatoes, turnips and manglewurzels. Some also kept cows and pigs. The result was that they were able to pay their rent through their own hard work. Gilbert also supported the idea because it fitted in well with his belief in self-help. The scheme was successful and she provided evidence to show that it was cheaper than providing parish relief. She was a very progressive woman and became a member of the Labourers' Friendly Society and later secretary of the Society for Improving the Conditions of the Labouring Classes, arguing that rural poverty could best be resolved by renting out land to unemployed farm workers.

She sent a report on her scheme to Richard Whately (1787-1863), Archbishop of Dublin. He had been professor of politics and economics at Oxford and his writings in the social sciences were well known. They included views which were hostile to trade unionists and appeared in text books still being used in Church of England National Society elementary schools long after Whately had died. One passage read:-

> Many 'submit to be ruled by tyrants who do not allow them to choose how they shall employ their time or their skill or their strength. These unhappy persons are those who have anything to do with trade unions and combinations. There will generally be found among the workmen some able and ill-disposed persons who feel envy, and endeavour to excite others against everyone who earns more than the usual wages. In this way they often persuade a great number of their fellow workers to form themselves into a combination and appoint these agitators under the title of committee men. The business of these committee men is to make laws for the government of the combination, and to punish all who break them.

Objections were raised at these writings in school text books at the Trades Union Congresses of 1879 and 1880 resulting in correspondence with the NSPCK with a view to having these text books removed. It is difficult to believe that given the general level of basic education in elementary schools and the infrequent attendance of pupils at the time how Whately had been able to persuade the SPCK Committee, 'that the children of the lower orders should be acquainted with political economy …dealing with titles of money, Exchange Commerce, Coin Value, Wages, Rich and Poor, Capital, Taxes, Lettings and Hirings'. His approach not only lacked any attempt at political objectivity but was completely unsuited in terms of comprehension to the age range of most of the children concerned; namely an exposition of classical economics. (18)

There was opposition from some landowners who feared that independent farm workers would not be available for casual seasonal work. However, Mary Gilbert proved a formidable advocate of improved methods of husbandry to help farm workers, advising them to install water butts, stack wheat on stone piles, stall-feed cows and fork soil. In an attempt to prevent rural workers 'wasting' their earnings on alcohol she produced a list showing what the price of two glasses of gin a day would pay for over a year; a man's cotton shirt, a pair of women's shoes or a pair of blankets. By 1835 there were 213 tenants most of whom were able to pay their rents from their work on the allotments. In 1840 she established two agricultural schools in nearby Eastbourne villages; one at Willingdon and the other at East Dean. The children of allotment holders who attended were taught reading, writing, account keeping,

Bible studies and husbandry. Teachers received an income from the small weekly fee paid by the pupils.

The *Sussex Advertiser* in 1844 devoted almost a complete broadsheet page to some of the problems facing agriculture in the country, drawing attention to experiments in allotment systems being tried in various areas and focusing in particular upon that being pioneered by Mary Gilbert. They wrote a report on a visit they paid to the self-supporting industrial schools, established at Willingdon and East Dean, by Mrs Gilbert

> There a single simple principle is made at once the basis and proof of its own truth, namely, that, the industrial occupation of a few hours in the afternoon upon the land, will nearly or entirely discharge the cost of the school-tuition of a given number of pupils and add a branch of instruction not less valuable to the scholars....The Willingdon self-supporting school is a neat little cottage building, combining, in a very small compass, the attributes of dwelling-house, school, dairy, cowhouse, with thrashing floor above, and various conveniences attached. The roof is surrounded by gutters, that convey the rain-water into a large tank, so that it is not only not wasted, but prevented from running away on the land. (19)

It needs to be remembered that there was no state system of primary or secondary schooling in the country at the time, only an annual grant to the two major religious groups of the time, namely the Church of England and Nonconformists, to subsidise the elementary schools they had established. Roman Catholic Schools did not receive a subsidy until 1845. Hence the system of self-supporting schools she established described by the report mentioned above needs to be seen against this background.

> Our visit was made at half-past one, in ignorance of the hours of the school, which was afterwards found to be from nine till twelve, the afternoon work commencing at two, and continuing till five: on entering the house we found the master, his wife, and children, and a stranger, seated at dinner, having before them pudding or dumpling, potatoes, and a by no means despicable piece of hot bacon. Finding the master so well occupied, we of course retired, leaving him to finish his repast, while we inspected the outbuildings. We first entered the cow-house, where we discovered two little fellows about seven years of age, waiting to go to work. Their proper hour was two o'clock, but there they were, spade in hand, ready for their afternoon's work. These children were the picture of strong and ruddy health and of thorough cheerfulness, and certainly quite reversed the usual order of things by the evident alacrity with which they came to their work, *before their proper time.* They were shortly joined by some more *playmates,* for though it was work, in one sense, it certainly was not in another, and they proceeded in a body and commenced digging on the ground allotted for their afternoon's employment. On questioning them we found that there was only one boy above nine years old, and he was the eldest son of the master. There were about a dozen children in all, and they were chiefly under 8, one even being but four years of age.

There is no doubting Mary Gilbert's good intentions to provide a number of children with information about modern farming methods, practical skills to carry them out and basic schooling. Yet when one considers the ages of those in the school, a century later, the four year old would have been too young to even be registered at an infant school whilst all the others would have only been two years into their junior school education. Child labour was the common experience of working class children in the Victorian age whether it be in factories, down coal mines, selling cheap goods on street corners, working on barges on the canal network or in the fields. When the beginnings of an elementary schooling system began to take place following the 1870 Education Act, the education of rural children was frequently undermined by irregular attendance, partly as a result of inclement weather and partly from the practice of work in the countryside having preference over school attendance. Such practices are recorded in school log books for most months of the year from tending cows and gathering acorns for pigs to beating for the local hunt, and in the case of older girls, carrying out housework for the local vicar, the very person who as chairperson of the local NSPCK School was supposed to encourage pupil attendance.

Carew Davies Gilbert (1852-1913)

Carew Davies Gilbert was the grandson and only two years of age when he inherited the Gilbert Estate so that his mother acted as guardian until 1872 when he came of age. In 1881 he married Grace Catherina Rosa, and they both spent a good deal of their time at Trelissick in Cornwall where he served as a magistrate. They travelled widely in Europe and South East Asia. He left the management of his Eastbourne estate to a steward but involved himself with the town by providing land for Princess Alice hospital which opened in 1883 and the churches of St Anne's, Norway Mission and St George's. He sold Gildredge Park to the Corporation in 1909. Like his father he was an ardent Conservative, President of the Eastbourne Division and founded the *Conservative Review* in 1885 in support of the local party. A lengthy obituary to Gilbert appeared in the *Eastbourne Chronicle*. He was described by the newspaper as an, 'ardent and loyal Churchman...In politics a Conservative of very decided and settled convictions, he was always an active and generous supporter of the causes as represented by the County and local electoral organisations. As President of the Eastbourne Division Conservative and Unionist Association he was much esteemed...He was a member of the Carlton and Wellington Clubs, London; the Royal Yacht Squadron, Cowes; and the Sussex Club, Eastbourne. ...He was an enthusiastic supporter of the Eastbourne Foxhounds and of the pack of harriers that preceded it. When opportunity offered he simply loved to follow the hounds.' (20)

7th Duke of Devonshire (1808-1891)

In 1782 Lady Elizabeth Compton, the daughter of the 7th Earl of Northampton, married George Augustus Henry Cavendish, 3rd son of the 4th Duke of Devonshire and brother of William Cavendish, the 5th Duke of Devonshire. The Eastbourne estates became the property of the Cavendish family. In 1831 George Cavendish was knighted as 1st Earl of Burlington and three years later died owning 8,577 acres including Compton Place. His grandson, the 6th Duke of Devonshire inherited and introduced a large building programme which left significant debts when he died in 1858. The 7th Duke carried on with the building schemes. The Devonshires invested in the town, public utilities and became a major influence on the local government board.

William Cavendish attended Eton and Trinity College, Cambridge. In 1829 he married the niece of the 6th Duke of Devonshire, Lady Blanche Howard, succeeding his cousin to become the 7th Duke of Devonshire. He inherited a considerable amount of land in Eastbourne from both his grandfather, Lord George Augustus Henry Cavendish and his wife, Elizabth Compton. (21) He provided the finance which made it possible to continue the planned development begun by the 6th Duke who had died in 1858, having displayed an extravagance coupled with 'a sense of financial responsibility which had never even dimly developed.'(22) This meant he left his successor with debts of around £75,000. The 7th Duke fell out with Berry who had played a large part in the early plans and construction of the town replacing him with Henry Currey, a relative and solicitor who drew up plans for further development of the town in 1859. A local board for a water company was set up and one for the supply of gas. By then the 7th Duke possessed estates in 11 English and 3 Irish counties which brought in a revenue of nearly £110,000 a year.

However progress was not always smooth. Speculation among building companies in the 19th century as at any other time was driven by the opportunity to make profits and problems over drainage were seen as the cause of an outbreak of scarlet fever, which in turn adversely affected trade. (23) The 7th Duke came to the rescue when the contractor for the drainage scheme went bankrupt. Eastbourne College, which aimed at attracting the sons of gentlemen, did not have its foundation stone laid until 1870, three years after the college's opening. The pier was only half built by 1870 but following these setbacks the town gradually made progress. The major hotels were constructed, the Devonshire baths and theatre completed and the pier, badly damaged by a severe storm during 1877, rebuilt with improved facilities. A sign that the town's growing success had been recognised was the granting of a charter for incorporation as a borough with G.A. Wallis, the Duke's agent, as the town's first mayor. (24)

By the 1880s the Sussex estates of the Cavendishes comprised some 11,000 acres making them among the largest in the country. They controlled the seafront, the area of the Meads and much else whilst the Gilberts were largely confined to the area north of the railway station, including Old Town. Apart from the Glebe land the remaining areas, less than one fifteenth, were owned by smallholders, agricultural labourers and fishermen.

The Duke entered Parliament in 1829 as member for Cambridge University and having supported the 1832 Reform Bill was not re-elected. Instead he was returned for Malton, Yorkshire in 1831 and then for North Derbyshire 1832-34. He gave up politics in 1834 having succeeded as Earl of Burlington and devoted much of his time to science and industry. He was chairman of the Royal Commission on Scientific Instruction and the Advancement of Science, Chancellor of the University of London 1836-56 and then Cambridge from 1861 until his death 30 years later. His devotion to science led him to endow the Cavendish Laboratory at the University.

Because of his varied interests and numerous residences he was 'never more than a short-term visitor' to Eastbourne, a situation which the *Eastbourne Gazette* commented on in October 1872 and again in 1880. (25) Nevertheless the town deferred to his aristocratic background, wealth and ownership of the major part of the town. Similarly, Wallis, as his agent, also gained great influence and wealth in the town. Like the Duke, he was a Liberal, indeed as was the town, but this was not so for the surrounding countryside. The 1884 Reform Act extended the franchise to a larger number of male voters and established the South (or Eastbourne) district of Sussex. Wallis, who was well regarded and popular in the town stood as the Liberal candidate. He received considerable support from the *Eastbourne Gazette* in the town but the assumption that he would win comfortably had not taken into full account the views of the rural population whose support for the Conservative candidate, Captain Field, enabled him to receive 3,561 votes as against 3,497 for Wallis.

Specific Buildings for the Working Class?

There is no doubting the splendour of the buildings by the Devonshires and Gilberts which made Eastbourne such an attractive place to higher income families either to buy a house and settle in the town or become regular visitors during the Summer season. One looks in vain for projects approaching anything like this scale specifically built for lower income groups in the town. The only one which easily springs to mind was not provided by either of the major landowners, namely Leaf Hall in Seaside. This building was constructed by Blessley, the same architect who built the Grand Hotel. It was financed by William Leaf (1791-1874) who had made a considerable fortune in the City. He was a devout Christian and wished to provide a building for working men which contained a library, reading room and lecture hall. Such facilities would give them the opportunity for self improvement. The building, looking somewhat like a church at first glance, was opened in 1864 and provided a programme of lectures covering a wide range of subjects. The lectures sought to compensate in some way for the inadequate provision of schooling before the 1870 Education Act. They gave many men a chance to gain greater knowledge of a range of subjects which took their interest. As a generalisation skilled workers made up most of the audience and initially at least there is no mention of women attending. Trade unions also held their meetings in the building in the late Victorian period.

It was a temperance institution and this would have discouraged attendance by some working class men. This restriction needs to be placed into perspective because broadly speaking there were two approaches to abstinence from alcohol. Some people believed that for religious reasons it was morally wrong to drink alcohol and certain Nonconformists groups took this approach. On the other hand there were others who wished to discourage the drinking of alcohol for social reasons in that they were aware low paid workers might spend money in the public house which was needed for the family household budget. An example of one problem in this respect was provided by Robert Noonan (Tressell) from his experience in the building trade in Hastings, where the men were required to collect their weekly wage from the foreman in a nearby public house. At times of unemployment buying the foreman a drink could help to secure a further week's work. (Tressell, R. (1914) *The Ragged Trousered Philanthropist*, (1965 ed.) Lawrence & Wishart) Leaf's intention, however naïve to some, was to provide an opportunity for working men to enhance the quality of their lives by offering them facilities similar to those available to higher income groups. Later an approach would be made to provide working people with the opportunity to study full-time with the opening of Ruskin College at Oxford in 1899, once more an enterprise developed by a wealthy philanthropist, the wealthy American Walter Vrooman. Leaf's enterprise was initiated a generation earlier.

Years later it would be criticised by George Meek when a proposal for a war memorial was being discussed in 1919, one idea of which was to establish a similar institution. Referring to Leaf Hall he wrote that such a building already existed:

> Which has always been a failure. I refer to Leaf Hall. Now this building which by the way, looks like a cross between a Sunday School and a police station, was erected for the benefit of Eastbourne workmen, under the will of a Mr Leaf, to achieve what Alderman Duke hopes the proposed YMCA building will do. i.e. keep the returned soldier (who will be in ninety-nine cases out of a hundred workingmen) out of the public house.
>
> Has the Leaf Hall done this? Do you see the working men crowding into that building of cocoa and buns, or ginger beer and ginger bread? Never! Never in the

long history, and the late Mr Leaf's good intentions have ended this well meant institution degenerating into a mere private cook shop, which would probably do better business if it was carried on in ordinary business premises.

Doubtless Meek's criticism of Leaf Hall's temperance approach was at least partly due to his liking for a drink himself. To the implication that for the low-paid alcohol might deprive a family of necessary income he wrote in his autobiography, that drink helped working people to endure the wretched conditions many faced daily. "Let the poor man drink and forget his misery ." It costs me less for a week's beer than it does for the wine consumed by some single members of the exploiting class at one meal." He was familiar enough with most of the public houses in his home town and produced a poem in which eight were named. (26) (Coxall, B. & Griggs, C. op.cit.,p. 221)

8th Duke of Devonshire (Earl of Hartington - 1833-1908)

On his death the 7th Duke had three surviving sons; the eldest, the Marquess of Hartington, was M.P. for Lancashire North 1857-91 and a prominent member of the Liberal Party. He became the 8th Duke of Devonshire. Frederick Cavendish was MP for West Riding, married to Gladstone's niece, Lady Cavendish and newly appointed Chief Secretary for Ireland. In the struggle for Irish Independence, Charles Stewart Parnell had been placed in Kilmainham Prison. He and Gladstone tried to reach an agreement to put an end to violence by striking a bargain which became known as the 'Kilmainham Treaty'. However a small group known as the 'Irish National Invincibles' planned to kill Thomas Burke, Under Secretary and the most senior Irish Civil Servant. On the 6th May 1882 he was walking in Phoenix Park, Dublin, with Frederick Cavendish who had arrived on that very day when they were both assassinated. This action put an end to discussions concerning Irish Independence for more than a generation until the compromise decision in 1921 to divide the island into the Irish Free State and Ulster.

There were other political consequences as well. Lord Hartington, Frederick Cavendish's older brother, was so appalled by the murder that he split with Gladstone and led a breakaway Liberal Unionist Association which along with Joseph Chamberlain's Radicals, also opposed Irish Home Rule. They were to give their support to Lord Salisbury who led the Conservatives to victory over Gladstone's Liberal Party in 1892. The third brother, Edward Cavendish, was MP for West Derbyshire. The three brothers together presented an example of landed gentry with entry to Parliament through patronage with the political influence it brought.

The 8th Duke was disturbed by the financial situation he inherited in Eastbourne. The 7th Duke had been quite willing to leave the business of his estate to his solicitors, the Currey family and George Ambrose Wallis, a civil engineer. The 8th Duke queried the efficiency of these appointees feeling that the revenue which should be available to the Devonshires was constantly being ploughed into developments in the town. There seemed to be a hint that perhaps more of this money had been diverted into the incomes of Currey and Wallis than was reasonable? The building of Hollywell Mount by Wallis in 1879 at a cost of £10,000 seemed to illustrate that he had certainly prospered from the management of the Duke's estate. The Duke was sufficiently concerned to arrange for Price Waterhouse, the accountants, and Mr Farrant, an engineer, to examine the administration of the Eastbourne estate. Their reports suggested that it would be possible to obtain a larger income for the Duke from the estate. (26) In 1892 Wallis resigned on the grounds of pressure of work. He died in 1895. However both Currey and Wallis wrote extensive reports arguing that the comparatively high expenditure on certain projects had provided important work upon which the prosperity of much of the estate benefited.

Unlike the 7th Duke who was not really attracted to political power, the 8th Duke, who was a Liberal Whig, (those members coming from the landowning 18th century Whigs), had a long Parliamentary career. He was a member of Gladstone's Government and led the Liberal Party in 1877. In spite of Queen Victoria's wish that Hartington would replace Gladstone, the Prime Minister she personally disliked, there was little real prospect of that taking place. He was not 'overawed' by the 'Grand Old Man' and opposed the 1884 Reform Bill for he 'had by this time lost all enthusiasm for extending the franchise or indeed for any significant measure of reform.' (27)

Writing in his diary in 1879 Lord Derby described his phlegmatic character as such; 'Although a quintessential Whig aristocrat in politics, he never got on particularly well with his fellow landed magnates, neither Derby himself, whom he once dismissed as no more than an owner of Liverpool rents, or Salisbury who was too much of a non-sporting intellectual for Hartington's taste and who, when they were working in close alliance in 1891, retaliated by complaining that 'Hartington is at Newmarket and all political arrangements have to be hung up till some quadruped has run faster than some other quadruped.' (28) Balfour 'knew the Duke's sense of honour far exceeded his intelligence'. (29) Catherine Walters was his mistress and he did not marry until 1892 when he was 59 years of age and then it was to Louisa Augusta van Allen.

It could be claimed that the 8TH Duke was too preoccupied with the political scene to spend much time in Eastbourne and even when he was made mayor of the town in 1897 he only attended three of the fourteen meetings. The office could never be more than ceremonial given the political obligations he had at the time as the local paper recognised when the idea was mooted; 'It seems almost too much to hope that the nobleman whose time is more or less engrossed with affairs of state, and who already holds many responsible public positions, will yield to popular wish in this matter.' (30) Yield he did but he was not really interested in the office any more than that of Chief Magistrate which was offered to him, and when asked to stand for another year as mayor he rejected the offer, only to find himself made the town's First Freeman!

Prominent people in the town always sought to exploit the aristocratic connection and it is a reflection of the social attitudes of the time that politeness and respect often gave way to sycophancy in speeches or written comment on occasions, such as the wording in the *Eastbourne Gazette* (26.10.1898) when the Duke had served his year as mayor: 'That the grateful thanks of this Corporation be accorded to His Grace the Mayor for accepting the office of mayor of this borough, and for the great honour His Grace conferred upon the town by so doing and by the generous manner in which he has filled the duties of the office during the past year.' (31) His equally emollient replies led to the Duke and the Council sounding at times like a mutual admiration society. (32) Open criticism was a rarity. 'It might be all very well for once in a way to have an ornamental Mayor, but as a rule, an office of this importance – at all events in a town of this character – ought to be held by someone who was prepared to give constant and assiduous attention to the duties' wrote 'A Large Ratepayer' to the *Eastbourne Chronicle* earlier in the same month. (33)

In reality it would seem that the aristocratic 8th Duke was completely out of his depth as a Government Minister in both intellect and interest in his role as Minister for Education. His performance was heavily criticised. Beatrice Webb gave an insight into the views of Robert Morant, Permanent Secretary at the Board of Education, concerning the Duke as nominal Head of Education. '...failing through inertia and stupidity to grasp any complicated detail half an hour after he has listened to it, preoccupied with Newmarket, and in bed till 12 o'clock.' (Banks, O. (1955) *Parity and Prestige in English Secondary Education* p.25, R.K. P.)

Salisbury was Prime Minister from 1892 to 1902 with two intervening periods; Gladstone (1892-94) and Rosebery (1894-95). Balfour took over in 1902. He now faced the problem of a conflict between the Liberals' long held views on Free Trade and the growing calls for a form of protection for British industry and the Empire; the most vociferous campaigner of who was

Joseph Chamberlain. Among the Liberal members, Charles Ritchie (Chancellor), George Hamilton (Secretary of State for India) and Lord Balfour of Burleigh could not bring themselves to serve in a Government which sought to abandon the policy of Free Trade which was so entrenched in Liberal Party policy. They sent in their letters of resignation to the Prime Minister. They clearly assumed the Duke as leader of their Party would also resign. He did have qualms about the issue but he did not resign at that moment. In the stance he first took he was supported by his wife, the Dowager Duchess of Manchester, who had 'not yet surrendered the ambition that he should become Prime Minister.' (34) She persuaded him it was his public duty to survive in Government. It therefore came as a shock to Balfour to receive his formal letter of resignation which 'virtually invited Balfour not to accept it.' In essence the letter 'was intended to meet the demands of honour by appearing to assert his solidarity with his free-trade colleagues. What at first sounded like an assertion of loyalty was really preparation for abandoning his friends. 'I could not honourably reconsider my position in any way without further communication with them.' (35) (ibid)

Having accepted the resignations of Hamilton, Ritchie and Balfour of Burleigh the Prime Minister had another meeting with the Duke who asked if he would reconsider accepting their resignations, a request which was refused. 'The Duke, having made his token gesture, then 'consented to withdraw (his) resignation.' (36) He attempted to justify this action to Ritchie, the result of which was to infuriate the former Chancellor who reminded the Duke in a letter that he had stated there was 'no chance of his (Balfour's) altering your determination.' (37) Two weeks later Balfour assumed that all was well but following his address to the National Union in Sheffield in which some enthusiasm was expressed for a retaliatory tariff the Duke resigned from the Government. It has been claimed that, 'He was looking for an excuse to clear his conscience and redeem his good name.' (38) Balfour's report to the King claimed, '"The Duke of Devonshire's conduct has been pitiable. Nor is it possible to excuse, or even fully understand, his vacillations without remembering that he has, without doubt, put himself somehow in the power of Mr Ritchie and his friends. He is forced to behave badly to me, lest he should be publicly taxed with behaving badly to them.'" (39) The Duke's 40 year political career was over. He died five years later.

In Balfour's 1905 Conservative Administration, in which the 8th Duke was President of the Council, it must have been assumed he would continue to support a Conservative Government as he had done previously. Balfour had hoped to retain the support of the Duke in spite of his free-trade prediction. 'He thought he had succeeded, and when Devonshire resigned two weeks later on a hair-splitting interpretation of Balfour's speech but really under pressure from other free-traders, he was not only very angry but, unusually for him, displayed his anger in a withering letter to the unfortunate duke.' (40)

References - Chapter 2

(1) Surtees, J. ibid., pp.16-17
(2) Cannadine, D. *(1980) Lords and Landlords; the Aristocracy of the Towns 1774-1967*, pp.233-235
(3) ibid. pp. 231-233

(4) ibid. p.258
(5) ibid
(6) The family tree of the Devonshires is complicated; for details v. Cannadine, D. ibid. pp. 231-233,
(7) For details of Davies Gilbert's life v. Todd, A.C. (1967) *Beyond the Blaze*
(8) ibid. pp. 207-209
(9) ibid. p.37
(10) ibid.,p.179; This may well reflect Gilbert's attitude but he had been dead several years before these words from the famous hymn 'All Things Bright and Beautiful' were written by Mrs Cecil Francis Alexandra in 1848.
(11) Parliamentary Debates (*Hansard*) Vol.lX,798, July 13th. Quoted in Simon, B. (1960) *Studies in the History of Education 1789-1870*, p.132.
(12) Todd, A.C., op.cit. pp.180-181
(13) ibid. p.270
(14) ibid.
(15) ibid. p.246
(16) ibid. p.278
(17) Kramer, A. (2007) *Sussex Women* p.41.
(18) Griggs, C. (1983) *The TUC and the Struggle for Education* pp.93-100; Goldstrom, J.M. (1966-67) 'Richard Whately and political economy in school text books 1833-1880'
(19) *Sussex Advertiser* 9.4.1844
(20) A lengthy obituary to Gilbert appeared in the *Eastbourne Chronicle* (6.12.1913)
(21) For details of the Devonshire family v. Stevens, L. *A Short History of Eastbourne*, pp. 14-15 and Cannadine, D. op.cit. pp.231-233
(22) ibid. p.286)
(23) ibid.), p.245
(24) ibid.
(25) *E.Gaz.* 9.10.1872 & 22.9.1880.

(26) Cannadine, D. op.cit. Ch.21
(27) Jenkins, R. *Gladstone*, p.489
(28) ibid. p.429
(29) Hattersley, R. *The Edwardians* p.113
(30) Cannadine, D. op.cit . p.399
(31) *E.Gaz.* 26.10.1898
(32) Cannadine, D. *op.cit*.p.342
(33) *E. Chron.* 1.10.1898
(34) Hattersley, R. *op cit.* p.114
(35) ibid.
(36) ibid. p.115
(37) ibid. p.116)
(38) (ibid., p.118)
(39) Royal Archive 1.10.1903, cited in Hattersley, R. op.cit.,p.119
(40) Blake, R. (1985) *The Conservative Party from Peel to Thatcher* p.180

CHAPTER 3

RELIGIOUS INSTITUTIONS & SOCIAL CLASS

Churches and their Congregations

Religious beliefs just like political philosophies can generate heated responses and emotions, so much so that local historians will sometimes shy away from them to avoid what may be seen as contentious issues. However effective this approach may be to protect the sensitivities of some it does not help in attempts to explain past events. To some extent these will always be a matter of personal interpretation and grounds for debate. For a town whose planners in the 19th century specifically zoned areas in terms of differences in incomes, occupations and interests it will be no surprise to note that the Established Church reflected these differences. The congregation of St Mary's Parish Church was in an area inhabited by various groups of people and originally catered for this diverse population. However as wealthy families were encouraged to move to the town to rent or buy property on the new estates being developed by the Devonshire and Gilbert families, so a source of tension arose at times. One response was to subdivide the existing parish though this did not 'grant complete autonomy at once to the new ecclesiastical districts...as Pitman, vicar from 1828 to 1890, continued to have the right to all church fees throughout Eastbourne...with the exception of All Souls....until his death in 1890.' (1)

One church frequented by the wealthy was St Anne's in Upperton Gardens, which was regarded as the Gilbert Estate's church, in which all pews were rented on the assumption that those attending could easily afford such fees. It was not until 1943 that they were abolished by when it was finally conceded that it was 'an out of date system'. (2) St John's, the Meads Parish Church, and All Saints, also catered for the residents who received above average incomes. The latter had a system whereby the pews provided for rent were on the sunny side of the building. Holy Trinity attracted a wider social range of worshippers being attended 'by some who had seceded from St Mary's after new stalls were installed in 1851, those who found Pitman intolerable, plus a few visitors, boarding house keepers and local tradesmen.' (3) The Rev'd Pitman appealed for funds to construct Holy Trinity which needed £2,500, promising to provide 540 seats of which half would be free for the use of the poor.' (4)

Rented pews were a cause for debate. At a time when churches were full for Sunday services they could be seen in some way as booking a seat for a theatre performance. The worshipper then knew that they had reserved a seat for the service. The payments were also clearly a source of revenue for a church. On the other hand they did make it apparent as to who could afford the cost and who could not, reinforcing the difference between income groups, especially where pews were grouped together. There was also the question as to whether people ought to pay to worship in church. In rural areas, where there was usually a Church of England parish church, the leading families had seats grouped together near to the vicar giving the sermon. This was one way in which the social hierarchy in a village was made clear to agricultural labourers and their families. It was one more custom, along with doffing caps and stepping aside when the squire and his wife passed by which these traditional social differences were perpetuated. (An elderly lady living in Ferring, West Sussex, related how her family, farm labourers, during the Edwardian period, stepped off the pavement when the Lord of the Manor or his wife were approaching. Such deference was expected of employees of major landowners in rural areas.) The Wesleyan Methodist Central Church in the town also had a proportion of rented pews which remained well into the 20th century and the numbers can still be seen on the seats.

It is doubtful whether Pitman's pronouncement of free seats for the poor arose from any great concern for their plight. He has been described as 'autocratic by temperament', was friendly with the 7th Duke of Devonshire, and believed in upholding the 'proper relationship of rank and class.' He ended evening services which had been attended particularly by working class families and returned the oil lamps used at it to the Rev'd Alexander Brodie's widow. His removal of the galleries in the Church further alienated him from the poor. St Mary's did retain a more balanced congregation due to the social mixture of the population in old town and although never becoming as exclusive as the churches in Meads and Upperton Gardens it did become more middle class as a result of Pitman's attitudes and the changes he made. In his plea to help Holy Trinity financially, especially the promise of free seating for the poor, it is possible that this was partly in the hope or intention that some of the poorer members of his own church might be persuaded to change their place of worship to Holy Trinity. This suggestion is reinforced by a comment on his time at St Mary's: 'In his 44 years as vicar of Eastbourne he had not exactly singled out the poor as the prime concern of his Ministry.' (5) His unsympathetic reputation results partly from comparisons with his predecessor, the Rev'd Dr Alexander Brodie, vicar of St Mary's from 1809 to 1828, who pushed for a better parish poor school and supported the work of three of his daughters, all of whom established infant schools in the town.

Some wealthy people were willing to give vast sums of money to finance the building of a new church. Lady Victoria Wellesley, great niece of the Duke of Wellington, provided £40,000 towards the building of All Souls (1881-1882) and George Whelpton from Hastings paid for the erection of St Saviour's Church; his son was then installed as the first vicar! Whether such generosity was purely philanthropic or in the belief that such actions would stand them in good stead in the after-life they believed in it is impossible to know.

Given that the teachings of Christian churches proclaimed that Jesus and his followers did not live a life of luxury and spoke up in defence of the meek it seems rather strange that some poorer members of a parish were not made to feel particularly welcome in the local church. Church missions are usually thought of as a product of earnest Christians going overseas to comparatively poor communities in the 19th and 20th centuries to provide help with education and medical care. Yet in Victorian Britain there were also 'missions' established to provide church services to some parishioners who did not feel comfortable attending their local church which seemed to cater more for the wealthier parishioners. Alienated by the idea of private pews which they could not afford and the disapproval they felt from some of the more affluent members of the congregation they chose to go to missions of that church. Missions were established in some of the poorer areas of the town and in the case of St Mary's only a short distance away on the other side of the road.

The Victorians were quite open about social divisions which they saw as the natural order of things, made clear in the words written by Mrs Alexander to one of the verses of the popular hymn *All Things Bright and Beautiful*.

> The rich man in his castle,
> The poor man at the gate,
> God made them high and lowly,
> And ordered their estate.

The Establishment of Missions

The reality was that the sharp distinctions in income were reflected in every aspect of life. Manual workers dressed according to their job and were often employed on sites with no washing facilities. They went to work clean enough but often came home grimy. By contrast higher income groups dressed in a formal style which made it clear that their workplace was comparatively clean. Sundays in many areas was a formal day and people dressed in their finery to attend church. The quality of their clothing marked them out from lower income groups. When attending the same church there were those among the affluent who would not wish to meet church members from lower income groups, some of whom in turn would resent the greater wealth of members of the congregation. One solution was to go to a mission of that church nearer to home and be among friends. This situation might have led to less potential discomfort within the congregation but it does seem at odds with the Christian message of brotherly love.

Hence the mission established in 1872 at Old Town by William, son of the Rev'd Brodie, and Emma, the fourth daughter, in a former excise office within easy sight of St Mary's. Upwick Mission room was opened, 'to provide a more suitable venue for a different class of people.' (6) It would later become St. George's Church. The Roman Catholics opened their new church, Our Lady of Ransom, in a central area opposite the town hall. Initially the Catholic population increased with the arrival of Irish labourers who participated in the building of the railways. At first they held services in a basement at 42 Ceylon Place before opening a church two years later in Junction Road with seating for 200. As the Catholic community prospered so they too established a mission, St Agnes, in the East end of the town in 1907. (7)

This pattern would be repeated by some nonconformist groups as well. The leading dissenters were usually comparatively prosperous; farmers, tradesmen and those who had chosen to retire to Eastbourne. They were respected members of the community and whilst some faced a measure of hostility, such as Charles Adams, who spoke out against church rates, this was not true generally for others, such as Alderman Duke, who would become town mayor on several occasions (1919-21), and Carlos Crisford, the builder of the Central Wesleyan Church. Again one can see a pattern with the major Wesleyan church in the centre of the town and the Primitive Methodist Church in Whitley Road in the poorer East end. In time there was hardly a nonconformist group without a place of worship; Presbyterian in Blackwater Road, Calvinistic Independent, Cavendish Place; Immanuel Free, Hyde Road; Baptist Calvinistic, Grove road; Baptist, Ceylon Place. Town guides at the end of the 19th century list more than a dozen C. of E. churches and a similar number of nonconformist chapels, a Synagogue, 2 Roman Catholic churches, Salvation Army Citadel and the Quakers' Friends House in Bolton Road.

The Salvation Army and the 1885 Eastbourne Improvement Act

The Salvation Army came to the town in 1890 and established a citadel in Langney Road. To that extent they were just one more religious organisation but their actions led to what would be termed the 'Eastbourne riots'. The town had passed the Eastbourne Improvement Act in 1885 in which clause 169 prohibited processions with music on Sundays. Having successfully challenged a similar custom in Torquay in 1888, the Salvation Army Band and followers on Whit Sunday, 1889:

> ...marched along Bourne Street, singing and playing, in direct contravention to the Eastbourne

Improvement Act of 1885 which forbade processions with music. After an open air meeting at Ashford Road, the band set off again, but the Town's Chief Constable pushed his way through the crowd of onlookers and halted the procession. The Band's Commanding Officer, Captain Bell, and and five other members (including one woman) were taken to court for breaking the Act. Five were sent to Lewes Prison. (8)

This did not deter members of the Salvation Army repeating their actions again that month only to be confronted by a mob, many of whom had been stirred up by ill-chosen words from the Town's mayor, William Epps Morrison, who 'was an implacable opponent of the Salvation Army'. The result was that elements within the crowd of onlookers, some emboldened by alcohol, violently attacked those in the procession, leading to injuries among both men and women marchers. They were also subjected to baton charges by the police and participants in the procession were convicted under the 1885 Act leading to fines or imprisonment. The Salvationists continued to march and were continually faced with violence. They had two aims; to overturn the 1885 Act aimed at no music on Sundays and to bring an end to alcohol being sold to the public on Sundays. They were successful in the first aim in 1892 and the Council's resistance cost the Eastbourne Corporation £30,000 in legal fees. The second aim had little chance of success as it lacked sufficient public support .

The Salvationists' wish to have marching bands on Sundays was only seriously opposed by some of those who considered themselves to be 'respectable residents' and resistant to most activities taking place on the

Sabbath, including bands at the Devonshire Park or Pier. For some working class people the Salvationists did have appeal in that they were unlike some of the older established churches in which they did not feel 'comfortable'. However, others were not keen on the 'military associations' of marching in public wearing a uniform. Becoming teetotal did not have wide support. In commercial terms any attempt to close public houses on Sundays was bound to be resisted by the influential licensed victuallers in the town and the growing holiday trade.

The Working Class and Established Church – a Measure of Indifference

Places of worship were well attended in the West and Central parts of the town but in terms of the proportion of people living in the poorer areas of the East end this was less so. There were exceptions such as the Primitive Baptists 'who were of humbler origins' but attracting significant numbers of working class people produced a challenge recognised by most churches. The Primitive Methodists based in the East of the town noted that 'the hall was in the midst of a non-church going, almost anti-church going population'. (9)

It was not fully appreciated by some of the middle classes that both working class men and women were often engaged in heavy manual work at a time when there were few regulations as to the limit of hours people could be required to work. For those so involved Sunday was often regarded as the one day they had an opportunity to relax a little, although even here there were always chores to be carried out. Whilst the more affluent took time to dress and prepare for their usual place of worship and listen to a church service, a large number of servants from nearby working class districts were busy carrying out their housework, preparing their Sunday lunch and undertaking other tasks thereby making church attendance easier for their employers.

The reasons for significant numbers of working families being indifferent to attendance at church in many areas, including Eastbourne, was well expressed by George Meek whose father was a plasterer in the town before emigrating to the USA in 1872 during a slump in the building trade. 'My people had been Church of England to the extent that they conformed to that communion when attendance at a place of worship appeared to them imperative: that is to say at christenings, confirmation, weddings and funerals of members of the family. Otherwise I never remember them attending any place of worship.' (10) He went on to state, 'I am of the opinion that the "gentry and clergy" were usually regarded as our natural enemies.'

There were good reasons for this general view. The Church of England was the Established Church. Most of their number identified with the Establishment. Ordained priests were nearly all educated at Oxford or Cambridge. In villages they often owed their living to titled gentry who helped to finance the Parish Church. On most occasions where there were disputes between farm labourers and landowners they took the side of the landowners. Joseph Arch, a Warwickshire farm labourer and Primitive Methodist after several abortive attempts formed the first successful Agricultural Workers Union in 1872. The Kent and Sussex Agricultural Union declined to attend the inaugural meeting of this national trade union but were to join later. Arch wrote, 'The

Vicar of Harbury convened a meeting in support of the Union, and there was a parson here and there who went with us openly; but the majority were against us, and others blew now hot now cold, and flew round like weather-cocks as squire or farmer or villager grew strongest at the moment. These shining lights of the church as by Law Established were but poor farthing rushlights to the agricultural labourer.' (11)

Nonconformist links with Middle and Working Classes

The treatment of agricultural workers in some areas was very harsh as was made clear by the Rev'd James Fraser's Report in connection with the 1867-69 Agricultural Commission's Report, in which he found only two parishes out of 300 'had the cottage provision appeared to be both admirable in quality and sufficient in quantity.' (12) An extreme example of the power of employers to force religious obedience upon workers was the imprisonment of two Cornish labourers 'for refusing to obey their master's lawful command to attend Church on Sunday.' (13) Both the Church of England and the Tory Party supported the status quo for much of the 19th century as will be seen in the alliance over the provision of elementary schooling. Early trade unionists tended to be nonconformists and supporters of the Liberal Party and some would go on to become MPs of that Party. e.g. Joseph Arch for West Norfolk [1855-56 and 1892-1900], Henry Broadhurst, who had been a stonemason by trade and later Secretary of the Parliamentary Committee of the TUC was in turn MP for Stoke 1880-85, Bordesley 1885-86, West Nottingham 1886-92 and finally Leicester 1904-06. Thomas Burt, a Northumberland coalminer, represented his area in Parliament 1874-1918 and a fellow coalminer, Benjamin Pickard of the Yorkshire Miners Federation was MP for Normanton 1885-1904. W.R. Cremer, a carpenter, was MP for Haggerston [1885-1908] and Ben Pickard, Miners Federation of GB for Normanton. [1885-1904] They were known as Lib-Labs.

There was an acceptance that in organisations in which the State was involved, compulsory religion was of benefit to those involved. This attitude was to be found in many countries whatever the dominant religion. Church parades for the armed forces are one obvious example. In England captive audiences such as workhouse inhabitants were taken to Church every Sunday, and prisoners were expected to attend weekly religious services. Meek recorded his experience of the practice when he was sent to Lewes Prison for falling behind with the rent on his bathchair for a total of five shillings.

> I had not attended church or chapel for a good many years, and I looked upon these services with contempt, considering them a bitter mockery both of the alleged God in whose honour they were supposed to be held and the people who were compelled to attend them. In my mind I jeered at and despised the class which had instituted them and the creature they paid to conduct them. He came in and went out locking the door after him like any other warder; for I considered him as being nothing but a superior sort of warder who paraded in a white surplice instead of a blue uniform.
>
> After chapel we were marched back to our section and locked into our cells till dinner time, the morning being broken by the governor's inspection. (14)

How far these views were typical of working men it is impossible to know but he experienced another example of what might be referred to as institutional religion when he stayed at a hostel to which he was admitted when searching for work in London.

> Sunday is the busiest day. At the top of the building and covering the whole of it is a large mission hall. Here the Sunday services are held. To them in the morning come such a crowd of tatterdemalion men and women as one can only see at such a function in a great city; for after the religious service another follows which is the cause of these poor wretches attendance: each is given a pint of steaming hot cocoa and a pound of bread. (15)

Youth Movements

By contrast in the youth movements founded in the late Victorian and early Edwardian years, although they all had religious associations, these were a genuine part of a broader programme to encourage young people to become good citizens. The Boys' Life Brigade founded in Glasgow in 1899 with a girls' equivalent three years later saw its aims as 'spiritual, physical, educational and social'. These values were also to be found within other youth movements of the time; the Boys' Brigade (1908), Girls' Brigade (1910), Boy Scouts (1908) and Girl Guides (1910). They were linked to various churches and participated in church parades but they also taught a variety of contemporary skills, such as morse code, and encouraged independence by activities such as camping. They provided positive role models for young children and often a measure of 'escape' for those living in poor circumstances. Examples of all these movements were established in Eastbourne; Two troops of scouts were formed in August 1908 (1st Willingdon and 4th Eastbourne) and registered with the Scouts Association in 1910, and a natural choice for children living in a sea-side town, the Sea Scouts, were formed the following year. Girls Guides, Brownies and Cubs rapidly followed providing organisations for young people which were very popular. By this time there were about 150 scouts in the town. Some were 'sponsored' and linked to a church; others were 'closed', such as those formed in private schools, most of which had disappeared by around 1940.

Surveys of Working Class Life

There were a number of factual surveys of working class life and conditions in Victorian Britain. Frederick Engels 'Conditions of the Working Class in Britain in 1844', Charles Booth's 'Life and Labour of the People of London' published over the years 1889-1903 and Seebohm Rowntree's 'Poverty; a Study of Town Life 1901'; the town referred to being York. These detailed surveys provided sound evidence of the need for social reform. There were also personal accounts of people who experienced the hard life of working people; Jack London's 'People of the Abyss' about Edwardian London and just along the coast from Eastbourne, Robert Tressell's (ie Noonan) 'The Ragged Trousered Philanthropists' describing the experiences of building trade workers in Hastings during a similar period. The importance of Meek's account is that he alone among all these writers, came from poor circumstances and apart for about a year, remained poor. He received only a brief and inconsistent elementary schooling, experiencing several changes of school including Eastbourne, Jevington and Willingdon, as he was left with grandparents first, then his mother before striking out on his own to get away from her and the new partner she had joined. To that extent his idiosyncratic account is written by one who really knew from his own experience how hard life was for the poor. To have written an autobiography, admittedly with considerable support from H.G. Wells, was nevertheless a real achievement.

To summarise, it would seem, that as might be expected, the place of worship in the second half of the 19th century was related to the prosperity of different parts of the town; the West with higher income groups occupying the Devonshire and Gilbert estates with the large churches of the Anglicans whilst some in the poorer East end of the town were started as missions of these churches and helped financially by the more affluent congregations of the former. Similarly the Wesleyan Methodist Central church where many of the more prosperous members of the business section helped their fellow Methodists in the poorer eastern part of the town and this pattern could be observed also among members of the Roman Catholic community. In the poorer eastern part with its rows of terraced houses, which were smaller and more densely populated as the town spread ever eastwards, so smaller places of worship were to be found catering for other denominations such as the Plymouth Brethren down Seaside. Whilst this is generally true there were always exceptions in which people in more affluent areas wished to identify with and give support to those living in poorer parts of the town. For example, James Attlee, one of Clement Attlee's uncles, lived in Bedfordwell Road and later Carew Road. He could be easily recognised by his long flowing beard and on Sundays he walked to Christ Church in Seaside where he often read the lesson.

Sunday in particular in Victorian Britain was a day on which attendance at a place of worship in the morning was expected and normal weekday events frowned upon. The expectation among the middle classes was that formal dress was expected, play frowned upon, as well as certain forms of entertainment. As to the opening of public houses, there were conflicts in opinion; publicans regarded it as an opportunity to make profits, people from many walks of life wished to enjoy a drink whilst some believed that drinking alcohol was something to be avoided on any day, but especially on a Sunday. A considerable number of nonconformists were teetotal, sometimes because they believed it diverted money from working class pockets when they often lacked expenditure for basic requirements. Certain tasks were frowned upon even though they were not illegal, such as hanging out washing on the Sabbath, a custom which few would consider breaking. Many would claim many of the unwritten rules which originated in the affluent West of the town heavily influenced at least those who might be termed as the respectable lower middle classes, some of whom considered their social advancement locally could be influenced by how far they adopted these conventions. The further one moved east the less were such customs observed, including attendance at a place of worship on Sundays.

References – Chapter 3

(1) Neville, G. (1982) *Religion and Society in Eastbourne 1735-1920*, p.10
(2) *E.Gaz.* 27.3.1943
(3) Surtees, J. ibid.,p.15
(4) Neville, G. ibid. p.16
(5) ibid.
(6) ibid.
(7) Proctor, J. (1951) *A Short History of the Catholic Parish of Eastbourne,* p.19, quoted in Neville, G., ibid. p.11
(8) *Century Herald 1883-1983*, Part 1, p.iii
(9) Neville, G. op.cit. p.17
(10) Meek, G. (1910) *George Meek – By Himself,* p.81
(11) Arch, J. (1966) *The Autobiography of Joseph Arch,* MacGibbon & Kee, p.57.
(12) Horn, P. (1971) *Joseph Arch 1826-1919; the Farmworkers' Leader*, p.35
(13) ibid.P.36
(14) Meek, G. op.cit. p.237
(15) ibid. p.205

CHAPTER 4

SCHOOLING IN THE EASTBOURNE AREA DURING THE 19TH CENTURY

Resistance to School Boards

The development of public elementary education in Eastbourne was not unique but it was unusual in that it never established a system of board schools. This was also true for Winchester whilst Salisbury had a school board but never built a board school. There are several possible reasons. The most obvious could be that there were sufficient school places so further schools were not needed. An explanation could be that the Church of England and its supporters were so powerful that they were able to resist all attempts to introduce board schools or that indifference to education of many residents made the issue of who provided schools of little consequence. Even an appeal to the 'respectability' of the town might seem possible.

At first glance these suggestions do not seem plausible when compared to other towns. Were not Canterbury and York equally strongholds of the Church of England yet they were unable to resist school boards.

Certainly Bournemouth and Cheltenham would be considered equally 'respectable' as the 'Empress of Watering Places' yet school boards were established in these towns. As is often the case no single explanation will suffice.

Although there were numerous elementary schools in the mid-19th century for working class children in England and Wales there was no system as such. In the towns provision was grossly inadequate and irregular attendance due to the demands of child labour undermined the educational progress of most children. In factories in the Northern towns, particularly those engaged in textiles, child labour was regarded as normal. Many parents accepted the situation because this had been their own experience as children. The few pence earned by children might be vital to keep the family at subsistence level. In the coalfields traditions of women and children working were well entrenched and in rural areas child labour was endemic. Employers exploited the situation and saw little need for education believing that given their prescribed role in life, as children of working class families, they were most probably destined to continue in the life-style and occupation of their parents. Even basic literacy was not a necessity. Schooling was not compulsory and usually a small weekly fee was required. Reformers pressed steadily for many years to limit the hours of child labour and remove them from exploitation but were constantly resisted by vested interests until the 1853 Act was passed limiting the hours of work for children and women. Because this effected some of the work carried out by men they benefited too and the result was that some of the worst of the early 19th century working practices were ended.

Caffyn's detailed analysis of schools functioning in 18th century Sussex and some of their predecessors provides a good indication as to the source of provision, financing and small numbers of children involved. For example, 'Alciston...The parish paid small sums to women to "school" individual children in the Easter-to-Easter years 1747-48 to 1758-9. The most paid in any one year appears to have been £1.2s.5d. to Dave Richardson in 1757-58 for schooling two children'. (1) Similar information is also provided for Alfriston, East Dean, Folkington, Friston, Heathfield and Westham.' Most were charity schools and had some links with residents in Eastbourne. For example 'From at least 1736 a small charity school at Westham was supported by the Cavendish family, the Compton Place accounts showing payments of £5 p.a. to a School Master for teaching 8 to 9 children. In 1784 the payment was made by Lady Cavendish to a school master, Richard Thompson. It appears that Pevensey children attended this school.' (2) In East Dean, George Medley paid £5 per annum from 1775 to 1779 for the schooling of 12 children from that village and Friston. (3) A parish school in Eastbourne was built against the church tower of St Mary's and a record for the repair of this building is given for 1638. A report showed that £6 should be paid out of the parsonage, in lieu of breakfasting including '£4 to be given to a schoolmaster to instruct 8 of the parishioners' sons in the Latin tongue, and £2, the residue thereof, to be given to a schoolmaster to teach 4 children, whose parents are not able to pay, to read and write.' (4)

In 1807 Samuel Whitbread introduced a Bill into the House of Commons which proposed to establish rate-aided parochial schools offering two years of free schooling for children between the ages of seven and fourteen who could not pay fees. There were two sources of opposition. 'When the Bill came before the

House of Lords the Archbishop of Canterbury argued it would go to subvert the first principles of education in this country, which had hitherto been, and he trusted would continue to be, under the control and auspices of the Establishment.' (5) Another Bill by Brougham in 1820 favouring the Church of England also aroused opposition from 'both Dissenters and Roman Catholics forcing it to be withdrawn.' (6)

Davies Giddy's opposition to Whitbread's Bill made it quite clear that he believed people should stay in the social position to which they had been born. (7) (v Chap 2, Political ideas of Landowners) The Sunday School movement of the 1780s associated with Robert Raikes, an evangelical churchman, made progress in helping 'street urchins' and was taken up by Methodists, evangelicals and the Church more widely. 'The purpose of the schools was simple – to teach children to read the Bible, and, in Hannah More's words, "to train up the lower classes in habits of industry and piety"'. (8) Employers were generally content to favour this move for two reasons: it took place on Sundays and therefore did not interfere with the six day working week which was the norm and the teaching of the Catechism and many of the New Testament stories underpinned the stated philosophy of the time, however much it might be divorced from the every day life of the majority of the labouring poor in 19th century Britain.

Early Government moves to assist elementary education

The first moves towards anything resembling some system of elementary education in England and Wales arose from the activities of Joseph Lancaster, a Quaker, and Andrew Bell of the Church of England. They adapted what were really factory methods of production to schooling. A teacher with a large class of 50 children or more would teach some aspect of a subject to ten monitors who would then teach it in turn to ten children. There is debate over who first thought of the method but Lancaster opened a school for poor children in 1798 and in 1808 the R.L.S.E.P. was formed. It would become known later as the B.F.S.S. Bell had developed his system in Madras which he described in a book in 1797 entitled *An Experiment in Education*. In 1811 the Church of England established the N.S.P.C.K. These moves received the general approval of government and the wealthy because they were cheap to run; only one teacher was required to deal with very large numbers of children. Whilst reading and writing were taught there was much emphasis on moral and religious discipline and social subordination.

In 1818 a Parliamentary Committee produced a Report 'on the Education of the Lower Orders in the Metropolis and Beyond'. They found that 'a very large number of poor children are wholly without the means of Instruction, although their parents appear to be generally very desirous of obtaining that advantage for them.' (9) Bills recommending some education for poor children and the regulation of conditions for children in cotton mills in 1802 and 1819 made little progress. Individual attempts to help children were successful in some places, one of the most famous being the introduction of schooling for the children of working people in the New Lanark Mills organised by Robert Owen, the founder of the Co-operative Movement. He believed that providing decent housing and working conditions for his workers was not only right ethically but led to improved production. Adults also received education and to aid children he produced some of the first school text books with pictures.

The Government was reluctant to get involved directly in the provision of schooling. They were concerned that ideas might become promoted which challenged Society but also conscious of some of the rivalry between religious groups wishing to provide schooling for the children in the clear belief that they had a duty to teach their religious beliefs in contrast to those of their rivals. The Catholic Emancipation Act of 1829 increased these pressures. As a way of avoiding involvement in the rivalry between the two principal religious groups in 1833 the Government provided an annual grant to be shared between them of £20,000. To put this expenditure into perspective it was the equivalent to that provided for the refurbishment of the Royal Stables at Windsor. (Roman Catholic Schools were included in 1845) Religious societies had to raise money for a school in an area which would then receive a grant from the Government. Constant appeals were made in churches to raise sufficient money to finance local schools. There were also charity schools and dame schools.

St Mary's appeals for financial support towards Church of England Schools

In rural Sussex the Church of England was dominant in the villages and schools were built supported by most of the population living locally. Dr Alexander Brodie, vicar of Eastbourne energetically supported education in the town and as a means of receiving aid to build a replacement school for St Mary's, had written to the National Society:

> It is the wish of those who have the management of the school at Eastbourne for the Poor in that and the neighbouring Parishes of East Dean, Jevington and Willingdon that the said school be united to the National Society. (10)

The rules and regulations for this unity were stated and included:

1. The Madras System of teaching is adopted.
2. The children are instructed in the liturgy and Catechism of the Established Church...to constantly attend Divine Service at their Parish Church...on the Lord's Day.
3. No religious tracts were used in the school but which are or shall be contained in the catalogue of the National Society. (11)

The St Mary's replacement school was built across the road from the Church in 1814 and a couple of years later a new floor was put in the original loft where the boys were accommodated with the girls on the ground floor. The cost was met by Charles Gilbert for although he died in that year the money required was left in his will for that purpose. Church of England schools followed in East Dean (1844), Jevington (1846) and Willingdon. (1851). Within the town Trinity was built in 1851 and Christ Church in 1866. Dr Brodie was also associated with three infant schools in Eastbourne, each run by one of his daughters; Maria at Compton Place

School built in 1836 for children of the workers on the Duke of Devonshire's Estate, Lydia ran Church Road and Julia, Christ Church, both of which were erected in 1852. A Sunday school for children in Meads which provided evening classes for adults was unsuccessful in its bid for a grant from the National Society. A new National School was opened on the same site in 1873 which lasted until 1899 when a further National School was opened in nearby Wellcombe Valley. (12) Of the two main local newspapers, the *Chronicle* first published on the 7th October 1865, supported the Church of England on the education issue and was sympathetic to the Conservative Party.

W.E. Forster's 1870 Education Act

Due to the increase in population during the second half of the 19th century it became clear that the various religious bodies had not been able to provide sufficient elementary school places for the nation's children. To deal with this problem the 1870 Education Act established a national system of School Boards which would be elected in each area where there were insufficient elementary schools. It was seen by many as a progressive scheme. The school board could raise money from the rates and frame bye-laws which would make attendance compulsory for children between the ages of 5 and 13. As ad hoc boards of between five to fifteen members all ratepayers were entitled to vote and this meant that some women were enfranchised nearly fifty years before they gained a parliamentary vote. By concentrating their votes on certain candidates, a practice which became known as 'plumping', minority groups were able to gain representatives on the board responsible for education in their area. To avoid religious disputes which had been a source of so much friction in past years the schools were nonsectarian and school assemblies limited to readings from the bible. Religious schools were given a year of grace to put forward plans for new schools where there was a shortage of places for children before a school board could be introduced. The result was that whereas in 1869 they had submitted 226 applications for building grants in the last five months of 1870 they applied for 3,003. There were to be no religious tests for teachers applying to work in a board school.

The first published response in the town to this Education Act came from the *Eastbourne Gazette*, founded in 1859, subtitled the 'Fashionable Intelligencer and East Sussex General Record'. It informed its advertisers and readers that it was 'the only Liberal journal printed in the town'. It suggested that 'The election of the various school boards throughout the country marks the commencement of the educational campaign, the war against ignorance...This educational reform...will prove one of the greatest social reforms ever effected in the United Kingdom.' (13)

The following year HMIs visited Eastbourne to examine the three Church of England Schools which had 'voluntarily placed themselves under Government inspection'; St Mary's, Holy Trinity and Christ Church. The local newspaper reported that:

> We are glad to find that, judged by this test, the parochial schools of Eastbourne appear to fulfil their mission in a most satisfactory manner and fully justify the confidence placed in them by the inhabitants, who

> feel that whilst the education given in them is up to the mark, and liberty of conscience secured alike to Churchmen and Dissenters, there is no necessity for a rate-aided school – the natural outcome of a School Board. (14)

The only school for which examination results were available at the time was Holy Trinity and these were impressive. Of those presented for examination 92% passed and in addition to the three Rs a whole range of extra subjects were presented by some pupils; for example 37 boys and 27 girls gained passes in geography and 19 girls in English history. The teachers' certificates were endorsed with favourable comments and 13 pupil teachers also presented themselves for examination. The pupil teacher system was like an apprenticeship whereby older pupils were taught outside school hours by the headteacher and worked in the classroom under the supervision of an experienced teacher. If they obtained high marks in their examination they could apply for a Queen's Scholarship which would enable them to attend a Teachers' College for a two year certificate course. This certificate in turn would entitle them to a higher salary. Eastbourne seemed to be well-served by elementary schools at this time. In addition to St. Marys, Holy Trinity had been added in 1851 and Christ Church in 1866.

Arguments over the sufficiency of school accommodation broke out from time to time becoming particularly heated in the 1890s. Between 1871 and 1891 the population trebled. Trying to assess the extent to which the town was able to keep pace with the growing need for school places was not easy. To begin with whilst the total accommodation remained quite high this could be quite misleading because in directories only private schools were listed. This was still certainly true as late as 1910. (15) These schools were well beyond the means of ordinary and poor residents.

Financial problems for elementary schools serving the Poor in the East

By contrast the areas of comparative poverty in the town were reflected in comments of certain local vicars. On at least two occasions, in 1869, Lloyd, vicar of Christ Church wrote to the NSPCK to explain why he had not made a donation: 'I hope to have a collection in my Church every 2nd year for the National Society. We have such serious difficulty in raising funds for the ordinary expenses of the Church that I cannot promise a collection every year.' (16) Later in the year he wrote again in a similar vein; a plea that was recognised by the Society. The poverty of Christ Church was expressed by later vicars too. 'There is in this very poor district a population of nearly 3,000 with at present only an Infant School and a National School (mixed), into which we are only able to admit a few boys under the age of 9 years...(17) The poverty of the district helped to justify the vicars' requests for grants from the National Society but the threat of a board school may well have been used to spur on the NSPCK into providing funds. 'We are making every effort to raise contributions to meet this crisis and at the same time to preclude the necessity of a School Board....The Parish is very poor. The town has done all it can, and the case is urgent, because of the imminent risk of the school board coming....which disaster has so far been averted. (18)

NSPCK. grants were by no means the major source of funding for schools and to put them into perspective they provided Christ Church with £40 towards a bill of £941. A few months before the HMI Inspection, when the results of Trinity School were reported upon favourably in the local newspaper, Revd. J.J. Irwin was commenting in a sermon at St Saviour's about the educational problem facing parts of the town. 'Notwithstanding the great efforts that had been made of late years, they had failed to keep pace with the rapid growth of population. Eastbourne could justly boast of its schools and colleges for children of the upper and middle classes, nor had provision for the children of the poor been neglected, as admirable and efficient national schools existed: but there was still a crying want of schools in the Christ Church District, where a population drawn together by the increase of buildings and works in the more favoured quarters, was crowded together in squalid dwellings, a large proportion of them the victims of ignorance, intemperance and improvidence...' (19)

The building boom of the late 1870s and early 1880s had been largely confined to the erection of large spacious houses. Whilst the wealthy would not contemplate sending their own children to public elementary schools they did recognise that schooling was necessary for the children of the lower income groups. The Church of England was already established in the town as the sole provider of elementary education in 1870 and although this monopoly was to be challenged, the wealthy people attracted to the town were not likely to be among the challengers. As the town had no manufacturing base there was less chance of a prosperous middle class nonconformist group arising to contest the

Church's Schools. Although there were some notable exceptions by far the majority of the town's prosperous and prominent people were members of the Church of England. Speaking in 1895, Mr Langham said, '...he always thought that in a town where the Church was so strongly represented and where there were so many wealthy residents, the necessary funds might be obtained'.. (for Church Schools.) (20)

Landowners links with Church of England

The Church connection was true for the three significant landowners; the Duke of Devonshire, the Gilberts and the rectorial glebeland. The 7th and 8th Dukes of Devonshire were particularly generous in donating sites for schools: the former provided locations for Holy Trinity, Christ Church, the Wesleyan School, St Saviour's and All Souls; the latter for Meads, Willowfield Infants and Higher Grade Schools as well as St Joseph's Roman Catholic School for £400. Gilbert Davies provided sites for St Andrews and Green Street; Lady Howard de Walden, 'whose gigantic fortune was the talk of London in the eighties,' donated £600 to build Meads School and Lady Victoria Long Wellesley, great niece of the Duke of Wellington, provided £1,200 towards the cost of All Souls School. With wealthy and generous supporters such as these the Church of England was in a most advantageous position. Any school board that might have been formed would at the very least have had to meet the expenses of purchasing land for their schools. Apart from the NSPCK other benefactors donated on a smaller scale, such as the LBSCR which gave £30 towards St Andrews in 1887.

As a generalisation it is true to link support for the Church and some other religious bodies to the Conservative Party; that for school boards to the Liberal Party, Nonconformists and the slowly emerging Labour Movement, in the form of trade unions at national and trades councils at local level. The wealthy occupants of Eastbourne seemed to provide a united front; they were in general strong supporters of the CUA giving some credence to the 19th saying that the Church of England was the Tory Party at prayer. (21) Carew Davies Gilbert, became Secretary of the Conservative and Unionist Association (CUA) when it was established in the town in 1865, a post he held for the next 15 years. He was active in the Church Party's resistance to school boards. A County Councillor of East Sussex, he pointed out to a ruri-decanal conference in 1901 that at meetings of the County Councils Association which met in London he had taken stock and '...with one or two exceptions, they were, he believed all Churchmen and all Conservatives or Unionists...' (22)

One might have expected some sympathy for school boards from the Dukes of Devonshire. The Seventh, then Lord Hartington, during the Education Bill debate in July 1876 declared that the voluntary system was, '...a remarkable and anomalous system. It is a system which places in the hands of the religious bodies and private individuals duties and powers which in every other country in the world are considered as appertaining to the State and should be exercised by it. (23) However as the 1885 Irish Home Rule Bill made the Seventh Duke a Liberal Unionist, after that he and his son supported the CUA. They were both generous donors to religious schools for working class children; the Seventh was also a generous benefactor to private schools.

The Eighth Duke was responsible for education in the country as President of the Council from 1895 onwards. It might have been expected that in this position he would have taken a neutral attitude to the dispute between rival providers of Religious and Secular Schooling. When the CUA was returned to power the following year, together with the Prime Minister Lord Salisbury, he expressed sympathy to a deputation of clergy led by the Archbishop of Canterbury who complained about the competition from non-sectarian school boards. In 1899 he became President of the newly formed Board of Education. When Admiral Field won the 1895 General Election for the CUA in Eastbourne the Revd. Lynch was reported as saying that Field's '...majority was won by the extra votes of voluntary schools and he'd got in. Admiral Brand, the Liberal candidate said he wouldn't support them (ie The voluntary Church School system) he hadn't.' (24) Field had gained not only the votes of the Church of England supporters but also those of Roman Catholics, some of whom had declared, 'they'd go to prison sooner than pay the school board rate.' (25)

The final source of support for religious schools came naturally enough from the Church of England itself. The Vicars of Eastbourne championed Church Schools, especially Thomas Pitman and Bickersteth Ottley, who covered 70 years between them at St Mary's. The churches used their pulpits both to appeal for financial support for their schools and to warn that dire consequences would follow if a school board was introduced into the town. (26) As Ottley told the congregation of St Mary's in a survey of the Church's work during the year; '...once a school board, however small and inexpensive at first, is introduced into any part of the town where hitherto the voluntary system alone has existed, then, of course the subscribers to Church Schools are also compelled to pay the School Board rate....so that the resources of the voluntary schools are thus slowly but surely undermined. Their 'neutrality' as regards religion he considered 'a fatal flaw in the school board system.' (27)

Local Support for School Boards

By contrast the forces ranged in support of school boards were weak. In 1869 the Wesleyans had established a Sunday school and four years later a day school was opened on a site provided by the Seventh Duke. Initially, there is reason to believe that this move was regarded favourably by the 'Church Party' because whilst it was no serious challenge to the NSPCK schools in the town, at the same time, by providing extra accommodation, it lessened the chances of school board supporters being able to demonstrate that there was a shortage of school places in the town. When it closed in 1893, Chambers saw this as a plot against the NSPCK schools and wrote later. 'The spirit which actuated the Dissenters at this time is sufficiently shown by their having put pressure upon the Education Department to decree the formation of a School Board, and by their having in a very spiteful spirit brought about the closing of the Wesleyan School in order to create a new deficiency which they expected churchmen would be unable to face, but in this our Dissenting brethren were sold short. (28)

A more likely explanation is that the school was closed because the managers could no longer satisfy the requirements of the Education Department. (29) As is often the case the situation was rather more complicated. On the site of the present Wesleyan Methodist Church which was built in 1908 there was a smaller chapel and on adjoining land a proposed school room was built but the size of this 'room' is unclear. (30) Planning for a double purpose Day School and Sunday School were also mentioned later: 'Shell of a school room has been erected so far. Building Committee now out of debt –interior now under contract.' (31) It was not in the interests of Wesleyans to have their school closed but given the size of the site which was shared by the earlier chapel it does seem as if the more ambitious demands of the Education Department concerning facilities would have been the major issue. That the Wesleyans would prefer to have a non sectarian School Board rather than the prevailing Church of England monopoly of schools was also true.

Chambers, was born on 1841 in Upton on the River Severn. His father was a doctor and the family moved to Colchester, then to London. His acquaintance with Eastbourne was due to regular visits for health reasons 'to escape the London air and water containing living creatures' which did not agree with him. His views on the issue of school boards were hardly neutral. His grandfather was Rev'd Dr Alexander Brodie, of St Mary's church, and sought the original grant from the National Society. Chambers was Secretary of the Church of England Schools Extension Fund and an active member of the CUA.

For many of the people living in the poorer east end of the town there is no evidence to suggest they were strongly in favour of religion or education. In many towns, trades councils were strong supporters of board schools and put up their own candidates for election to the Board. In Eastbourne trade unionism was comparatively weak in these years. The social structure of the town and absence of substantial industry provided little scope for organised Labour.

The opposition to school boards however, as has been demonstrated, was led by the most influential forces in the town; strong and very well organised. A series of committee structures were able to raise funds to maintain Church Schools and at least for a decade or more following the 1870 Education Act, provide sufficient school places for the growing population of the town. Both the School Extension Scheme and later the Voluntary School Building Company enabled the Church to control Eastbourne's elementary schooling without serious challenge until the 1890s when opposition gradually increased and some voluntary subscribers began to doubt the wisdom of continuing the system as it was.

Initially Church organization was rather spasmodic and not particularly effective. A vestry meeting was held in 1872 to consider school accommodation in the town. In 1881 a 'Committee of Gentlemen' met to oppose school boards (although one year later the Revd. Allen was complaining of their inactivity). A vicars' meeting was held in 1884 also protesting about school boards; to be followed one year later by a meeting of the Town Committee which suggested that £4,000 needed to be raised to increase the provision of school places in the town. It is probably as a result of this meeting that the Eastbourne Elementary S.E.S. came into existence. From about this period of time onwards the shortage of school places became increasingly apparent although the exact number needed was always a matter of heated debate.

The Church of England and its supporters had been in a seemingly unassailable position for the two decades following the 1870 Education Act. The 1890s witnessed a series of challenges to them and an increase in the intensity of the arguments concerning the provision of elementary education in Eastbourne. The first sign of the challenge to Church supremacy came in the Spring of 1892 with the pronouncement from the School Attendance Committee that the town was between 800 and 900 school places short. This was reinforced with a statement from the Education Department that according to HMI's the shortage was nearer to 1,200 places. The School Attendance Committee had come into being as a result of Sanderson's Education Act of 1876 which authorized such committees in areas without school boards. It was unpopular with the Church School supporters. Before its pronouncement concerning school places the editorial of the *Eastbourne Chronicle* had attacked the Committee for failing to prosecute persistent non-attenders. 'If anything will force upon the borough a School Board it will be the painfully lax arrangements that obtain for securing a proper attendance at school....prosecutions for non-compliance with the Education Act are practically unknown in Eastbourne. (32)

The reports of shortages sparked off a series of meetings of clergy and laity culminating in a conference at the Town hall (16 May 1892) where a scheme was submitted and approved to build school places for 1,000 children; 500 at Christ Church in the east end of the town, 250 in the central District and 250 in 'Old Town'.

The cost was estimated at £6,000 and a subscription list was opened with early promises of £1,000. This was followed up by a high-powered conference attended by the 90-year-old Dean of St Paul's, J.R. Diggle (who was chairman of the London School Board yet hostile to school boards! Twenty five other members of the clergy were present and Dr Dunford, Bishop of London, who told the audience that, '...such schools as the Church possesses are good for all...' (33)

The main arguments of the Church and their supporters were that school boards were expensive because they made demands upon the rates whereas Church schools were cheap for the town's inhabitants. The latter were financed by school pence, voluntary subscriptions and substantial government grants. In addition school boards were claimed to be anti-religious. Referring to the 1870 and subsequent Education Acts which had made the introduction of board schools possible, Chambers proclaimed, 'It was an unmistakable fact...that the Education Acts tended directly to infidelity and atheism and were distinctly atheistic in essence...' (34) whilst the Rev'd R. Allen argued that,'...instruction, divorced from religion, not only produced a godless but a criminal community...' (35) There was always an element of concern for converts behind the sectarian squabbles of the nineteenth century as Canon Sanderson made clear at a ruri-decanal conference at the turn of the century. '...the Church was losing its influence over a vast number of children that were being brought up and taught in this country and was allowing these children either to fall into religious indifference or to subsist on a colourless religious teaching as implied by the term undenominational religion. (36)

Voluntary Schools falling behind with Provison of school places

With the publication of both the School Attendance Committee's Report and the statistics produced by the HMIs it now became possible to suggest that at the very least the Church had not been entirely successful in providing elementary education to all who were entitled to it by law. The Nonconformists and Liberals were not slow to exploit these apparent shortcomings and add further criticisms about the near monopoly of church schools within the town in the past. They never accepted the view expressed by some Churchmen that the latter alone were in favour of religious education. Frederick Allen claimed that: '...only 3% of school boards decline to have the Bible taught. Is it seriously feared that Eastbourne might go the way of the 3% and not the 97%....It is surely not suggested that Eastbourne, with its 10 or 11 churches will ever have such a school board...(37)

As for the argument put forward by Dr Durnford, that it was necessary, '....to save the voluntary schools of the Church in Eastbourne from threatened extinction ..' (38) the Hon. Lyulph Stanley from the London School Board replied at a meeting in support of school boards that, '...the Bishop and the holy men who surrounded him...must perfectly well know that there was nothing ...in the Education Act...that would be brought to bear to create a school board which would in any way threaten the voluntary schools in Eastbourne with extinction. The Act of Parliament was most precise in that respect. It safeguarded the interests of all existing voluntary schools, and the most the Department would do was to supplement any deficiency of accommodation which might be needed owing to the growth of the population beyond the present supply of schools. (39)

The Church of England and its supporters used two main arguments to resist school boards. One already referred to was the accusation that school boards denied parents the religious influence which permeated Church schools; the other had a far wider appeal because it held out to the inhabitants the promise of lower financial contributions for education within the town. School boards by their funding from the rates were portrayed as extravagant institutions and the towns folk could avoid the extra demands they might make by supporting religious schools on a voluntary basis. The situation was in fact more complex and in some ways the financial burden was spread rather unevenly. It was possible for some parents to avoid requests for donations and pay only the school pence demanded by attendance, whereas a school board system would have made them contribute according to the value of their property which in turn usually reflected their income. It was argued that for some parents their contributions through rates towards the cost of the school board would be greater than that which they paid in school pence for the year. A letter to the *Eastbourne Chronicle* commented, 'Do Eastbourne parents know that in 1888 the Government paid £2,630 towards their Children's education, that kind friends gave more than £900, and that their children's pence amounted to some £1,500 or £1,600?' (40)

The spread of schools did not reflect the religious beliefs or lack of beliefs of the population throughout the school board period. Some parents objected to paying through their school pence for education at a school belonging to a religious sect which seemed hostile to their own religious ideas. For all the money raised voluntarily an increasing proportion of it began to come from the State and this was provided by tax payers of all and no denominations. With school boards at least the local populace had some control over expenditure of money contributed by the community and the management of the schools. For Church schools there was taxation without representation. This was typified by St Andrew's School in the poor district of Norway Hamlets. The Trust Deed showed that the land had been donated by Carew Davies Gilbert and that the Minister was '...to have the superintendence of the religious and moral instruction given in the day school and entire control of the Sunday School.' The Committee was to comprise the,...'Incumbent of Christ Church for the time being; his licensed curate...if appointed by him...five other persons, members of the Church of England, subscribers of at least 20/- per annum... Vacancies to be filled by election. Electors to be subscribers...at the time of the election of at least 10/- per annum...members of the C. of E....Declaration of Church membership. Master or Mistress to be members of the Church of England...A Committee of not more than four ladies, members of the Church of England may be appointed annually in March. (41)

Hence in Eastbourne between the years 1870 and 1902, with the exception of the Wesleyan School and St Joseph's Roman Catholic School which opened in 1895, no teacher who was not a practising member of the Church of England could be employed in any one of the elementary schools of the town. Moreover whilst poor salaries were suggested as one cause of the lack of pupil-teacher candidates in the town once more only members of the Church of England were permitted to take up such appointments in the schools. Managerial and committee roles were restricted to Church members in comfortable financial circumstances. Moreover, 'the fact remains that they consist in each case of the Vicar and his nominees, and are in no sense elected representatives of the people – or ...of the subscribers either. Their meetings are also conducted in camera so that there is no means of judging how the important work of school management is conducted.' (42) The freedom of religion much quoted by Church supporters against the school boards did not seem to extend outside the boundaries of the Established Church in school matters. Even the lack of elected local representatives on school committees was pronounced as a virtue because it allowed the Town Council to avoid the 'expensive machinery' of a school board including the cost of triennial elections. (43)

Whilst the Church of England School supporters were comparatively well organised there were meetings held in favour of the introduction of a school board. To take but one example, it was reported that 'a meeting in the town hall was held in December 1892 by certain gentlemen who desire to see a school board set up in the borough.' They included Lyulph Stanley of the L.S.B. and George Gladstone of the Hove School Board The latter underlined the situation. 'Every school in Eastbourne at the present, excepting the Wesleyan, was in the hands of the Church of England, and it could not be pretended that the whole of the population of the town was Church of England with the exception of a number of Wesleyans. Therefore he urged there should be a variety of schools. The monopoly which it was said School Boards wished to have really existed on the part of the clergy.' (44)

Claims that school boards would prove more expensive to ratepayers were also challenged. The Rev'd J.B. Fletcher had warned in the Spring of 1889 that a school board in the town would require one shilling. Mr Diggle told the meeting this was not the case and that this claim made three years earlier showed a lack of understanding of the system. He provided examples of local towns who had school boards. For Brighton it was 6.5 pence but they were educating 10,000 children. At Hastings it was 2.75 pence, Folkestone 3.5 pence and Rye 3 pence.' (45)

More fund raising organisations for Church Schools

The Schools Extension Scheme which came into being in the mid 1880s to cope with increased demand for places can be seen as an umbrella organization under which two other committees developed: the Building Fund Committee and the Maintenance Fund Committee, both established in 1892. These last two committees worked in alliance and their respective tasks were to raise money to extend existing school accommodation and then provide sufficient money for their maintenance. A number of new church schools were built from their efforts and opened in 1894, namely Green Street (Upwick), Whitley Road and further buildings at St Andrew's in response to the serving of one month's final notice from the Education Department that a school board would be formed in the town. (46) The new schools finally cost around £11,000. Nearly £8,300 was raised by a subscription list, the remainder being obtained by a bank loan, part of which was paid off the following year from the proceeds of a 'Fancy Bazaar' held in the Devonshire Park over a 4-day period. The remaining debt of about £2,000 was gradually repaid by contributions from Church supporters.

The considerable increase of Church schools in the town meant that gradually the question of maintenance began to supersede that of construction. The maintenance Fund Committee was reconstituted in 1894 with the amended title of E.V.S.M.F. This revised Committee included local dignitaries such as J.G. Langham (Hon.Sec), H.D. Davenport (Chairman) as well as all Eastbourne vicars whether they had schools in their parish or not and delegates elected by the managers of each of the six school parishes. The main purpose of this Committee was explained by Langham as '…raising a common fund to assist in the maintenance of the schools and to make good such deficiencies as would otherwise occasion a lessening of the annual parliamentary grant.' (47) Hence apart from the subscriptions made within a parish for an individual school this central fund distributed payments according to estimated need to maximise government subsidies and the more prosperous parishes thereby helped the poorer ones. In 1895 the estimated needs of the schools' managers were as follows:

> Holy Trinity, St Saviour's and Meads nil; St Mary's and All Souls £122, Christ Church £156 and St Andrew's £246, making a total of £646. The system met with considerable success and within a couple of years two other areas, Wimbledon and Winchester,

adopted a similar scheme. Whilst Eastbourne raised on average about £850 annually the other two areas raised £3,000 to £4,000, a result which Davenport held up to the townsfolk as an example of what might be achieved if more people would contribute. In fact the fund was always in a precarious state. About 400 subscribers made contributions; these included, in 1898 for example, the wealthiest of the Church's supporters such as the Duke of Devonshire £58, the Dowager Lady Howard de Walden £50 and Carew Davies Gilbert £25, together with business interests such as the Eastbourne Gas Co. and Eastbourne Water Works £50 each, Barclays Bank, Eastbourne College and Electric Light Co., £10 each, London Brighton and S. Coast Railway £25. These notables were prosperous enough but they were simultaneously receiving demands from other similar funds also working on behalf of Church Schools. E.g. The Diocesan Confederation of Church Schools. By September 1901 the Maintenance Fund faced demands for £1,200 in financial aid but could raise only £882.

The *Eastbourne Chronicle* had been continually hostile to the idea of a school board, and whilst it faithfully reported meetings of both Church and School Board supporters alike its editorial always favoured the former. One regular column entitled 'Stray Notes' by Nimrod provided steady support for the church schools. To give but one extract, the writer posed the alternative to the present voluntary system for the town, whether the people, '...will sacrifice these advantages to the expensive luxury of a School Board, to a colourless and uncertain system of religious teaching, to a heavy and increasing rate and to a triennial saturnalia of faddists with a mission. (48)

Almost a School Board for the Town?

Yet the disappointing response to the subscription appeal found Nimrod the following year ending his column in a somewhat pessimistic mood: '...between the lethargy of the Churchmen and the determination of the Education Department, a School Board appears unmistakably to be looming in the distance and I have yet to see the wisdom of fighting the inevitable.' (49) A few months later still he was asking,'...is it rather the weakness of a sentiment than the wisdom of statesmanship to prosecute the struggle?' (50) The editorial also expressed doubts deciding to set before its readers, 'the facts of the case from a purely business point of view' and after comparing the difference between the money raised by subscriptions and the costs of providing extra school accommodation concluded by asking 'whether the friends of voluntary schools would not do more wisely to put forth all their strength to lose nothing of what they have, rather than strive to occupy new ground." (51) Even Hesketh Jones, chairman of the Eastbourne Branch of the English Church Union wrote to the local newspaper in despair at the failure of the Church supporters to raise sufficient money, stating, 'I am by no means the only churchman who is convinced that a School Board is inevitable...' (52)

In April 1899 the S.A.C. created an uproar by passing a resolution stating that it was 'absolutely essential' that additional places be created in the East and Western Districts as the town was over 500 places short. The SAC wrote to the Duke of Devonshire, who was of course Head of the Board of Education at the time, informing him that they agreed with the Education

Department's requirements and stating that it had their support in proceeding to order the election of a school board. The Voluntary School supporters claimed the report had failed to mention new accommodation provided at Meads and Willowfield. The *Eastbourne Chronicle's* editorial claimed 'a majority of the SAC have determined to lose no opportunity of forcing a School Board upon the town...' (53) and a letter to the paper said of the SAC,'...the body is notoriously opposed to the Church of England.' (54)

In spite of considerable pressure upon the Church to consolidate its position supporters now launched one further organisation, the Eastbourne Voluntary Schools Building Company under the patronage of the eighth Duke of Devonshire, the Bishop of Chichester, the Archdeacon of Lewes and Carew Davies Gilbert. The directors were familiar names of those associated with the Eastbourne Church Schools; Langham, Chambers and Davenport. This joint stock company which offered 10,000 shares at one pound each, of which the Duke purchased a £500 share, set out to build schools for rent to local school managers. Adjoining sites were provided by the Duke at a small rent of £12 annum for Willowfield Infants, which was opened in 1899, and a Higher Grade School opened three years later. The income of the schools would include 'the Parliamentary grant and fee grant' and if this was insufficient 'a share of grant in aid'. The maintenance fund was still in existence to provide help if it was needed. As the schools were the absolute property of the company they could be sold if the need arose to a school board. The company prospered and offered a dividend of 4%. The church supporters were delighted by the company's success. At the

Church Congress in September 1897 the Revd. W.A. Bathurst, '...alluded to the fact that it had the support of the Duke of Devonshire and that its special object was to prevent the necessity of a school board.' (55)

Duke's Conflict of Interest in School Provision

However a few years later at a Free Church meeting the Duke's role in this enterprise was questioned. The Rev'd. J. Hurst Hollowell, having been called to task for incorrectly stating that the Duke was Chairman of the Company wrote a lengthy statement as to the nature of the objection:

> The Duke of Devonshire, Lord President of the Council (and thus Head of the Administration of Education of England and Wales) took shares in the company to the amount of £500...he is guardian of the educational rights and interests of the whole country and it is his official duty to order the formation of a School Board wherever there is a deficiency of school supply. It was therefore, a matter for great regret that his Grace, while holding that position should become patron and shareholder of a company which aimed to prevent the formation of a School Board and to make a profit out of the transaction...Had his Grace been Chairman of the company itself his connection could hardly have been closer, for the first meeting of the company was held in October, 1897, at the Duke of Devonshire's Compton Estate Office. (56)

Eastbourne's school experience had been different from most of the remainder of the country. Had it been better or worse? In terms of the quality of schooling examples can be provided showing there was sometimes insufficient accommodation; in the East end of the town, 'the law requiring regular attendance cannot be enforced if school managers are driven to the necessity of refusing admission to fresh children.' (57) At other times there were glowing reports such as one achieved by St Mary's: 'Highest grant received for every subject from Education Department. Highest standard of efficiency further attested by fact that special recommendation of HMI's annual examination due in February 1896 is withdrawn.' (58)

That education might have been provided more cheaply without school boards could suggest that it was provided 'on the cheap'. There is some evidence to suggest that the Church Schools were forced to provide the minimum standards because their financial position was often an uncomfortable one. (59) Referring to the 1902 Education Bill the *Eastbourne Chronicle* praised the Conservative Government for attempting to lift the 'Voluntary Schools out of the slough of poverty and inefficiency'. The Revd. R. Allen wrote to the National Society in 1881 telling them that '...the builder would be glad to have his money...' and a few months later wrote 'The contractor is pressing me for payment....' (60) St Andrew's when constructed was described variously as 'a granary, a barracks and a cowshed'. (61) Tenders for building Green Street (Upwick) Boys ranged from £3,670 to £2,100 of which the lowest was accepted.' (62)) The salaries of teachers varied according to gender and who controlled the school. They were respectively for masters and mistresses; Wesleyan £172 and £84, School Board £154 and £108, Church of England £120 and £72; and Roman Catholic £113 and

£64. (63) It is possible to suggest that board schools might be able to attract better teachers than some religious schools because of their higher salaries.

Some Church supporters believed that because they were among the first in the field to provide elementary education for the children of the town they had the right to continue with this provision whatever the change in circumstances might bring. Squabbles between the religious bodies depicted by a cartoon in *Punch* showed children being prevented from entering the school door because the entrance was blocked by two people from rival religious groups arguing, implying that some would rather children went without schooling than be taught by a rival sect. The arguments over Eastbourne's education system were partly disputes over school provision and partly over religious and political control. In these matters the combined forces of the Church of England, the Conservative Party, the principal landowners and the wealthiest members of the community proved far too strong for the opposing forces of Nonconformity, Liberalism and a burgeoning but as yet weak Labour Movement.

By the mid 1890s it seemed as if the scale of the problem was beginning to grow beyond the control of the Church and its supporters. The continuous appeals for money were starting to try the patience of many. At a meeting of the town council the mayor declared, 'All I can say as one subscriber is that I amongst many others are becoming tired of it.' (64) It does seem as if all but the most fervent Church supporters believed a school board was inevitable and imminent. However the faith of the Church supporters was finally rewarded when in 1902 the Conservative Government, just like the cavalry, came to the rescue with the passing of the Education Act which abolished school boards throughout the country. Eastbourne suddenly found itself in tune with all other local providers of schooling! The Voluntary School Building Company duly sold both of their Willowfield schools to the local council for a profit. (Cost of Schools £4,694; sold for £5,995. (65) Chambers lost his seat on the County Council in 1904 after fifteen years according to him due to 'furious opposition engineered by political Dissenters, who made great and successful efforts...to obtain a dominant position to control the Education policy of the Councils in the interests of Dissent, and to the detriment of the Church'. The very opposite policy towards which he had spent so much time, raised such funds and organised supporters of the Established Church to enable them to retain a near monopoly of the control of Eastbourne's elementary schools.

Fee-paying schools

Just as income and social class were reflected in the area in which people lived so too was the school children attended. The provision of elementary schooling for lower income families was separate from that provided for higher income groups, which in turn was subdivided by the numerous further divisions in incomes of the more prosperous in the town. Various estimates as to the number of fee-paying schools in the town have been made. Chambers wrote in 1910, 'I know not the present number; but as far back as 1894 they had grown to more than 200, a fact which I found out when acting as Secretary of the Elementary Schools Extension

Committee.' (66) This is misleading because the term 'school' was being used to cover such a wide range of institutions which advertised in local newspapers and directories. Significant numbers of these 'schools' were either short-lived or seasonal, offered tutoring to boys but mostly girls, of middle class families arriving for the holiday season of several weeks. Numerous advertisements of the curriculum for some of these small schools provided for girls usually included classes in drawing, music, deportment and social accomplishments, in keeping with the expectations of the clients. They were often accommodated in large Victorian houses which catered for between 10 and 20 pupils. Large numbers of them came into existence for a few years and then closed, moved within the town or amalgamated with others similar in size and ambition.

Fewer in number but more serious in terms of education were a series of fee-paying establishments, usually with a considerable number of boarders, established largely during the second half of the 19th century. The Duke of Devonshire was persuaded to be patron of Eastbourne College in 1865. The college was opened two years later on land he provided at a much reduced rent. 'By the end of his life, he was not only the majority shareholder with holdings of £5,580, but he had also lavished an additional £12,468 on buildings, and endowed two entrance scholarships of £90 each.' (67) New College, a nonconformist establishment, was founded in 1875 by Frederick Schreiner, the same year as Moira House, a progressive School for girls which offered a wide curriculum including serious studies of the arts marking it out from many other girls' schools in Victorian times. Examples of other private schools among the many which opened in the town were Clifton House (1868), Eastbourne Ladies College (1870), St Saviour's (1879), St Winnifred's Girls' School (1880) and Avenue House, which started as a private house in The Avenue, a location favoured by several other fee-paying schools. Another which became quite well-known was Asham School (1893). Many others were opened but most did not enjoy immediate success.

There were wide differences between the numerous schools within the fee-paying sector. This was less the case between the local elementary schools in the town. The clientele between the public and private sections were distinguished primarily by the social class of the parents. At the fee paying schools they ranged from the children of considerably prosperous parents at the larger boarding schools to the 'sunken middle classes', lacking in substantial income but anxious to distinguish themselves from the working classes, partly by an exaggerated attention to etiquette, as per Pooter. (68) The Elementary schools of the town catered for the vast majority of children. In the directories of the time, usually only the fee paying schools are listed, which can provide a misleading picture of schooling in Eastbourne. This may be merely a reflection of the fact that fee-paying schools paid for entries in directories. However many years later when the BMA celebrated their 99th Annual General Meeting in the town in 1931 they produced a booklet for members at the Conference which devoted 83 lines to a description of the fee-paying schools and 7 to the local authority schools catering for the vast majority of the town's children. (69)

Corporal punishment was widespread in Victorian society; savage floggings were carried out in the armed services and in prisons leading to severe injuries and on occasions even the death of the victim. Caning was a common feature of elementary school life and teachers were issued with canes shaped like a walking stick. To some extent punishment was limited by the fact that children went home at the end of the school day and could report to their parents, who may well accept the chastisement, given attitudes of the time, or visit the school if they believed it was undeserved. Moreover teachers of elementary schools often lived within the local community.

By contrast this was not the situation in the fee-paying sector especially for those who were boarders. They were under the control of both teachers and prefects, with little chance of appealing to their parents who lived far away from the school, significant numbers often even in a different country. The scale of beatings given as a punishment to many boarders was truly horrific both in number and severity. There is overwhelming evidence that harsh punishments were widespread, almost routine, and their continuation difficult to understand knowing that many fathers who sent their sons to these schools were fully aware from personal experience of the regime they would experience. It was a situation which had been going on for decades with all manner of instruments being used for beatings within a variety of idiosyncratic rituals, some measure of which has been recorded by Jonathan Gathorne-Hardy. (70)

The consequences for some boys were traumatic. At the extreme even death. One example concerns William Gibbs, a twelve-year-old at Christ Church in 1877. 'After a caning for gross insolence to the gym master and then, having run away to his sister, a public flogging (was to be given). He became too terrified to return to the school. He was forced back by his father and locked into a room to await his fate. "He looked defiant," said the master. "He looked as if he did not care much what happened." How much Gibbs cared can be gauged from the fact that two hours later he was found dangling by a cord from a window, strangled to death.' (71) Letters to *The Times* and a public outcry followed including a Home Office Inquiry but no action was taken.

Eastbourne Schoolboy Beaten to Death

Doubtless corporal punishment was prevalent in many of the fee paying schools in Eastbourne as it was the norm for private schools. By no means typical was the case of Thomas Hopley who set up a school at 22 Grand Parade for the sons of gentlemen.

> He was a severe disciplinarian, but successful, and published pamphlets advertising physical exercise and chastisement to harden children. There were only six pupils, all sent because of special needs, and on 21 April 1860 Reginald Cancellor, 14, a backward boy with 'bad habits', was called to Hopley's study following 'intransigence' and beaten for two hours. The next morning the boy was found dead. But the inquest verdict was natural causes. The following day the boy's brother came to Eastbourne, saw bruises on the body and demanded a post-mortem, and when this showed horrifying injuries Hopley was arrested, charged with manslaugther, found guilty and sentenced to four years. (72)

To a great extent private schools were irrelevant to any shortage of school accommodation for the majority of children in the town because their fees were well beyond the means of most parents, especially those in the eastern area which had the largest population and one that was continuing to grow. In any case the ability to pay fees was not the sole requisite for entry to Eastbourne College any more than they were for golf enthusiasts seeking to join the Royal Eastbourne Golf Club. Alfred Ryder owned a successful book shop in South Street and was captain of the Eastbourne Downs Golf Club but was barred from the 'Royal' because he was 'in trade'. Eastbourne College Council displayed the same snobbish attitude which was prevalent in so much of Victorian society.

> At their second meeting in the Spring of 1867 the Council had been faced by applications for shares in the company from some Eastbourne tradesmen, and, as these shares would have given the holders the right to nominate boys to places in the school, the Council had taken fright. Legal advice had been sought, and, although they were warned of the importance of offending the local tradesmen, a resolution was subsequently passed that shares were not to be issued to them. (73)

This ban on the sons of tradesmen was first broken by Thomas Ryder, Alfred's son, a fine sportsman who was the first to win a scholarship to the college. He won an M.C. in 1918. He later sent his own sons to St Cyprians. (74) The name of the Royal Eastbourne Golf Club features again indirectly in the case of Eric Blair. (George Orwell) His mother Ida, having returned to England from where her husband was working in the Indian Civil Service, wanted Eric to have a public school education but could not afford the fees. (Orwell later would describe his family situation as 'lower middle class') Her brother in law, Charles Liouzin, lived on the South Coast. He was a proficient golfer and like the headmaster of St Cyprian's, a member of the Royal Eastbourne Golf Club. When they met at the Club, Limouzin persuaded him to help Eric Blair to gain a scholarship and private arrangements were made for the family to pay only half the required fees. In fact Blair was later to claim that he hated his time there, writing very disparagingly of it later in *Such, such were the Joys*. (Written earlier but published posthumously in 1952.) Yet in terms of teaching the school served him well as he obtained a scholarship to Wellington and in fact went on to Eton. Needless to say working class children had no prospect of being considered for the college. Fee-paying schools and elementary schools providing for the majority of the children were not part of a single education system but separated by financial and social circumstances in the 19th Century and the years ahead.

References – Chapter 4

(1) Caffyn, J. (1998) *Sussex Schools in the 18th Century*, p.37
(2) ibid. p.215
(3) ibid. p.108
(4) ibid. p.105
(5) Barnard, H.C. (1967) *A History of English Education*, p.55
(6) Morrish, I. (1970) *Education since 1800*, p.11
(7) v. Ch. 2
(8) Lawson, J. & Silver, H. (1973) *A Social History of Education in England*, p.239
(9) Maclure, S. (1979) *Educational Documents; England and Wales 1816 to the Present Day*, p.18.

(10) Dr Brodie to National Society, 2.11.1814, National Society Archives.
(11) ibid.
(12) *E. Chron,* 25.3.1899
(13) *E Gaz,* 7.12.1870
(14) ibid. 15.11.1871
(15) v. *Pike's Eastbourne Blue Book & Directory,* p.89
(16) Rev'd Lloyd to National Society, (N.S.) 29.5.1869
(17) Rev'd J.J. Irwin to N.S., 26.4.1871
(18) Vicar of All Souls to N.S., 12.2.1889
(19) *E. Gaz,* 17.5.1871
(20) Meeting of Maintenance Fund 1895, *Eastbourne Chronicle,* 19.1.1895
(21) v. Ch.2, Politics of the Town's Principal Landowners
(22) *E.Chron.* 7.12.1901
(23) ibid. 23.1.1877
(24) *E.Chron.* 7.3.1896
(25) ibid.
(26) ibid.
(27) *E.Chron.* 26.11.1892
(28) Chambers, G. *ibid.,*p.193
(29) Forargue, H.W. (1933) *ibid.* p.157
(30) *E.Gaz.* 22.6.1870 & 12.10.1870
(31) ibid. 5.4.1871
(32) *E.Chron.* 2.5.1891
(33) ibid. 5.11.1892
(34) ibid.
(35) ibid
(36) *E.Chron.* 7.12.1901
(37) ibid 12.11.1892
(38) ibid. 5.11.1892
(39) ibid. 10.12.1892
(40) *E.Chron* 15.2.1890
(41) NSA particulars of Trust Deed, St Andrew's 23.7.1886. v. also trust Deed for Christ Church School, 24.6.1869

(42) v. letters to *E.Chron.* 19.5.1900
(43) ibid 18.11.1899
(44) ibid.
(45) *E.Chron.* 10.12.1892
(46) ibid. 24.6.1893
(47) J.G. Langham to *E.Chron.* 9.6.1894
(48) *E.Chron.* 17.12.1892
(49) ibid. 21.1.1893
(50) ibid. 17.6.1893
(51) ibid. 18.3.1893
(52) ibid. 22.7.1893
(53) ibid. 29.7.1899 & 5.8.1899
(54) ibid. 12.5.1900
(55) ibid. 2.10.1897
(56) ibid. 14.6.1902
(57) ibid. 28.7.1900
(58) ibid. 25.5.1895 & 7.3.1896
(59) ibid. 5.4.1902
(60) Rev'd R. Allen to National Society 28.12.1881 & 3.2.1882
(61) 'Stray Notes' *E.Chron.* 10.3.1894
(62) ibid. 23.12.1893
(63) Report of the Committee of Council on Education, p.298
(64) *E.Chron.* 18.11.1899
(65) Forvargue, pp.55-56 & *E.Chron.* 25.2.1899 & 8.3.1902
(66) Chambers, G.F. *op.cit.* p.191
(67) Cannadine,. D. *op.cit.* pp.278-281
(68) Grossmith, G. & W. (1892) *Diary of a Nobody*
(69) Budgeon, W. (Ed) (1931) *The Book of Eastbourne* pp.81-83
(70) Gathorne-Hardy, J. (1979) *The Public School Phenomenon*, Ch.3
(71) ibid.
(74) Surtees, J. op.cit. p.9

Part 2
The Edwardian Years

CHAPTER 5

CHALLENGING THE POWERS THAT BE

Trade Unionism in Eastbourne

Trade unionism was weak in Sussex with only Brighton having what might be described as the core of a labour movement with Hastings a poor second. In the 1890s the county had a trade union density of less than one to every two hundred of the population but Durr has suggested that :

> 'it is more helpful to consider if there was any trade union membership among the occupational groups and trades that were functioning in the country: for example, Engineering, Building, Carpentry, Transport, Railways, Clothing, Printing, Paper, Woodworking... This group nationally made up 60% of the British Trade Union movement in 1888...These occupations were no more than 19% of the total working population, so prior to 1889 no more than a handful of workers had a trade union to join....even so, within the group there was no more than 3% membership.'(1)

An examination of the structure of the population and occupations of Eastbourne in 1901 showed that females outnumbered males by approximately 3:2, (21,422 to 14,134). About half the females were retired or unoccupied as opposed to a quarter of the males. Occupations were related to the demands of the town with around 2,000 women engaged in clothing, food, laundry and domestic service whilst males worked in building, conveyance, goods, food, drinks and lodging. With regard to women the national picture is described by Laybourn.

> 'It is clear that women, a not insubstantial proportion of the workforce, failed to be effectively organised within unions. In 1901 women formed 30 per cent of the workforce but only 7.5 per cent of the total number of trade unionists. The nature of their employment was part of the reason for their poor organisation.' (2)

Applying that to Eastbourne, much domestic work was carried out by women employed part or full time, visiting individual homes, mostly by themselves, occasionally with others, where the size of the dwelling required a considerable amount of labour for its upkeep. Their very isolation would mean that union membership would be impractical and largely pointless. If anything it might be a reason for dismissal! This situation would undergo considerable change in the Edwardian period, by which time some women were employed as clerks, in banks or insurance companies, nearly always in junior positions. A National Clerks Association was formed in 1893 and made some progress in major cities where clerical work had expanded rapidly with government and investment companies providing increasing employment beyond traditional financial services. However it was one thing to join a union and be one among many other clerical employees; something quite different to be one of a few in a local branch of a company in a comparatively small town like Eastbourne. Not only would it be considered an unwise move for an employee's career prospects but for most clerks themselves, any organisation remotely linked to that of manual workers, whether skilled or not, would not be something with which the majority of them would wish to be associated. There was a feeling among many clerical workers that union membership was associated with manual working class occupations which many of them considered to be of a lower social class than white collar employees.

Even in areas with considerable concentrations of industry, such as textiles in Lancashire, during the mid 19th century, there was little sign of unity among workers because there were so many different skills involved in a manufacturing process that attempts to form one big union for the trade initially made little progress. (3) How much harder was it in Eastbourne where working people were scattered in small numbers and unlikely to have a focal point to discuss any common grievances they may experience?

Of the comparatively few occupations which did have trade union membership in the country there was an understandable reluctance for working people in the town to become active members of a union, for it could be seen that taking action might lead to severe consequences. For example among many bitter disputes between coal mine owners and miners, in South Wales a crowd of miners in 1869, demonstrating against poor conditions and inadequate wages, were faced by troops who fired on them killing four and wounding twenty-six. (4) Such actions, whilst not typical, could nevertheless, deter those in small isolated groups, in other areas of the country from joining trade unions.

Local means of transport

Some forms of transport relying upon both residents and visitors were dependent on the holiday season and the weather. From 1873 to 1876 licences were required for those working with certain classes of vehicles granted by the Local Board 20 years before the Watch Committee of the Borough Council took over this duty. (5) Places designated with a metal plate indicated where these forms of transport could be found and were expected to wait for hire; for example HCS stood for Hackney Carriage Stand and BCS for bath chair stand. Categories listed were hackney carriages, saddled donkeys or ponies, bath chair-men and luggage porters. (Eastbourne Local History Society arranged for these plates to be restored and returned to their original sites by the Borough Council) These services were classified into various categories. For example, the number of horses pulling the carriage and how many passengers it could take. There were well over 100 of these in the late Victorian period but their numbers would fall when local omnibuses appeared. Similarly bath chair-men and porters' services were in steady decline. A knowledge of the town's geography was required and considerable strength to pull some of the bath chairs which weighed about 100 kilograms (2 hundred weight). With much 'unskilled' work in a town where the labour market was so precarious and reliant upon the holiday trade and weather there was no shortage of people willing to take on such work, if only for the 'season'. Many waiters and servants were also reliant on the success of the holiday season. This was to some extent dependent upon the weather but usually experienced a decline after October, rising again from March onwards.

Bath chairmen – an example of poorly paid seasonal work

To take just one of the vehicle categories, that of bath chairmen, we have considerable knowledge of the details of this trade through George Meek's autobiography in which he describes his experiences of life in the town spent largely in this trade. (6) Among all those listed above in terms of 'classes of vehicle' the bathchair men were the only group to ever form a trade union. This was a considerable achievement given the situation of these men. Some owned their own chair, some rented a chair whilst others might own several, working one and letting out the others. The Watch Committee set the rate at which bath-chairs could be hired. In 1892 a Bath Chairman's Union was formed and a year later they asked the Committee to limit the number of licences they issued as there was insufficient demand for the men to make a living from their work. The Committee refused but did limit applicants to those who had lived in the Borough for at least a year. Like many other working people in the town where working conditions were so precarious, their bargaining power was weak. It was not until 1911 that the number of licences were finally restricted. (7) Given the social composition of the town the idea of working people combining to gain some protection against the low wages available for many of the jobs required in the town's economy would have received scant sympathy from those living in the western part of the town, if only because they had little perception of the lives experienced by most working class families.

It is not easy to know the number of those working in the bath chair trade because the records available from *Gowlands Directories* only list proprietors rather than the numbers plying for trade. Meek claimed there were about 60 when he started in 1891. An examination of the number of proprietors from 1893 to 1912 shows about a total of 12, rising slightly to 1914 and then a steady decline to 5 in 1929. A Mr Tarrant had at least one chair from 1893 to 1925 and a Mr Bradford from a similar period to 1917. There were two men who are recorded as having chairs well beyond these years; Mr Farrier 1936-1940 and Manser 1935-1953. By this time they had become a seaside novelty.

For those who rented they kept a quarter of the earnings and Meek claimed he was attracted to the job by tales of men earning £2 per week in the Summer months during the 1880s. This would have been high earnings indeed for those years but would seem to be an exaggeration, at a time when skilled workers received little more than half of such a figure. (8) Yet such a tale may well have persuaded him to try this work although in reality his lack of skills left him with few choices within the labour market. Like many others in such seasonal work he tried to earn extra money from other casual employment; cleaning jobs in hotels and working behind the scenes at the Devonshire Park Theatre. There is no reason to believe that his experiences were any different from those of his colleagues. They shared the experience of so many seasonal workers; uncertainty of work and therefore no regular income. He recorded his experience of such conditions graphically in his autobiography:

> If you would know the horror of black despair go out with a bath-chair day after day, with the chair-owner or landlord worrying you for rent, food needed at home, and get nothing. Stare till your eyes ache; pray with aching heart to a God whom you ultimately curse for his deafness. And this not for a few weeks, but year after year. (9)

He also described a couple of acts of charity but they were rare for how would the more affluent be aware of the plight of those engaged in such work?

> On one Sunday at the turn of the century Meek had been waiting on the corner of Wilmington Square for twelve hours from 8 a.m. onwards without a single fare. He was just moving off home when a gentleman hailed him and not as it turned out to be for the hire of his chair but merely to ask him for a light. "Very busy?" he asked Meek whereupon the latter told him how he had spent the day. "That's hard lines, here's half a crown" and on learning that Meek had a family added "Here's another five shillings."(10)

The Building Trade

The majority of trade unions formed in the town during the late 19th century were related to the building trade: the Amalgamated Society of House Decorators and Painters (ASHDP) 1878; the Society of Operative Stonemasons, 1890; the Operative Bricklayers Society, 1891 and the Amalgamated Society of Carpenters and Joiners, (c.1891). The building trade was difficult to organise for a variety of reasons. Building companies may have retained some key skilled workers but employment for the remainder was reliant upon the season, weather and length of time needed for any particular project. These issues alongside slumps in the trade made membership of a union difficult for workers. Those who might complain about working conditions were not likely to be hired again.

There were always men desperate for work who could be persuaded to accept a lower rate of pay which undermined a building worker trying to maintain the rate at which he had been hired. The work was by its very nature dangerous and accidents common. Injuries sustained during work on a site might well prevent a workman being able to continue in a job but this would just be considered 'bad luck' and a common enough aspect of work on a building site. For example the use of heavy wooden ladders used to reach considerable heights on which painters were expected to balance, was a task made all the more risky when it was windy. They were aware that refusal to do so would mean that with most building companies they would lose their job for there were always others searching for work willing to take their place. At the same time building firms were aware that competition was fierce and that they always had to worry about being undercut by another company who might be less scrupulous in the working conditions they adopted. There is no evidence to suggest that conditions were any different on most building sites throughout the country during these years.

The arrival of Winter not only led to an increase in inclement weather but also a reduction in the length of daylight restricting or at times halting building projects. For casual building workers this would mean a reduction in earnings for in general, with the exception of a number of key skilled workers, no work meant no pay. Superimposed on this pattern of temporary unemployment were the major cycles of slump in this industry when supply of housing outstripped the volume of demand during many of the years between 1885 and 1896. (11) The lack of significant industry in the town meant that employment opportunities for working class people were very limited and when proposals were made which would have attracted some industry, they were rejected by the dominant groups in the western areas of the town. Regulations covering working practices meant that this was a hard industry in which to be employed. Robert Noonan's story of building workers in Hastings during the Edwardian period is written as a novel yet firmly based upon the experiences of the author, a house painter in Hastings, during these years. (12) He graphically described not only the conditions faced by building workers but the unscrupulous practices employed by companies in order to reduce their costs in such a competitive business.

Whilst these conditions for building workers were widespread some areas fared better than others. The monthly Trade Circular of the Amalgamated Society of House Decorators and Painters reported for the month of February 1881, the state of trade. It included 25 areas in England and Wales, in order that their members might know where trade was 'slack' in order to avoid such areas where possible. The numbers in the union are given providing some idea of their strength together with the 'State of Trade'. It is possible to note that seaside towns are among the worst effected in terms of both union membership and trade conditions but such comparisons can be misleading if coastal towns such as Exeter or Southampton are included alongside Eastbourne and Hastings. A few examples must suffice here:-

Branch	No. of members in branch	State of Trade
Exeter	3	Very Bad
Eastbourne	26	Improving
Hastings	53	Bad
Camberwell	33	Dull
Paddington	68	Dull
Plymouth	54	Very Dull
Swansea	40	Very Bad
Weston-Super-Mare	14	Bad

It can be seen that in comparison with some other areas Eastbourne was experiencing reasonable conditions but like most towns they also suffered periods of depressed trade in building: 'By the late 1880s, the orgy of building had spent itself. Indeed, the years 1886-8 were among the worst of the century, for the slump was longer and more damaging than that of the early 1870s had been.' (13) The *Eastbourne Gazette* claimed that:

> "The fact must be faced that Eastbourne has been very much overbuilt...It is no secret...that a very large number of houses are unoccupied...about eight hundred: eight hundred houses in a borough of thirty thousand inhabitants! ...Now many builders are in

liquidation and those who own houses find them a drag on the market..." (14)

Building firms went bankrupt and many among those in the trade became unemployed. Several years would pass before the major landowners put into progress new road and housing schemes which helped to reduce the uncertainty and unemployment in the building trades.

The Amalgamated Society of Railway Servants (ASRS)

The ASRS was comparatively strong in Brighton and Newhaven had an active branch. The London and Brighton South Coast Railway (LBSCR) had reached Lewes in June 1846. Later in the same month it almost reached Hastings with a station at Polegate, but it was not until 1862 that a double line connected it to Eastbourne. (v. Ch.2, para 1). Given that the Amalgamated Society of Railway Servants (ASRS) was not formed nationally until 1872 and there were only a comparatively small number of railway workers in the town probably explains why it was nearly 20 years before a branch of the union was formed in Eastbourne. There had been disputes between the managers of the LBSCR and employees on several occasions before the union was formed and in general these had not lasted long for two reasons. The first was that in the early years of the railways there were insufficient numbers of qualified railway drivers so that they were paid considerably above average wages before the 1870s. The other reason was that there were many different grades of railway staff including firemen, guards, porters, pointsmen and signalmen. Managers were sometimes able to persuade one grade to carry out the work of another group threatening to or taking industrial action. As railway workers became more organised this practice would decline. As a generalisation railway workers were reasonably well paid compared to many other workers with a measure of security in their work. As early as 1852 the LBSCR had published a statement concerning potential industrial disputes:

> The directors are in principle opposed to combination of any description for the purpose of interfering with the natural course of trade. They think that masters and men should be left in every establishment to settle their own terms, and arrange their own differences without foreign interference or dictation.[1852] (15)

The very terminology used of 'masters and men' may be seen to indicate the social divisions which were so much a matter of everyday life in Victorian times and this can be detected even among the railway workers themselves in the choice of words used in the title of one of their early trade unions, namely 'The Amalgamated Society of Railway Servants'. Although trade unionism was comparatively weak in the Eastbourne area there was a growing sympathy throughout the country for railwaymen forced to work excessive hours which were seen as contributing to serious accidents. 'By the reports of the Board of Trade inspectors on railway accidents the public were being made increasingly aware of the dangers to public safety of excessive hours of labour.' Among many examples was that quoted by an inspector 'Colonel Yolland, (who) reported that a contributory cause of a collision which occurred on the London and North Western Railway near Daubhill on January 22, 1865, was the fact that "the signalman's working hours were 5.30 am to frequently after 9 pm..."' (16) Such reports were of concern to those using the railways and led many to look favourably upon employees' attempts to seek improved working conditions. By the very nature of railway work, in which many of them were travelling frequently, information concerning activities within the system rapidly became common knowledge. Moreover, members of the ASRS were not an isolated group in Eastbourne but part of an industry-based organisation with a membership of hundreds within their own network and thousands nationally. Towards the end of the century they were in a position to act as a national body.

National Union of Elementary School Teachers

There are no minutes surviving from any of the Eastbourne local branches of these national trade unions with one exception; that of the best organised white collar trade union in the country at this period, the National Union of Elementary School Teachers. It was an achievement, given all that has been written about the social attitudes of the most prosperous and dominant members of the town, that this union should have been accepted as a respectable organisation to speak on behalf of teachers, school pupils and education within the town's elementary schools. They knew their situation and acted with tact and pragmatism. In addition it was generally accepted that school teachers had received a reasonable formal education and their members were respected in the community. Indeed in some villages they were among the few who were formally educated. The national union had been formed in June 1870 at a meeting in King's College, London University. In any case the school leaving age was only ten in 1876 and whilst there were some National Schools in villages few children experienced regular schooling. In some rural areas close to the town there were children who only went to school when they were not required to help at home or on the farm. Teachers were frequently frustrated when they found it difficult to keep to a planned programme of work for children when some were away for an important area of a subject which provided the groundwork for what was to follow and sometimes previous absence of other pupils meant they had forgotten material covered earlier.

On 7 November 1874, in St Saviour's National School a meeting of schoolmasters and school mistresses was held to form an association in connection with the Brighton District Union. Mr Joseph Welch, headmaster of Eastbourne's oldest elementary school, St Mary's, stated:

> that their aim was 'chiefly to promote unity and kindly sympathy in carrying out the work of education, to discuss the various topics of educational legislation, and to secure to teachers that amount of consideration which the importance of the work in which they are engaged demands.' (17)

Mr Welch had been appointed headmaster at 20 years of age; not as unusual during the 19th century as it would be years later. He had been born in Bedfordshire in 1835, the son of a farmer and became a pupil-teacher at All Souls School, Langham Place, in London. He had obviously been an outstanding pupil for he went on to Cheltenham College for a one year course from which he left with a Teachers Certificate. (v. Obituary E. *Chronicle* 19.9.1914) Most teachers were poorly regarded at the time:

> '....discarded servants, or ruined trades men; who cannot do a sum of three; who would not be able to write a common letter; who do not know whether the earth is a cube or a sphere and cannot tell whether Jerusalem is in Asia or America; whom no gentleman would trust with the key to his cellar...'

Such was the stated opinion of Thomas Babington Macaulay in the House of Commons on 19 April 1847. (18)

This claim would rapidly become out of touch as the first teacher training colleges were established in the 1840s. It does explain why initially those with a teacher's certificate were in considerable demand. The two routes to qualified status were to work as a pupil-teacher in a school where tuition was given by the head teacher on Saturday mornings and tested by an HMI in order to gain a teaching qualification. Those who did well could apply for a Queen's Scholarship to one of the few Teacher Training Colleges in the country, such as Borough Road, St Marks and St John and Cheltenham College. Whilst not detracting from Joseph Welch's ability, such early success was not unique. For example George Collins, born in 1839 near Bath began teaching at Borough Road School which was attached to the

Training College of that name. After five years he won a Queen's Scholarship of £27 and began the one year course in 1859. He left with a first class certificate to become headmaster of the elementary school in Newbury, Berkshire. (19) He would have a successful career as a teacher, founder member of the National Union of Elementary Teachers, (NUET), joint editor of their journal, the *Schoolmaster*, a founding member of the London School Board and the first Parliamentary candidate from the Teachers' Union. For all their proven ability many elementary school teachers did not always receive the credit their skills deserved because their one year certificate was not considered equivalent to a three year university degree course in terms of knowledge gained. This is not to ignore the fact that in terms of teaching experience and proven talent in the classroom they were sometimes more able teachers than those who came straight from university. Towards the end of the 19th century the overall accomplishments in education of a number would be recognised; James Yoxall who succeeded Collins as NUT President became an MP, as did Ernest Gray, and T.J. Macnamara.

Joseph Welch, as headmaster for so many years in Old Town, had become a well respected member of the community. He was interested in numerous issues in the town. Canon Pittman had made it clear that he did not believe Welch should consider becoming involved in local political issues. He made it clear that he disapproved of him standing as a councillor. It was a difficult situation for Welch but was finally resolved. Pittman died on the 3rd May 1890; Welch was elected as councillor on the 9th March 1891 for Old Town due to the death of Thomas Young . He became an Alderman in

1907 and was involved in so many aspects of the local community; Parish Clerk for 48 years, hon treasurer of the Eastbourne Cricket and Football teams, Secretary of the Rifle Club, a member of the Tyrolean Lodge of Freemasons and a member of the first Volunteer Corps. He died from injuries received when run over by a cyclist in 1914.

For all its shortcomings one positive element of British trade unionism, unlike some of its counterparts on the Continent, was that it managed to avoid division on religious lines. This was very important for the NUET, because after the 1870 Education Act establishing non-sectarian school boards, the union represented teachers in both these schools and those controlled by religious societies, the most numerous of which were the National Schools of the Church of England. Teachers avoided this potential problem in Eastbourne and the surrounding area for whilst the opinions expressed in some discussions were fairly predictable according to the school at which a teacher was employed they did not allow differences at national level to feature in their approach to local issues. The choice of the Eastbourne and District Association of the National Union of Teachers (EDTANUT) officers elected illustrate this clearly:

President: Mr Drury, St Saviours National School
Vice Pres: Mr J.C. Wright, Wesleyan School
Treasurer: Mr Towler, Hailsham School Board

This cooperative and pragmatic approach probably played a part in gaining support from influential local people. For example, the Revd Canon Lowe, Vicar of

Willingdon, was chairman, and the Bishop of Chichester, the Revds Canon R.S. Sutton (RipeVillage) and R. Sutton (Pevensey) were also supporters of the association. In 1888 Mr Wright believed they should concentrate efforts on the three S's: security, superannuation and supply, the last of these to be kept limited in order to safeguard wages. (20) In terms of schooling, the association expressed concern at the lack of action taken by Eastbourne's School Attendance Committee (SAC). They were particularly incensed that the statement by newly elected councillor Welch, had been branded a 'falsehood' by Alderman Keay, a response they believed to be 'most evasive and reprehensible'. (21) The SAC were under attack from both the local press and voluntary school supporters for failing to prosecute persistent non-attenders. The editorial in the *Eastbourne Chronicle* (2.5.1891) stated 'If anything will force upon the borough a school board it will be the painfully lax arrangements that obtain for securing a proper attendance at school...prosecutions for non-compliance with the Education Act are practically unknown in Eastbourne'. (22) This reluctance of the SAC to act firmly was not uncommon at the time. (23)

The Eastbourne Association sent a copy of their critical resolution to the Town Council and received a reply from the Town Clerk, inviting their secretary, Mr Towler, 'to attend a meeting of the School Attendance Committee and examine the books to see what had been done in respect of School Attendance'. (24) At the end of the year the Association's annual report stated that 'The outcome of Mr Welch's controversy with the School Attendance Committee showed that (the) Association had the power to help members. Greater exertion (had been shown) on the part of the

SAC since.' (25) There is evidence here that their organised pressures could be seen to be of positive benefit to local children and some recognition of their standing in the community. This did not stop various half or full day unofficial holidays linked to some customary event taking place as the log books, a form of diary introduced into schools in 1863, illustrated: 'No school today as Forester's Fete took place' (26); 'Children had a half-holiday this afternoon as there was a cricket match in the village, which is made a kind of general holiday (27) Holidays were also recorded for May Day, Sunday school outings, a visit by Princess Christian, the relief of Ladysmith and the Proclamation of Peace in 1902.

School attendance was an ongoing problem as absence was often connived at by some employers and parents; the former seeking cheap labour, the latter often needing the extra pence to add to the family income. It took many forms. In the surrounding rural areas customs were strongly embedded in the patterns of village life with children helping with farm work or at home to earn a few pence extra for the performance of errands and deliveries. Teachers were frustrated by these actions and the Secretary of their Association sent a letter to the *Eastbourne Chronicle* pointing out that the union had taken legal advice on the question of children being absent to run errands and had been informed that; '..the employment of such children during the recognised school hours is illegal, even though such employment extend to only half a day in every week....' (28) At their AGM that year the social consequences of absenteeism were raised:

> Surely we ought in season and out of season to insist that regularity of attendance shall be strictly enforced by

those who have the power, but shirk the responsibility, and then, forsooth, bewail the spread of Hooliganism, having the temerity, moreover, to attribute this latest phase of juvenile and youthful depravity to the "school", when it is undoubtedly the product of non-attendance, and therefore may be laid at the door of the Magistrates, who display at times lamentable leniency, or worse, inane indifferentism. (29)

This suspicion was confirmed by Reginald Graham, a Barrister at Law and Deputy Lieutenant of the County of Sussex in his book *Eastbourne Recollections* published in 1888:

However well intentioned, this Act (1870 Education Act) has worked a great deal of hardship...I believe most magistrates feel great repugnance to imposing penalties on the poor under this Act. In poorer families it is of greatest importance that their children should, as early as possible, make some little addition to the small family income by their labour: and it is often impossible to spare the elder girl from helping in the charge of young children, and indeed of the household, if the mother is ill.

The views of school teachers and some higher income persons in terms of regular school attendance were not easily reconciled. For the former regular attendance was important to ensure that children were able to achieve at least a basic education, without which, they could not gain the opportunity to break away from the poorly paid and 'unskilled' work which had kept their family in poverty. For the barrister he felt sorry for the family circumstances and was reluctant to apply a law which would punish them. However there is little doubt that he would not allow his own children to miss school because he realised the importance of education. The implication that it was fine for older girls to help their mother look after younger siblings was quite common, even if the mother was not ill. These social customs among lower income groups had a detrimental effect on the educational opportunities of many of the older girls in a family.

The behaviour of young people, especially those of school age, was of serious concern to teachers and the Association put forward a resolution to the NUT Conference of 1903, 'That in view of the alarming increase among young boys of the habit of cigarette smoking, this conference is strongly of the opinion that steps should be taken to render illegal the sale of tobacco to boys under the age of 15.' (30) The influence of schools on juvenile behaviour was a frequent matter for discussion, not only among teachers, but also among the leading members of the local community, and one upon which newspapers often commented. In 1890, Mr Towler, that year's Association president, referred members to a meeting in Seaford Girls' School to,'...the diminution of the number of juvenile offenders since the passing of the Education Act (1870?); and the salutary effects of Education generally.' (31)

Opinions on the benefits of schooling differed. In a column by 'Censor' for the *Eastbourne Gazette*, in an article favourably disposed towards teachers, it was written, 'To the incomplete character of the training given in some elementary schools we may attribute the complaints so often heard from employers and householders. A steady reliable errand boy is not easily obtained; and the behaviour of some domestic servants is constantly being made the subject of complaint.' (32) As one teacher commented, 'With regard to work done in the town, some think we teach too much, some too little, some think boys are educated above their station, or girls do not make perfect cooks...but we do something towards training good citizens and workmen. In a great many cases the schoolmaster is not able to influence (the) career of boys, as parents object...'(33)

One example of anti-social behaviour around this period was that of five poorly clad boys ranging in age from nine to twelve years of age brought before the magistrate in Eastbourne, Colonel Shaw, accused of stealing four bottles of marking ink from a draper's shop. It was claimed that pins and some bread from another shop had also been removed. The mother of one of the twelve-year-olds said, 'she took her son to school on Tuesday morning and did not see him again till he was in custody. She had punished him by feeding him on bread and water. The boy went from shop to shop and stole.' Another mother pointed out that she had taken her boy home after he had slept out for three nights and gave him a good tanning. One of the parents suggested that 'a birching would do the boys good.'

Having listened to the case and views of the mothers present Colonel Shaw declared: 'It seems to me that the juveniles in this town are going from bad to worse. Time after time we are called here to sit in judgement on boys and girls. It neither reflects credit upon the parents, nor, apparently, on the schools they have been at... (magistrates) were always unwilling to send young boys and girls to gaol, but if there was nothing else to do they must. Unfortunately, the legislature prevented them from ordering a whipping until a certain age.' (34) The boys were remanded in custody and removed to separate cells where 'they treated their position no longer as a mere joke, but cried out aloud for some considerable time. Two of them had already been before the bench earlier accused of stabbing someone with a knife.' (35)

'Censor' commenting on the case put most of the blame on neglectful parents, claiming that many of these cases were really a matter for the NSPCC. He doubted that the schools were really to blame. 'That Colonel Shaw is justified in suspecting that the schools are not all that they should be is only too clear. From personal observation I can testify that the existing system is at fault. The teachers are underpaid; they are often overworked; and, as a natural consequence, they cannot throw themselves heart and soul into their work. When the classes are very large it is practically impossible to exercise personal influence over individual boys. The Eastbourne Assistant Teachers' Association ought to take this opportunity of asking for the fair treatment to which they are entitled...the truth is that the people of this country do not attach sufficient importance to education; and they must pay the penalty of neglect.' (36)

There was also a social aspect locally to membership of the NUT. Summer outings were arranged which gave members from different schools an opportunity to meet in the surroundings away from that of their school. (e.g. A Char-a-banc outing to Battle for a lunch followed by a stroll and game of rounders in September 1895 and an outing by train to Heathfield in 1901) Whilst common issues might arise and be discussed the emphasis was on enjoyment with colleagues, a by-product of which was greater attendance at meetings during the year.

The Association promoted self-improvement for teachers in terms of personal education and information specifically designed to help their teaching. An example of the former was a paper on Wordsworth at the end of a local meeting, (37) whilst on one Saturday in March at the Devonshire Park Pavilion they organised an address by an HMI on the New Primary Drawing Circular recently issued by the Board of Education which attracted an audience of 300 teachers. In thanking the speaker the Association's secretary suggested that in future when school circulars recommending new ideas for schools were issued it would be helpful if a specific grant of money was provided for any new apparatus needed and in response to Government recommendations for a reduction in the present size of classes there was a wish for adequate funding to allow for a corresponding increase in the number of staff in the school. Class sizes were around 40 or more pupils in most Victorian elementary schools. Certificated teachers were paid more than uncertificated who often complained they were given the most difficult children to teach and female teachers, even when equally qualified to male teachers and carrying out the same tasks, received lower salaries.

Given the spread of teachers in the town and surrounding villages it is a measure of the Union's success that in 1896 at their AGM they could state, 'At present there are probably less than half a dozen non-members in the district'. (38) This achievement was due to the approach taken to restrict matters largely to local issues specifically related to education. They refused to become involved with wider political issues confronting the Labour Movement, such as the request for a donation to give support to the Penrhyn quarrymen during a strike of 1896-97, not because of the lack of sympathy of most members but because they realised that such action would lose them the support of many in the town. Whilst acknowledging that help could be seen as supporting the right of other working people to negotiate their working conditions with their employers they also realised that it would be seen by some as giving support to a political dispute. This could easily undermine the broad support within the town for their aims and actions. (39) It was for this reason that equality of pay between men and women teachers and the extension of the franchise to women was a dilemma for some members. Given the large number of women employed in schools most teachers supported equality of pay because it was seen as directly related to education and conditions of employment whilst the extension of the Franchise might be considered a 'political' issue. At the end of the 19th century equal rights for women were still many years away from being resolved satisfactorily.

In comparison other trade unions, for reasons already suggested, did not fair so well as the elementary school teachers. The lack of industry and the seasonal nature of much of the work have been mentioned but the one potential source of an expansion in employment, the railway, was rejected by the Chamber of Commerce. In Brighton with its much larger population nearly 2,000 people were employed on the railway. On a smaller scale, Newhaven too was often claimed to be a 'railway town'. In 1901 there were discussions between the mayor and the chairman of the LBSC Railway Company concerning a possible site for the construction of an engine works at Eastbourne. (40) This would have provided secure employment for many men in the town and increased the strength of the National Union of Railwaymen Branch in Eastbourne. It would also have swelled total membership within the region. The business community was 'horrified at the thought of a colony of artisans', in the town and duly condemned the scheme.

A similar proposal to introduce electric trams into the town also saw this suggestion being supported and challenged on lines of class interest. It was a contentious issue in other towns as well; Bexhill, Bournemouth, Brighton, Hastings and Torquay all initially opposed tramway systems but succumbed in the end. Eastbourne and Folkestone did not. A tramway system along Seaside and as far as Beachy Head was first proposed in 1896. It would have provided a cheap form of public transport for working people in the east of the town. The residents in the Western end of the town were 'chary of proposing anything that would in any way tend to lower the high tone of which the town is so justly proud'. (41) According to Chambers, 'in 1899, a proposal was made by some London speculators for the formation of an East-Bourne and Pevensey Omnibus and Tramway but nothing came of it... The route was quite extensive starting at Terminus Road and running to Langney Bridge, whence a loop was to be made to Pevensey Station, through Westham to Pevensey Village and back to Langney Bridge again. No invasion of the fashionable residential parts of town was included in the scheme.' (42)

Chambers, was well educated, both affluent and influential in the town, but unlike many of a similar social situation, supported the introduction of a tramway system. He was critical of the motor omnibus which he described as 'hideous, noisy, and stinking and no sufficient or satisfactory substitute,' for the tram. (43) There were debates over the issue including 'a great public meeting at the recreation ground, Seaside ... which may have numbered a thousand,...various speakers, including councillors, discussed the chronic condition of the motor buses and the question of trams.' (44) During the period of 1898-99:-

> The British Electric Traction Company, Ltd., suggested that the Corporation should consent to their applying for an order authorising the construction and working of electric light railways in certain streets in Eastbourne, or that that the tramways should be owned by the Corporation and leased by the Company. The Council were of the opinion that the Corporation should make application for an Order if tramways were to be constructed and that they should be worked by them. The Borough Surveyor prepared plans for the construction of tramways in the town. (45)

Inevitably there were considerable arguments over the routes proposed and pressure by different groups to make amendments to parts of them. The borough surveyor's initial proposal was for the following routes: Fort Road to the Town Hall via Pevensey Road and South Street; then to Eldon Road via Grove and Upperton Roads. Also from Upperton Road along the Avenue, Lewes Road, King's Drive to Hampden Park, with a connecting line from Seaside to the Upper Avenue via Terminus Road. The whole idea of a tram system was not popular with some residents, especially among some people living in the Meads area. An Opposition Committee was formed to resist the proposals and when a Motion was proposed for the construction of the planned system although a majority voted for it by 17 to 10, this was not a two thirds majority and so the motion was lost. A further proposal from the Company to construct a light railway from Eastbourne to Pevensey was also lost.

The arguments were reported in the local newspapers. All to no avail. An omnibus system was introduced in 1903 which would claim to be the first municipal bus service in the country. Most of the residents of the West end were pleased although their 'victory' had been won at the expense of the poorer residents of the East end. It would be decades before the issue of the greater pollution from petrol driven vehicles as opposed to those driven by electric power would become an issue. To that extent the residents of the West end had unthinkingly chosen the 'dirtier' form of public transport for all areas of the town, ironically, including, their own.

A Measure of Compensation?

Whilst the more affluent in the town rejected the development of industry, there were in any case no large deposits of coal or iron ore nearby on the scale which had provided the raw materials for the industrialisation which had taken place in the north of the country. The plans of the major landowners were specifically designed to attract residents of considerable wealth. This meant providing an aesthetically pleasing environment with commercial development strictly controlled. This did mean employment for working class people was largely restricted to service industries in which wages were comparatively low but there were benefits to all residents in terms of health.

Mortality rates in Seaside towns in general, and Eastbourne in particular, were well below those of other towns. Death rates per thousand in 1863 were 22 for Brighton and 17 for Eastbourne. These rates would improve further still to wards the end of the 19th century:

	1899	1904
Eastbourne	10.8	10.2
Hastings	14.5	13.2
Brighton	19.0	16.6
Scarborough	19.3	14.8

By comparison in 1899 the rates for Liverpool, Manchester and Birmingham were 22.6, 21.3 and 19.9 respectively. (46) In many northern towns, working class people toiled long hours in factories and suffered the constant effects of pollution from heavy industry. To be poor in Eastbourne was clearly not a pleasant experience but in Victorian times with few means of ensuring decent working conditions there were compensatory factors in terms of general health associated with life in a seaside town. This was true for most of the town's inhabitants.

References – Chapter 5

(1) Durr, A. (1982) *'The Socialist Revival in Sussex'*, Seminar Paper, University of Sussex,
(2) Labourn, K. (1997) *A History of Trade Unionism*, p.77.
(3) Lane,T. (1974) *The Union Makes Us Strong*, p.58.
(4) Hutt, A. (1962) *British Trade Unionism; A Short History 1800-1962*, p.28
(5) *Eastbourne's Historic Street Furniture* (1984) pp.9-10
(6) Meek, G. (1910) *George Meek, Bath Chair-Man – by Himself*, Chs. 26 – 28.
(7) *Eastbourne's Historic Furniture* p.8

(8) Meek, G. op.cit.,p.164
(9) ibid.,p.175
(10) Coxall, B.& Griggs, C. (1996) *George Meek- Labouring Man: Protege of H.G. Wells* p.103
(11) Cannadine, D. op.cit. pp. 370-376
(12) Noonan, Robert (1870-1911) Bellamy, J. & Saville, J. (Eds) *Dictionary of Labour Biography*, Vol. 10, pp.156-162
(13) Cannadine, D. *op. Cit.*,p.247
(14) *E.Gaz.*,6.10.1886 – cited in Cannadine, D. *ibid.*,pp. 247-248
(15) Bagwell, P.S. (1963) *The Railwaymen*, p.15
(16) ibid., p.36
(17) *The Schoolmaster* 28.11.1874, p.. 312
(18) Betts, R. (1998) *History of Education,* Vol. 27, No.1
(19) ibid
(20) Mins. EDTANUT 14.3.1888
(21) op.cit. 13.6.1891
(22) *E.Chron.* 2.5.1891
(23) Davison, L.M. 'Rural Education in the Late Victorian Era; School Attendance Committees in the East Riding of Yorkshire 1881-1903' *History of Education Bulletin, No.45, Spring 1990*
(24) Mins EDTANUT, 12.9.1891
(25) op.cit. AGM. 1891
(26) Willingdon School Log Book, 7.6.1877, Lewes County Record Office
(27) op.cit 13.7.1877
(28) *E.Chron.* 26.11.1898
(29) ibid.
(30) Mins EDTANUT 6.12..1902
(31) op.cit. 18.7.1890
(32) *E.Gaz.* 5.10.1898
(33) Mins. EDTANUT 2.12.1899
(34) *E.Gaz. Op.Cit.*

(35) ibid.
(36) ibid.
(37) Mins. EDTANUT 13.4.1889
(38) Griggs, C. (1991) 'The NUT in the Eastbourne Area 1874-1916; a Tale of Tact and Pragmatism' *History of Education,* Vol.20,   No.4, p.231
(39) Ibid. pp.336-337
(40) Cannadine, D. *Op.Cit.* p.372
(41) *E.Gaz.* 15.7.1896, Quoted in Cannadine, D. *Ibid.*
(42) Chambers, G.F. (1910) *Eastbourne Memories of the Victorian Period 1845-1901,* pp. 139-140.
(43) Ibid.
(44) Spencer, D. (1992) *Eastbourne Bus Story,* p.18
(45) Forfargue, H.W. Op.Cit., p.43
(46) Cannadine, D. Op.Cit. p.266

CHAPTER 6

EARLY SOCIALIST GROUPS - LATE 19TH CENTURY

During the last two decades of the 19th century numerous groups arose influenced by ideas of Socialism on the continent. They had certain features in common; their membership was comparatively small, several were short-lived, they often had charismatic leaders and frequently, alongside strong beliefs, there was constant bickering within and between these organisations. The oldest was the Social-Democratic Party formed in 1881 by H.M. Hyndman. In response to an article he wrote attacking the lives of the wealthy, Lady Warwick, a Mistress of Edward V11, went to remonstrate with him only to end up joining the organisation. She became a champion of its causes. Three years later it changed its name to the Social Democratic Federation. (SDF) At one time or another a whole stream of nationally recognised Socialists were members; Tom Mann, John Burns, Will Thorne, George Lansbury and Ernest Bevin. In the General Election of 1885 it fielded three candidates but became discredited when it was revealed they had received money from the Conservative Party. In the same year William Morris led a breakaway group, the

Socialist League, but this in turn collapsed after bitter internal disputes over the influence of Anarchism.

For all the disagreements within, such as the expulsion of the founder when he attempted to support Imperialism during the First World War, the SDF lasted for 30 years, finally uniting with other groups to form the British Socialist Party in 1911. (1) It produced a successful newspaper *Justice* which had considerable influence. The SDF gained considerable sympathy when in 1887 a march of 20,000 supporters made its way to Trafalgar Square to be met by 4,000 constables, 300 mounted police, 300 soldiers from the Grenadier Guards and 350 Life Guards. Hundreds of marchers were injured, 2 killed, 300 arrested and over 100 policemen injured. (2) The event became known as 'Bloody Sunday', and at the funeral of Alfred Lindle, who was crushed by a police horse, a massive demonstration of 120,000 Londoners turned out. The violence shown to the demonstrators convinced some within the Labour Movement to doubt the wisdom of these tactics. The result was the formation of the Independent Labour Party (ILP) led by Keir Hardie, an MP, who alongside others urged working people to work for election to Parliament. Leading members such as Ben Tillett, H.H. Champion and Jim Connell joined with Hardie. There was greater co-operation with trade unions which the SDF had neglected. The Trades Union Congress (TUC) dated back to 1868 and the London Trades Council to 1891. The former comprised the representatives from the major trade unions; the latter from London trade unions. The absence of a trades council in Eastbourne during the 19th century reflected the weakness of trade union membership in the town.

Other like-minded groups came into being; the Fabian Society in 1884 pushing for peaceful change by gradual permeation of the ruling class and its organisations. They were to produce numerous booklets providing a critique of the economic and social conditions within the country. Whilst their numbers were not large initially they became influential through their writings. Among their members were Bernard Shaw, Beatrice and Sydney Webb, and H.G. Wells. Finally in 1900 the Labour Representation Committee was formed by the Fabians, ILP and the TUC. There was no individual membership at first and all their candidates who stood in the 1900 Election failed. Keir Hardie became leader; Anthony Snowden and Ramsay MacDonald both joined. By 1906 individual membership was introduced and the Labour Party came into being in the form which would become familiar throughout the country.

One more significant but completely different organisation was *The Clarions*. After some years in the army and working as a storeman when he began to write short stories, Robert Blatchford joined the *Sunday Chronicle*. In a short time he gained considerable experience and became highly paid. (i.e. About £1,000 per annum in 1890!) Having observed the slums of Manchester he became a Socialist and in 1891 established *The Clarion* newspaper, a weekly, which was lively and interesting. It would become the most successful Socialist newspaper for more than two decades. The slums of Manchester had been vividly described a generation earlier in a detailed survey by Frederick Engels (3) A number of articles Blatchford wrote were published in a booklet form in 1892 as *Merrie England* selling three quarters of a million copies in its first year.

It would be mentioned as an influential text by many people who became active in the Labour Movement.

The *Clarion* became more than a newspaper. *Clarion* cycling clubs were formed and groups cycled out to a town where they would set up a stand to address an open- air meeting and like missionaries attempt to persuade their audience as to the virtues of a Socialist society. In some places they established hostels for members. The *Clarion* movement from the newspaper to the active members was a considerable success during the 1890s but divisions arose within the membership when Blatchford supported the Boer War and then later, more controversially, the 1914-18 War. Significant numbers of the membership opposed the idea of working people of one country agreeing to fight and kill those of another; a disagreement which became quite bitter when significant numbers became conscientious objectors. Just like the leader of the SDF, Hyndman, many saw Blatchford as betraying the ideals of Socialism; a similar split which would occur in the new Labour Party by 1914.

The impact of Socialist Ideas in Eastbourne

Most of the organisations mentioned so far had their origins in industrial areas, including London. For reasons already mentioned, radical views were difficult to spread in rural areas or towns where there was an insignificant manufacturing base. This has been clearly demonstrated with regard to seaside towns in which work was largely related to the provision of services for the holiday season and the more affluent residents in the western parts of the town. Yet there is evidence that there were public meetings at which speakers from

Socialist and other organisations addressed audiences, sometimes in small numbers, other times of considerable size. They were more frequent than might have been considered given the assumption that the town was overwhelmingly conservative minded in most aspects of life. These meetings suggest a greater interest among working people of challenging political ideas that it might have been assumed were held by almost all the town's residents. Both the *Clarion* and local newspapers often covered these events. A few examples for the year 1895 can suffice to give an indication of the content and nature of some of these meetings.

> A meeting of Socialists will be held at Welsh's Dining Rooms, Susan's Road,
> Tuesday 14th, 8 pm. Object – to discuss the desirability of forming a Socialist
> Society or Club in Eastbourne. Will *Clarion* readers please attend. (4)

> The next meeting of the newly formed *Clarion Club* will be held at Wadey's
> Hotel, Friday 31 May, 8.30. Will all *Clarionettes* please attend or communicate with the secretary, C. Chapman, 2 Cricketfield Cottages.
> 25 May, p.166) (5)

> Eastbourne *Clarion Cycling Club* report membership of 20 and prospect of 20 more. Would like copy of some other clubs' rules.
> 8 June p.182) (6)
> C. Chapman, Secretary

The local newspapers also carried notices of future meetings and reported on them.

Meeting Bakers Temperance Hotel. Mr Russell Smart – commercial traveller.
Independent Socialist candidate for Huddersfield in Summer ..G. Meek presided
R. Smart said 'the object of the Socialists was to make use of the various collective and organised municipalities and democratic institutions of the country in order that the resources of the country might be utilised for the welfare of the people in that country and not merely for the benefit of a few private individuals who use the resources of the land, the instruments of production and the working classes themselves merely as the wheels of a machine which ground profit for their benefit only. He proposed the solution was to adopt the methods being adopted by areas in Huddersfield, Nottingham and Glasgow – municipilisation, by which industries such as gasworks, electric lighting, waterworks, tramways and free libraries were being provided by the local authorities. A lively discussion followed and Mr George Quirk, a local Liberal, expressed his view that 'Socialism was impossible'. (7)

For some it must have seemed Utopian; for others, however desirable – difficult to achieve considering the powerful and controlling vested interests involved.

The *Gazette* reported the meeting in detail devoting 22 column inches (65 cms) to it under several subheadings, including "Collectivism in Municipal Politics", 'An Independent Socialist Candidate' and 'Mr Russell Smart in Eastbourne'. It was a straightforward factual account of what was said at the meeting with no attempt by the paper to give an opinion on the views expressed.

CLIVE GRIGGS

Karl Marx and Frederick Engels in Town

Eastbourne was the favourite sea-side town of two of the most well-known Socialist thinkers of the time; the Germans Frederic Engels (1821-1895) and Karl Marx (1818-1883). The *Eastbourne Gazette* subtitled 'The Fashionable Visitors Record and Guide' included Engels in the guest list of Astor House, 4 Cavendish Place, with an asterisk placed alongside his name denoting he was a gentleman of some importance. He had been a regular visitor to the town enjoying in particular the walk along the sea front and up to Beachy Head. Marx and his wife Jenny sometimes accompanied Engels. Earlier in July 1881 they had all stayed at 43 Terminus Road. Engels stayed there again in 1883 and 1887, when he was accompanied by Helen Demuth, who had been housekeeper to the Marx family, a role she continued with the Engels Family.(8) Engels was aware in 1894 that he was suffering from cancer of the throat. On the 14th November he added a codocil to his will, that his body be cremated and ashes thrown into the sea off Beachy Head. He wrote his last letter from Eastbourne dated 23rd July 1894, returned to London and died the following week on 5th August. After the funeral on the 27th August his request was carried out by Eleanor Marx, Edward Aveling, Edward Bernstein and Frederick Lessner. Unfortunately for them the sea was very stormy on that day.

One question that arises is why these two famous men who were good friends with many of the radical thinkers of the time including Keir Hardie, William Morris, John Burns and Tom Mann, seem to have made no effort to contact those seeking to establish the small embryonic Socialist groups which began to emerge in Eastbourne. There are at least two possible explanations. The simplest could be that given the hectic lives they lived in London with countless meetings, hours devoted to research and writing, they used their days in Eastbourne as an opportunity to recharge their batteries. More likely is that the dates when they were most active did not coincide with events taking place locally. For example, by the time that some progress was being made towards forming a branch of the *Clarions* in the town in 1895, Marx had been dead 12 years and Engels died in that same year. They had arrived in England in 1848 after being expelled from Paris; by then the biggest radical movement in the country, the Chartists, who had been pressing their six demands upon Parliament, had peaked after ten years of activity. Strictly in terms of these demands they had failed in their ambition. During these years of great activity their leading members had been imprisoned and some transported. The movement broke up and only Ernest Jones became friends with the two emigres in the years which followed. (9)

It needs to be emphasised that in other respects Chartism could claim some credit for social reforms which had been achieved by their support; the Ten Hours Act (1833) which limited hours of work for children to 48 per week and prohibited under 9 year olds from working in textile mills, the Mines Act (1842) prohibiting women, girls and boys under ten from working underground and the Factory Act (1844) which limited the hours of children under thirteen to 6.5 hours and women to twelve hours per day. Moreover, as organised labour began to grow in the last two decades of the 19th century many of the active members were found to have been former Chartists.

CLIVE GRIGGS

Eastbourne's 'House of Commons' – another source of opinion

Local parliaments – each with a Government and Opposition following parliamentary rules were extremely popular institutions in Victorian England, representing another aspect of the public appetite for participation in the struggles between the political parties. They had been stimulated by the Reform Acts of 1867 and 1884. The Parties increasingly sought to gain support from these new sources of potential voters and established clubs to cater for their recreation to draw them into the Party if possible; the Liberal Club opened in 1885, a year after the opening of the Conservative Club. They both provided a wide range of facilities including meals, alcoholic and non-alcoholic drinks, and recreation. A reading and writing room, billiards room and one for games such as cribbage, chess and draughts were also available. They were open weekdays until about 11 pm but closed on Sundays. Eastbourne's first attempt to introduce a 'local Parliament' in 1882 was a brief one because 'a violent, abusive attack upon the Conservative leader, F.G. Pownall, appeared in the *The Courier*, edited by Alexander Bancroft, a Socialist Radical, who refused to provide a written apology, which led to a Conservative walk-out.' (10)

Nearly a decade later the idea was revised with Liberals in a small majority over the Conservatives (67 – 60 seats) and 42 Independents, including George Meek as the only declared Socialist member. Each participant paid 2/6d. per session at a time when the wages for building workers on the South Coast were about five old pence per hour with most working a fifty hour week. (There were 240 old pence to a pound and 2/6 was one eighth of a pound.) George Meek, in spite of poor financial circumstances, was willing to subscribe the required fee because of his interest in political matters, the opportunity it provided to express his views, and like many other participants, to see them reported in the local newspapers.

This 'local Parliament' tried to copy as accurately as possible the model at Westminster. Women were excluded here just as they were in the National Parliament, a situation which would continue for many more years until Lady Astor succeeded her husband as MP for Plymouth in 1919. 'Members' were not elected but paid a subscription and could choose which constituency they were supposed to be representing. It was all taken very seriously although to some extent those taking part were in effect 'acting' out a part. There was a Speaker and Deputy, a Prime Minister and other Cabinet ministers listed. The Chancellor of the Exchequer had no access to funds for recommendations which might be made and the PM no real power yet it is clear that the procedures, announcements and debates, followed those of the National Parliament as closely as possible, including the language, which was at times both stilted and pompous:

A Mr Brown, 'threw himself on the indulgence of the House' (11)

Certain statements have been circulated of late which in my humble opinion are derogatory to the dignity of this honourable House...and moreover.... (Mr Fenmorf?) (12)

There was a Queen's Speech made...Gentlemen of the House of Commons.

> The communication which I receive from Foreign Powers assure us of their continued Goodwill. I have called upon China to bring the authors of the recent outrages upon English missionaries to justice. I am happy to say the demand has been complied with. A Bill will be submitted...for the shortening hours of labour of shop assistants and railwaymen..and for the promotion of conciliation in trades disputes with a view to the prevention of strikes...Proposals will be laid before you for the better regulation of the liquor traffic, and for the abolition of the system of tied houses. You will be asked to provide a fund for granting Old Age Pensions.

Mr J. Trowell rose to move this humble address.

> ...be presented to her Majesty, and thanking her for her most gracious speech. (13)

Those attending acted just like MPs at Westminster with criticisms at times, approval at others and also humour. As a means of raising serious matters and drawing them to the attention of local people such as the long hours worked by shop assistants, it would serve a useful purpose but the Eastbourne House of Commons had no power to take action. Was China really going to comply with a demand which came from 'MPs sitting occasionally in Eastbourne Town Hall? What notice would the National Government make of their requests for Old Age Pensions? The answer to that is quite clear. It would not be a part of the political programme of Lord

Salisbury's Conservative Government of that same year in 1895 or that of any other Conservative Government of the time. Old Age Pensions would have to await the election of the Liberal Government in 1906 when a non-contributory scheme came into being in 1908 by which those over 70 years of age, whose income did not exceed £21 per annum, would receive five shillings a week. The Liberal Government of Campbell Bannerman also brought in a system of school meals following reports of the poor physical condition of many Boer War recruits who had lacked sufficient nutrition when children. Both of these measures were due to the activities of two genuine reformers; Lloyd George as (the real) Chancellor of the Exchequer and Winston Churchill at the Board of Trade.

Perhaps the Eastbourne House of Commons should be seen more like a debating society where points of view on matters of both local and national interest were discussed by men, reports of which appeared in the local newspapers. At the very least the attention of the local people was alerted to proposed developments in the town which were of relevance to many, such as the excessive hours worked by railwaymen with obvious relevance to all in terms of safety. On other issues the major landowners made decisions which had little prospect of being challenged by the majority of the town's population.

There were some views expressed which might be considered as fitting the stereotypical view of conservative attitudes in Eastbourne. 'Mr Wheeler (Conservative) speaking in reference to the Second Chamber, said that they (the Conservatives) agreed with the hereditary principle of the House of Lords (derisive Ministerial laughter and opposition cheers.) The hereditary principle, he took it, was the descent of father to son. The sons of noble lords, he believed, were educated up to political functions (cries of 'No', laughter and opposition cheer). 'What about the idiots?' and further cries of 'No' and 'Yes'. (14)

By contrast, Mr G.E. Quirk (Liberal) stated that, 'In the interests of commerce, public economy and the welfare and prosperity of the people it is expedient that Parliament take the necessary steps to acquire the ownership of the railways of the United Kingdom'. (Applause) (15) A call which was taken up again a fortnight later when he contended that, 'the railway system was essentially a monopoly and one of those public institutions which ought to be controlled by the Government of the country. He instanced the post office and electric telegraph as being under the administration of the State in the interests of the whole community and said he could not conceive of arguments that applied to the control of these institutions by the State which did not comply with tenfold force to the similar administration of the railways. Claims were made that fares would be lower, the transmission of food products to the market better, that in countries which had adopted such a scheme passenger numbers had increased due to lower fares made possible by a greater volume of traffic. The motion was put to the 'House', 'and was received with loud cries of "Aye" and a few feeble "noes". A clear majority in favour of the nationalisation of the railways; nearly fifty years before it materialised!

Various social attitudes were raised and discussed. F. Wilson called attention to the 'blasphemous, seditious and indecent character of certain speeches reported' at various public places around the 5th November when Guy Fawkes night was celebrated with marches and bonfires at which anti-Catholic sentiments were made by a minority within the crowd. This was an issue raised on more than one occasion even although most of the crowd gathering to watch bonfires did so purely as a means of seeing the ritual as an opportunity for fun and pleasure. Mr C.F. Simmons (Conservative) called for 'the better treatment of the aged and poor in our Unions and the removal of the badge of poverty they wore, so that when they had their day out they would not be ashamed to see those they had known in better days.' (16)

The local newspapers gave extensive coverage of the discussions that took place at the town's 'House of Commons' which ranged far and wide. The scheme did allow for numerous public and national events to be considered. It clearly lacked any power at local level and there was nothing particularly democratic about its membership. Indeed Mr. J. Fuller held what would later be considered anti-democratic sentiments. He 'expressed his opposition to manhood suffrage, as the working classes, who outnumbered all other classes of the community, would have the government of the country entirely in their hands.' (17)

Trade Unionism in the 1890's – an overview

During the 1890s there was a steady expansion of trade unionism within the country; a trend which would continue into the early Edwardian period. Socialist organisations, especially the ILP were also making their presence more widely known. Some of the latter thought that trade unionists would be their natural allies but in this they were far too optimistic. 'In the 1890s...the vast majority of trade unionists maintained an allegiance to the Liberal Party, and, to a lesser extent, the Conservative Party.' (18) Yet from 1893 onwards, when the ILP was formed there were strong moves in some areas for it to capture trade union support.

There is some evidence to suggest that there was a gradual move away from the Liberal Party taking place although the special circumstances in the town, low trade union membership and limited documentary evidence suggests caution is needed for this view. Meek's autobiography describes his personal change of allegiance, although there is always the consideration that the hindsight possible in his interpretation of past events may have influenced details of his account. There was more than one factor involved in his move away from Liberalism, including a source of well-paid employment in his work for the Party and his new-found choice of contemporary political newspapers; namely *The Clarion*, *Justice* and *The Workman's Times*.

> Influenced by the new political creed, he drifted away further and further from orthodox Liberalism until, in the Spring of 1893, after holding an open air meeting and advising his hearers to form an ILP group, he was expelled from the Liberal Party. The cost to Meek of following his convictions was by no means negligible, although it might have been even greater. He had been on the Liberal Executive Committee and District Council and Brown, the agent, had promised him before the 1892 General Election that, if the Liberal candidate won, Meek would be appointed to a permanent post as assistant registration agent at a good

salary. The defeat of the Liberal candidate had removed this possibility about nine months before Meek was expelled from the Party but he was still forfeiting the chance of occasional lucrative work which, for an unskilled man who had just had a bad season with his bathchair, was a significant sacrifice. (19)

It needs to be born in mind that changes in political attitudes were not necessarily a sign of conversion, for many people remained committed to certain ideas in spite of altering social circumstances which might have taken place, even if the changes were detrimental to their own circumstances. Familiarity and loyalty were strong influences for continuity of belief. Sudden changes of events such as younger people entering the work place who might be unwilling to accept the status quo might be more likely to identify with new political groupings. Episodes such as 'the strike in 1891 in response to the Manningham Mills directors' attempts to reduce wages which lasted 19 weeks, the Liberal-dominated Bradford Watch Committee seeking to prevent the strikers holding meetings, the events which led to the calling in of troops and the reading of the riot act, all demonstrated to many working men, that the Liberal Party was against the economic interests of the mill workers.' (20) These actions suggested to many that there might be need for a new political party focused more on improving the working conditions of ordinary people than the Liberal Party. It would take more than a decade for significant numbers of working people to accept such an idea but some new leaders were 'waiting in the wings' working hard to see such an ambition fulfilled.

References – Chapter 6

(1) v. 'Hyndman and the SDF' in Hobsbawm, E.J. (1964) *Labouring Men*
(2) Morton, A.L. & Tate, G. (1989) *A People's History of England*, pp. 385-6
(3) These had been described vividly in the mid-19th century in Engels, F., *The Conditions of the Working Class England in 1844.*
(4) *The Clarion* 11.5.1895, p. 157
(5) ibid. p. 166
(6) ibid. p.182, 8.6.1895
(7) *E.Gaz.* 16.10.1895, p.12
(8) Fagan, H. 'Engels in Eastbourne' *E.Gaz.* 24.4.1976; 'Engels in Eastbourne' *Visual History,* No.1, August 1975
(9) Wheen, F. (1999) *Karl Marx*, pp.195-196
(10) Coxall, B. & Griggs, C. (1996) *George Meek – Labouring Man; Protege of H.G. Wells,* pp.66-69, and footnote 71, p.79
(11) *E.Gaz.* 13.10.1895
(12) ibid.
(13) ibid.
(14) *E.Gaz.* 26.10.1895, p.6
(15) ibid.
(16) ibid. 9.11.1895, p.2
(17) *E.Chron.* 23.11.1895
(18) Laybourn, K. p.81
(19) Coxall, B. & Griggs, C. op.cit. p.59
(20) Laybourn, K. op.cit.

CHAPTER 7

EDWARDIAN DAYS 1901-1914

Keeping up Appearances

Both housing and district were clear indicators of a family's financial situation. The obsession in the Victorian age with all aspects of social class continued into the Edwardian years albeit with increasing challenges to the hierarchical structure which attempted to hold back change. Initial judgements concerning a person's class were still used as a means of characterising them; the way a person spoke in terms of accent and vocabulary, the school they had attended and their interests. Many people accepted the place they seemed to have been assigned to in life. There was always a thinking minority who did not believe that some were of greater worth as human beings than others simply because they were wealthier. Gradually like-minded people began to come together and form organisations which challenged some of the social and political assumptions of the previous century. Groups were formed either focusing on a central theme, such as ratepayers calling for elected councillors to undertake greater scrutiny of the finances in their district or suffragists demanding equal voting rights for women to those already granted to men.

A series of political groups calling for fundamental changes to what they believed to be the vastly unequal and unfair distribution of power and wealth within the country also began to increase in numbers. These political groups with their origins in the late Victorian period would gain in influence slowly as the 20th century progressed. It was not just a case of trying to convince large numbers of the population as to the justice of their cause but also to overcome vested interests which stood to lose from certain social changes. It would be incorrect to suggest that Eastbourne or any other South Coast resort, with the possible exception of Brighton, was a major force in these national trends but a reading of both local and specialised newspapers sympathetic to Socialist ideas, reveal that such activity was far more widespread than previously thought. The fact that these movements and ideas were to be found mainly in the poorer eastern part of the town may explain why less has been known about them in the past. One example of the slow pace of change in the country was the issue of equal pay for teachers. Those working in the schools of the town had to await protracted discussions nationally over a quarter of a century before the case was approved. e.g. The National Federation of Women Teachers (NFWT) campaigned for equal pay within the NUT who adopted the policy in 1919. A 1946 Royal Commission recommended equal pay in 1946; it was agreed to in 1955 and phased in over the next 5 years. The Edwardian period witnessed growing support for women to be granted the franchise on equal terms to men. The majority of Asquith's 1908 Cabinet were opposed to the principle thereby stimulating growth within organised women's movements.

In general clothing was strongly related to income and occupation. Those engaged in hard manual work wore clothing appropriate to the nature of the task in hand; building workers needed warm clothing and heavy boots. Some wore overalls but many were dressed inadequately for the nature of the work they were undertaking. Small building firms in a competitive market needed to offer clients low prices to gain contracts; in turn the wages they offered were low, especially for the unskilled. This meant poorly paid labourers often lacked waterproofs or the appropriate footwear needed for their work. Gloves would have been considered unmanly among some building workers, whatever the weather. There is no reason to believe that the problems documented in Robert Tressell's novel about the building trade in Hastings, *The Ragged Trousered Philanthropists*, during this period were unique to that town. Dress therefore marked out manual workers, reinforced for many by the fact that they returned home displaying the grime inevitably associated with the nature of their work. In many places of work, especially building sites or farms, washing facilities were not available to most workers. Coal miners came home still blackened from the hard task of hacking out coal in cramped dimly lit dust filled conditions which took a heavy toll on their general health, especially in the debilitating disease of pneumoconiosis. Workers employed by large companies, such as the railways and buses, were provided with uniforms which made them easily distinguishable to the public and often indicated their grade of work, such as porter or locomotive driver. Uniforms also provided a form of publicity for these companies and in turn gave a measure of prestige to workers, especially if they indicated a level of skill, such as a driver or signalman.

There was an army of women in the eastern part of the town who provided the services for those in the more prosperous West. They also needed to wear appropriate clothing for much of the housework they undertook. Their clothing therefore distinguished them from both their employers and ladies living in the large villas which made up the Western part of the town. Those engaged in retail or offices of commercial firms were able, indeed required, to dress formally; men in suits, white shirts and a tie, women in long skirts, blouses, (usually white), and a jacket. The formality was partly related to the class of the customers they were serving and also by the fact that formality was the norm and casual clothing mainly reserved for particular occasions such as sporting events or a walk in the countryside. People sat on the beach in their ordinary clothing, including their hats, which could serve as a shade against the sun, with ladies wearing bonnets and some men buying a straw hat for the season.

Photographs make it quite clear that most people wore hats in everyday life. In really hot weather some men would discard their tie but most people were expected to make few concessions to warm weather, even if they were at the seaside. Sea bathing in a formal way on the beach could take place by the use of a hut with large wheels which was pulled down the beach to the sea and when it had reached a position where the water was about two feet deep a door or curtain was opened allowing the bather either to walk down a short ladder or jump into the sea. These bathing huts would be hauled up the beach later by a horse. Costumes for women started with loose leggings down to the knees and short sleeved blouse-like garments covering the body. Over the years the costumes would come to fit the body more closely and reveal at least the arms and legs with necklines becoming lower. For men swimming trunks, often with a matching vest and belt were worn. This was the kind of attire to be seen in the central areas of the beach. Away from the popular areas children swam in less formal and shorter 'costumes', or for those who could not afford such a luxury, they just went into the sea naked.

Those on higher incomes dressed formally nearly all the time, whether they worked in the professions or lived off lucrative investments and did not need to attend a place of work daily. Their attire attested to the fact that they did not carry out every-day chores. For these tasks they hired help; gardeners, cooks and domestics to clean the home, run errands or carry out the cooking. There was little need for most of the higher income groups to think of wearing clothing which might be exposed to dirt or dust. Professionals were in a similar category in terms of dress, if not in terms of income. Like others in the community they dressed in the manner expected of them, which generally helped them to retain the due respect to which their occupation entitled them. Hence, almost alone, dress made clear the social standing of a person. Nothing needed to be said. The clothing people wore in everyday life acted almost as clear an indicator of their social position as the insignia displaying rank on the uniforms of those in the armed forces, even if the ability to command obedience was weaker

Leisure time

These numerous social divisions in the work place and everyday life were carried over in most instances into the world of leisure. In general, membership of golf and tennis clubs was determined by the scale of fees to join and this meant they were beyond the means of the working class. A membership committee would also consider the applicant's social position to determine whether they would 'fit in' with other members. In turn there was a pecking order among the clubs in terms of the scale of their fees. (Apparently this was not the case in Scotland where golf was more widely played.) The oldest club in Eastbourne was the Royal Golf Club founded in 1887 in the year of Queen Victoria's Golden Jubilee with her grandson as patron. Willingdon followed eleven years later in 1898 and the Downs in 1907-8. 'Alfred Ryder, who ran a bookshop in South Street.....was at one time captain of the Eastbourne Downs Golf Club. He was barred from the Royal Eastbourne because he was in trade...' (1). In that year the Downs started the Artisans section, a movement taking place nationally to allow lower income groups to play golf with certain restrictions; generally these were that they had to play early in the morning or later in the evening. Fees were much lower than those of 'ordinary' members. Membership for women was also not a straightforward matter of paying the required fees. Most clubs had a separate bar for men from which women were excluded. Again tennis was not a game played by large numbers of working class people. Membership fees were comparatively high; tennis clothing and equipment expensive.

By contrast soccer was always a working class game and rugby union more middle class, partly because fee paying schools tended to play the latter in the 20th century. Again there is a contrast with rugby being more popular in Wales. Cricket was widely played although the clothing varied between those who played the game in the park in their everyday clothing to those who wore the traditional white shirt and flannels of local clubs, too expensive for most working class boys and men. Sports chosen by fee-paying schools and council schools were influential in encouraging games to be followed when youngsters left school. There were fewer opportunities for girls to participate in sport. From an early age much of their 'free time' was taken up by helping their mother in the house with various chores including looking after younger brothers and sisters. This often meant that they could not continue with team games in which they had participated in at school. Sporting commitments for girls within many families did not take a high priority; certainly not compared with shopping for groceries or cooking. These are generalisations but they are not difficult to substantiate.

The separation of leisure time pursuits was also a matter of the fact that working class people worked very long hours and many had neither the energy nor spare time to become involved in organised sporting activities. On Sunday mornings, after dutiful attendance at church, the separation of social groups was depicted quite publicly with the parade on the well-kept lawn in front of the Grand Hotel. This was an opportunity for the town's prosperous inhabitants to dress in their finery and walk on this open expanse of land facing the sea. It was regarded as a social occasion for meeting friends, for families walking out together, young ladies in groups hoping to catch the eye of young smartly dressed men, who in turn were aiming to strike up a conversation with a girl who caught their attention.

Parents often looked on, trying to assess the worth and character of the young men strolling with their friends. Quality and style of dress accompanied by manners (which were assumed to be a guide to 'breeding') were sufficient to deter all but the boldest young people from the eastern part of the town attempting to take part in this social display of the town's finest.

If this area was claimed by higher income groups for their display, in turn many of them did not feel 'comfortable' walking East of Queen's Hotel, opened in 1880. 'It marked the start of the eastern working class part of the town, for before 1939 it was said that no lady would walk east of the Queen's Hotel'. (2) The hotel 'was deliberately planned as a visual barrier to divide the high-class hotels area of the west from the boarding area to the east'.(3) From there onwards the houses were smaller, built closer together in terraces with small gardens back and front, and generally outside toilets. The roads were narrower and density of population greater. It was classic Victorian working class territory as would be found in many towns but the lack of heavy industry generally limited the extent of grime to that produced by the coal fires of each house, mainly in the Winter.

George Meek of Eastbourne (1868-1921)

At this stage it is worth looking at George Meek, not only because he would become a key figure in encouraging Socialist ideas in the town but also because his life was fairly typical of that experienced by many working class people. Moreover he was one of the few from this social class who wrote of his experiences of life as an unskilled poorly paid worker. Such men were among a small minority in the South East to have been attracted to ideas concerning Socialism or to have the courage to admit to these views, and even more to openly campaign for them. Employers were in general hostile to various sections of the Labour Movement such as trade unions which enabled working people to organise in groups and confront employers together rather than as an individual worker who could easily be ignored or replaced. Similarly, those joining organisations such as the ILP or SDF which challenged the outcomes of a society stratified by differences in wealth and income were generally regarded with some suspicion. To be one among hundreds in industrial areas was one thing; to be one of a very small number in a South Coast town was completely different. In these circumstances a person was isolated and vulnerable to those with influence and power. They might be victimised or experience hostility from some employers for in small towns having radical ideas well outside those of mainstream political parties would make them stand out.

George Meek was a bathchairman in the town; a poorly paid insecure job reliant upon the tourist trade and good weather. (4) His wife worked in the laundry at the Grand Hotel. His son Jocelyn, born in 1898, died before he was four months old. By contrast, Mildred his daughter was born in 1902, and lived for more than eighty years. Meek knew hardship from personal experience and spent most of his life living on the edge of poverty. His father, Joseph, from Hastings, was a plasterer in the building trade and met Sarah Humphress when he was working in Eastbourne. They were married in 1868 and George was the eldest of seven children of whom three died in infancy.

Emigration to the USA

In 1871 there was a slump in the building trade and Joseph had to take relief in the winter, breaking flints on the Grand Parade. Somehow he managed to save sufficient money to pay for a passage to the USA where he found work within a week and began to prosper. He sent for his wife who took her second child with her but left George with his grandparents, who had moved for work to Jevington. All of Joseph's brothers would move to North America, some legally, two of them by jumping ship when they were in the Royal Navy visiting a North American port. George went to Jevington Church of England school at which he believed the headmaster, Mr Dimmer, an ex-naval man, treated the poorer children less favourably than those from more prosperous families. However his grandparents treated him very well. Whether his parents would have sent for him in time is not easy to know. It seems his mother showed little affection for him because of his appearance; his eyesight was poor and he would later undergo surgery at the Eye Infirmary in Brighton. The result was that he completely lost the sight in one eye which had a cloudy appearance and retained only restricted vision in the other.

Joseph Meek had gone to an evening performance at the Brooklyn Theatre on 5th December 1876 where the audience was about one thousand strong. In the last act of the play a fire broke out on stage and the theatre was engulfed in flames. There was panic and as people scrambled to reach the exits, the stairways collapsed under the sudden increase in weight, hence some were crushed, others burned. A total of 350 people died. It was the worst theatre disaster in New York history and led to the banning of naked lights on stage. Joseph was identified afterwards from his pocket watch. A full report appeared in *The Times* within a few days. Sarah decided to return to England with two of her sons, Arthur and Joe. Meanwhile George's grandfather had died so that the remaining members of the family all went to Willingdon, where George attended the local elementary school. After a short time his mother, now pregnant, left the family and moved in with a cabman in Susans Road, taking George, Arthur and Joe with her and leaving his grandmother and a cousin Harry, in Willingdon.

Youth

Like many working class children of his age George left school and took a job as an errand boy for Gilberts the baker only to find that a small 12 year old was not up to the task of carrying a large heavy basket of bread around a town whose geography he did not know sufficiently well, and when wearing new boots! He was sacked after four days. He then obtained another delivery job with another baker, George Vine which lasted several months. His mother continued in her efforts at dressmaking. She still treated George badly taking all his wages and only giving him a penny back on Sundays. He decided to leave home and walked along the coast to Brighton stopping at Seaford where some ladies took pity on him and made a collection for him. He spent the night with a watchman in his hut. At Brighton he bought a ticket to New Cross station assuming he would find work in London. He walked the streets looking for work and finally fell asleep under a bridge.

He was awoken by a policeman. Fortunately, he was able to persuade him, he was an orphan. His luck continued when among the crowd of people who had gathered around him some collected enough money to provide him with a meal and lodgings by Ludgate Hill station. He was then directed to a boys' home at Clapham where he worked for his keep by shining shoes under the Archway at Clapham Road station. He returned to Eastbourne and undertook a number of errand boy type jobs with his mother still treating him poorly

In the Summer of 1883 following on many months of his mother's harsh treatment he left home once more and walked to Stone Cross where friends of his from the *Eastbourne Gazette* gave him some money, food and told him of an empty house in which he spent the night before walking on to Heathfield, where he had breakfast, then continued on to Tunbridge Wells (via Mayfield and Rotherfield) which he reached in the afternoon. He had walked in all the best part of 24 miles yet he was only 15 years of age and partly as a result of a comparatively poor diet, not particularly robust. Moreover these journeys were along poorly surfaced roads, in everyday clothing without strong waterproof shoes or a raincoat.

In Tunbridge Wells he met a crowd of hop-pickers bound for the Kentish fields who persuaded him to accompany them. Upon reaching their destination they were provided with an open cattle shed in which to sleep and he learned that the rate of pay was tuppence a bushel. It was his first example of casual seasonal farmwork and it was a great improvement on the life he had been living at home. One important improvement was the food; 'bread and butter and tea for breakfast and supper, and bread and cheese, with onions or apples, for dinner, with a rasher or piece of steak fried over a gypsy fire for a change on Sundays...I doubt if I ever enjoyed anything more heartily... ' (5)

With several weeks pay in his pocket he teamed up with a companion and walked through the rain to Sevenoaks, where they lodged for the night before taking a train to Woolwich. Having spent most of their money they were forced to stay overnight at the Casual Ward at Woolwich, commonly known as 'the Spike'. Here conditions were primitive; a plank bed, two coarse rugs, bread and skilly for breakfast and supper, with bread, cheese and water for dinner. He was set to picking oakum the following day to work off the 'hospitality of the "Spike"', an experience which made him determined to walk the street the next night rather than spend another night in a similar manner. The next day he was directed to a home connected to Dr Barnado's where he spent a week doing various cleaning jobs in the home. A visit to Limehouse church each Sunday morning was compulsory. In all he spent nine months in this way in London. In that time he had earned over eight shillings and bought a train ticket to Croydon before walking on to Cuckfield, where he stayed the night in an inn. The next day he walked to Lewes, then went by train to Polegate, before continuing by foot to Willingdon, to his grandmother, who had heard rumours that he had been imprisoned or even killed. She informed him that his mother had died and his two younger brothers Joe and Arthur had been sent to the workhouse in Eastbourne. He saw Joe in his workhouse uniform once before he was sent on to Melton Mobray for some basic training. Arthur had already been transferred there so he never saw him again. They were both sent to Canada as part of a youth emigration scheme.

The cabman had remarried and wanted George to move back to Susans Road but having gained his independence he had no intention of surrendering it. He became employed by the Strettons who had a bakery in the town. The sons had been at school with George and they were all good friends. He worked there for well over a year until the bakery fell upon hard times due to numerous unpaid bills of customers. George took off for London once again where he got a job in an East End chopping yard but within a few weeks he was back in Eastbourne with a completely new experience awaiting him.

Farmwork in Wyoming, USA

He had been corresponding with his grandmother's brother for some time. Like so many of Meek's family they had emigrated to the USA and he now received a letter with an enclosed prepaid ticket from London to Warsaw, Wyoming, inviting him to join them. It seemed a great opportunity and he left Eastbourne for the USA late 1885 when he was 17 years of age. It was in fact an adventure for him; the journey to Liverpool to board the SS City of Richmond, the Atlantic voyage, and the arrival in New York where he was worried about his appearance, not from his clothing but his eyes which did not look 'normal'. American eugenicists expressing concerns about the scale of immigration and worried as to the health of some were having an influence on new arrivals; some were being rejected if it was believed they were carrying dangerous diseases or were unfit in some way. After a few hours in New York he boarded a train for the remaining 700 miles of the journey. He also remarked on the quality and low price of American tobacco for he was already an addicted smoker. On arrival at the farm where his relations lived he was met with a remark by an aunt who upon looking at this relatively small youth declared, 'You will never do' because she had been expecting a strong tall looking young man who would be able to work hard on the farm. He was passed on to other relations who seemed to be more willing to accept that he could help with their farm.

In his autobiography he described in some detail his experiences for what would later become common knowledge years later but was not so in the 1880s when few people had the opportunity to travel. Differences in the weather, harsher than anything he had ever experienced before were related and whilst he did help on the farm it does not seem as if there was a great future for him in such work. He left the USA to return to England just over six months after his arrival. It had been an unusual experience for a young boy with such meagre financial resources. Apart from commenting on the life of the people in that area he made one reference to a young man, 'Hohenstein...who had worked in the car-building shops at Buffalo, and had left owing to labour troubles. He was a member of the "Knights of Labour". We soon became good friends.'(6) How far they discussed politics is not known but the organisation was one of the oldest in American Labour history. Founded in 1869 as the Noble and Holy Order of the Knights of Labour by a group of tailors in Philadelphia led by Uriah Stephen, it was initially quite secret due to the fear of members being dismissed from their jobs. It was remarkably progressive for its time given the social history of the USA. Membership was open to both men and women, black and white. It campaigned for the eight hour day, termination of child labour and convict labour which was used to undercut costs and a belief in equal pay for equal work. It reached its peak membership of around 700,000 in 1886, the very time Meek was in the USA. (7) Whether Meek was persuaded by Hohenstein as to any of its aims is not known but as someone, who, from his own short experience of life up to that time, would have been very aware, there were wide differences in income and wealth in England as well as the USA. Within a matter of weeks he was on his way back to Eastbourne with no specific explanation in his autobiography as to why he returned. As he received board and lodging in return for working on the farm his passage was paid for him.

He returned to Eastbourne via Glasgow and found that a Liberal Club had been opened. He became a member. A Conservative Club had been opened by Davies Gilbert in 1884. Both clubs were in many ways social places in which members could get refreshments, play billiards and darts or just relax and meet with friends. It did not follow that they were interested in political ideas or supported the Party which ran the clubs although naturally there was a hope from the proprietors that they would at least be sympathetic to their views. Meek favoured the Liberal Party and there is some evidence that he was influenced in this choice from quite an early age. When he was eleven years of age and still at school in Willingdon he became friends with a local shoemaker who was a strong Radical. He told Meek that the Liberals were the friends of the poor working people. Meek therefore supported them and was delighted when Gladstone won the 1880 General Election.

He became involved with the Liberal Party and Club, (8) cleaned the premises, tended the bar. and was provided with a room at the club. For this work which was only considered part-time, the wages were low but at times they were boosted by registration work for the local Liberal Party. In time he became frustrated with the rate of progress of the Liberal Party's Reforms and having read a number of Socialist newspapers such as *The Clarion* and *Justice* at an open air meeting in 1893 he advised people to join the Independent Labour Party. He was duly expelled from the Liberal Party and considered himself a Socialist from then onwards. He went to London once more in search of work and whilst there he established contact with the SDF and the Fabian Society. He attended large public meetings and heard some of the well-known Socialists of the time speak, such as John Burns and George Bernard Shaw. He returned to Eastbourne enthused by what he had heard and organised a local Fabian Society. He arranged for H.R. Smart, (a Committee Member of the ILP), and (John Ward, an active Socialist who later became a Coalition Liberal MP in 1918), to address open-air meetings in the town. Disappointed by the lack of support in the town Meek took no more part in political activity for the next decade.

Liberal Party Landslide 1906 and Local Political Consequences

By 1906 the Conservative Party had been in Government for seventeen years with the exception of Gladstone's

Administration of 1892-94. The Liberal victory of 1906 was a landslide. 'At the General Election in January the Liberals won a sweeping victory over the Unionists by 400 seats to 157 whilst their electoral ally, the Labour Representation Committee (LRC) gained 30 seats and, once at Westminster, quickly formed itself into the Labour Party with Keir Hardie as its first chairman.' (9) The LRC was founded in 1900 when various organisations of the Labour Movement came together; seven representatives from the trade union movement, two from the ILP, two from the SDF and one from the Fabian Society. From the two 'Labour' MPs who had been successful in the 1900 General Election, Richard Bell of the ASRS and Keir Hardie of the ILP, the scale of increase in the number of Labour MPs in 1906 acted as a stimulus to all sectors of the Labour Movement. In Eastbourne Mr H.S. Beaumont was a part of the Liberal's success; he polled 5,933 votes to Sir Lindsay Hogg's 5,303 for the Conservatives. A similar win could be recorded for Brighton and Hove with two Liberals being elected, Ernest Villiers and Edward Ridsdale. However most of the South East remained Conservative: Lord Edmund Talbot for Chichester, Harvey du Cros at Hastings and Sir Henry Aubrey-Fletcher at Lewes. Yet even in some of these towns the results were reasonably close such as the record poll at Hastings where the Conservatives polled 4,348 to 3,935 for Freeman Freeman-Thomas the Liberal candidate, who lived at Ratton Manor, in Eastbourne.

In Eastbourne the defeat of the Conservative candidate gave encouragement to the small groups of trade unionists, ILP and SDF supporters. Those active in these organisations realised they had to enrol people sympathetic to their views knowing full well that it took some courage to declare support for radical political groups in a town which was traditionally conservative in its outlook. George Meek, one of the few active Socialists in the town at this time, also thought this was necessary. He realised that the means of increasing support which was spread thinly over the large area in the South East, was to link up the various groups so that they could combine to form a more powerful force. To that effect he proposed the foundation of an umbrella group which he named the South East Federation of Socialist Societies, appealing in particular for the support of the few well known Socialists in the area; Joe Young at Brighton, the Cruttendens at Hastings and E.J. Pay at Tunbridge Wells.

Socialist Societies in the Town

There is little doubt that the scale of the sweeping Liberal victory in the 1906 General Election and the election of twenty Labour MPs brought fresh hope to the various Socialist supporters in the area. Notices concerning their meetings began to appear in some of their national papers; the *Clarion* published by the Clarion movement, *Justice* (SDF) and *Labour Leader* (ILP):

Under the heading 'Social Clubs'.

> Very successful meeting held at the *Railway Arms* (The Dolphin, South Street), Wed. 23rd May. Election of officers, decided Wed. Public meetings every 4th week in same place. The business of the meeting immediate future is to discuss ways and means of furthering Socialism locally. G.E. Meek-Secretary. (10)

Just a month later Meek's appeal seems to have been very effective.

> Great meeting of Clarionettes, SDF'ers, ILP'ers and unattached Socialists is to be held on Easter Sunday, July 29th. T.F. Richards, MP for Wolverhampton is to speak in the evening. The rest of the day we hope to spend in entertaining the Tunbridge Wells Socialists' Sunday School and in holding a conference to devise some sort of Federation of Socialist Societies in the S.E. Counties; Kent, Surrey, Sussex and eastern half of Hants. Calls for those from – (and a list of twelve towns from Southampton to Canterbury were mentioned.) (11)

These ambitious attempts by Meek to bring together Socialists scattered widely throughout the South East together at first must have seemed like wishful thinking but in fact he was so active in publishing future events, in keeping up a steady stream of correspondence with local secretaries throughout the region that meetings began to grow in size. They were usually held on Sundays as this was the day most men and women were free from paid employment and public transport the only way of travel open to the majority of people, although at times, depending upon numbers, some groups hired a bus for the day. Following the successful bank holiday meeting and to keep the momentum going, another gathering was planned for the next week-end, to be held at Leaf Hall, followed by a tea at Cooks Dining Rooms. Again Richards was the principal speaker. Requests for people to bring their SDF Song Books made it clear that the audience would also be encouraged to sing songs, some of which would have a Socialist content. Over 50 people turned up. (12)

The first sign of a positive response to the appeals from Meek, Joe Young and E.J. Pay to encourage different Socialist groups to get together took place at a Conference held in Eastbourne in early August 1906, at which it was resolved to form the South East Federation of Socialist Societies (SEFSS) for these three counties. The aims of the organisation were to facilitate an interchange of speakers and endeavour to open up new places of activity within the area. In time they hoped to persuade Socialists from as far afield as Bournemouth in the West to Ashford in the East to co-operate. Meek was elected as Secretary; Edmunds from Ashford as Chairman and Delves from Eastbourne as Treasurer. (13)

Meek seems to have been the driving force behind the SEFSS judging by the number of notices he placed in the Labour Press to publicise their activities:-

Paper:		Date
Clarion	24th August	7th Sept 7th Dec.
Justice	25th Aug	1st Sept 8th Sept
	6th Oct	13th Oct 3rd Nov.
Labour Leader	24th Aug.	18th Sept, 9th Nov

Branches of the SEFSS were established at Epsom (SDF), Ashford and Reigate (ILP), Brighton and Tunbridge Wells (SDF) and Clarions at Brighton and Hastings.

Meek produced a steady stream of information concerning future dates and meeting places for the SEFSS which the separate organisations had agreed to attend. For example on the 16th September at an open air meeting in Eastbourne at the fountain which was in the middle of Seaside Road. (Since moved to the pavement on the Northern side of the road) Councillor Evans from Brighton addressed a crowd with a talk entitled 'Why I am a Socialist'. J.H. Reed from Leeds and Mr Roberts from Tunbridge Wells spoke at two meetings on the following Sunday. Collections were taken at these meetings and supporting literature sold. During the Winter months lectures were held indoors in the Committee room of the Town Hall where Evans spoke to the meeting on 'Municipalisation and Socialism'. Meek too spoke in other towns including the first meeting of the SDF in Hastings at the Fishmarket in 1906. Reports of meetings of the Hastings Trades Council appeared in the local paper. (14)

The Labour newspapers regularly informed their readers of forthcoming meetings and events as well as carrying reports of them later. They gave an impression of steady progress with the formation of new branches of the numerous societies, including the SEFSS. Notices appealed to those in Socialist societies who became increasingly involved and sometimes tried to persuade their neighbours and workmates to attend one of the meetings. A measure of progress was the ability of these groups to attract outside speakers; not an easy task given the cost of fares and the parlous state of their finances. T.R. Richards has already been mentioned but within a year of his appearance, J. Parker, MP for Halifax, was addressing residents of the town at the Congregational School with the Rev. E.J. Eastbrook presiding. Parker pointed to the unfairness of present society and claimed that life would be fairer for all when Socialism was established:-

'When trade began to prosper poverty flourishes with it. Last year when the imports and exports of the country amounted to more than one thousand million sterling there were half a million unemployed begging brother men to give them leave to toil. (Shame!) Cobden and Bright's …..Free Trade was alright but John Bright saw that if he wished to get cheap labour to manufacture carpets he must have cheap bread to do it...with the result he got his cheap bread and his cheap carpets. The manufacturers in Yorkshire and Lancashire employed children who toiled 12 hours a day...resulting in physical degeneration...The results of the worst years of the factory system.

Socialism would make society a real social human organism and not a batch of competing units fighting against each other. Individualism treated mankind as a disconnected mob. Socialism would teach mankind to act together as brothers; individuals defined wealth as that which satisfied desire. Socialism defined wealth as the well being of the community. As John Ruskin had very well said,'…Our God was spelt with four letters instead of three, 'Gold' was the real thing which we worshipped in England here and now.' (15)

It was clear that J. Warren, writing to the *Gazette* later fundamentally disagreed. He was worried about the way the town was developing and against any increase in Socialist ideas:

> (The) municipal bus service was supported by the rates. He doubted the benefit of electric lighting... Seaside places must be quiet and select if they are to attract visitors. The Socialist must not gain ground here but if the present apathy continues he assuredly will and Eastbourne will follow other seaside resorts and lose the high character it now has of being the best seaside resort in the U.K. (16)

Clearly someone with a measure of authority saw Socialism as subversive and at meetings in Brighton, Eastbourne and Hastings people began to notice that police were writing down the names of several attending these open air events. 'Both ourselves and the ILP have been favoured with their attention, although apparently no action has been taken in regard to the Salvation Army and a host of leather-lunged hot gospellers on either side of us. (17)

> According to Police Constable Burr, who later became secretary of his branch of the old Municipal Employees' Association, the police used to intimidate people by taking the names of those attending SDF meeting and posting lists of names in the police station. This name-collecting had been a police method against trade union movements for a very long time all over the country.
>
> In addition to the police, employers' associations then and since, kept 'blacklists' of such people, who could then be refused employment all round and forced to find other work outside their trade, usually to their great disadvantage.
> E.J. Pay…of Hastings, was one such who was finally obliged to leave the town and go to Tunbridge Wells where he again joined the SDF and became a well-known "agitator", this time sustained by his own little pedlar's business.
> Alf Cobb was also forced out of his employment and had to take a street barrow to get a living. (18)

Meek had worked so hard as secretary of both the Eastbourne Clarions and the SEFSS that he could not cope financially with the costs of postage to groups of the Clarions, ILP and SDF throughout the South East. He duly passed over the secretaryship of the former to G. Delves. His income from bathchair work was very precarious depending as it did upon the season and weather. His problems were increased when the proprietor of the bathchair he rented moved away from the town and sold his chair so that Meek could no longer rely on a chair on any one day. He had been the driving force in bringing together the different Socialist societies in the South East who were increasingly cooperating by participating in joint conferences and meetings. Numbers within all the different groups had increased within the year 1906-07. It came therefore as a bitter disappointment when he learned that Ramsay MacDonald had called for ILP members not to cooperate with the SDF in direct contrast to the support for cooperation which had gained approval from so many members of the different Socialist groups. Ramsay MacDonald had made his opposition to this cooperation quite plain in a letter to a branch of the ILP advising against this policy:

House of Commons, May 9, 1907

Dear Sir,

As a member of the Westminster Branch of the Independent Labour Party I sent a letter strongly advising them against cooperating with the Social-Democrat Federation in propaganda work. My reason for doing so being that wherever that co-operation has been tried it has been injurious to Socialism and the Independent Labour Party. I propose to repeat the advice on every occasion it is asked for.

Yours faithfully,
J. Ramsay MacDonald

J. Ramsay MacDonald (1866-1937) joined the SDF in Bristol in 1885, the Fabians in the 1890s and the ILP in 1894. Whether his hostility to the SDF came from his experiences as a member, because he saw them as a rival to the ILP, and later to the LRC [of which he became Secretary], is uncertain. His later political career could be interpreted as a matter of pragmatism, flexibility or pure ambition but ended with him being largely despised by the Conservative Party and expelled from the Labour Party.

Meek 'On the Tramp'

MacDonald's letter infuriated Meek after all the hard work he had put into organising the SEFSS which had led in turn to an increase in the membership of all the different Socialist groups. These results, largely brought about by the co-operation between them all, were considered by most of the members to be a real success. To read MacDonald's letter which undermined all his hard work infuriated him. Meek had been the driving force behind the SEFSS and was genuinely surprised to think that the co-operation which had increased support for Socialist ideas in the South East was considered to stand in the way of spreading ILP ideas even though in practice all the societies had gained from working together. Having lost his bathchair job in Eastbourne he decided he would go 'on the tramp' round the South East to rally support for the Federation. He set off from Eastbourne by train on the 16th May to Hastings and then continuing in an anti-clockwise direction, on to Ashford, Folkestone, continuing round the coast to Sheerness, Gravesend and London. He was welcomed in all these places by the local Socialist groups, helped with accommodation and food with collections made for his travelling expenses. Even so he walked long distances: Appledore to Ashford, Sittingbourne to Lewisham via Sheerness and Dartford. His return journey from London to Eastbourne also included lengthy walks including Bromley to Brighton via Sevenoaks and Tunbridge Wells. In his discussions with local groups he found strong support for co-operation. He also had lunch and a long discussion with H.G. Wells at his home in Sandgate, tea with Margaret McMillan at Bromley, and Joe Young at Tunbridge Wells. (19)

In reality whilst there was good will at local level between supporters of the SDF and ILP there were fundamental differences. The ILP was committed to the policy of a loose 'labour alliance', encompassing the trade unions, most of which were still non-Socialist, and those Socialist groups affiliated to the Labour Representation Committee; it was prepared to enter into electoral pacts with the Liberals. By contrast the SDF gave highest priority to its Socialist objectives, challenged the politics of the 'labour alliance' and disaffiliated from the LRC in 1901. After 1906, divisions on the Left intensified, with the policy of parliamentary moderation pursued by the Labour leaders becoming subject to increasingly heated criticism from a significant minority of grass-roots ILP-ers, Blatchford's *Clarion* and the SDF. Victor Grayson, who won the Colne Valley by-election in 1907 as an 'Independent Socialist', was the figurehead of this movement to recall the party to "the politics of unadulterated Socialist propaganda". Grayson would cause a stir when he visited Eastbourne and spoke at the town hall in 1912.

Meek's response to Ramsay MacDonald's Policy

Upon his return to Eastbourne in June, Meek was saddened to find that MacDonald's influence as chairman of the ILP had undermined attempts to encourage co-operation between the Socialist groups in the area. Instead the ILP were developing their own network of groups in the area, particularly in Kent, and showing considerable antagonism to the SDF. He wrote to the ILP newspaper (20) to express his annoyance and disappointment. His lengthy letter of ten column inches (25 cms) was the first in the 'Correspondence' section. As he explained the SEFSS with its co-operation between the different Socialist Societies went very well for a time. Then it came to his attention that MacDonald had written to an ILP branch telling them not to co-operate even though their annual Conference had recommended they, 'co-operate with Socialist bodies wherever possible'. Meek had written to MacDonald raising the matter and received a copy of the letter sent out to an ILP branch in May. He now realised that the *Labour Leader* was no longer printing his letters. An exclusive ILP Federation had been set up in Kent and branches recommended to withdraw from the SEFSS. Meek visited the branch and discussed the issue with members, as a consequence of which they agreed to retain membership. He visited other branches with the same satisfactory result. Spontaneous resolutions were passed at ILP meetings within the country condemning MacDonald's approach. According to Meek, ILP leaders then attempted to get delegates into the SEFSS's annual meeting to criticise their activities in the South East only to find the meeting condemning MacDonald's activities instead.

The SDF's membership was disproportionately in the South East so MacDonald must have seen them more of a threat than if they had been spread more evenly across the country. Given the lack of industry in the area they were less likely to be trade union members although this needs qualifying when the London area is included. Here the docks alone contained hundreds of trade unionists sympathetic to Socialist ideas given the harsh working conditions they faced daily. Eastbourne had little in common with working people employed on such a scale. To favour radical ideas within part of a large working force was an entirely different situation to working within a small group of only half a dozen people.

In Eastbourne in spite of arguments originating from MacDonald's tactics, the Clarion Fellowship remained active. In August two meetings were held on a Sunday. At the evening event the name of the visiting speaker, Jordan, and the Chairman, were taken by the police and reported for obstruction. In the dispute which followed the police advised them to hold their meeting elsewhere but the chairman claimed they had chosen the area best suited to their activity. The police did not pursue the matter and the following Sunday two more meetings were held addressed by Beckenham and Hardy of Brighton. 'Good collection, no police interference' was written into the summary of the Clarion Fellowship's activities in *Justice*. (21)

Meek was still sympathetic to the ideas of Socialism but his direct involvement in local politics declined for a number of reasons. His disappointment with MacDonald's activities has already been mentioned. His energies were now diverted by his attempts to write an autobiography with the help of H.G. Wells. Having read some of H.G. Wells's books he clearly thought he could produce a book on similar issues such as science fiction or a history text. He had written to Wells on several occasions putting forward his ideas. Wells must have received dozens of such letters from aspiring authors but having met Meek, been impressed with his struggle against adversity he replied, perhaps with a touch of exasperation:

> Why, instead of writing about things upon which you are necessarily ignorant, don't you realize that the only thing anybody has any right to produce books about is a personal vision of life? You must know no end of things, and have felt no end of things I, as a writer, would give my left hand for. Try and set some of them down. (22)

Meek took his advice and initially Wells considered using the material for a character in a book but after some time believed it would be possible for Meek to produce an autobiography. Given the demands upon Wells' time his generosity is apparent from the time he took reading through Meek's handwritten account, having it typed up and edited. Given Meek's poor eyesight it shows something of his determination in writing about his life as an unskilled, poorly and infrequently paid worker. It was a considerable achievement and if it had not been for Wells' agreement to write an introduction and support the project it is unlikely the book would have been published. Throughout the time his employment was precarious but he was as always supported by his loyal wife Sarah, working at the Grand Hotel. The book was published by Constable in 1910 and widely reviewed. It helped by not only the support of Wells but also by his literary friends, Maurice Baring, and Hilaire Belloc. He enjoyed a short period of national recognition. Understandably he now saw himself as a writer but whilst he would go on to write some articles for local newspapers in his own idiosyncratic way it is possible that Wells' earlier advice about writing on issues of which you have some real knowledge was probably as valid for him as for anyone else.

A third reason for Meek's disappearance from the local political scene was that by chance he received a visit from his Uncle Joe who like most of the Meek family had emigrated to North America. He had settled in British Columbia and prospered. On learning of Meek's plight he offered to pay for the family to move to Canada where he would provide him with a rent free house. They agreed but whilst they did finally make the journey it was only after a most protracted wretched experience during which he was financially supported by Wells and his friends and intervention by Belloc in his role as an MP. Needless to say there were no real employment opportunities for a small man in his forties who could not undertake heavy manual work in an area where there was little call for an unknown author of one book. Hope turned to despair and the family were back in Eastbourne before a year was up, deported because they could not maintain themselves financially. (23)

Primrose League in Eastbourne

A large audience in the New Hall, Seaside Road, attended a public meeting of the Primrose League. Col Sir Charles Fitzgerald presided, supported by Mr &

Mrs Rupert Gwynne, Col Henry Bowles, Col Sir Duncan Johnstone and other worthies of the area. The chairman stated that…'the League was an organisation that represented unchanging devotion to Conservative principles and that dwelt in the hearts of the majority of their fellow countrymen and women….three principles, the maintenance of religion, the estate of the realm, and the imperial ascendency of the British Empire. Atheists, Little Englanders and Socialists they did not admit.' The League had been founded by Lord Randolph Churchill in 1883 and within a decade had recruited around one million members, half of them women, and whilst there was a an active social programme the even spread of membership provided the Conservatives with a large force of volunteers during times of General Elections. (24)

Sir Charles told the meeting:

> 'they had an arduous campaign before them…and would enter the fight with light hearts knowing they would be victorious. Before next March they would have held twelve meetings, some teas, two balls, and a social meeting. The Primrose League was an organisation that represented unchanging devotion to Conservative principles and that dwelt in the hearts of the majority of their fellow countrymen and women…'

The principal speaker was Rupert Gwynne, who would become the town's Conservative MP in 1918. Remarking on the growth of Socialism he told his audience:

> It was a great pity that men like Mr Keir Hardie and Mr Victor Grayson were born too late; our forefathers would have known what to do with them. He did not

know what their fate would have been if they had lived in the time when men were hanged for stealing a sheep. Socialism reminded him of a disease mentioned in the Bible, where we read of people being possessed of the devil. (Laughter and applause) It possibly might be that it was now only a microbe, but it was an impetuous one because it was growing. (Renewed laughter) The Socialists' programme seemed to be: "Get what you can and do nothing for it." He hoped they would fight Socialism hot and strong. (Hear,hear) (25)

A view endorsed by Colonel Bowles who believed the Government was pandering to a class which in a few years time they would find to be a great danger to the State. Perhaps surprisingly, whilst the comments of Rupert Gwynne might go down well with an audience of the Primrose League, the response in the letter column of the *Eastbourne Gazette* was not so favourable. One reader, who was not a Socialist herself/himself commented 'in earnest, men were anxious to better the conditions of their fellow-workers. Socialists are at least entitled to fair play in controversy....I believe one of the fundamental ideas of Socialists is that all men should be made to work. This may be the reason why it gives some people "the jumps"'. (26) 'Publica' in his column 'Local Notes' referred to criticism about Socialists holding meetings in parks and making collections. 'In the ancient town of Lewes two methods of opposing the advent of the apostles of collectivism have been advocated. Some militant persons favour the use of such rough and ready arguments as flour and eggs of an uncertain age and dubious origin. The more sagacious and far-seeing residents urge that the Socialists should be left severely alone; this is the course which is likely to be most effective in the long run'. He went on to criticise Rupert Gwynne for some of his remarks which 'were likely to bring down on him the wrath he so pungently assisted.'

Victor Grayson in Eastbourne

Whilst Grayson had lost his Parliamentary seat at the 1910 General Election he had retained his reputation as a controversial speaker and visited Eastbourne in 1912 appearing before an audience at the Town Hall at an event organised by the British Socialist Party (BSP). Over 400 attended, a number which would probably have been larger if there had been no entrance fee. Whilst some were sympathetic to his ideas there were also those who opposed his views but wished to hear what he had to say, including a leading local Conservative speaker, G.W. Cancellor. His subject was 'Socialism and the New Epoch'. The reporter from the *Eastbourne Gazette* wrote, 'His voice is exceptionally strong and clear. He speaks very fluently and confidently'. (27)

Grayson told his audience he did not criticise the personalities of leading politicians such as Balfour or Asquith but their policies admitting, that 'I wish you to believe that I have committed mistakes. I am conscious of this.' The main thrust of his lengthy speech was one that was becoming increasingly familiar among Socialists during the Edwardian period. Namely that those producing the wealth of the country through their labours received in return far less proportionately than those who did not. He provided an imaginary conversation to illustrate the situation as he saw it.

John Jones, (a worker) and Archibald Majoribanks (a capitalist)....the former, being a land animal, had a right to claim means of subsistence by labouring on the land...the great bulk of the land of Great Britain was owned and controlled by a small gang of parasites, who never did anything to justify their existence.

There were more Joneses than there are Archibalds. Justice is on your side. Don't ask him to get off your back. Throw him off your back. Do it nicely. You need not get excited about it. He is in power now to control your destinies because you have placed him in power. He will remain in power as long as you are willing to let him remain in power.

The message was that all should be engaged in productive work if they expect to receive a proportion of the goods produced by working men and women and that the economic and social system worked against such a philosophy, sometimes rewarding those most who did the least and denying a fair share to the majority of working people. When it was time for questions Mr Cancellor asked whether under Socialism the working class might be worse off? He suggested, 'There must be somebody to look after them to see they do their work.' Grayson replied that under Socialism there would be no other people but the working class. 'A well-organised society would not need any persons in wide hats and with whips.

Grayson's appearance generated correspondence in the *Eastbourne Chronicle*.(28) Mr Cancellor agreed with others that the Town Council should 'not let the Town Hall in future to Socialist speakers because they may express opinions with which the writers disagree'. This in turn generated letters arguing that free speech was important for others might object to meetings held by the Primrose League or the Liberals. Apart from the intolerance expressed by Mr Cancellor and Dr Martin 'it would be exceedingly comical if the Town Hall were to be let only to those ratepayers or even rank outsiders, with whose opinions Messrs Martin and Cancellor agreed... The Town Hall belongs to the inhabitants of Eastbourne and should be available to all on the same terms. (George E. Quirk) This letter was typical of several others.

Victor Grayson had been an apprentice engineer before being supported by the Unitarian Church, of which he was a member, to attend Manchester University in order to train as a Church Minister. He spoke passionately about the curse of unemployment and was highly critical of all the political parties because of their failure to concentrate their energy and the necessary resources to tackle the issue. After some while, criticisms began to arise concerning his personal life which were bound to affect his standing among some of the electorate. He became a heavy drinker and developed a habit of staying in expensive hotels, a luxury far beyond the means of the majority of his supporters within the constituency. He had difficulty in managing money.

Grayson's end was mysterious. His wife died in childbirth as did her baby but his fate is unknown. Groves believes he fell foul of Arthur Gregory who was involved in the sale of honours scandal of Lloyd George. Gregory also worked for M15 and was busy spreading rumours about Grayson who wished to investigate the honours scandal. Grayson's 'disappearance' was a mystery; Groves has put forward claims based on circumstantial evidence that it was engineered by Gregory. (29) v. Groves, R. (1975) Ch.IV) A political journalist,

Sidney Campion,, claimed he saw Grayson with a lady on a District Line train in the late 1930s, and he said to her when they reached Westminster station, "Here's the old talking shop" but Campion had to alight at this station and there was nobody else who knew Grayson present to corroborate his claim.)

George Lansbury at the Hippodrome

Within a few months another well-known Socialist came to the town; George Lansbury, the MP for Bow and Bromley. He was also founder and editor of the *Daily Herald*. The BSP also sponsored his visit which attracted a large audience to the Hippodrome, mostly sympathetic to his views, including a significant number of local Suffragists. A resolution was proposed to the meeting 'That this meeting of Eastbourne citizens request that the Libraries Committee of the Town Council, in order to be fair to all its citizens, should at once place the Labour paper, the *Daily Herald*, upon its reading stands at the central and branch libraries.' (31)

In a lengthy speech Lansbury called attention to the fact that in no period in the history of mankind, so far as they knew, was the production of things they needed for the well-being of the community so plentiful as today, and yet men and women were dissatisfied both with themselves and with the condition of their fellows. Even the rich people with their wealth were dissatisfied because they were beginning to understand, through investigations and observations, that in our midst misery accompanied their wealth, and so they were asking themselves why it was in the midst of plenty, while they had every comfort, pleasure and leisure, there was all this destitution and misery.

He commented that when he first came to the town he always kept to the seafront and took a walk to Beachy Head which he found so exhilarating but when one goes to the working class part of the town there is 'overcrowding and people squeezed together in a condition that would make them ask whether land was scarce, and if there was not proper room for the people to spread out'. He espoused the cause of Women's Suffrage and observed that the brunt of the trouble during unemployment fell upon women. He expressed himself as strongly in favour of giving women the vote and went on to argue that, 'Cabinet ministers, archbishops and bishops and clergymen of all denominations had got to understand that the first vital thing was that each individual human being in the community was of equal value and each man and woman entitled to as high a standard of living and development as they claimed for themselves'. An aim which many might agree with as desirable if unlikely to be fulfilled.

The main thrust of his speech was in many ways little different to that made by Grayson only a few months earlier but it did not cause the same furore. This was probably because the tenure of the delivery was less harsh, his reputation less controversial and it took place in the Hippodrome rather than the Town Hall so the audience may have contained fewer people opposed to the ideas expressed. These factors may also account for the lack of critical letters to the local newspapers generated by his pronouncements.

Eastbourne's First Town Council Elections in 1883

There is a need to go back a few years in order to make some comparison between a late Edwardian local election and one from the last decade of the Victorian era. The *Eastbourne Chronicle* covered them both but the tone of reporting was markedly different reflecting the changes which had taken place within the 30 years which separated them; especially in the use of language and social attitudes towards the aspiring candidates. Eastbourne Borough was incorporated in June 1883 and local elections followed in November. There were four wards; East, West, Central and St Mary's with no less than 50 candidates contesting 24 seats. The winners included several whose names were already familiar to the town's inhabitants or would be over the next few years. For example, Mr. G.F. Chambers, a barrister, elected as a Conservative councillor in 1883, who would make his views very well known about the suitability of candidates a generation later in the 1913 Local Election. A very detailed report of numerous contemporary aspects of the 1883 election appeared in the *Eastbourne Chronicle*. To read parts of the report is almost to believe that there were no differences in the political or social views of the candidates and that the results for the town were the best possible that could be imagined.

> The fight is over, the battle won, and Eastbourne rejoices in the possession of its first Town Council, constituted of a body of men than in whom it is almost impossible the burgesses could have made a fitter or more commendable choice.

This kind of almost detached reporting continued in a similar vein.

> No doubt the enthusiastic support given to the advocates of municipal enfranchisement was mainly stimulated by the prospect of radical alteration in the voting system, and it is equally clear that, but for the substitution of the new electoral basis for the anomalous state of things hitherto in vogue, the present contest would have been provocative of far less interest than appears to have been centred in the event. Rarely was an election carried on with greater fairness. Its dissociation from political considerations raised it at once far above the level of similar elections in the majority of corporate towns, and gave it such a character as was calculated to elicit the honest and independent views of the burgesses on the merits of the various gentlemen seeking position on the council.
>
> There is an acceptance 'of the circulation of squibs and both a pungent and harmless type' but these were obviously of moral consequence.

One is left wondering if those elected disagreed on any fundamental issues. Certainly such uniformity of agreement was unlikely to be found among the town's population as a whole. After all this was the decade of the violent attacks upon the Salvation Army marching to music in the town.

The *Chronicle* concluded:

> The so-called working class candidates suffered utter municipal annihilation, but the trade element managed to secure pretty complete success. The general feeling, we venture to represent, is one of satisfaction at the upshot of the stirring non-political campaign, and

of the confidence that entrusted to the gentlemen elected, the future government of the town will be well looked after.

The poor showing of 'so-called working class candidates' was primarily due to the small numbers in organised parties within the town, most of which, such as the ILP and SDF were still in their infancy, alongside the lack of industry which in other areas had encouraged trade union membership. The 'trade' element had reasonable funding and organisation but were still not quite 'accepted' by all the influential figures in the town, some of whom fought a rearguard action to prevent their entry to certain facilities from golf clubs to educational establishments. The observations on the election results of the *Eastbourne Chronicle* suggest the main requirement for success at the local election was the social standing of the candidate, hence the references to 'gentlemen'. Working class men, by the very nature of their work were generally regarded as unsuitable in this regard and lacking in formal schooling to be capable of dealing with affairs relating to the government of the town. As for the thought that women from any social group might become competent councillors this was not even contemplated as they were not allowed to stand for such an office until 1907.

Labour – Early Signs of Political Progress

By May 1913 there were signs of improved trade union and Labour Party organisation. The Eastbourne Trade and Labour Council (ETULP) had been established in 1911 with A.J. Marshall as first chairman. Shortly afterwards it held a meeting on a Friday evening at the Central Wesleyan School Room in Langney Road, attended by Ex-councillor Evans from Brighton, Mr A. Gordon Cameron, the Labour candidate for Jarrow, and the Rev. John Glennell, Minister of the Eastbourne Primitive Methodist Church. Evans claimed that 'It was in towns like Blackburn, Leeds and Newcastle that "the brass" was made, and it was spent in such places as Brighton, Hastings and Eastbourne. Everything sprang from labour, which was the one thing in the whole world which was consecrated, although he was afraid that fact was not recognised...The sons of the workers were taken from school all too soon. Fourteen! Why, a boy's education was only beginning when he was fourteen. Look at the wealthy classes. They kept their boys and girls at school until they were eighteen.' Mr Cameron went on to express surprise that the Eastbourne Town Council refused to pay the trade union rate to the carpenters and joiners employed by them....They would have to take into consideration the running of trade union and Labour candidates of their own, as that would be the only way to get trade union conditions adopted by the Town Council. (32) This was precisely what they decided to do.

The secretary, W. Pitfield, first wrote to the Town Council asking for a deputation from the ETULP to be received to put before the Council their views concerning rates of pay. The mayor approved of this suggestion but in the discussion which followed it was considered that the deputation could not be received because the matter was one for the Highways Committee. Councillor Breach proclaimed, 'I have a contract under the Government and my instructions as to the wages I have to pay....All I am compelled to pay is the usual rate of wages current in the town, what more do the members of the Labour Council want?....They forget the probability that if these bricklayers and carpenters did not work for the corporation they would not get a job. Councillor Rawles said, 'They don't represent our employees officially. Someone steps in and interferes with our men.' More correspondence followed with the final letter to the Trades Council stating, 'That he (ie. the ETULP secretary) be informed that the carpenters in the employ of the corporation are perfectly satisfied with the terms of their employment, and that the committee does not propose to enter into any correspondence with the Trades and Labour Council on the matter.' (33)

This assumption as to the contentment of the town's employees was challenged in the same newspaper three weeks later in a letter from Mr M. Evans who claimed that whilst the conditions described by Alderman Keay are true for some council employees it was not true for others, '...the Council employ carpenters for short periods, and pay men who do not receive these two-penny-half privileges 4s. 8 per week less than an outside contractor would pay....(some) bricklayers working on the new surface water drain...under the same conditions as an ordinary contractor's workmen, lose time when it rains, stand off when they are not wanted; yet the Council pay them a penny per hour less than would be paid by a private contractor. In plain language, the work is being done by sweated labour, while a Borough official has a large increase in his salary for his share in the business.' Other examples were given, including workmen digging trenches for lower wages from the Electric Lighting Department.

When Mr Keay repeated his claim that he had received no complaints from the workmen the reply came, 'Of course not. I can give you the reason. Recently the men employed at the gasworks sent in a petition for an increase in their wages. The Gas Company replied by discharging the men whose names came first on the list.' A short letter signed 'One Who Knows' appeared on the same page discussing conditions of work for some Council employees. 'I consider that the Corporation gardeners, who do so much to beautify the town, are worthy of consideration, as at they are greatly underpaid. It would be a great surprise to many people to hear that these deserving men do not receive what may be regarded as a living wage.' The result of this seeming impasse was that the ETULP decided to contest three of the five wards in the forthcoming borough elections. The results were a great surprise for the town.

The Municipal Election of 1913

The Eastbourne Borough elections took place in November with five of the borough's nine wards being contested; Cavendish, Central, Hampden Park, Roselands and St Mary's. Labour candidates stood in Cavendish, Roselands and St Mary's. Most other candidates did not openly declare their political allegiances although local people usually knew the opinions they held in general. The final verdict was clearly a surprise, the *Eastbourne Chronicle* declaring 'Most surprising results in the history of the Borough'. (34)

Cavendish	A.J. Marshall (Labour)	488
	S.E. Buckland	291
	Majority=	197
Central	Frank Carter	242
	Dr Fielden Briggs (Unionist)	213
	James McCann	121
	Majority=	29
Hampden Park	J.W. Pearson	100
	E. Claude Martin	96
	Majority=	4
Roselands	J.T. Miller	265
	J. Prior	410
	M.T. Evans (Labour)	182
	Majority=	228
St Mary's Ward	F.J. Huggett (Labour)	422
	A. Avard	420
	H.R. Leach	265
	Majority=	2

A large crowd of 'no fewer than three thousand' gathered at the town hall in eager anticipation of the results announced by Alderman Welch, the returning officer. Huggett, a postal worker, experienced the narrowest of victories polling 422 votes to the 420 of A. Avard and 265 of H.R. Leach. The narrow victory by F.J. Huggett, a postman, in St Mary's ward was greeted with much cheering by the Labour supporters, pleased by the election of the first Labour councillor in the borough's history. He told his supporters, 'It is a splendid victory for Labour in this town. It is a working man's victory.' Mr Avard, a local builder, came forward to speak but many of the crowd were already walking away. He did say that the closeness of the vote should necessitate a recount but accepted the close verdict with good humour being assured by some supporters that 'he would have another opportunity of re-entering the Council at no distant date.' The news of the victory in Cavendish, of A.J. Marshall, a railway driver, brought further cheers from supporters to which he duly responded; 'Fellow workers – I thank you for placing me at the top of the poll by an overwhelming majority. You have demonstrated to-day the solidarity of the workers on the housing question and in regard to fair wages not being paid by the present Council'.

Large numbers of Huggett supporters marched to the Technical Institute, removed a horse from a carriage 'in order that the victors might be drawn along in triumph by their friends.' They sang a song which had been printed on a leaflet in the campaign; 'March of the Men of Hardnecks' to the tune of 'Men of Harlech'.

> Working men, now ease your slumbers,
> Rent too heavy you encumbers,
> Rates increase each year in numbers
>   Seek the reason why!
> Wake at once, for time is slipping'
> Landlords fat with joy are skipping,
> You exist on bread and dripping,
> And work until you die.
>
> Chorus: Councillors retiring, for your votes aspiring,
>
> Preach to you of what they'll do,
> With efforts most untiring;
> Yet remember, each November,
> When elected as your member,

They forget you in December.
Labour members try.

Now while for your votes they're praying
For your good they live, they're saying,
While council workmen underpaying!!!
    So their axe they grind.
With their virtues I'll not bore you,
But this time I do implore you,
Seize the chance that's but before you,
    Don't be left behind.

Chorus: No more be kept under,
    This time make no blunder,
    Strong unite, for Labour's right,
    Make them shake with wonder;
    And remember, this November,
    If you choose a Labour member,
    He'll stand by you in December,
        He's no axe to grind.   (35)

After the singing of the song there was a hush whilst Alderman Welch pronounced the result which led to more cheers, then another break for Alderman T.B. Rowe to announce the result for Cavendish which led to even more cheers. A crowd of Labour supporters moved down to the open space in front of the Technical Institute, There is little doubt that the election of two Labour councillors was a surprise for many of the residents of the town. Thus for the first time in Eastbourne Labour had sought and secured direct representation on the Council, and it was stated that further candidates supporting the cause would be put forward next year.'

The need of affordable decent housing was recognised as a central issue during the election.

Labour's Huggett was not the only candidate to make an appeal by verse. Frank Carter, an upholsterer, in a triangular contest in Central ward against J. McCann, a retired builder seeking re-election, and Dr Fielden Briggs, had produced a rhyme on a leaflet which read:

> Remember, remember the 1st of November
> By your votes put Frank Carter on top;
> And don't forget, too, he lives amongst you,
> And both of the others do not.
> Poll early for Carter. (36)

The tone was amusing enough but there was a pointed reminder to the electorate that he lived within the community. Dr Fielden Briggs addressed the crowd when the results had been announced for Central but seemed to misjudge the mood of the lively crowd in terms of his tone. In a calm and even voice he said, 'Ladies and gentlemen, this field, as you all know, I entered at the last moment. 'Which prompted a person in the audience to shout out, "Hard luck!" 'I thank all those who supported me, he continued'. More interruptions followed. 'Next year I hope these 213 (voters) will poll again for me.' "Never!" came a voice from the crowd. His call for 'fair play' made little impression and as for his claim that he would have more time to prepare the next time this only brought another shout from within the crowd, "You will never have a chance."

One of the most interesting contests was in Roselands where the popular James Prior was defending his seat against Labour's Maurice Evans. The *Eastbourne*

Gazette believed Labour had made 'A Great Tactical Error' by nominating 'their most able candidate in opposition to James Prior, 'who for many years, has devoted himself heart and soul to the interests of the workers'. He had recently been suffering from an illness 'arising from excess of zeal in their service'. He was unable to attend the evening celebration meeting but his service was duly recognised by Mr F.W.Allcock a close friend who told of his conscientious approach as a councillor: 'During the last six years he has attended over 600 meetings of the committees and the Council, and at every meeting that he has attended he has done his level best for the benefit of the whole of his fellow workmen in the Roselands ward in particular and the town in general'. His Labour rival was just as generous in his praises for Mr Prior. '...my friend Mr Councillor Prior has, by his unfailing industry, and his consideration for the electors of the Roselands Ward, won for himself a place in your affections which I, a mere "carpet bagger" in the constituency, was unable to usurp.' In fact he recognised it had been a mistake to stand against Mr Prior recognising that the Councillor worked very hard for working class people in his ward.

The assessment in the *Chronicle's* editorial concerning Evans would seem to have been valid. Many would also have agreed with the newspaper's verdict that the main reason for Labour's success was the housing situation. 'The victories of the Labour candidates in St Mary's Ward and the Cavendish Ward are particularly attributable to legitimate dissatisfaction on the part of the working population – dissatisfaction arising from the failure of the Council to grapple with the housing question.' The newspaper believed they had failed to take advantage of the Housing and Town Planning Act. Maurice Evans had told the audience gathered for the results at the Town Hall, '...we have been rather troubled lately about the housing question in Eastbourne. You know that we have made such a stir that even the Council has taken notice of it'. (Laughter) An opinion rejected by the Council but half way through November there was news of '100 cheap dwellings to be constructed together with a recreation ground of 5 acres at Roselands'. How far this decision was influenced by the election results it is difficult to know but it clearly points to the fact that a shortage of housing in the town was a real problem at the time. Maurice Evans agreed with the *Gazette* on this issue and went on to point to the financial situation facing many of the town's residents.

> You know that Eastbourne is the worst paid town of its size in the country, having regard to the cost of living. According to the Board of Trade Return there are only three towns where the cost of living is higher than in Eastbourne, and those towns are Woolwich, Kingston-on-Thames and Croydon. But the rate of wages is something like 30 or 40 per cent less in Eastbourne than it is in those towns. Therefore you see what you have got to make up in order that you may have the same comfort and the same standard of living. Our local Town Council do not pay the ordinary standard rate of wages that is paid by outside contractors to their workmen. We think it is time they should do so. A town council or corporation should be model employers and not "sweaters". (Applause) That is one of the reasons for standing at this time. The Labour Party in this town is of very recent growth. We have

not been in existence fifteen months, and you see what we have done.

'Sweating' was usually associated with homeworkers, in particular women, who worked at home producing many articles needed for the clothing industry. They usually needed to supplement the family income but having small children too young to attend school could not go out to work. Some of the companies who employed them were well aware of their circumstances; working in an isolated situation, needing extra income and in no position to bargain with an employer. Councils were under constant pressure from ratepayers' associations wishing to keep local rates low in their own interests regardless of or indifferent to the effects upon wage rates of council employees. The Eastbourne Branch of the Christian Social Union invited Mr. J. Mallon, the Secretary of the 'Anti-Sweating League', to give a talk on the current situation of wage rates. He was able to inform them of some measure of success in the passing of the Trade Boards Act which had set a minimum wage of home workers of two and a half pence an hour thereby putting an end to the exploitation of women chain makers receiving one penny an hour. He quoted the Duchess of Marlborough who had informed a conference the previous year that 'in organised industries alone there were probably 300,000 women who earned less than 12 shillings for a full week's employment'. The Christian Social Union claimed it wished to apply the moral truths and principles of Christianity to the social and economic difficulties of the present time.' It was in this spirit that the lectures had been arranged. (37)

The 1913 Eastbourne Borough election resulted in a heavy poll with high percentages of the electorate recording their vote as the details made clear;

Number of electors in contested wards:

	On the roll.	Polled.
St Mary's	1399	1107
Central	784	576
Cavendish	1489	1044
Roselands	923	592
Hampden Park	223	196

There were people in the town who were worried and concerned with the idea of Trades Council representatives standing in local elections, some believing that their policies would be too radical whilst there were also indications that they were really not the right kind of people to be councillors. Among those who had been and those aspiring to be councillors were a retired builder, a shop owner and a 'working man', yet prior to the election a letter in the *Eastbourne Chronicle* (38) was highly critical of A.F. Marshall because he was an active member of his trade union:

> I am afraid he will get very little support outside of his own particular calling. And considering that most of the trouble and accidents are caused – according to the men's officials – by the number of hours the men have to work, I should think this candidate has quite enough on hand already, and that there would probably be fewer accidents if these men gave a little more attention to their work and left such matters as municipal affairs to gentlemen who have the ability and time at their disposal to carry out the duties they undertake. (With reference to railway accidents.) (39)

Cavendish Ward Elector (Oct 29th)

Clearly a majority of the electorate in Cavendish did not agree with such sentiments. The writer of the 'Stray Notes' column in the *Eastbourne Chronicle* (40) thought that feelings of alarm at the prospect of Labour Councillors being elected were misplaced.

> Any idea that the Labour members will exercise a disruptive influence upon the proceedings of the Council may be dismissed as an idle chimera. They would hardly do it if they could, and they certainly could not do it if they would. Until the contrary is shown, they are entitled to be seen as men animated by the same public spirit and the same sense of right and wrong as the other members of the Council, and it will be time enough to visit their policy and conduct with protest or condemnation when the confidence of the electorate is proved to have been misplaced.

Chambers did not believe working class people would make suitable councillors and almost a year after the elections he wrote again to the *Eastbourne Chronicle* (41) 'Be it always remembered that a town like Eastbourne depends for its permanent prosperity on capital and capitalists, and that for its local management to fall into the hands of nobodies, with nothing to lose, will be fatal. What in the world can a postman or an engine driver know about municipal government and how to work it for the general good?' The 'Stray Notes' column in the *Eastbourne Chronicle* commented, 'Unpalatable and even regrettable, from a certain point of view, the return of several Labour extremists may seem; but it would be easy to exaggerate the significance of this success of the Trades Council nominees.' (42)

These sentiments he expressed together with his stated opinions on so many local issues brought a lengthy reply the following week from George Quirk, a well-known local Liberal:

> Whatever may be the virtues, or vices of Mr George F. Chambers as a politician or social reformer, one thing at least may always be depended upon. If there is anything disagreeable to be said, maladroit or callous, he can always be relied upon to say it….No one ought to have a finer discrimination in the use of words, and their different shades of meaning, than Mr Chambers; but no one uses language with a more reckless disregard for propriety and proportion than he does….. Just a word on local questions. It has never been the avowed policy of the Liberal party in Eastbourne to capture the Town Council. It is contrary to its constitution as an organisation. By its rules it is expressly precluded using its funds or machinery for local elections, and has never done so. As an "ardent Liberal", one who believes that progressive enlightened administration is not less imperative in local than national affairs, I have continuously and persistently urged the Liberals, so far as I could, to imitate the Conservatives in this respect and fight on political lines. Avowed or unavowed,(*sic*) this has been the "settled policy" of the Conservatives since I can remember. My principal reasons for urging this are: 1. Moral. It has a great influence on larger imperial issues. It is also educative. 2. It keeps the election machinery bright and in working order, besides preserving the *esprit de corps* of the fighters. I have always deplored the apathy of the local Liberal leaders in local elections, and their acquiescence in the opposite party's monopolisation of all offices and appointments.

It is I perceive, a sore point with Mr Chambers that at the last municipal contest in Eastbourne three Labour men were returned, and he urges a rally of "the Conservative and educated classes," notice the implication, "to fight all local elections on party lines," as if they had ever done anything else. Mr Chambers must admit that the working class comprise a large, if not the larger portion, of the electorate. Surely they are entitled to some representation. Three out of thirty-six is hardly a fair, not to say undue proportion. Mr Chambers apparently thinks that the duty of the labouring classes is to labour and pay rates: to fight and pay taxes, but not to have any voice in administration. And just as he, and those he speaks for, (if any) are frantically urging us to be "patriots" and fight, he and they (if any) will be just as frantic to deprive us of both representation and votes, and to perpetuate the existing "constitution in Church and State," as Mr Chambers terms it, plural voting and every other political anomaly.

Yours truly,
George E. Quirk (43)

For all Mr Chambers' disparaging thoughts about representatives from working class movements being on the Council the reality was that they were becoming increasingly well organised. For example in the annual publication entitled *Eastbourne, Hailsham & District Blue Book* (1918-1919, p.22) a notice appeared which indicated clearly the numerous organisations using the premises of the Eastbourne and District Trades Council at 112-114 South Street, those responsible for the administration of the services offered and notice of the facilities being provided:

President: Mr A. Dilloway Vice President: Mr. T.B. Hasdell
Secretary: Mr S.C. Ball Asst. Secretary: Mr H.J. Boniface

Headquarters of:-
Eastbourne & District Trades & Labour Council, Eastbourne Labour Party,
Local Branch I.L.P., National Association of Discharged Soldiers & Sailors,
Journeymen Butchers' Federation, Amalgamated Society of Carpenters & Joiners, Amalgamated Society of Operative House & Ship Painters, Amalgamated Society of Engineers, Amalgamated Society of Locomotive Engineers & Firemen, Amalgamated Society of Tailors & Tailoresses, National Union of Railwaymen, Railway Clerks Association, Workers' Union [4 branches], Typographical Society, National Union of Coal Porters, National Amalgamated Union of Shop Assistants, Warehousemen & Clerks' Postman's Federation, Manchester Union of Odd Fellows.

In addition to the above meetings, there were rooms to be let at reasonable rents, also reading rooms, card rooms, billiard rooms and a Concert Room. The Club was open from 6 pm, till 10.30pm each evening, and 2.30pm till 10.30pm on Wednesdays and Saturdays.

During these years it was not just working men who were pushing for greater equality in representation at local and national government level, but also other areas of society which had been the preserve of higher income groups. Women too were seeking greater equality in all areas of society; from equal opportunities to men in most places of work to equal pay for the same work as men, from school teachers to doctors, and a whole range of work denied to them for reasons of tradition, bigotry and cost. For example the salaries of women teachers were below those of their male colleagues even when undertaking the same work in a school which meant it was cheaper to employ them for a position to an equivalent man. Significant numbers of women were becoming involved in the campaign to give women equal voting rights to men and these views were becoming increasingly promoted by women, including through the local newspapers in Eastbourne.

Changing Times - Trade Union for Domestic Servants

The ripples of social change in so many aspects of life from other areas of the country were beginning to reach Eastbourne. Within the country at the turn of the century there were 1,740,800 women domestic servants. There were still many in Eastbourne 14 years later. The thought of them joining a trade union in order for them to improve their conditions of work was anathema to many of their employers, whose thinking seemed to be from an earlier age. The suggestion certainly sparked off a storm of protest in the *Eastbourne Chronicle* during the Summer of 1914. It began with a letter from a domestic worker asking why they should not be organised into a union, 'the same as other workers, including clerks, shop assistants, etc, to improve their position and interests generally. We as a class of workers are not treated as human beings, but as mere machines (although there are exceptions) working about 16 hours every day, with about 3 or 4 hours freedom once a week. I feel sure domestics are not too proud to join a union (if there was one)...is there not someone who will take our cause up, so that we can demand improved advantages, as other workers have done and are still doing'. (44)

Whether solely in response to this letter or from a general feeling that domestics ought to join together to establish a trade union which would act on their behalf is not clear but the following month there was a report of a meeting in Coli's Restaurant, Terminus Road, for the purpose of starting a branch of the Domestic Servants Union. R.S. Maginess, Secretary of the ETULP was in the chair and among those supporting the aim were the Rev. J. Clennelli, Mrs F. Allen and the two elected Labour Councillors. The special speaker, Miss McNeill was from the Union in London. There was a good attendance of domestic servants.

Miss McNeill dealt with two main issues; the conditions of domestic workers at present and the objects of the union. She pointed out that the average working day was 16 hours which was 116 per week. Whilst not always at work they were always on duty. Unlike other workers they did not always have their meal times to themselves but were liable to be called at any time. They were at the beck and call of their employers.....Their average wage was less than £18 a year, which worked out at less than a penny an hour.....they got board and lodging but there were many places where food was insufficient and inferior whilst sleeping accommodation was such as would be condemned by sanitary authorities. It was not right that they usually had to meet the full cost of their uniform. She stated the aims of the union were to raise the status of domestic work to that of other work. Their employer's home was not their home; but a workshop for them and it should be subject to visits by inspectors as other places of work were. A hostel in each town would obviate the need for many to sleep in and there were hundreds of girls under fourteen undertaking arduous work. A number of domestics joined the union at the end of the meeting.

A leaflet was produced for distribution to domestics working in the town which read:

A FEW STRAIGHT QUESTIONS

ARE YOU SATISFIED with the present condition of Domestic

Service, both as regards your own case and others in a worse position than yourself?

Are you quite satisfied with your WAGES, your FOOD, your HOURS OF WORK, your holidays and the attitude adopted towards you by your employers, and by the community as a whole?

If not, HOW DO YOU PROPOSE TO ALTER THESE THINGS?

HOW HAVE OTHER WORKERS BETTERED their CONDITION and gained greater respect from their Employers?

Only in one way – by COMBINATION.

JOIN THE
DOMESTIC WORKERS UNION

Which stands for the Bettering of the lot of the Domestic Servants, helping them to get justice from unjust Employers, for providing you with money when you are out of a place, and for securing better conditions all round.

Such a leaflet came into the possession of 'A School Mistress' who complained to the newspaper how one of her 15 servants 'went out to post a letter and was greeted by one of these female agitators and asked questions about her working conditions...it is an outrageous thing that a paid spy and agitator should be allowed to linger outside houses where servants are employed and stop the maids as they come out to cross-question them about their employers and their methods. Surely such a person can be arrested for loitering and obstruction? The mistresses who treat their maids badly are few and far between. We have to pay heavily for unskilled labour...we mistresses ought to make a stand for our own union and demand better work for the present high wages we give instead of the present incompetent standard of labour.' (45)

She was supported by 'An Employer of Servants' in the Meads district the following week who claimed that 'The present difficulty of obtaining and retaining suitable domestics was unheard of 15 to 20 years ago. The change had come about with the reign of the paid professional agitator, the whole intention and drift of whose policy is to create a spirit of unrest and dissatisfaction amongst those who would otherwise be perfectly happy and contented. The impressionable nature of the average domestic renders her an easy prey to the wiles of agitators, who are less concerned about the girls' material welfare than they are about setting class against class....'

A new member of the Domestic Workers Union in Eastbourne wanted to know if the lives of domestics were so good 'why do we hear every day the servant problem so frequently talked over in drawing rooms or wherever mistresses meet? Simply because girls nowadays will not enter into domestic service. She prefers to go and work in factories, laundries or anywhere instead of entering domestic service, and can you wonder at it?'(46) The Hon. Secretary of the Union in the town highlighted the problems domestics faced. 'There are a good many ladies who put servants in rooms to sleep where they would not put their pet dog. We of the servants union do not wish to strike; what we ask for is better conditions, a fixed number of working hours daily, a little more liberty and decent sleeping apartments.' (47)

Councillor Huggett wrote of how with Councillor Alfred Marshall, he had supported the formation of the Domestic Workers' Union. He suggested 'School Mistress' should teach her pupils 'How class privilege, luxury and idleness is based upon a monopolistic system, which exploits the toil, necessity and misery of the poor. (It is unlikely she would follow his advice.) He quoted Victor Hugo, "The Paradise of the Rich is erected upon the Hell of the Poor". Huggett wrote, 'The Union is come to stay and the status of domestic servants will not remain unaltered.' (48)

Women still disenfranchised

Women had been fighting a campaign to have equal voting rights with men for at least 40 years. Numerous organisations to achieve this fundamental right had been established. In fact a small number of women had been entitled to vote during the early years of the 19th century but this right had been removed by the 1832 Reform Act. There is evidence that in Litchfield some women voted in 1843 for the Assistant Overseer of the Poor. (49) The 1869 Municipal Franchise Act gave the vote to some women ratepayers in local elections and the 1888 County Council Act gave women the vote for County and County Borough elections. In 1907 they could serve as Council Members. What continued to be denied to them was equal voting rights with men.

Among the most well-known women's movements were the National Society for Women's Suffrage (1872) and the Women's Social and Political Union (1905). There was a Suffragist movement in Eastbourne, members of whom had attended George Lansbury's meeting two years earlier. Under a sub-heading entitled 'A Demoralising Movement' a critical unsigned article appeared concerning 'Suffragists and Socialism' which described how 'the Woman Suffrage movement has allied itself with Socialism…justifying their alliance with Socialists, they adopt a mingled attitude of apology and defiance…They are not responsible they say, for a man's views on other matters than the suffrage question; then they add, in any case the Labour-Socialist Party is the only one that is solid for female enfranchisement and for this reason has to receive their unqualified support (but) when once votes have been granted to women, Suffragists will duly return to the normal state of their political mind.' (50) The following week the paper published another lengthy article 'Against Woman Suffrage', in which the writer suggested 'The vote is an instrument of government, and government is the enforcement of the will of the one or of the many on the remainder of the nation – good government being the enforcement of this will in the interests of the community as a whole, bad government the enforcement of this will in the interests of a section only of the community.' (51) Lengthy articles in this vein were not uncommon and many recognised that whilst most Liberals, along with the emerging Labour Party favoured equal voting rights for women, Asquith, the Liberal Leader did not. Most in the Conservative Party were opposed to such a measure.

In May 1914 a meeting was held in the Special School, Whitley Road, presided over by the Rev J. Clennell, in which the main speaker, Victor Duval, in a lengthy speech denounced the Government for its refusal to grant women equal voting rights to men. He informed the audience of a Men's Union formed four years earlier and now numbering thousands of men of all political parties working to support the women's cause. They worked side by side with the Women's Social and Political Union. They endorsed entirely its aims and objects, namely; "...to secure for Women the Parliamentary franchise on the same terms as it is or may be granted to men". The main argument within the meeting came from Mr F. Allen, a Liberal who believed the speaker was too critical of the Government and tried to excuse them for the imprisonment of women campaigning for the vote, especially the forced feeding of those on hunger strike, often carried out in a brutal manner. Mr Allen put forward numerous hypothetical scenarios, for example whether a convicted murderer who went on hunger strike should be released or force fed, although this was really irrelevant as the women imprisoned did not come into this category. Tempers rose until the chairman intervened to suggest, 'We are getting away from our subject. We are here to organise a Men's Union. There may be men holding different opinions, but we may quite agree on the central principle'. Mr Maginess of the Trades Council spoke briefly to support the aims of the Men's Union 'proudly announcing his adherence to socialistic principles'.

As a generalisation it is fair to say that Conservatives were the most likely to oppose women being granted equal voting rights to men but as with many politicians pragmatism played a part in their attitude. Their Party had dominated Parliament for the best part of 32 years only being out of office for about 9 years. The all male Parliamentary franchise seemed to have served them well. Could they afford to take a risk with the extension demanded, regardless of the social justification of adult suffrage? There was considerable support for women's right to adult suffrage from the Primrose League whilst the Liberal Party was disunited over the matter. Only the Labour Party could claim that it was their policy to grant adult women equal voting rights to men.

References – Chapter 7

(1) Surtees, J. p.67
(2) Ibid. p.50
(3) Spears, H. (1981) *Eight Town Walks in Eastbourne*, p.44
(4) Coxall, B. & Griggs, C. (1996) *George Meek – Labouring Man, Protege of H.G. Wells*
(5) Meek, G. op.cit.,pp.54-55
(6) ibid. p.96

(7) Hofstader, R., Miller, W. & Aaron, D. (1967 ed) *The United States; The History of a Republic*, pp.535-536, 539-40.
(8) For full details of the work he undertook v. Coxall & Griggs, *op.cit*, Ch.4
(9) Coxall, B. & Griggs, C., *Meek*, p.113
(10) *The Clarion*, 1.6.1906
(11) ibid. 20.7.1906
(12) ibid. 27.7.1906
(13) *Justice* 4.8.1906
(14) *Hastings & St Leonards Observer* 13.10.1906
(15) *E.Gaz.*1.5.1909
(16) ibid. 28.8.1907
(17) *Justice* 25.5.1907
(18) Ball, F.C. (1973) *One of the Damned*
(19) A map showing full details of his route is included on p. xix, and Ch.7 in Coxall, B. & Griggs, C.,op.cit., 1996
(20) *Justice*, ibid. 1.8.1907
(21) ibid 1.8.1907
(22) *George Meek – Bathchairman*, p.*ix*.
(23) Coxall, B. & Griggs, C. op.cit. Ch.10, *E.Gaz.* 30.10.1907
(24) Pugh, M. (1994) *State and Society; British Political and Social History 1870-1992*, pp. 32,61,82 &102.
(25) *E.Gaz.*30.10.1907
(26) ibid.
(27) *E.Gaz.* 22.5.1912
(28) ibid.
(29) Groves, R. (1975) v.Ch. 4, *The Strange Case of Victor Grayson*
(30) Clark, D. (1985) *Victor Grayson; Labour's Lost Leader*, Quartet Books
(31) *E.Chron.* 21.9.1912
(32) *E.Gaz*, 21.5.1913
(33) ibid

(34) *E. Gaz.* 8.11.1913
(35) *E. Chron.* 5.11.1913
(36) ibid.
(37) *E Gaz.* 26.11.1913
(38) *E.Chron.* 10.10.1914
(39) Bagwell, P.S. (1963) *The Railwaymen; A History of the N.U.R.*, pp.36-38, pp.47-52
(40) *E.Chron.* 17.10.1914
(41) ibid. 10.10.1914
(42) 'Stray Notes' *ibid,* 8.11.1913
(43) ibid. 17.10.1914
(44) ibid . 9.5.1914
(45) ibid. 27,6.1914
(46) ibid. 4.7.1914
(47) ibid.
(48) ibid
(49) v. Richardson, S. *Political Worlds of Women; Gender and Politics in 19th Century Britain..*
(50) *E.Gaz.* 14.5.1913
(51) ibid. 21.5.1913

CHAPTER 8

THE OUTBREAK OF THE 1914-18 WAR

An account of what was one of the most widespread and devastating wars in Europe is well beyond the aim or scope of this local study. In reality the War was a product of the Imperialism of the 19th century in which various powers sought to expand their territories and influence whilst others sought to defend the lands they had gained earlier. The reaction of some European powers to what seemed to them to be aggressive ambitions of the German Empire following the Franco-Prussian War (1870-1871) and a series of treaties, (some secret), which committed various countries to come to the aid of others if they were attacked, were major facts which led to the War. Between June and August, it spread from the time of the assassination of Franz Ferdinand on the 28th June 1914, through to the 3rd August when Britain entered the War following the invasion of neutral Belgium by German troops. Japan joined Britain under agreements made in 1902 and 1911; Italy entered on the same side in 1915. The Ottoman Empire and Bulgaria came to the support of Germany in November 1914 and October 1915 respectively. The entry of the USA finally in 1917 spread the participation even further. For those wishing to study the subject in greater detail there is no shortage of studies of the conflict from those covering the whole War to others concentrating upon a specific campaign.

The immediate response of 'Stray Notes', a regular columnist in the *Eastbourne Chronicle*, to the news of the outbreak of the War, would seem in time to appear quite bizarre, almost frivolous, because it focused attention on the immediate practicalities facing the holiday resort:

> 'The Eastbourne Season'
>
> The war could not have broken out at a more unfortunate time for the holiday resorts. The high season having only just opened when the outbreak occurred, the disastrous effect of the international hostilities will cover nearly the entire period upon which traders and boarding and appartment-house keepers rely to replenish gaping coffers and to establish a state of preparedness for the quieter months of the year. Hopes are still entertained that the season may not turn out so bad as appearances seem to threaten; but it must be confessed on a slender hypothetical foundation. Eastbourne is certainly no whit worse off than any of its neighbours. The number of visitors is admittedly below average for August, and the prospect of any revival is now remote; considering, however, the seriously disturbed condition of things and the widespread spirit of uneasiness, not to say of alarm, we may count ourselves fortunate, perhaps, that local conditions present no more disconcerting aspect. (1)

Concern was expressed as to the impact already being felt by tradesmen from 'the presence of soldiers on commandeering bent....the men in quest of horses and other means of transit have a simple and irresistible way of annexing what they fancy. Sometimes the trader's premises are visited and a summary intimation given to somebody in authority that a certain number of horses and vehicles are required....During the last few days local traders have been divested of scores of horses and carts by the easy formula prescribed by military law in war time.'

The mood throughout the country rapidly became one of overwhelming patriotism and Jingoism. Eastbourne was no exception. The newspaper columns reflected the new mood, which was just as prevalent in Germany and the other countries who became involved in the conflict. Extracts from poems by Sydney Beckley and George Meek are typical:

'THE CALL'   A modern Nero – mad with lust
of War
Demands such sacrifice as Rome ne'er
knew or saw;
To satisfy his selfish greed for power
Our bravest march to their great glorious
hour.

March on, brave countrymen! And leave to
God
His way of vengeance on the braggart's
brood;
He will make plain the grand old human
story
That honour's path is *still* the way
to glory.

And from George Meek '1914'
> Hark! The blare of countless trumpets,
> And the roar of countless guns;
> England, called to war unseeking,
> Needs the help of all her sons.
> In the fight for right and freedom,
> Shall their answer be delayed?
> See them answering in their thousands,
> Resolute and undismayed.
>
> But-and it is ours to answer
> While we hear our country's call-
> We must stand a race united,
> *All for each and each for all.*
> Each our little all can render
> To the people and the State,
> And they also serve who only
> Calm and patient stand and wait.

Within a month Meek sent in another five verses in a similar vein:

> Not driven to battle
> Like Germans or cattle,
> The Britishers take to the gun,
> They're partial to freedom,
> Free nations, - they breed 'em,
> And that's how their day's work is done.

(2)

More amusing and therefore probably more memorable was a limerick 'From the Front' by A.B.:

> A Monarch who's known as the Kaiser,
> Of Belgium was once a despiser;
> He tried in his rage
> To capture Liege –
> And now he is older and wiser.

Support for the War

Support for the War came from all manner of societies who voiced their views in the local newspapers. Some were offering support to servicemen in one form or another. Others, moral support based upon what were considered to be the justice of Britain's actions. However as correspondence to the local newspapers would illustrate, for regular church-goers the thoughts expressed through letters or church services could be confusing. The Society of Friends were faced with a predicament given the pro-War atmosphere in the town and their usual belief in non-violence. 'The Christian conscience must be awakened to the magnitude of the issues....it is of vital importance that the war should not be carried on in any vindictive spirit, and that it should be brought to a close at the earliest possible moment.' (3) Unfortunately, the very nature of war ensures that it is carried on in a vindictive spirit. Chambers writing in the *Church Family Newspaper* posed the question 'whether war is compatible with Christianity (and) decided that there can be no doubt whatever that cases will occasionally arise when it is not only permissible for a Christian individual and a Christian nation to resort to the sword, but it is even a duty to do so.' (4)

At St Mary's Parish Church the vicar told the congregation, 'that by upholding their hands in prayer the people of the nation could take a great part in securing the victory of the right. It was right to pray for the victory of our army and navy – it was a poor man or woman who was not a patriot'. He added, 'they should also pray for God's mercy and pity even upon their enemies'. (5) The Rev J. Westbury Jones at South Street Church told his congregation that, 'In serving their country Englishmen serve their God' and that 'He that hath no sword let him sell his cloke (sic) and buy one for surely we all prefer to die rather than submit to the ruthless tyranny of German militarism'. (6)

'A correspondent' who attended the English Episcopal Church told how like many of the congregation she 'felt humiliated and grieved at the sentiment which the first psalm for the day called upon them to express...they were made to say to the Almighty – "But now Thou Art far off, and puttest us to confusion, and goest not forth with our armies. Thou makest us to turn our backs upon our enemies, so that they which hate us spoil our goods. Thou lettus us be eaten up like sheep..." She stated Britain is only doing her duty and has no cause to fear that God is going to deliver her into the the hands of her foes and requested a selection of more appropriate psalms should be selected in future services.

It seems as if whatever idea was tried by someone to help with the War effort there was always someone else who disagreed with their approach. Towards the end of August there was criticism of the patriotic music being played by the Devonshire Park Orchestra: 'at practically every concert... at which I have been present recently, it has concluded with the singing of "Rule, Britannia" two or three times by the audience followed by cheering and finally the singing of the National Anthem....I certainly think this (frequent) practice should be discontinued...'. He suggested the National Anthem at the end of a concert would be sufficient. 'Yours, British to the Core'. (7) By contrast a letter then appeared complaining at the music being played at the bandstand. 'Surely these are not the days for ragtime variations, but rather for inspiring martial favourites...' Yours, Patriotism'. (8)

Anti-German Feelings

Anti-German and Austrian sentiments began to appear. A 'Loyal Subject' recounted his experience of a lunch in a London hotel and 'to my utter surprise found myself waited upon by an Austrian waiter. I called the attention of the floor manager to this, and received the reply that it was "under consideration of the manager". Under consideration indeed! When there are hundreds of English waiters out of work! British subjects should give a wide birth to any hotel staffed by alien enemies.' (9) An issue taken up by Meek in the same edition referring to a similar situation in Eastbourne.

> An opportunity now occurs for hotel and boarding house keepers and others, who have sinned so greatly in the past by giving encouragement and support to what were all the time possible, and have now proved to be actual, enemies of their country, by giving preference to alien waiters, to make amends by filling up their places with so many Englishmen who, from physical and other causes, cannot serve their country in the field.'. (10)

Some people wished for music by German composers to be removed from concerts and one church, perhaps by coincidence, provided an organ recital of music entirely by English composers. Meek had decided that Germans had no merits at all; '...it is a sign of the times that while England has produced such men as Tom Hood, W.W.Jacobs..., France such as Le Sage and Dumas..., Spain her Cervantes, America its Mark Twain..., Germany with all its first-class writers has given the world no humorist of the first rank.' (11) He never ceased to denigrate almost every aspect of both Germans and their country. In one of his regular columns for the *Chronicle* he ended by pointing out that in Canada people from China had to pay a landing tax and an annual poll tax of £30. 'We, in England, should treat at least the German and Austrian "Schnieders" in the same way. They have proved themselves to be quite as uncivilised and dangerous as any "Chink". A "Schnieder", in German, means a "rotter"'. (12)

The recruitment drive was ongoing as realisation dawned that the War was not going to be over within twelve months as many had thought at first. Appeals were made at many events to young men to join the armed services. Rupert Gwynne, the town's MP made such pleas in the town and surrounding areas such as Seaford. 'Following the rendering at the bandstand of a patriotic selection of music and poetry by Kipling, at a given signal, the Union Jack is raised and names taken of new recruits. (13) A well-organised recruiting campaign took place in Sussex with the promise that unlike other areas where there was no guarantee as to the regiment to which a man was placed when signing up, if they signed up now they would be guaranteed to be placed in a Sussex Brigade. As the recruitment team moved around the county 'women were taking a prominent part.' In a question to the Under Secretary for War asking how many more men were needed, Colonel Lowther, a Sussex MP was told, '…that as far as could be seen this million now being recruited for Kitchener's Army will be the last million.' Sussex he was convinced would wish to shine in this last million. It appeared that there were still 50,000 men in the County unenlisted of military age. People knew there was a good possibility that conscription would be introduced in the future. It became a reality in January 1916.

There is little doubt that young men were made to feel very uncomfortable if they resisted joining the armed services; the charge being either that they were unpatriotic or, worse still, a coward! One man, quite willing to provide his name complained at the experience he had undergone concerning White feathers. 'Is it not pitiful that certain so-called "patriotic people" who are prosecuting a recruiting campaign should resort to such contemptible methods as distributing white feathers to, and asking for petticoats for, those unfortunate males they consider cowards? Is it not sufficient that one, like myself, must endure the mortification of having been rejected by the Regular and Territorial Armies for medical reasons? Or is it necessary that one must also be a target for the studied insolence and insinuations of these good people?...do they not realise that all men worthy the name would come forward of their own free will to serve their country without being dragged by the scruff of their neck...'(14) In the same edition a letter from 'Fair Play' gave support for the young men who through no lack of bravery and loyalty to their King and country, but for true and justifiable reasons are unable to accept the call of duty....(some are) working early and late for those dependent on them..it is disgraceful they should have their brave and hard lives made harder by being branded as cowards.' (15)

Given the widespread support for the War and constant encouragement for young men to join their contemporaries in the armed forces there were also attempts to shame those who for one reason or another resisted the intense recruiting campaigns.

FALL IN by Harold Begbie

What will you lack, sonny, what will you lack
When the girls line up the street,
Shouting their love to the lads come back
From the foe they rushed to beat?
Will you send a strangled cheer to the sky
And grin till your cheeks turn red?
But what will you lack when your mate goes by
With a girl who cuts you dead?

Where will you look, sonny, where will you look
When your children yet to be
Clamour to learn of the part you took
In the War that kept men free?
Will you say it was naught to you if France
Stood up to her foe or bunked?
But where will you look when they give the glance
That tells you they knew you funked?   (16)

The Labour Movement and the War

Initially there had been serious attempts by working class organisations to oppose the First World War. 'The International Socialist Bureau issued a manifesto calling for vast demonstrations against the War ...in every industrial centre .....calling for Workers, (to) stand together for peace...Up with the peaceful rule of the people!'. (17) The following day Arthur Henderson, Keir Hardie, George Lansbury, Will Thorne and other leaders addressed a mass demonstration in Trafalgar Square against the move to war. 'We stand by the efforts of the international working-class movement to unite the workers of the nations concerned in their efforts to prevent their governments from entering upon a War. ... The Government of Great Britain should rigidly decline to engage in war....' (18) Ramsay MacDonald still registered his party's disapproval: 'Whatever may be said about us, we will take the action....of saying that this country ought to have remained neutral, because in the deepest parts of our hearts we believe that was right...' (19) Small groups would continue to protest about involvement in a European War but with the exception of some members of the ILP, once Belgium had been invaded, support, even enthusiasm for the War, became overwhelming from then onwards: '..throughout the war the left was divided and defensive, while the patriotic right was self confident and more or less united.' (20)

The division among leading Socialists was not a simple one between Left and Right. There were surprises. Among those remaining opposed were Willie Gallagher, Keir Hardie, Arthur Henderson, George Lansbury, John McLean and Will Thorne. By contrast, Victor Grayson, who had been so radical and anti-establishment, toured the country using his speaking skills to persuade young men to enlist. Robert Blatchford who had founded the Clarion Movement and newspaper of that name gave the War his full support. In his visit to Eastbourne he warned an audience:

> 'The day has come; Germany is making war with the utmost violence and the destinies of five great powers are in the melting pot. At last British people are obliged to own that the German menace was real...and must now be met... (Yet)..watching the holiday crowds... Thousands of young men and women were walking on

the promenade, lounging on the beach...the band playing..and this was more than a fortnight after our Government had declared war with Germany.'

We are at War. We are committed to a war that will be desperate and terrible in its action, and in its results appalling. And here are young men flirting, laughing, riding, swimming...

Every one of those merry, careless young men ought to have a rifle on his shoulder...'

Any outright opposition in the Labour Party quickly disappeared once they had entered into the Coalition in Parliament. A widespread Government campaign was launched with the famous poster of Kitchener pointing outwards and declaring 'I want You' which was so effective that thousands of young men flocked into recruitment stations almost overwhelming the authorities. Men were required to be 5 feet 3 inches in height! Just as with the Boer War many were judged unfit to be soldiers; a result of the inadequate nutrition of large numbers of working class young people and one reason for the introduction of school dinners, initially in parts of London and elsewhere by certain local schemes and later with government support in the inter-war period.

Final Months of the War and formation of Eastbourne Labour Party

Many of those who became actually involved in the fighting found it difficult to talk of their experiences afterwards because the full horrors affected them so deeply and they found if almost impossible to explain the reality of the ferocious fighting and terrible suffering of so many of the combatants. To take just one example from the history of the Royal Sussex Regiment during the War, the Battle of the Boar's Head which took place at Richebourg L'Avoue, on the 30th June 1916, in which the 11th, 12th and 13th (Southdowns) Battalions were engaged. It was an example of the relentless trench warfare of the Western Front. After heavy bombardment of the German trenches the Battalions were ordered 'over the top' to charge the German trenches in the face of relentless machine gun fire. The battle raged to and fro for several hours. The result was 366 men dead and a further 1,000 wounded or taken prisoner. It became known as 'The Day Sussex Died'. It was hardly mentioned because the following day, the 1st July, the Battle of the Somme began in which 20,000 died on the first day. It seems as if the Battle in which the Sussex Regiment was involved was a 'diversion' and it remained unmentioned in official histories of the War. It is difficult to know how those who survived that day thought about the familiar Jingoism which had been so widespread in the early days following the entry by Britain into the War in August 1914. A sentiment which was widespread among most of the countries which participated..

In the Spring of 1918 the Germans launched a major attack on the Western Front which was unsuccessful. From that time onwards people in the UK began to believe the end of the War was now in sight even if it was recognised that this was still some way ahead. In Eastbourne, as in other towns, local considerations still dominated council discussions. For example an application from the town's branch of the Workers' Union had applied for an increase in pay and reduced hours of work. Councillor Hasdell, who was a member of this trade union supported the proposal pointing out that their income had fallen behind due to the increase in the cost of living and the steady inflation which had taken place during the War. (21) At the same meeting the town clerk drew attention to an enquiry being considered to introduce proportional representation for electing Sussex MPs. A request for a private bathing area opposite the Wish Tower was rejected. A proposal to consider the purchase of land from Mr Marchant at Tutt Barn for allotments was discussed resulting in Mr Burtenshaw being asked to act on behalf of the Council to consider the valuation of the site. (22) More controversial was the suggestion by Councillor Wood that they should have teachers on the Education Committee, which was seconded by J. Pulsford but rejected by the Council, some of whom claimed that this would lead other occupations to make a similar claim for representation on various sub-committees.

Pulsford pointed out that they were found to be on over 200 committees in the country but the proposal was 'strenuously opposed' by Councillor Duke who argued that they regularly called upon head teachers to act in an advisory capacity. Bolton claimed that 'the resolution if acted on would bring about a state of things akin to Bolshevism.' Ignoring the appeal for 'No politics', he went on to say that 'Bolshevists appointed committees in the Army and Fleet, and the result was that both became disorganised rabble. They did not want Bolshevism in any of the institutions of this country. He did not suggest that any of the Councillors were infected with Bolshevism but they had perhaps not seen the logical result of the resolution.' (23) The motion on being put to the vote was lost. The fear of Bolshevism spreading within Eastbourne Town Council faded.

These are just some of the ordinary matters which were discussed at the Council, alongside bus services, libraries, street lighting, highways and drainage, housing and pleasure grounds. At such times the War must have seemed far away. The opposite sentiment must have been felt for the servicemen engaged in the ongoing conflict.

Attitudes and Policies of Political Parties

All three major political parties were in general agreement that following the numbers of British, Commonwealth and Allied troops who had been killed or wounded in the War the opposing nations of the Central Powers, Germany, Austro-Hungary and their later allies should be 'Made to Pay' for the terrible destruction caused by the War. Understandably emotions ran high and the demand for compensation was incredibly strong at the time even though it would be proven to be completely unrealistic in later years. Nevertheless, in 1918, bitterness at the suffering resulting from the Conflict was the dominant mood and this was true for all political parties.

In August a meeting of the newly formed Labour Party took place in the hall of the Baptist Forward Mission. The *Eastbourne Clarion* report (24) had two sub-titles, 'Local Propaganda Meeting' followed by 'Social Reforms Demanded'. Tommy Hasdell was elected to the chair by J. Thompson, H.G. Kille, T.W. Johnson and S.C. Ball, the branch secretary. Hasdell told the meeting that, 'The rich controlled the land; two thirds of the wealth of the country was in the hands of people who did not help to produce wealth. There was a need to sweep away the conditions which had prevailed before the War.' He gave an example of a firm in Rye paying four and a half pence an hour – the pre-war rate – with the manager priding himself on those wage rates.

Mr Kille told the meeting that the only hope of working people was a party of their own. 'He emphasised the utter importance of environment and referred to the slum property in which the majority of the working class lived. There was drunkenness, but this was the fault of the environment. If a man had a decent home and garden he would have less use for a public house. He approved of the promised changes in the educational system but claimed, '...the ruling classes would see the working classes were not educated more than they could possibly help. The poor man's children should have the same chances of education as the children of the rich. If they had, then in 25 years the whole social system of the country would be altered.' They needed to depend on their own party, and above all, trust their leaders. The proposed changes were well received as the way forward to improve the lives of the working class; however the comment about leaders would be severely tested in the inter-war years.

The following month Tommy Hasdell presided over a meeting of Eastbourne Labour Party attended by Mr Peters, the National Agent, together with Mr H. Roberts, the London Organiser at Marine Hall. (25) The visitors expressed delight in the rapid progress of the Labour movement in such counties as Sussex. Mr Peters pointed out that 'the War had tended to strengthen the ranks of trade unionism. The country had passed through a kind of revolution – the 1918 Representation of the People Act giving votes to women over 30 years of age placed a new weapon in the hands of the working class. The number of electors had increased from 8 to 20 million, nearly 7 million of whom were women; the majority of them the wives of working men. As the election would be held on the same day there would be no more motor cars from London and elsewhere to help win the seat for Toryism.'

Many towns in Sussex had already chosen their Labour candidates; Hastings, East Grinstead, Brighton, Chichester as well as several in Surrey. Unlike some parties the meeting was told, local Labour branches choose their own candidate. The Labour programme called for decent housing, a minimum wage and equal pay for women. Roberts drew particular attention to the first item on their programme. 'Some of the nation were housed in places that were a standing disgrace to a country which called itself Christian...tremendous profits were made from these hovels and the most effective remedy for these evils was to send a man from their own class to Parliament.'

Hasdell was chosen as the Labour candidate for Eastbourne. He was born in Northampton and came to the town in 1899 when 30 years of age. He established a shoe maker's business in Green Street and became co-opted onto the Town Council in March 1918 due to the resignation of A.J. Marshall who was serving with the Army in France. In May he was made a Magistrate and became President of the recently established local Labour Party. He was later Vice Chairman of the Trades and Labour Council and an organiser for the Workers' Union which would eventually amalgamate with the TGWU.

The Party held another meeting in October, this time at the town hall with guest speakers Mr T.C. Cramp,

President of the NUR and Labour candidate for Middlesbro and Dr Marian Phillips, Chief Woman Officer of the Labour Party. Cramp told a crowded room that 'It was a sign of the times when in a highly respectable and aristocratic town like Eastbourne so many people had assembled to listen to the gospel of Labour; '..the conditions of the future would make it absolutely imperative that for the salvation of this country Labour must rule, and unless it was prepared to assume and accept its responsibility, the future was going to be blacker than the past had ever been....the railways should become the property of the nation and by the people who worked upon them...the object of Education should not be to lift children out of their class, but to lift up their class and give them the opportunity they ought to have.' (26)

In December Hasdell spelt out the programme he supported for the Labour Party; it was radical by contrast to many of the ideas that had prevailed in so much of Edwardian society which had only been challenged by the 1906 Liberal Government. After people had been asked to sacrifice so much during the devastating War there was little chance that they would all return meekly to the oppressive living conditions which had been the experience of so many working class men and women prior to 1914. Some of the demands were for an extension of schemes introduced earlier; others for root and branch social reforms. There was strong support for the formation of a League of Nations to prevent another major War and the abolition of Secret Diplomacy which had played a considerable part in expanding the Conflict. An end to military conscription was sought and a massive programme of national reconstruction, especially for local authority housing programmes supported by grants in aid to provide decent housing for the thousands of families forced to live in inadequate dwellings.

To improve the conditions of working people an eight hour day should be introduced, an ambition dating back to the 1860s at a meeting of the International Association of Working Men, in memory of which a number of silver pocket watches had been produced with the words 'Eight hours for Work, Eight Hours for our own Instruction and Eight Hours for Repose'. (27) Other improvements demanded were a minimum wage and equal pay for equal work. An increase in Old Age Pensions was sought and a reduction in the qualifying age from the present 70 years. Given life expectancy in Edwardian times a significant number of adults never lived long enough to receive any payment. The franchise to be the same for women as it was for men; instead only women over 30 years of age were granted the vote. Education to be free for all from Nursery School to University together with the provision for teachers of all kinds and grades, pensions, training and opportunities for advancement commensurate with the high social importance of their calling. The railways, canals, coalmines, iron and steel industries to be nationalised and Ireland to have the right of self determination. Finally the appointment of a Ministry of Health, that the State should take over all the hospitals and Institutions now maintained by charitable contributions and to establish a National Medical Service to deal with this matter; a generation before the National Health Service (NHS) was finally introduced! This programme must have seemed Utopian at the time for whilst the vote was finally given to women on equal terms to men in 1928 it would take until 1944 for most of the other proposals to come to fruition. A National Health Service was introduced by the reforming 1945 Labour Government against considerable political opposition in Parliament. In the case of some reforms, such as the minimum wage, the wait would be even longer, 1999, whilst many changes, having been implemented, would be reversed by Privatisation schemes years later.

In November there was a public meeting in support of Sir Alfred Callaghan, the Liberal Party candidate at the Pitman Institute in Old Town. If returned he told them 'he would be prepared to support the Government as far as lay in his power to bring about a just and lasting peace and in carrying out measures of construction…but not bound without the opportunity of criticising any measure…too much in a Tory mould.' His wife, Lady Callaghan spoke in his support dealing with 'the question of the disabilities under which women were suffering' and promising her husband would do what he could to remove these. Sir Callaghan also produced a sixteen point programme for the General Election scheduled for Saturday, 14th December, including Coalition Government, the League of Nations, Women and Social Justice, Education and Housing. It was printed in full in the *Eastbourne Chronicle*. (28)

The Constitutional Club in Seaside was the venue for the Conservative Party's pre-election meeting. Their candidate, Robert Gwynne, was delayed at another meeting and so Charles Jewell, the president, started the proceedings stating that the Central Powers should be made to pay for the War – 'they had caused all the horrors, misery and mortality.' He claimed that 'They who had made their money abroad were very pleased to help their country by paying high taxation, but the Labour Party were desirous of conscripting their capital and being very lenient as to the indemnity from the Germans – quite a wrong policy.

He told the audience that he thought, 'Britain had lost more men than any other country and were going to exact this indemnity.' In this statement he was incorrect as the statistics would demonstrate later although the precise figures would never be known. Approximate numbers of total dead would read France 1,397,800; Russia 1,811,000; UK 886,939; Germany 2,050,897; Ottaman Empire 771,844 and Austro-Hungary 1,100,000. Britain's lower total casualty result was partly because the country was not invaded. In any case each death was a tragedy whatever the nationality. For every death recorded there were 3 seriously wounded, some of whom were able to recover their health whilst many others were much less fortunate. The war monuments in Eastbourne and the surrounding villages bear testament to the terrible loss of life. Gwynne arrived later and called for support for the Coalition led by Lloyd George 'who had shown he was out against the Germans. That was the man they wanted, for many years, to keep out the scoundrels; do not let them have German goods dumped here. Intern all of them and do not let Germans become naturalised.'

A pre-election meeting of the 'Eastbourne Habitation of the Primrose League' expressed similar attitudes towards Germany and her inhabitants. They offered membership to 'all who adopt our principles, but for the Bolshevist, the Pacifist and the Defeatist we can find no room. The League itself is essentially "democratic," and is represented on the Council by men and women of different social positions.' They were strongly anti-German and saw the War as a struggle between Germany (standing for world domination) and Anglo-Saxondom (standing for freedom.)...it is absurd that in their present temper their styling themselves "Democrats" or "Socialists" would make the least difference.... her treachery, savagery and brutality has never been equalled....There must be no more dealings with Germany....' Part of the strength of feeling can be explained by the time of this strong declaration; just a few months before the end of the War. (29)

'Stray Notes'in the *Eastbourne Chronicle* (30) on sale the same day as the General Election forecast the probable result: '...we do not profess to be very sanguine when anticipating a somewhat decisive victory for the Coalition candidate. The conditions are exceptional, and any effort to gauge the relative strength of parties is complicated by the wholly novel experience for Eastbourne of having three candidates in the field. That the Labour Party are a force to be reckoned with, even in a non-industrial centre, must be admitted; but after making full allowance for Councillor Hasdell's enthusiastic reception in certain parts of the borough, one cannot believe in an absolute triumph for that gentleman. Sir A. Callaghan, the Liberal candidate, between whom Mr Gwynne, despite a rather heated interchange of criticisms, there are probably more points of agreement than divergence, has been engaged in an uphill fight as was inevitable after his belated arrival on the scene....from a dispassionate survey of the position, we fail to discern any tangible promise of an impending Liberal victory.' The analysis turned out to be correct.

The General Election took place on Saturday 14th December and the outcome was no real surprise. The result was:

Mr Robert Gwynne (Coalition)	11,357
Mr T.B. Hasdell (Labour)	4,641
Sir Alfred Callaghan (Liberal)	1,852

Gwynne had been Conservative MP for the town since 1910. His background was not untypical of many of the MPs in his Party. He had inherited Wooton Manor, the family home in Polegate, was educated at Shrewsbury and Cambridge before training as a barrister. It came as no surprise either to find a large number of those who worked to get him elected were invited to a celebration at Eastbourne College 'kindly lent for the occasion by the Head Master'. A list of some of those who had helped him during the Election appeared in the *Eastbourne Chronicle*. (31). Among the 110 names printed there was one colonel, one Lt. Colonel, two majors, two ladies, a Knight of the Garter and three councillors.

The low Liberal vote was a surprise. Sir Alfred, speaking from the town hall balcony alongside the other candidates said, 'He stood before them a beaten candidate – very much beaten.' By contrast, Tommy Hasdell claimed 'the greatest victory of all the parties, for they had for the first time in Eastbourne a candidate who represented the workers and who got his living by his hands.' He met with his supporters at the Labour Club in South Street for a 'splendid concert arranged by H. Jowett to celebrate their participation in the General Election, at which Tommy Hasdell told them,

'Personally he was proud of his position as the first Labour candidate and did not think they should be downhearted by the result.' (32)

References – Chapter 8

(1) *E.Chron.* 8.8.1914 'Stray Notes'
(2) ibid. 5.9.1914
(3) ibid. 15.8.1914
(4) ibid 5.9.1914
(5) ibid 22.8.1914
(6) ibid. 12.9.1914
(7) ibid. 29.8.1914
(8) ibid 5.9.1914
(9) ibid 22.8.1914
(10) ibid
(11) ibid 26.9.1914
(12) ibid 3.10.1914
(13) ibid 5.9.1914
(14) ibid Sydney Wale
(15) ibid
(16) ibid.
(17) Morton & Tate (1973) *The British Labour Movement*, p.256
(18) ibid.
(19) Pelling, H. (1976) *A Short History of the Labour Party*, pp.35-36
(20) *McGibbon, R. (1974) The Evolution of the Labour Party 1910-1924*, pp88-89
(21) *E.Chron.* 6.4.1919
(22) ibid 7.12.1918
(23) ibid
(24) *E.Clarion* 31.8.1918
(25) *E.Chron.* 7.9.1918
(26) ibid. 19.10.1918

(27) Birch, L. (Ed) *The History of the TUC 1868-1968*, p.9
(28) *E.Chron.* 30.11.1918
(29) ibid. 26.10.1918
(30) ibid. 14 12 .1918 'Stray Notes'
(31) ibid. 4.1.1919
(32) ibid.

Part 3
The Inter-War Years

CHAPTER 9

THE COAL INDUSTRY AND THE 1926 GENERAL STRIKE

The 1914-1918 War – The Human costs!

This terrible War led to the death of thousands of service personnel on all sides of the conflict. There is no way these disastrous events can be covered in a history concentrating mainly on local events. There are numerous excellent studies of the war as a whole and detailed accounts of particular conflicts, such as the struggle in Northern Italy, the widespread onslaught on the Eastern Front and the fighting on the Western Front. For British people and many allied soldiers it is the latter which became a familiar picture of the War which would be reinforced in books and films. Here soldiers from both 'sides' attempted to over-run the trenches of their opponents by infantry charging across muddy shell-holed stretches of land, criss-crossed with barb wire, only to be faced with rapid machine gun fire, which led to widespread casualties. For example the Battle of the Somme in November 1916 'developed into the bloodiest battle in world history with more than a million casualties' whilst the following year the Battle of Passchendaele in 1917 led to 'British casualties of at least 300,000'. In large cemeteries throughout Europe long rows of tombstones give witness to the scale of losses in general whilst monuments in villages and towns give some indication of the personal sacrifice within local communities, such as East Dean, Hampden Park and Pevensey. The War Memorial in central Eastbourne was unveiled in 1920 whilst a list of those who died in the conflict was carved on a wide wooden panel which can be seen on the first landing of the staircase in the town hall. (1) For a detailed account of the effects of the War upon the people of Eastbourne the reader should consult R. A. Ellison's study. (2)

Economic and Political Problems in the British Coal Industry

At least some part of the issues of the 1926 General Strike were related to the outcome of the 1914-1918 War as detailed studies have made clear. (3) Different international pressures arising from the results of the 1914-1918 War and conflicting interests played a major part to the manner in which the events unfolded. 'In their wisdom the peacemakers at Versailles issued a dicktat that Germany was to meet part of its reparations to the coal producing nations of France, Belgium and Italy in coal. The world groaned under a flood of the black mineral and within a year the export price of British coal slumped by more than half. Forced to balance the coal budget at a cost of £5 million a month, Lloyd George ordered the immediate return of the mines to private ownership and abandoned the miners to wage cuts of up to 40%...British coal exports slumped from 42 million tons in the first half of 1924 to 35 million tons in the first half of 1925.when their twelve month agreement came to an end.' (4)

A series of pre-war Royal Commissions into the mining industry had impugned its management and convinced the miners that only nationalization would solve the industry's problems. 'A further Royal Commission was set up in 1919 under Lord Justice Sankey to study the immediate issue of wages and hours and the longer term question of nationalization. The Government undertook to adopt its report "in spirit and in letter". However the Commission which was made up of 6 miners' nominees, including Sydney Webb, 3 coal owners and 3 industrialists, was unable to reach unanimity on anything.' (5) Each group produced a report but could not agree on the key issues of wages, hours and nationalization, although, perhaps surprisingly, all favoured various forms of nationalization. Lloyd George ignored these recommendations; the result was that the miners in general believed he had broken his pledge and refused to discuss the issue further. When the 1926 Crisis did arise, Baldwin would declare, 'In this as in so many other things Lloyd George left us with a legacy of trouble.' (6)

Winston Churchill's efforts to become an MP had been thwarted by electoral defeats in 1922, 1923 and a by-election in 1924 before he was successful standing again in the General Election of the same year. He had moved from the Conservative party to the Liberals and back again to the Conservatives which led some to regard such actions as political opportunism. Baldwin made him Chancellor of the Exchequer whereupon he promptly returned Britain to the gold standard at pre-war rates of $4.86 to the pound making the British currency too strong and thereby reducing the ability of the country to export. Philip Snowden, the Labour Chancellor of 1924 supported this move; John Maynard Keynes argued that it would lead to widespread unemployment. As mine owners found it increasingly difficult to export they sought to reduce costs, hence their moves to reduce wages and increase the hours of miners, which were resisted by their trade unions, who campaigned under the slogan, 'Not a penny off the pay, not a minute on the day'. The coal owners gave way leading to what became known as 'Red Friday'. Based upon their success the TUC pledged to support the miners in any future disputes.

Those politically aware within the parties to the dispute, miners, coal owners and Government, all realised this settlement was really more like a sullen truce than a victory. Planning for the next stage of the conflict began to take place among all those who had interests in any potential conflict within the coal industry. Maurice Hankey, permanent secretary to the Cabinet, wrote to the King, 'Public opinion is to a considerable extent on the side of the miners' whilst Neville Chamberlain, at the Health Department declared, 'The owners were not a prepossessing crowd.' Because of such attitudes Baldwin did not wish to be too closely associated with the coal owners and so diverted criticism from activists within the trade union world to one of a constitutional challenge to Parliament; a far more effective tactic. Greater sympathy was shown to what were considered 'moderates' at the TUC and the Political Right emphasised the role of activists as 'militants' and 'Reds', a description which would be used a few months later at a meeting of the 'National Citizens' Union in Eastbourne.

One difficulty with the situation was that many communities were still suffering from the effects of the 1914-1918 War in which thousands had died or suffered from terrible injuries. Were these sacrifices to be so quickly forgotten or ignored with so many coal miners in particular expected to face redundancy, lower wages and a longer working day? At the risk of grossly oversimplifying the situation at least two major approaches were possible within the TUC. There was the Syndicalist policy of Arthur J. Cook who believed they should confront and challenge both coal owners and the Government as opposed to that of Ernie Bevin who believed from his experience that industrial action – or even its threat – was an important weapon for trade unionists to use when necessary if faced with intransigent employers but not to challenge government.

Having experienced the War ordinary people were unwilling to return meekly to the social situation which had prevailed during the Edwardian age in contrast to some of the more affluent members of society who wished for precisely that. Moreover there had been major upheavals and changes in Europe and the Middle East. The Empires of Austro-Hungary and the Ottamans had been swept away, there had been a successful revolution in Russia in 1917 followed by two failed attempts in Hungary and Germany two years later. (7) The Government was clearly aware of these developments although there was no such serious threat of similar events taking place in the U.K. However the situation was not helped when on the 14th October 1925 warrants were issued for the arrest of a number of members of the Communist Party (C.P.), including Albert Inkpin, party secretary and Harry Pollitt, both charged with 'seditious libel and incitement to mutiny' for calling on servicemen to refuse to fire upon demonstrating workers! The result was that they were sentenced to a year's imprisonment. There were protests from well known public figures such as Bernard Shaw and Lady Warwick; in Parliament Labour MPs, including Ramsay MacDonald, together with Lord Simon of the Liberal Party, complained of these actions. A petition was signed by 300,000 people urging their release. At a large meeting at the Albert Hall George Lansbury repeated many of the calls made by those imprisoned which helped to add to the pressure upon Baldwin. Raids on offices of the C.P. in London and the provinces resulted in 'some 1,200 of its members being brought before the courts.' (8) Baldwin partly took this approach to appease some of his back-benchers but politically it was rather unwise because it provided considerable publicity for the C.P. and some sympathy for its members, especially among trade unionists.

Negotiations between Coalmine Owners and Coal Miners

Negotiations between coal owners and the MFGB on the 1st May almost reached agreement but broke down over a lack of firm assurances concerning wage rates. This failure led to a lock out of one million miners which in turn brought an amendment from the TUC that a general strike would take place 'in defence of miners' wages and hours' to begin one minute to midnight on Monday 3rd May. It was to include railwaymen, transport workers, printers, dockers, iron and steel workers; what was regarded as the key front line workers. Even at this late stage there was still a slight chance of an agreement being reached between TUC representatives and Baldwin but at 1.30 am, the Prime Minister called them all together to announce all negotiations were at an end because at the *Daily Mail*, Thomas Marlowe, the editor, had written a leading article entitled 'For King and Country', highly critical of trade unions which the printers refused to produce. The result was an unofficial stoppage which confronted Baldwin with a claim that 'freedom of the press' was being denied. The failure of the *Daily Mail* to be printed led one of Baldwin's aids to phone the King at Windsor to explain that this newspaper had not been published. There was no need for concern came the reply: 'We don't take the *Daily Mail* or *Daily Express*! (9) The scale of support for the Strike surprised both the TUC and the Government. There could be no doubting the harsh working conditions faced daily by miners nor the general sympathy they evoked. For example, King George Vth in response to suggestions they were revolutionaries replied, 'Try living on their wages before you judge them.'10) Cuthbert Headlam, a Conservative MP in the coalminng area of County Durham recorded in his diary 'The Government has not managed the business cleverly…one could not have risked a general upheaval of labour…without being convinced that the great mass of public opinion was against the miners. Thanks to the [owners'] tactless stupidity it was nor.'(11)

Many working people in Eastbourne had no direct experience of such work either but they could sympathise with people undertaking such dirty, dangerous and hard daily work for their conditions were usually far from ideal either. Their wages were comparatively low, being a sea-side resort work was often seasonal and subject to the general prosperity of the town, so that the building trade fluctuated in line with variations in the demands for new housing. Some were more able to sympathise with miners and those working in heavy industry if they were members of trade unions. Many were also aware that private owners of the coal mines were now facing increased competition from overseas, such as the USA and Germany in the post-War period. To maintain their profits they increased the hours of work for miners and reduced their rates of pay. Such moves were not confined to the mining industry but contrasted sharply with the comparative prosperity and higher wages of the war years when demand for coal had been high.

The General Strike – Conservative Government Action

With regular newspaper supplies under threat the Government contacted the *Morning Post*, edited by H.A. Gwynne and owned by the Duke of Northumberland, and Lord Beaverbrook for help in producing a daily paper which would put forward the Government's point of view on the strike. J.C.C. Davidson, who had been elected as a Conservative MP in a by-election in 1920 and had served as PPS to Bonar Law, was Deputy Chief Civil Commissioner by 1926 and as such involved in the early discussions which led to the establishment of the *British Gazette*, a daily paper of which Winston Churchill was made editor. Churchill's aim was twofold; to portray the industrial strike as a challenge to government and to undermine the confidence of the strikers. The latter would be achieved by the falsification and distortion of events in which he was quite successful. Even the General Council of the TUC who were genuinely amazed at the unanimity of the strike, were surprised at claims made in the *Gazette*. For example the London Underground was described as running at full service although only 8 out of 29 trains were running on the Central Line and only a total of 43 out of 315 trains operating in total. (Figures given for London from another source were even less supportive; 15 out of 1,500 underground trains running, 9 out of 2,000 trams whilst all 4,000 buses were off the roads (12)

Churchill had asked the BBC to broadcast the sound of the presses in action producing the *Gazette*; they refused to do so. (13) Two days later he proposed that the Government should take over the BBC and use it to broadcast official news! The Cabinet rejected this. (14) His lack of any attempt at objectivity as editor led Davidson, who would go on to become Chairman of the Conservative Party, to write 'never have I listened to such poppycock and rot.' (15) (Lloyd George referred to the short-lived *Gazette* as a 'first class indiscretion, clothed in the tawdry garb of third rate journalism'. (16) More predictable perhaps was the opinion of the *New Statesman* – 'One of the worst outrages which the country had to endure – and pay for – in the course of the strike, was the *British Gazette*. This organ, throughout the seven days of its existence, was a disgrace alike to the British Government and to British journalism'. (17)

As with most disputes the parties wished to win the sympathy of the public for their claims to legitimacy. There was not too much sympathy for the owners of the coal mines so Baldwin's approach was to claim that the strike was a challenge to the Constitution, 'a challenge to Parliament and the road to anarchy and ruin'. For the Trades Union Congress it was an industrial strike in which trade unions were supporting the miners against the harsher conditions being imposed on their working conditions by the private owners of the mines. When Councillor Martin repeated the claim that 'the strike was against the constitution' at a meeting of the Eastbourne Council the idea was challenged:

> Hasdell: Can I ask of the Town Clerk on that matter, whether it is constitutional or not?. The Mayor: 'No, I am not going to enter into that.'
> Hasdell: It has been challenged. I am a loyal constitutionalist, and I object to anyone saying otherwise.
> The Mayor: I suggest that the merits of that question need not be pursued further.
> Councillor Chatfield: ...the fact that the Labour members had not tried to alter the constitution of the Committee when it was first appointed was proof that the strike was not a deep-laid plot against the constitution, as had been alleged otherwise...

Effects of General Strike in Eastbourne

The *Eastboune Gazette* (18) received a special message from the Press Association describing the national situation:

General Strike blow fell at midnight last night and reports show that both in London and the provinces the call to cease work met with a remarkable response, and the stoppage is practically complete....A meeting of the TUC was held in London to review the situation and discuss the position generally and in a final message the council laid the responsibility for the crisis on the Government.

The newspaper described the situation in Eastbourne which 'like every other town in England, awoke, yesterday to find itself in the throes of a general strike. The disaster, causing about 3,000 local workmen "to be idle", of course, had been foreseen and that accounted for the calmness with which people adapted themselves to the novel situation. Whilst a few trains ran between London, Brighton and Guildford, there was no service to Eastbourne. An analysis of the 3,000 not working in the town produced the following approximate numbers:

National Union of Railwaymen	300-400
Associated Society of Locomotive Engineers & Firemen	100
Railway Clerks Association	Unknown
Engineers Union	50-60
Carpenters & Painters	300-400

The number might have been larger if the strike notices had not been delayed through the irregular postal service. Like the railwaymen, the bus crews ceased working on the Monday night with Corporation and Southdown men joining the 3,000 strikers in the town whilst a few non-union men continued to work. (19) At the Eastbourne Labour Club, the Strike Committee and

Council, consisting of every trade effected sat throughout the night, with large numbers of strikers remaining at the Club to keep in touch with events. Mr J. Pritcher, Secretary of Eastbourne's Trades Council and Labour Party, stated 'He thought the Strike would last a week. When the union funds were exhausted the men would "fight on their stomachs."' He refuted any suggestion of revolution and said, 'If there was a revolution it would be started by the Tories and Fascisti'. It was important that 'those two bodies kept their heads – the strikers would'. (20) He emphasised public opinion was with the miners and he thought, 'it would be interesting to know how many of the men who volunteered to do emergency work had undertaken the duties of the miners.' (21)

In the face of the strike the Eastbourne Branch of the Organisation for the Maintenance of Supplies which had been provided with an office in the town hall, appealed for the names of those wishing to help with the greatest need being for 'motor drivers, skilled men, mechanics and men who could work on railways'. All work in the building trade had ceased with the exception of that related to housing or hospitals.

Many of the strikers in the town assembled in Cornfield Lane, by the headquarters of the Trades and Labour Council. A bus conductor named Wells, ex-Sergeant Major of the Guards during the 1914-1918 War, led the march down Seaside Road to the Recreation Ground where an open-air meeting was held. 'The procession, which included a group of women, numbered between six and seven hundred persons, many of whom wore their war medals. A band provided the music and the banners displayed included those of the N.U.R.

and Workers' Union, and others inscribed "We say no reduction in miners' wages," "Our motto: Live and let live," "Miners were comrades in 1914," and "Still comrades to-day." The Rev'd C.R. Farnswork of Southover church held a service for railway workers from local branches of the N.U.R., R.C.A, and T.G.W.U.

The first speaker, Mr Honeysett, Chairman of the local Labour Party, called for three cheers for the miners, then read a telegram from Mr Cramp, industrial secretary of the N.U.R., saying that the position was never better and that there was tremendous enthusiasm amongst the railwaymen. He contradicted a statement in the Government's *British Gazette* that 12,000 men had returned to duty on the Southern Railway. (22) Labour councillor Marshall referred to the employees of a local transport firm who came out on strike as 'heroes'. These men, he said, had been threatened with dismissal but, if after the strike, the company employing them 'rode the high horse' and refused to take them back, he would see to it (he was a member of the N.U.R) that there were no more trains running into and out of Eastbourne Station than there were today. The statement was received with cheers. (23) Mr P. Jeeson of the B.T.O.S., speaking at the same meeting said it was an understood thing that if there were any cases of hardship among the local strikers those of them who were in a position to do so would render help. Reporting on the gathering the *Eastbourne Chronicle* wrote 'the procession was free from disorder and unseemly incident. Even the speeches, though rather flamboyant, were neither inflammatory nor provocative, and the proceedings generally were marked by cordiality and good humour.' (24) Similar comments concerning related activities of trade unionists throughout the strike were mentioned on a number of occasions. (A photograph of the demonstration at the Recreation Ground appeared in the *Eastbourne Gazette* (5.5.1926) which gave an indication of the size of the crowd. Unfortunately the lack of clarity in such an old newspaper means that it cannot be reproduced.)

A considerable number of people responded to the appeal for 'Volunteers' as special constables; 184 by the 8th May, including 43 who had been sworn in the day before. 'The Chief Constable, Mr W.H. Smith expressed himself very gratified by this response and also by the fact that they were all of the best possible type for the purpose.' (25) Those who came forward offering to try and carry out the work of those on strike were not always regarded in the same light by many working people who were more likely to regard them as 'strike breakers'. There was no driving test before 1934 which meant there was no official way of knowing for certain the competence or safety of some of the volunteer drivers. Writing many years later about the General Strike the author of the article in (26) mentioned his experience as a young man in Eastbourne. 'The writer remembers it all, and, being young and unpolitical, conducted a bus "for the excitement of it," in Eastbourne.' One example is hardly representative of the dozens who became involved temporarily in such work. It is doubtful whether those who earned their living regularly as member of a bus crew considered it as particularly exciting. When a train arrived from London during the week-end it was claimed that the passengers made a collection for the driver and fireman. It was reported that Mr Wynford-Wright, son of the late Rev. F.

Wynford-Wright and Mrs Wynford Wright, of Eastbourne 'is driving a train daily on the London tube and working twelve hours each day.

By contrast there were those who worked as volunteers to support the strike. Percy Wood who had joined the army during the 1914-1918 War when 16 years of age, (he explained that he was 'tall for his age' and those recruiting did not challenge him given that the height required for recruits was five feet three inches and there was a pressing need to replace the large number of servicemen badly wounded or killed in the conflict). He drove a supply van for the Co-operative. He knew from experience how hard life was for many working people. He married in 1921 and received a redundancy notice on the same day. He became a Labour Councillor for Roselands in 1934. (27)

Understandably there were concerns as to the effect the strike would have directly on the town. In the 'Stray Notes' column of the *Eastbourne Chronicle* (28) it was pointed out that the town 'had lost most of its visitors and trade being more or less depressed by the general upset and the not unnatural reluctance of the public to speculate. Given favourable conditions later it may happily be possible partly to repair present deficiencies, and the inhabitants must at least be thankful that the strike has occurred at a comparatively slack time, and not in the season, when it must have operated disastrously upon all seaside resorts.' (29)

One significant event which coincided with the strike was the National Chamber of Trade Conference scheduled for Eastbourne during May. When the assembly met at the town hall the General Strike was already under way so it was thought there would be a need to curtail part of the programme arranged for the event. Initially it was thought most of the sessions would need to be cancelled; 'no reasonable alternative to entirely abandoning the session for the conference proper (and) the social functions fixed to take place on Tuesday and the following days.' (30) The banquet at the Grand Hotel was cancelled for 'Even if there were a sufficient company to justify the gathering, the feeling prevailed that it would not be seemly in the present crisis.' (31) However when it was pointed out that as businessmen they ought to realise that the cancellation of the dinner would be a financial loss to the Grand Hotel, a show of hands decided the dinner should not be cancelled.

At the luncheon which took place at the town hall a number of people were asked to speak including the local MP, Alderman Sir Reginald Hall, who inevitably made reference to the breakdown in the early negotiations between coal mine owners and the men who worked for them. 'No-one would be foolish enough to prophesy what was going to happen, but he submitted to the company that....it behoved each one of us, whether we agreed with the Government or not, to stand behind them and ensure peace within our borders as well as overseas...he had the greatest confidence, affection and respect for the prime minister...' (32)

After a couple of days the *Eastbourne Chronicle* provided a brief summary of the effects on the town. 'As far as Eastbourne is concerned, business has been carried on much as usual, except for the almost total curtailment of railway facilities – only one, or at the most two trains between here and London in the day – no serious inconvenience has been caused to the public. Some 3,000 men, members of the Unions, have ceased work, among them the Corporation bus drivers and conductors, but volunteers have filled their places to some extent...' (33) The newspaper went on to state, 'That there is a feeling of sympathy for the miners is evident... The N.T.C. showed only "brotherly sympathy" in coming to the support of "colleagues in distress," and had they limited their sympathy to moral support the whole country would be with them.'

In the surrounding areas there was also support for the strike among the comparatively few people working in industries in which the T.U.C had called for their support; railways and bus companies being the most important at the time. At Seaford, 'the railway service was at a complete standstill and the station deserted.' On the Wednesday afternoon 'a party of the strikers, numbering just over 100, marched over from Newhaven and held a brief open-air meeting'. (34) There was limited activity at Lewes and Rottingdean but more substantial strike action at Newhaven and Brighton.

Emergency Committee and Trade Unions negotiate the end of the Strike

A special meeting of the town council was called for Wednesday 12th May but when they met to discuss the situation they learned that the possibility of a national settlement was being seriously discussed in London. Councillor Hasdell, suggested a delay in their planned discussion: 'in view of the good news that is reported to us, this matter should not come for discussion today.... until we get the official news through and the terms of the settlement. At this moment there is nothing but good will on our side. We all realise that this is not a local dispute. We feel that it is perhaps unfortunate that we could not have got the official communication by the time this Council met. If the council adjourned it would save any unnecessary remarks. The Mayor agreed saying that his suggestion 'was distinctly a good one' and adjourned the meeting until the next day when they would be in possession of all the facts. Alderman Thornton said '...it should be a cause of great satisfaction to the Council and the town that those strike notices have been withdrawn.' This measure of agreement between councillors was the easiest part of the dispute to settle; other related issues would prove more challenging.

Meanwhile throughout the afternoon a crowd of strikers had gathered outside the Labour Party Headquarters in South Street. A notice had been pinned to the door: 'No official instructions received. Stand firm. No man to return to work. J. Pitcher, Secretary for Council of Action'. Shortly afterwards another notice read: 'Council of Action. Official announcement will be posted here at 8.15 pm.' At that time Honeysett appeared at an upper window to announce the receipt of a telegram from the T.U.C as to the termination of the strike and giving instructions that men were to return to work in an organised manner.'

There were two main contentious issues before the Council. Who should be included on the Emergency Committee and the reinstatement of those trade union members who had followed the instruction of their executive committees and come out in support of the strike. The question of membership of the Emergency Committee arose because it was linked to the second question; the fate of the strikers. The membership of the former had been appointed in April and comprised of the Mayor, Chairman of finance Committee (R.G. Thornton), Alderman Soddy, Councillors Avard and Woodnough. Councillor Soddy argued that the purpose of the Committee was to maintain essential services and relieve problems emanating from the strike, in which Labour councillors were playing supporting roles. However Hasdell pointed out that the Mayor could be said to represent private residents, Sir Charles Harding and Alderman Thornton the professional classes, Councillors Avard and Woolnough the business men and Alderman Soddy the tradesmen; but the organised and other workers were practically unrepresented on the Committee. It was a very dangerous precedent to set up a committee with one-sided views, anti-Labour, and expect the workers to accept that committee.

Councillor Marshall pointed out that Labour was represented on Food Control Committees and other organisations throughout the country. He suggested two of the councillors had businesses which had lost money because of the strike and might well feel some bitterness towards those who had taken part in the strike. Only the five Labour councillors voted for a motion, namely Chatfield, Hasdell, Higgs, Marshall and Packham. This meant that the Emergency Committee members alone would now decide who among the strikers should be reinstated and who should not. Councillor Carter said he was not going to argue whether councillors Woolnough and Avard were fit and proper representatives to be on that Committee 'but I do take the stand that, if the Council decide that they are, then Labour ought to be represented...Therefore I am going to support their claim to be included in the Committee.'

The Committee had no say concerning railway workers who were employed by Southern Railway. It was the buses which were the area of contention. Mr Turner, manager of the private Southdown Bus Company received a letter from the local Council of Action asking that he meet a deputation from his employees which he declined to do. He stated that because the company now refused to recognise trade unions they no longer intended to engage union labour. The Company had sent all their employees a circular which they would all be expected to sign agreeing that they would no longer be members of a trade union. Out of 21 who went on strike 14 did not return.

The Emergency Committee by deciding to make such decisions over who should be retained and who should not among the Corporation's bus crews meant they were faced with questions such as what should be done about those who had been volunteers during the strike and now wished to gain employment which could only be granted at the expense of those who had been on strike. It seemed as if although some volunteers had come forward at the time in a belief that it was the right thing to do in helping the community some others had seen it as an opportunity to gain employment themselves at the expense of the regular bus workers. Having taken upon themselves the decision as to who would be employed on the Corporation's buses the Emergency Committee found themselves confronted with questions such as what was to be done with those who had taken over the jobs of the regular bus workers and now wished to remain? How would they deal with bus workers who had gone on strike at the request of their own trade union? (35) They decided that the

Committee should meet with the bus workers seeking re-engagement. Some favoured giving preference to those who had temporarily taken the work of the regular bus workers, yet such a decision was bound to lead to further problems, especially in the light of telegrams arriving at the local Labour Party headquarters which were read out by D.G. Honeysett:

> Where employers meet in spirit of reconciliation men to return at once, but members must not resume work in any form where there is an attempt on the part of employers to insist on new agreements or to victimise members. Act with other Unions in so far as this policy is observed.

There was another telegram from C.T.T. Cramp, the industrial secretary of the N.U.R, calling upon all railwaymen to continue the strike until we receive satisfactory assurances.

The terms of the settlement between Prime Minister Stanley Baldwin and T.U.C. General Council had been no victimisation on either side and men to return to their posts as they had left them under the old agreements. However the Emergency Committee in the town by contrast was informing some of the busmen that their services were no longer required. They had continued to state that they would interview all bus workers from those who had worked for the Corporation before the strike and those who had temporally filled their jobs and now hoping to become permanent employees. Whilst this impasse continued those who had been on strike refused to go back to work. When the Mayor was asked at a meeting of the Emergency Committee whether any of the 'temporary men had been promised permanent employment he replied that 'they recognised they were acting in an emergency. No time had been fixed for the duration of their services...' (36) On the 15th May the Emergency Committee met a delegation from the Corporation's busmen and discussed with them the conditions for their return to work. Emerging from these talks they joined with colleagues waiting for them and marched together along to their South Street headquarters and considered the terms put before them. (37)

There were lengthy discussions about the possible fate of the Corporation's busmen. Forvargue, who was town clerk at the time recorded that, 'There was considerable trouble with regard to the reinstatement of these men after the strike terminated'. ((38) It is to the credit of the trade unionists and town councillors that the issue was finally settled to the satisfaction of most of the parties involved. This was eventually achieved by negotiations between the Emergency Committee and the five busmens' representatives. The Committee invited the busmen to meet them having produced a statement which read:

> The Committee think it is desirable to state publicly that the Council have not decided that all shall not be re-engaged

They posted a notice outside the town hall which read:

> The Committee have invited all the men to meet them and not representatives . The invitation still holds good, but the Committee are not prepared to discuss

> matters with representatives only before this meeting had taken place. The Council approved of the Committee's suggestion that they should have a conference with the men and they adhere to that suggestion. The Emergency Committee will be at the Town Hall at 11.30 a.m. on Saturday, 15th inst. For the purpose of meeting the men.

It was signed by the Mayor. On the Saturday afternoon the men marched from their headquarters in South Street to the Town Hall and met the members of the committee. The Mayor explained to members of the Press that some of the proposals had not been accepted by the men and further discussions would now take place. Councillor Hasdell, the district organiser, was accompanying the men. Detailed negotiations followed and a settlement reached in which 'all the men were to be reinstated and the settlement described by Hasdell as 'quite satisfactory'. The terms of the settlement need to be set against the situation at the time in the town. The Town Council had a Conservative majority and many of the inhabitants were either indifferent or hostile to trade unions. Given that none of the five Labour councillors were represented on the Emergency Committee, a situation to which the Labour councillors had protested, in the circumstances the recommendations were reasonable.

All the Corporation's bus staff were to be re-instated unless they had been guilty of violence or intimidation. (For full details of the Agreement v. Appendix 2) The one sting in the tail was that those 'volunteers' who had been employed during the dispute would be given preferential consideration if there was any need to make anyone redundant. Given the circumstances of the time and comparing the manner in which the Southdown

Company had treated their regular employees the agreement could be considered reasonable. A similar verdict of the settlement by David Spencer, 'In the circumstances of the time the council busmen found the terms acceptable.' (39) A view also endorsed by the columnist 'Stray Notes' in the same edition of the newspaper.:

> ...there were moments during Saturday's protracted sittings when the chances of an immediate and satisfactory issue to the negotiations seemed none too rosy. Thanks, however to the Committee's wise handling of the matter and to the reasonable, conciliatory bearing of the bus hands, a settlement was reached which, while it involved no sacrifice of principle or surrender of official dignity or public interest, was accepted by the men as being fair and considerate under the special circumstances. (40)

The result was a continuation of the good will which had existed between the bus corporation and their staff suggesting that honest negotiations were more likely to prove productive and help to maintain the mutual respect which had existed before the strike. This approach was in direct contrast to the dictatorial approach of the private Southdown Bus Company which had led to widespread staff dismissals.

When the Strike ended on May 12th there were still arguments about the action. As a generalisation Conservative councillors and members of the Party were opposed to what they saw as a challenge to Government by Trade unionists; Labour Party members and many working class people gave general support for what they had claimed all along was an industrial dispute. It needs to be born in mind that significant numbers of the population, especially among the more prosperous, did not necessarily take a stance of opposition to working class people as such but simply had no conception of what life was like for coal miners in terms of working conditions, accidents, severe injuries and fatalities. It was a time before pit-head baths so men walked home in their overalls black with coal dust and when they arrived in their Victorian terraced house lacking a bathroom, stripped off their dirty clothing and stepped into a tin bath which had been hanging on the wall in the yard. Placed indoors in the warmth their wife filled it with hot water. The telling cough and difficulty in breathing was recognised in mining communities but the deadly disease of Pneumoconiosis which affected miners, and many years later among those working with asbestos, meant little to those in towns such as Eastbourne located far away from areas of mining, heavy polluting industry or hard manual work inside vast factories. To that extent many were truly 'ignorant' of the lives experienced by large numbers of the population.

Eastbourne aid to Miners' Families in Rhymney

Making generalised statements about people can be a product of lazy thinking and this is made apparent by contrasting reactions in the town towards the plight of miners and their families in South Wales. Whilst some might have been against the strike because they considered it a challenge to the Government there were those in the town aware that although the Strike ended on 12th May the miners struggled on alone for a further six months; many of them and their families facing destitution, trying to exist on donations from other trade unions and subsidised food from local Co-operatives. In Eastbourne some churches had made collections to help the wives and children of the miners. During the period 1928-1929, 'In view of the prolonged and widespread unemployment of miners in South Wales, Eastbourne "adopted" Rhymney to relieve the distress in the town. The sum of £2,530 was collected, £1,000 being sent to the Lord Mayor's Fund for general assistance in South Wales. The remainder was sent to the Local Distress Committee formed by the Urban District Council, and was utilised to relieve sick members of the families of unemployed men, for the rendering of assistance to sons and daughters who obtained work away from home, and the provision of work for the unemployed.

The scheme operated for 124 weeks, and benefited at least 120 men and youths.' (40) Really useful and essential work resulted from the support given and the Eastbourne Local Committee kept in regular contact with the Rhymney Committee. Help continued with Eastbourne sending clothing and other useful items in time for Christmas 1928. Meads Councillor Mr W.E. Wood, (1857-1931), played a large part in the organisation of aid which was greatly appreciated by the Welsh town. He had enjoyed much success in many fields before coming to Eastbourne. For example, he was a founder of the Cookery and Food Association as well as the Catering Syndicate which operated in connection with the Royal Horticultural Shows and involved with a series of charities. A staunch Conservative, Freemason and an original Knight of the Primrose League he was involved with so many aspects of life in the town from working to support hospitals to helping with communal kitchens in Seaside Road at which he was seen 'handing out salted herrings to the poorer residents of the town.' It was this genuine sympathy for those in poor circumstances which explains his major contribution to the mining families of Rhymney (41)

Flag Day for Miners' Wives and Children

However when the Labour and Trades Council of the town proposed a flag day with proceeds to go to miners' wives and children to ease their hardships councillors seemed to take a more critical approach. At the Council a Committee of five people was appointed consisting of the Mayor, C.J. Knight, the Deputy Mayor, R.G. Thornton, and Alderman J. Haster and two Labour Councillors, Hasdell and Higgs. Yet within a few days the first three had resigned which meant that the remaining two could make no progress. Were their sudden combined resignations designed to sabotage the proposed flag day? It was no secret that they had all strongly condemned the Strike but as support for Rhymney indicated they were quite willing to provide help to the families of the miners who had been on strike for many weeks. Was the real objection to the fact that this appeal had been proposed by the Labour councillors and might be construed as support for the Miners' strike rather than only for their families? The Mayor had suggested a proportion of any money collected should go to others who had been adversely affected by the strike, to which Hasdell had agreed. (42). Originally the flag day had been planned for 20th June but the sudden resignations had now left this in doubt. In fact the Trades and Labour Council held the flag day three days later and were able to announce that they had collected £182,17 shillings less 11 shillings expenses. (43)

Sir Charles Harding at the next Council meeting suggested that the money should be handed over to the Salvation Army to distribute perhaps implying a lack of faith in the Trades and Labour Council (TL&C) which had undertaken the collection. This idea was supported by Hollins but Woodnough thought that those who had undertaken the collection and had it in their possession should be left to distribute it and the Council should 'have neither lot nor part in its allocation'. Prior supported this suggestion asking why the Salvation Army should be involved pointing out that other churches, including his own, had made collections 'for the miners' wives and children'.

There were clearly political undertones to much of the discussion:-

> Councillor Chatfield wanted to know why Sir Charles Harding thought that the people who collected the money could not administer it quite as properly as the Salvation Army.
> The Mayor – I don't know whether I can call upon Sir Charles to answer that.
> Councillor Chatfield – I should like him to give me an answer.
> Councillor Hasdell said that the Trades and Labour Council worked very hard in getting the fund together and surely it was not fair or even common justice to ask them to hand over the fund to a body who had nothing to do in the collection. He did not think (they) would agree to such a proposal. He would say quite frankly that he considered the proposal unfair and he suggested the Council appoint a sub-committee to meet

members of the T&LC and decide what proportion of the fund should be devoted to others who were suffering in consequence of the industrial dispute.

Councillor Higgs, in seconding, said he thought the matter was satisfactorily arranged at the last meeting but unfortunately there was a certain amount of wire pulling on the part of political parties and that caused a split in the committee appointed by the Council.
The Mayor – Oh no! I cannot allow that to be said.
Higgs – I have, expressed my opinion and I withdraw it at your wish.
The Mayor – No, not because I wish it but because it is inaccurate.
Higgs – It is a most regrettable thing that after the first meeting three of the members resigned leaving him and Councillor Hasdell to carry on. The flag day was held and his wife took an important part in the collection…but she had never been subject to so much abuse from people of importance. (laughter) Everybody who took part in the collection was subject to the most gross abuse.

Councillor Marshall observed there seemed to be a great deal more enthusiasm over the distribution of the money than there was in the collection of it. Certain members of the committee appointed by the Council retired from the committee and he supposed they did that because they were not very friendly to the idea of having a collection. The only people who contributed were those in sympathy with the miners' wives and children and, generally it was a question of the poor helping the poor. The collection did not (arouse) very much sympathy among people who lived on rent, interest and profit.

> Woolnough moved and Morgan seconded an amendment to the effect that as the fund was collected by the T.&L.C. the distribution should be left to that organisation. It was carried 'by an overwhelming majority'. Sir Charles Harding, Hollins, Keay, Haster, Eden, Hodgson and Miss Thornton voted against. A national political issue which had generated strong feelings had influenced a local issue. (44)

Antagonism over issues believed to be related to the General Strike continued to be played out in the Council Chamber with each side protesting their approach to matters was unrelated to the events. In a debate headlined in the *Eastbourne Gazette* (45) 'Uproar at Town Council – Mayor's Threat to Councillor Chatfield' Councillor Woolnough 'made a statement to the effect that Labour members had induced the Motor Bus Committee to make alterations in the bus service in order to find work for the busmen who went out on strike. The Labour members, while strenuously denying the charge declared that Woolnough was determined to victimise the busmen. A heated altercation occurred between the Mayor and councillor Chatfield on account of the latter's defiant attitude towards the chair. The Mayor several times threatened to have the Councillor removed from the Council Chamber under the new standing order which provides for this drastic course in cases where a member refuses to obey the ruling of the Mayor.

The Bus Company reported that at their meeting they resolved that a 15 minute service be instituted between the Archery and the Lodge Inn forthwith, but the chairman of the Committee, Councillor Wood, said that the route had been tried and there had been a heavy loss. He therefore asked the Council to consent to the

Committee's recommendation being withdrawn. Councillor Hogdson seconded. Councillor Chatfield urged that while the route might not be profitable it was a great public convenience to those people who lived at the end of the town and thus helped the housing trouble. On the whole the motor bus undertaking was very profitable – so profitable that at a recent meeting the borough Accountant was perturbed with regard to income tax. Sir Charles Harding asked that the motion be put and it was carried. Chatfield now wished to know why the service had been deleted without the consent of the bus company committee and the Council. Alderman Keay asked if the Committee had the power to discontinue any service they think fit? No answer was given.

Councillor Woodnough said he believed the Labour members had rushed alterations in the bus service in order to find work for the bus men who had been out on strike and that all the spiteful talk about the manager of the Bus Department was due to the strike, a claim that brought angry disclaimers from councillors Chatfield and Marshall. The Mayor called upon Chatfield to keep order, remarking 'I shall take other steps if you don't obey my ruling,' to which Chatfield responded angrily, 'You can do that if you like. I come here for business, not this sort of thing.'

A measure of irritation between the two sides was apparent, partly because the Labour members were in a minority and however much in theory the Mayor as chairman was supposed to be neutral his political sympathies were fully known:

> Mayor – I shall not speak again. If you persist in interrupting I shall ask somebody to take steps under Standing Orders.

(Chatfield rose to speak)
Mayor – Please sit down. I am not listening to you at all.
Marshall – Are we to sit here and be insulted?
Mayor – The insults usually proceed from your side.
Marshall – That is an insult from your side.
Chatfield – Let Councillor Woolnough substantiate or withdraw.
Mayor – Councillor Woolnough has a perfect right to express what he thinks right. He is expressing an opinion as to why he thinks these services were put on. I don't think he has named any of you.
Chatfield – Yes he has.
Mayor – No he has not. "Sit Down"
Chatfield – I call upon you to ask him to withdraw his statement
Marshall – You allow others to insult us.

The argument went back and forth until Woolnough said 'The Labour members are very keen on making profits out of...which brought an immediate response from Marshall, 'That is direct enough – "The Labour members" and when Woolnough replied 'Yes the Labour members', Chatfield immediately asked the Mayor, 'Did you not ask us Mr Mayor, not to use the term Labour or Conservative? The Mayor conceded that he did 'think it a pity to use the word Conservative to designate some of us.' Woolnough stuck to his claim that the Labour members are keen to make profits out of the bus company 'and I am convinced they would never have put on that bus to lose money unless they had some other motive.'

In turn his motives were suspected. 'It was Councillor Woolnough's intention to victimise every busman who had come out on strike,' stated Chatfield, and 'he must not think that others were prepared to act on such dirty lines as he was.' This heated argument was unusual. Councillor Lower regretted the recriminations which had taken place ...it was the first time he had seen such behaviour as they had witnessed that afternoon. Councillor Woolnough's amendment was lost.

Related to the bus strike yet from a completely different aspect, Herbert Hardy who had worked as a volunteer to replace busmen on strike in Eastbourne was brought before the magistrates and found guilty of theft. He claimed that he would not have needed to steal if the Council had kept its promise to keep on drivers who had undertaken such work when the strike ended! Sir Charles Harding on the bench decided to take 'a lenient view' and put him on probation for twelve months In general such leniency was not so readily forthcoming.

Response of All Saints' Vicar

The Rev. G.M. Hanks, Vicar of All Saints' in Carlisle Road, one of the more affluent areas of the town, commented upon the strike in the June edition of 'Parochial Notes':

> We saw that the same spirit that made the British soldier unbeatable in the war rises in its full strength to resist any attack upon the Constitution and the national life – that great inconvenience can be endured in the resistance to tyranny....(An) important factor played a great part in the conduct and sequel of the struggle; That was the religious character of our people. The Prime Minister did not hesitate to speak publicly of praying for guidance, and many thousands

of the people waited upon God in earnest and daily supplication. The broadcasting which played an entirely novel but admittedly influential part in the matter was unfeignedly religious throughout...

What can be said of the Trades Union Council?...they took a step which was both morally wrong and tactically foolish. It may be said that a mistaken expression of sympathy with the miners misled them...by some of their colleagues in the Labour World their action is branded as cowardly and a betrayal...

His views on the actions of striking trades unionists may well have reflected those of many of his parishioners but they showed little understanding of the issues behind the strike, the sacrifice involved in loss of pay in supporting the miners and no recognition of the early actions of the mine owners.

References - Chapter 9

(1) Meek, G. ((1996) op.cit., Ch.14 *'The Eastbourne War Memorial'*
(2) Ellison, A. (1999) *Eastbourne's Great War 1914-1918*, S.B. Publications
(3) Farman, C. (1972) *The General Strike May 1926* and Skelly, J. (Ed) (1976) *The General Strike 1926*
(4) Farman, C., op.cit., p.30.
(5) Ibid. p.31
(6) ibid.p. 32
(7) v. Gilbert, M. *A History of the Twentieth Century, Vol.1, 1900-1933.* Ch.23
(8) Farman, C., op.cit., p.244
(9) ibid.,p.140
(10) Sinclair, D. (1988)*The Making of the Modern Monarchy,* P.155

(11) Clark, A. (1998) *The Tories; Conservatives and the Nation State 1922- 1997* . p.71.
(12) *Look and Learn,* 18.1.2012
(13) Gilbert, M. (1992) *Churchill - A Life,* p.475
(14) ibid.
(15) Farman, C. op.cit., p.167
(16) ibid. p.168
(17) ibid. p.159
(18) *E.Gaz.* 5.5.1926
(19) Spencer, D. (1993) *Eastbourne Bus Story*, p.37
(20) *E.Gaz.,* 5.5.1926
(21) ibid.
(22) *E. Gaz.*12.5.1926
(23) ibid.
(24) *E.Chron.* 8.5.1926
(25) ibid.
(26) *Look and Learn,* 18.1.2012
(27) Interview with Percy Woods, 4.2.1986
(28) 'Stray Notes' *E.Chron.* 8.5.1926
(29) ibid.
(30) ibid.
(31) ibid.
(32) op.cit. 8.5.1926
(33) ibid.
(34) *E.Chron.* 15.5.1926; *E.Gaz.* 19.5.1926
(35) *E.Chron.* 15.5.1926
(36) Spencer, D...p.37
(37) ibid. p.37.
(38) *E.Chron.* 22.5.1926
(39) ibid.
(40) Forfargue, H.W. op.cit. pp.132-133
(41) v. Obituary, *E.Gaz.* 18.3.1931
(42) *E.Gaz.* 16.6.1930
(43) ibid. 7.7.1930
(44) ibid.
(45) *E.Chron.* 29.5.1926

CHAPTER 10

COMPETING POLITICAL PRESSURE GROUPS –1930s

There can be few better concise summaries of the struggles and outcome between the major political parties during the inter-war period than that given by Mellers and Hildyard:

> ...the domestic consequences of total war were, for millions of erstwhile Edwardians, socially frightful. Whether or not the Liberal Party was already, before 1914, doomed to be overtaken by Labour, it is beyond reasonable doubt that in fact the Great War sealed its fate. This watershed for British political life condemned progressive politics to adversarial class warfare and in practice ensured twenty years of Conservative hegemony punctuated by two feeble minority Labour governments, lasting less than three years between them. (1)

Nowhere was this more true than Eastbourne which returned Conservative MPs throughout the whole period without a break, regardless of the name the Government went under in Parliament, and even when there was not a Conservative majority Government; e.g. Coalition (1916-1922), Labour (1924 and 1929-31) or National

(1931-40). By 1936 membership of the Conservative Party in the town had risen to 2,500. It needs to be born in mind however that in any case the town was strongly associated with all things conservative and traditional by no means limited to political matters.

1926 to the early 1930s – Political Parties and Pressure Groups

Eastbourne was a town with a multitude of societies catering for a wide range of interests. There were at least a dozen freemason lodges, sports clubs covering many games, special interest groups and others which would be less familiar to visitors, such as the 'Ancient Order of Shepherds' and the 'Improved Independent Order of Oddfellows'. The three major political parties, Conservative, Labour and Liberal were all represented in the town with their own meeting places:

Conservative & Unionist Party	1925-1934 143 Terminus Road
	1935-1951 3 Bolton Road
Constitutional Club	1925-1951 75 Seaside Road
Central Liberal Club	1926-1932 61 Terminus Road
Eastbourne & District T.C.	1938-51 48 Seaside
Labour Party	Ditto
Independent Labour Party (ILP)	1930-1946 The Red House, Beamsley Road
Liberal Party	c.1928-1930s 3B Junction Road
National Citizens' Union (NCU)	1925-1937 9 Cornfield Road
	1937-1939 18 Gildrege Road
Primrose League	1925-1936 9 Cornfield Road; 1937-1939 18 Gildredge Road

CLIVE GRIGGS

The Conservative Party

Although usually Party members supported their general points of view, this naturally does not mean that each one agreed with all the policies of the Party. The Eastbourne Association of the Conservative Party was established in 1865 with G.F. Chambers as Secretary for the next fifteen years. He was well known in the area being a member of many organisations, such as the County Council, Lay representative of the Rural Deanery Conference, Director of the Voluntary Schools Building Company and President of the Technical Committee. Davis Gilbert was President of the Conservative Party in the 1880s and established a Conservative Club in 1884. The new Liberal Party Club followed a year later. Their Chairman from 1890 onwards was Admiral Brand who had preceded Chambers as President of the Technical Committee. In addition there was the Primrose League founded in 1883, with the declared purpose of gaining support for Conservative principles. At the first meeting in the Carlton Club many notable members of the Party were there to support such aims, including Winston Churchill, Sir John Gorst and Percy Mitford. This view was reinforced by John Slater, the Conservative MP for Eastbourne speaking at the Corn Exchange in Hailsham. 'The Primrose League has always been the nursery of Conservatism. The motto, for God, for King and Country was never greater in its appeal and never more important than it is today.' (2) The Upperton branch in the town had over 600 members and included social events in their calendar such as a visit to the Albert Hall. (3) At their AGM of that year they referred to three great crises the Government had surmounted: the General

Strike 'caused by revolutionary and insane trade union officials, the sending of troops into China to protect British property and the expulsion of "Bolshevik emissaries"'. They called for people to vote for a 'party that stood for private enterprise, the British Empire, the State and Church ....' (4) There was never any attempt to pretend that the League was anything other than a supportive part of the Conservative Party. Given their origins and philosophy there was no surprise when at the League's Summer School in 1926 the main speaker commented that 'the town's Mayor had reacted with a twinkle in his eye when he had said that the Primrose League "was not a political organisation"'. (Laughter) (5)

In the New Hall, Seaside Road, a large audience attended a public meeting of the Primrose League at which Col. Henry Bowles presided, supported by Mr and Mrs Rupert Gwynne, Col. Sir Duncan Johnstone and other worthies of the area. The chairman stated that 'the League was an organisation that represented unchanging devotion to Conservative principles and that dwelt in the hearts of a majority of their fellow countrymen and women...three principles, the maintenance of religion, the estate of the realm, and the imperial ascendency of the British Empire. Atheists, Little Englanders and Socialists they did not admit.'

Mr Rupert Gwynne met with a very flattering reception, having mounted an attack on the Liberal Government's policies. He told the audience, 'There was only one consolation; that when the time came for Sir Henry Campbell-Bannerman and company to leave this world he did not think they would go up, but would go down.' (laughter) Alluding to the growth of Socialism he said, 'it was a great pity that men like Keir Hardie and Mr Victor Grayson were born too late; our forefathers would have known what to do with them. He did not know what their fate would have been if they had lived in the time when men were hanged for stealing sheep. Socialism reminded him of a disease mentioned in the Bible, where we read of people being possessed of the devil. (laughter) It possibly might be that now it was only a microbe but it was an impetuous one because it was growing. (Renewed laughter) The Socialist programme seemed to be "Get what you can and do nothing for it". He hoped they would fight Socialism hot and strong. (Hear,hear.) When the 1918 General Election approached the Primrose League attempted to claim they were 'politically independent.' Such speeches contradicted this suggestion!

The NCU and other conservative organisations

The inter-war years witnessed a multiplicity of new organisations supportive of various conservative agendas; some pursuing a particular theme of the Conservative Party, others emphasising a more extreme version of a policy. Among these, several of which were comparatively short-lived, were the National Citizens' Union, the Most Noble Order of Crusaders and the Empire Crusade. They usually stated they were non-party political; a claim not always easy to sustain in the light of views expressed by some of their speakers. The Middle Class Union was founded in 1919 by Lord George Askwith, former government chief industrial commissioner, to safeguard property following the 1918 Franchise Act the year earlier which had increased the number of working class people eligible to vote. (6) It was short-lived being absorbed in 1922 by the National Citizen's Union (NCU) under the leadership of Askwith. 'Prominent members of the NCU professed an allegiance to fascism, such as the Conservative MP and Irish landowner J.R. Pretyman Newman, Conservative MP for Finchley and Colonel Sir Charles Burn, formerly Conservative MP for Torquay, who would become a member of the British Fascisti's Executive Committee.' (7) Its initial issue was a call to restrict 'alien' immigration, which in reality referred to significant numbers of Jewish people from eastern and central Europe. Sir Robert Burton Chadwick (1869-1951), shipping magnate and Conservative M.P. (1918-31) was a member of several right wing organisations – notably the British Fascists. Charles Burn (1859-1930), another Conservative MP was also on their Executive Committee.

In 1927, the anti-semite Colonel A.H. Lane of the Britons became the NCU Chairman while another Britons notable, the Reverend Prebendary Gough, also joined. (The significance of the Britons in pushing forward anti-semitic views is discussed briefly by Lineham. (8) By 1938 the NCU was collaborating with the extreme anti-semitic and quasi-fascist body, the Militant Christian Patriots.' (9) It does not follow that all members were fully aware of every aspect of the NCU's policies or the relationships they had with other bodies. Among their stated aims was opposition to increases in taxation and rates, including the financing of pensions for local authority personnel. It was these ideas which were particularly popular with numerous middle class residents in Eastbourne and many other towns. There were 139 branches of the NCU in the country and one of the largest, with 1,600 members, was to be found in Eastbourne.

Oliver Becker Lampson, MP, spoke to a 'crowded audience at a great patriotic meeting held at the Winter Gardens' arranged by a branch of the NCU on the theme 'Clear Out the Reds' claiming that there were subversive activities of the Reds in this country'. On the platform were Vice Admiral Sir Reginald Hall, MP, with Mr H.J. Temple in the chair. Mr Relf sang 'Land of Hope and Glory', the refrain of which was sung in chorus. Commander Lampson, accompanied by Mrs Lampson, and the Vice Admiral were warmly applauded as they walked up the centre of the Floral hall, preceded by the Union Jack. Members of the Conclave of the Most Noble Order of Crusaders formed a guard of honour.' Mr Temple informed the audience that this was not a political meeting but 'revolutionary agents were working for the overthrow of the constitution and our empire, which generations of our forefathers had built up and handed down to us.' (10)

Two weeks later at a meeting of the ILP at the Hippodrome, Emanuel Shinwell, ex-Minister of Mines, challenged the theme of the NCU meeting. 'The commander believed that behind every bill, there lurked a "Bolshie". Holding a copy of the *Gazette* in his hand, he gathered that the recent demonstration of Conservative opinion might very properly have subjected itself to the imposition of the entertainment tax...' (laughter) (11) Give the men decent wages; give the working class safe tenure of employment; make production consistent with distribution and eliminate private gain and when they have done these things there was no reason why the Labour Party should exist a moment later.' (12)

In the New Year at the AGM of the NCU a packed hall was addressed by Rev Prebendary Gough from London. The content of his speech made it difficult for the NCU to maintain its claim that it was non-party political. 'Socialism was against progress, because it was emotional, (it) was the greatest reaction that had ever fallen on the civilised world, there was nothing in it that was progressive….(it) was dominated by morbid piety… it was slavery under tyranny.' (13) All the sentiments he expressed were enthusiastically approved by the audience. Eastbourne was now clearly a venue for public speakers dealing with political themes whether they identified openly with a political party, such as the ILP, or spoke at meetings by well organised pressure groups whose sentiments were clearly to the right of the political spectrum.

The ILP organised meetings at which Andrew MacLaren MP spoke followed by W.R. Wallace, prospective MP for Walthamstow, on the tragic waste of unemployment and trade disputes inherent in the present economic and political system. (14) Wallace suggested that the House of Commons of which the country was particularly proud, seemed today to be a place where directors of companies met…So composed a Parliament could hardly be expected to discharge its duties…in the interests of the mass of the people…'

In March 1927 a report appeared in the *Eastbourne Gazette* of a meeting of the NCU credited to 'Notes of a Member'. The unsigned article provided a supportive account of their meeting and comments made by speakers such as, '..all workers…should save, in order to invest; and get rid of the habits of spending all he earns, and then demanding higher wages.' The NCU 'reporter' also praised the 'common sense views expressed, free from prejudice, and animated by goodwill.' (15) Sir A. Holbrook, a prominent member of the NCU asked the Minister of Labour whether he would 'direct applications from such bodies as the NCU to be favourably considered for representation upon local employment committees but was informed by Sir Montague Barlow, Parliamentary Secretary to the Ministry of Labour, that there was no provision for this and doubted the 'expectancy of giving the direction suggested'. (16)

By contrast the writer also provided this local newspaper with an account of the speech given by Andrew MacLaren at the ILP meeting. He suggested that the MP's proposals to increase rating and taxation of capital land values, 'as a case of the "have nots" seeing a chance to grab the property of "the haves". This writer was now provided with a space to give his views on a variety of local and national political matters. (e.g. *E.Gaz.*, 1927 - Mar 2nd, 23rd; April 6th, 10th; June 29th; Aug 3rd, 31st; and so on through 1928 to1932, etc) How this arrangement came about is unknown but the contrast in tone of the reports by 'the member' and those of the professional journalists at the *Gazette* stood out in stark contrast; the former, very opinionated, the latter, factual, leaving the reader to come to their own conclusion. In 1930, perhaps as a move to distance the partisan reporting of 'Notes of a Member' from the 'neutral' views of the paper, a note appeared above the article concerning the NCU stating 'The views expressed by our contributor in the following notes, are those of the National Citizen's Union'. (17) Future articles published went back to the familiar title, 'Notes from a Member'.

Shortly afterwards the 'NCU member' was expressing his views on the large numbers of unemployed people in the country who were receiving 'dole' payments.

> I would have every man Jack who is out of employment and living on the dole in full swing in less than twelve months, even if some of them had no other quality than that of chopping sticks or cleaning windows. I should like to see the time when all men who are willing to work may have it, and those who are indolent and shirk, made to.
> A further expression comes from a man who can be fairly described as a great administrator; namely Mussolini. The Duce declared himself an opponent of the dole system on the grounds that it tended to accustom the worker to idleness. (18)

This was not the first time that Mussolini had received praise in an article carried by the newspaper. Two years earlier the artist Wynford Dewhurst (1864-1941), who had served on the Buckingham County Council and sent three of his children to the Meads Boarding School, wrote two lengthy articles for the *Gazette*; one in 1928 of 65 column inches spread over four pages and another the following year of 60 column inches over two pages. In the second he wrote a critique of local government:

> I am heartily sick of the old fashioned, time and patience wasting procedures of Councils and committees, resolutions and amendments, party manoeuvres and personal jealousies, and I therefore propose (apocryphally, of course) to handle the reins of your municipal governance for the next three years, as an autocrat

of the Mussolini type, who knows exactly what he wants and also the quickest way to get it.... Conservatism is my political ideal, and "For King and Country" my motto.... Seeking neither honour nor profit, I shall upon completion of my job, retire, with mind content to the bosom of family life....(19)

The NCU was gaining in strength in the town with speakers showing less concern in their pronouncements about party-political neutrality. At their Empire Day rally at the town hall at which H.J. Temple presided, Admiral Sir Reginald Hall, the town's Conservative MP, Rev S.M. Warner and the principal speaker, Rev Prenbendary Gough, the chairman stated the obvious; they had become 'very definitely anti-Socialist'. Gough spoke on Patriotism:

They belonged to a great race, and their country deserved the most vehement and loving support... England was any other than an essentially masculine race – not a feminine type – although he did not mean any single word of disrespect to the ladies (laughter)... the 'feminine' man was profoundly anti-British, yet he had attained an enormous influence and was doing everything possible to weaken the country. (20)

By 1929 pretence that the NCU was non-party political was exposed again when their Eastbourne chairman H.J.Temple 'received a wireless message from Ceylon informing him that Lt.Col. Newnham was willing to stand as a Conservative candidate.' He was an Eastbourne resident, chair of the NCU nationally and had contested Rotherham division for the Conservative Party. (21) The following month at the Meads AGM,

Mr Weller Kent, chairman of the NCU for Eastbourne revealed that the Grand Council had passed the following resolution. 'The GC of the NCU urges all members to support the anti-Socialist candidate who is most likely to secure the highest quota of votes at the next General Election...be they Liberal or Conservative'. (22) Kent would be one of the many councillors who stood successfully as an 'Independent' for Meads, although the NCU was always listed in Kelly's annual directories in the same section as 'Political Clubs' alongside the major political parties in the town. Just as the Labour Party shared the same buildings for its headquarters as the Labour and Trades Council from 1925 onwards so too did the NCU and the Primrose League, first in Cornfield Road and then from 1937 onwards at 18 Gildredge Road.

The approach of the November local municipal elections did not spark off a lively contest. J.W. Woolnough was invited to stand in the Roselands ward in place of C.H.Taylor but otherwise there seemed to be little demand for a contest. The NCU did not propose to intervene on the present occasion.' (23) They did not need to as most candidates supported their policy of pushing for low rates. The official Ratepayers Association did not run their own candidates but supported those they believed to be suitable. i.e. Supported their principal demands to keep rates as low as possible. It was considered unlikely that either the Mayor, Col. Roland Gwynne or the Deputy, Councillor Lachlan MacLachlan, would be opposed as they stood again for Central and Devonshire wards respectively. Reselection of current councillors seemed to be accepted; Weller Kent (Meads), Avard (St Mary's), H.J.Hodgson

(Upperton) E.C. Martin (Hampden Park) with T. Hadsell and Mrs Kenyon (Redoubt). Whether candidates openly stood representing the views of political parties or not most residents knew or could soon ascertain their social and political allegiances.

A common theme of the NCU and many others was the hope and wish to restore or at least maintain the British Empire of the late 19th century. This was partly because a considerable proportion of members were old enough to have lived through such times, as members of the armed forces in their youthful years during the Edwardian era. Just one example among several organisations with similar ideals active in the town was the 'League of Frontiersmen' composed of ex-servicemen from the Boer War and First World War founded by Roger Pocock of the North West Canadian Mounted Police who established the organisation in London in 1904. They formed a battalion which participated in the 1914-1918 War. A meeting of members in the town appeared as late as 1933. (24) Significant support for the NCU came from the appeal to keep taxes and rates as low as possible. Self interest can be a good recruitment for any cause. Other organisations might have made similar appeals, such as the Freedom Association, but they never attracted the mass membership locally of the NCU. (25) However by the late 1930s they had lost some of their creditability and appeal when some members became 'associated with pro-Nazi elements'. (26) He believed that most of their records had been taken over by the Economic League and were inaccessible.) They never ceased to demand reductions on many forms of public expenditure. The pursuit of these goals led to policies which would inevitably have meant going back to conditions of a generation ago. Two examples must suffice. At its 13th AGM the Eastbourne branch of the NCU, having rejected a suggestion that they secede from the national organisation went on to call for a restoration of a second chamber's right to veto Money Bills in Parliament. This would mean an unelected House of Lords would be able to reject bills on public expenditure introduced by the elected Government in the House of Commons; a power they had relinquished under the Parliament Act of August 1911 when under sharp criticism from many members of the House of Commons.

The second example was from among the various resolutions their meeting had passed 'calling upon the Government to take action to restrict drastically the unnecessary extravagant expenditure on education, and so materially reduce the cost to taxpayers and ratepayers of carrying out the Education Acts and Regulations'. (27) The 'extravagant education system' in operation at the time was one in which approximately 80% of children received only elementary education. In reality the NCU were clearly out of touch with education thinking at the time in terms of national needs. (28) H.J. Temple, another 'Independent' councillor returned 'unopposed' for Meads whilst well-known for his NCU's activities, wrote a letter of resignation to the *Eastbourne Gazette* (29) from Ceylon where he had been staying for some time managing his business interests which were facing difficulties due to the problems of world trade. 'I am very grateful to the electors of Meads Ward for their confidence in me in twice returning me unopposed, and I can only say that I much regret that I have to resign as I had hoped to have some years service on the Council.' [Rangala, Ceylon, 31.1.1932] His contacts with Lt Col

Newman in connection with the Conservative Party have already been mentioned.

It has been suggested that the NCU began to lose some of its influence in the early 1930s. An unsigned article in the *Eastbourne Gazette* by 'A Student of economy' who clearly supported their aims, pointed out that it 'was months since the NCU held a public meeting in the town or any of the wards' and claimed that 'the NCU used to speak with genuine authority for the private resident, and particularly those of Meads and Upperton....they had provided the protection of the great middle class from the continuous "squeeze" of an intolerant, swollen and supercilious bureaucracy.' (30) If their public presence had declined it would seem that their influence had not. They canvassed successfully in the 1932 local elections for Charles Mathews and Colonel Church in Upperton ward where they had always retained considerable presence.

The *Gazette's* comments concerning the election in Cavendish were not strictly neutral. Reporting on the candidates in Cavendish ward they wrote that 'People are asking whether the presence of Horace Simmons in opposition to councillor Richard Terry will split the moderate vote and thus allow Mr A.J. Marshall to secure a seat in the Socialist interest.' Referring to the contest in Old Town the *Eastbourne Gazette* stated that, 'Councillor Higgs was retiring, leaving Frank Uphill, who has taken a prominent part in the councils of the local labour organisation. Opposing him in the moderate interest will be Mr Vaughan Wilkes who will make a strong appeal to many moderate Labour people.' Rather subjective descriptions of the Labour candidates.

Noble Order of Crusaders

Perhaps the strangest of all these organisations was 'The Noble Order of Crusaders' who easily attracted attention by the costumes they wore on ceremonial occasions; that which they imagined crusaders of the 11th to 13th century wore when they were attempting to capture Jerusalem. Full armour with swords, shields, helmets and a white garment with a red cross displayed on the chest and back. Only men in this organisation paraded in these costumes but whether women were members in some capacity is unclear. The organisation was founded in 1921 by Colonel Walter Faber. Membership was secret except for the ruling council. The Duke of York was its patron and whilst its agenda was stated as 'Class Unity', it had many fascist overtones and it initiated an annual eve of Derby fundraising dinner for the Conservative Party. 'It was designed to include ex-servicemen on a 10th Crusade against the forces of evil which would be extinguished in a holy fire'. Members included Sir Archibald Boyd-Carpenter (Conservative Minister 1918-37), Captain Gee (Conservative candidate for Newcastle East, 1923), Major Solbert (US Military attache), Duke of Northumberland, founder of the Anti-Semitic Patriot and owner of the *Morning Post*, Lord Younger, Tory treasurer, Geoffrey Dawson, editor of *The Times*. (*Wikipedia*)

They held annual services at St Marys (1927), St Andrews (1928) Holy Trinity (1929) and St Andrews (10.9.1935). A photograph of about 40 men in full regalia appeared in the *Eastbourne Gazette* in June 1929 and another in 1936. (31) The colourful display attracted considerable attention and the *Gazette* described their annual service at St Marys:

> Picturesque and impressive, its stately and solemn pageantry, seems to have succeeded in reviving for the benefit of the present age much of the spirit of the days when "knights were bold", and when chivalry and assistance to the unfortunate and the oppressed were carried on in, perhaps, a more ostentatious, but a no less sincere and effective manner....The church was packed when the three Eastbourne Conclaves, the Williams Green, the Oswald Fitzgeralds and the Robert Arbuthnot Conclaves, moved into their places, the procession being led by Ensign, and consisting of those holding special offices, pennon bearers, Grand Officers, companions, esquires, freemen and ordinary members. The regalia of the 250 was a brilliant array of green, khaki, grey, red, white and blue, and it stood out vividly in the central part of the church against the public occupying the other parts. After the processional hymn, the whole assembly joined in singing the National Anthem followed by the 'Song of the Crusaders'.

More details followed of the ceremony, hymns sung, with further activities by men holding more elaborate titles, such as the sword of the Conclave being handed to the Abbot who placed it on the Altar...more sermons followed, then the "Last Post" was played, followed by "Reveille" and the singing of Blake's Jerusalem". This seemingly bizarre all male organisation did not continue for many years. The costumes attracted attention; the philosophy less so. Their participation in the large gathering of the NCU in October 1926 give some indication of their political sympathies. They were clearly still active in 1935 when they attracted 900 people to a ball held at the Winter Garden (32) and three years later. (33) They seemed to have 'disappeared' by 1941!

The United Empire Party was a product of two powerful press barons; Lord Beaverbrook in 1929, with support shortly afterwards by Lord Rothermere, who used his newspaper, the *Daily Mail*, to promote their ideas. The Eastbourne Division of the organisation gained a considerable membership and their secretary Gordon Fraser, invited the town's Conservative MP to become a member. He declined and sent copies of the correspondence to the *Eastbourne Gazette* which revealed the organisation had invited Mr Marjoribanks MP to become a member. In his reply he explained why he had declined the invitation:

> I am sure you will understand that for a Member who is elected under a Conservative banner it would be quite impossible to join another party without consulting his constituents at a by-election. (34)

Fraser clearly did not accept this reasoning and in his reply wrote:

> You claim to be an Independent Conservative, and in your speeches you have not only declared yourself in favour of the United Empire Party policy but expressed a willingness to vote for Empire Free Trade against the dictates of your leader. It is very difficult indeed for my committee to understand your attitude in which you are unable to accept a courtesy office without a by-election especially when that party unconditionally offers you its support as an Independent Conservative and in no way aspires to be an opposing force in the constituency. (35)

Marjoribanks' response began cordial enough but then made the differences quite clear as to where his views concerning the UEP and the Conservative Party parted company.

> It is true that I have claimed that right of independent action which is the privilege and, I think, the duty of every Member of Parliament to maintain. My views on Free Trade are well known. I remain, however, a member of the party under whose banner I had the honour of being elected, whose "Whip" I receive, and upon whose strength any Imperial policy must depend. In my view to have formed a separate party in Eastbourne was unnecessary.
>
> I am unable to distinguish between the declared policy of the United Empire Party in its essentials and that of the Conservative Party, as I understand it but the United Empire Party has other branches besides that of Eastbourne. I cannot help remembering that your organisation opposed not only the other Conservative candidate at South Paddington but also the representative of the Empire Crusaders and that Mr Redwood, who founded the United Empire Party at Eastbourne spoke for the Empire Crusade candidate and against the local United Empire candidate at the same by-election.
>
> Much more effective was the policy of the United Empire Party at Bromley; but if the United Empire Party were to poll proportionately well in every constituency at the next election the mathematical and certain result would be an enormous Liberal and Labour majority...It is for this reason that I opposed the formation of the United Empire Party in Eastbourne at the outset as part of a wider organisation which is calculated to defeat its own object....

The two candidates on this occasion did hold many viewpoints in common but Marjoribanks recognised only too well the potential danger of allowing his Party locally to become linked publicly with another group promoting similar policies on some issues but not on all. Both were staunch advocates of economic policy based upon tight controls of public expenditure.

In the Meads there was a contest between two people in an election for councillor. They were similar in their political views. Of the two candidates, Miss Campbell, a cousin of Lord Hailsham (who also happened to be the half-brother of the town's MP!) was a holder of various prominent posts, including national president of the Young Women's Christian Association. The other was Mr Weller Kent, K.C., who had been chairman of the Eastbourne branch of the NCU. Whilst both similar in many of their outlooks, Miss Campbell was also using her candidacy to point to the position of women in the town and the country at large. She stated :

> Women's representation on the town council is not sufficient...Remember there are only five women out of a total membership of 36...Meads has only one woman councillor at present, although I am informed, women voters out-number men by a proportion of three to two...

In spite of her appeal she lost the election. This contest therefore could be seen as illustrative of issues in the town and much of the country in general in which women were denied equal opportunities; it would continue to be an issue in the area of local government in many areas for some years to come. In this respect the town made good progress. There were signs of change, for example, in relation to the appointment of the town's mayor; Miss Alison Hudson was mayor in 1926 and 1927, Miss E.M. Thornton in 1934 and 1935 and Miss A. Hudson again in 1943 and 1944. Mr Weller Kent voted against the appointment of a woman.

The reasons for comparatively poor wages in the town and seasonal work have already been mentioned. As a generalisation during these years the major hotels attracted the wealthier holiday makers whilst boarding houses catered for those less prosperous but it needs to be remembered that most working class people could not afford such holidays. There were few adequate facilities to provide an escape from the wet or cooler weather which might be a part of any British Summer. This was a major reason for the arrival of holiday camps such as the one in Skegness, pioneered by Butlins, which opened in 1936. The inhabitants of some resorts were sometimes unsure of how far such establishments were a positive attraction for their town. During the inter-war period traditional heavy industry in the North of the country and Scotland continued to decline, whilst the new light industries were being developed in Southern areas of the country, especially in the London suburbs, such as the Western Avenue with Hoovers, Lyons and Walls and Kodak in Harrow. They employed thousands of men and women. There was no equivalent in Eastbourne in particular or the South Coast in general, where significant numbers working in the service trades had not undergone a similar lengthy period of training; so many would not be classified as 'highly skilled'. Wages reflected this fact and were therefore comparatively low and sometimes unreliable where work was seasonal..

To that extent it is all to the credit of Caffyns, a local employer, who in negotiations with the National Union of Vehicle Builders as early as the 24th July 1929, conceded two weeks annual holiday with pay. They already paid good wages. In addition, they reached an agreement to provide a non-contributory pension fund for their employees, who would receive this on reaching 65 years of age. To put this into perspective most manufacturing companies did not provide holiday pay until the post 1945 years.

Eastbourne's Inter-War M.P.s

Regardless of the National Government at every parliamentary election in the first half of the 20th century which this study attempts to cover, Eastbourne returned a Conservative MP. The one exception was when H.G. Beaumont (1864-1922) gained the seat during the 'Liberal Landslide' of 1906. His parents were 1st Baron Allendale and his wife Lady Anne de Burgh. He was educated at Eton and Oxford. Throughout both the inter-war period and the years down to 1951 the town's six Conservative MPs were R.S. Gwynne, Sir George Lloyd, Admiral Sir Richard Hall, Edward Marjoribanks, John Slater and Charles Taylor. Robert Gwynne (1873-1924) had been elected in 1910 and served through until 1923. He was the third eldest of nine children of James Gwynne of Wooton Manor, Polegate. Like most elected as MPs for the town he had attended a public school; Shrewsbury, followed by Pembroke College, Cambridge. He trained as a barrister, married Stella Ridley and they had four daughters. He died suddenly of kidney failure having suffered from a weak heart resulting from rheumatic fever in his early years.

George Lloyd (1879-1941) succeeded him but only for a year. His father, Sampson, was wealthy and involved with Samuel Lloyd. He attended Eton followed by Trinity College, Cambridge before joining the family firm of Stewart and Lloyds, working in the commercial department and then the foreign office. In 1910 he was elected Liberal Unionist MP for West Staffordshire. He travelled widely and during the 1914-18 War was with T.E. Lawrence for some time. At the end of the War he was made Governor of Bombay. He was an Anglo-Catholic, anti-semite and an elitist who believed in 'the unique ability of the British upper classes to rule a colonial empire.' Elected MP for Eastbourne he resigned within a year when he was made Baron Lloyd and appointed British High Commander in Egypt and Sudan.

In the by-election Sir William Reginald Hall (1870-1943) was elected as Conservative MP for the town. He had followed his father into the navy at 14 years of age, later attending Greenwich Royal Naval College and becoming an admiral. Also, like his father, he became involved with naval intelligence, especially code breaking. He continued this work with the intelligence services, encouraging links between MI5, MI6 and Special Branch New Scotland Yard. In 1919 he joined with a group of industrialists and financial companies, including leading British banks, to form an organisation entitled 'National Propaganda', to be renamed later as the 'Economic League'. They sought to produce lists of active trade unionists and socialists to many branches of the business world; in effect blacklisting people they considered 'subversive'. It has been alleged that he was involved in the Zinoviev letter plot of 1924. He was MP for Liverpool West Derby 1919-1923 and for Eastbourne

1925-1929. He resigned as an MP due to poor health. In the General Election of 1929 at Eastbourne there were four candidates; Edward Marjoribanks (Conservative), C. Burt (Liberal), R.S. Chatfield (Labour) and P.E. Hurst (Independent). The votes cast were respectively 18,157; 7,182; 8,204 and 2,277.

The 1931 General Election; the Eastbourne Gazette takes sides!

In October 1931 it was announced that there was to be a General Election. The *Eastbourne Gazette*'s response to this news in it's leader column entitled 'An Uncontested Election for Eastbourne?' must have come as a surprise to many of its readers:

> For many years now the *Eastbourne Gazette* has stood aside from participation in party politics. We have reported impartially the speeches of all parties in our news columns, but we have given our allegiance to none, preferring to maintain a position of complete independence. That is a policy which our readers have appreciated in the past, and nothing less than a grave national peril would have induced us to take sides on political questions. It seems to us, however, that a situation has now arisen in which all caring men and women who are deeply concerned for their country must do what they can to support the national cause and to oppose those who, for whatever reasons, cannot see their way to do so.
> In the coming election the National Government will have our unstinted support, and we hope that our readers will show, in the only practical way, that they approve of the decision we have taken . (36)

They declared that a Liberal-Labour alternative Government is an unthinkable proposal and would be an unpatriotic move. Within days they were to find that this view would not go unchallenged as Labour declared it would contest the election as was their right to do so. The following week the Leader Column was entitled 'Is it a Joke?' when they learned that the local Socialists intended to run a candidate in opposition to Mr Marjoribanks.

> Their choice (so it is said) has fallen upon Mr Alfred Marshall, who was a former member of the Town Council...it seems impossible to believe that at a time when the nation is in the direst financial peril there is a considerable body of men and women in the Eastbourne Division who would be unpatriotic enough and wasteful enough to vote for the defeat of the National government when quite obviously its overthrow would involve this country in a state of which one dare not contemplate. It is practically certain that the Liberal executive will adopt the patriotic course and not put forward a candidate. (37)

The *Eastbourne Gazette* related how the Liberals were holding a meeting that evening and that they might be recommended to vote for the 'Socialist candidate' but it was not clear 'how far advice of this character will appeal to Liberals, who, in the past, have not been without a measure of patriotism in their make-up, only the polling booth verdict will tell.' (38) The suggestion in the *Gazette's* editorial two weeks running that it was unpatriotic to stand against a National candidate was both unfortunate and ill-chosen for Labour's candidate, Alfred Marshall, had resigned as a councillor, (Tommy Hasdell taking his place) and spent three years in the

Royal Engineers serving in France, during the 1914-1918 War. The newspaper had made its support for the National candidate clear and whilst it treated the Liberals with a measure of respect at a time when the voting intentions of many were uncertain there was no similar reluctance to attack the programme of the Labour candidate who they described as 'a Socialist who admittedly swallows the Henderson programme in all its hocus-pocus entirety'. (39)

At a meeting held in Red House, Beamsley Road, the headquarters of the Independent Labour Party, Alfred Marshall described it rather differently declaring, 'as an undiluted Labour candidate I shall stand by the full Labour manifesto as agreed at the Scarborough conference and issued by Mr Arthur Henderson which criticised attempts to reduce unemployment pay by following the dictates of the TUC rather than the international bankers.' (40) He told the meeting, 'You have thought fit to select me to represent the Labour cause in Eastbourne...I ask myself "why?". There are others more capable than I am. I am getting a bit rusty. I am out of practise through not fighting the Town Council, day after day, and month after month....this election would be the first time that the Labour Party had been able to get to grips with the Conservatives in a straight fight. Socialists were out for a new social order. Capitalism was breaking up.' The National Government '...made cuts at the dictation of the bankers – the almighty powers of this country, who will be such until the banks are reorganised, and taken from private hands and put into public hands.' (41) A reporter at this meeting of the Labour Party at the Red House wrote of how 'an atmosphere of excitement pervaded the adoption meeting and at the conclusion the members gave vent to their feelings by singing "The Red Flag".

The clear declaration of support for the proposed National Government and criticism of any party considering to oppose it at the General Election broke the *Eastbourne Gazette's* proud boast that it had done its utmost to take a neutral stance as far as possible in reporting on political events in the town. It does have to be remembered that they were serving a conservative minded town in which many residents did not see the Labour Party so much as representing a different point of view as an anti-patriotic Party. This would be true to some extent of many of their readers and those with significant business interests were also likely to be unfavourable to Labour Party policies. Whilst not adopting such a partisan stance in later national or local elections they were not always even handed to the Labour Party during local elections. For example, in the local election of 1933, the *Gazette* (42) devoted 312 words to Mr G. Newman the business candidate but only 36 to Alfred Marshall, the Labour candidate. The report began, 'To-day the electors of Cavendish Ward will have the opportunity, which it is confidently believed they will be quick to seize, of returning a sound business representative to the Town Council in the person of Mr Newman... (his)..candidature has the endorsement of the leading businessmen, through the support of the Chamber of commerce, Hotel and Catering and Caterers' Association.'

Later in the same year, at the election in the Redoubt Ward, over 16 column inches including a photograph was included for Alexander Robertson standing against Alderman Chatsfield, Labour, who received less than one column inch. Like so many local election candidates standing during the inter-War period, Robertson who had been living in the town for 17 years pledged no support for a political party, but his 25 years in Singapore where he worked as a stockbroker was likely to give some indication of his political sentiments. He modestly admitted he would need to learn about local government issues but 'held the view that local rates are too high and that I cannot understand where all the money goes. If I am elected I intend to go very carefully into this question'. Any hint that a councillor might be able to reduce rates paid by residents was likely to be popular until the effect of the consequent reduction in funding upon local services was realised.

By contrast leaders of Conservative opinion from all parts of the Division attended a private adoption meeting which soon nominated Mr Marjoribanks as their prospective candidate .He spoke to the audience for half an hour explaining why it was essential to support the National Government. He made it quite clear he was standing as the 'Conservative and Unionist candidate because there was no intention of forming a National Party, nor could there be in the time available, even if such a course were held to be desirable.' (43) John Slater, the chairman of the Eastbourne Association told them, 'In very few words it was a fight between national constitutionalism and Bolshevism, and any vote otherwise than for the National Government would be a stab in the back of the country'.

One new development at this election in the town was the arrangement made by the local newspapers with the Press Association for results to be thrown on a screen by means of a lantern slide. This, combined with 'a free cinematograph show consisting of films and animated cartoons' helped the crowds while away their time between the results being displayed. Hundreds of people had gathered to learn the election results, which brought cheers or groans, according to the outcomes announced. At one time when transport was being discussed a rumour circulated that the Labour candidate had driven a train to London that morning but the story was soon found to be a hoax!

Electoral Success and Suicide of Edward Marjoribanks

The outcome of the 1931 General Election in Eastbourne was 31,240 votes for Marjoribanks and 5,379 for Marshall. It was a record vote both in total votes cast and by the margin of victory of Marjoribanks over his sole opponent, the veteran Labour candidate A.J Marshall. Marjoribanks was a bachelor, barrister, author and a politician. He had just completed the first of a three volume biography of Edward Carson. He was the half brother of Quinton Hogg. Yet within six months this talented man had become very depressed, a condition it would seem to be related to the fact that he had been jilted for a second time. His step-father invited him to come and stay at Carters Corner Place in Hailsham, an offer he accepted after explaining that he first had to go to Paris. Upon his return he telephoned to say he was ill and unhappy. His doctor had prescribed sleeping draughts. Lord Hailsham was concerned about his health and telephoned the doctor who informed him that he was 'worried about Mr Marjoribanks' condition and suggested that he should go away for a sea voyage with a friend'. (44)

Lord Hailsham explained later that on the Thursday, Edward took a sleeping pill but did not sleep and on Friday there were indications that he was in for a nervous breakdown. It was thought it would be best for him to stay there quietly. On Saturday he seemed better…He said he had slept a little but still had a splitting headache. Lord Hailsham suggested he should go for a walk, but it was raining lightly so he decided not to. He was discovered the next day sitting on a chair in the billiards room with a wound about the size of a shilling in the left chest'. (45) Obviously the event was a severe shock to the town and at his funeral large crowds attended composed of a wide range of people.

Lead up to 1931 General Election

The manner in which the *Eastbourne Gazette* had intervened with such open hostility during the 1931 General Election pouring scorn on anyone not supporting the National Government and referring to such opposition as unpatriotic was largely, a reaction to the economic slump and the nine years of short lived governments which had proceeded the 1931 General Election. To understand this approach, regardless of whether it is believed the *Gazette's* policy was justified, there is a need for some knowledge of the governments which preceded it commencing with Baldwin's 1923-24 Conservative Government. In 1923 he dissolved Parliament over the issue of Tariff Reform. His action was a surprise; the election results which followed a disappointment for him. Whilst the Conservative Party remained with the largest number of MPs, with 258 members, the Liberals improved their position with 158 seats whilst the Labour

Party advanced further with 191 seats. The Liberals agreed to support Labour to form a Coalition in January 1924 with Ramsay MacDonald, an ex-pupil teacher from Scotland, as Prime Minister. Given the strength of the Liberal numbers in Parliament certain reforms which Labour MPs were keen to promote were out of the question. The one major successful social policy was John Wheatley's Housing Act which provided government aid for a programme of council house building. This brought help to a large number of low-income families. It also had the effect of stimulating the economy. (46) (There were aspects of this house building programme which helped to bring employment to building trade workers which were pursued later by Eastbourne borough council.)

MacDonald also acted as his own Foreign Secretary making considerable progress but this did not gain the attention of the majority of the electorate. He attempted to normalise relations with the Soviet Union negotiating a loan to them in the hope this would provide export orders for British companies and thereby help to reduce the widespread unemployment in the country. For Baldwin this was the first of three opportunities to attack the Labour Government and imply they looked favourably upon Bolshevism. (47) Next came the 'Campbell case' in which John Ross Campbell (1894-1969), the sub-editor of a Communist journal with a small circulation, produced an article calling upon soldiers not to fire upon working people when they were engaged in demonstrations. Similar appeals were common at many political rallies. Two Conservative Party politicians appealed to the newly installed attorney general, Patrick Hastings, referring to the Mutiny Act of

1875. However when Hastings looked further into the issue he discovered that Campbell had fought throughout the whole 1914-1918 War, been severely wounded and decorated for 'exceptional gallantry'. As a previous defence lawyer he knew that there was no chance of gaining a conviction. The charge was withdrawn and the opposition claimed that this was due to pressure from MacDonald 'behind the scenes'. This was not true but he was faced with a Liberal Party amendment supported by the Conservatives. He stated if it was passed he would go. The amendment was passed by 364 to 198 votes. The first Labour Government had been defeated. (48)

Four days before the General Election which followed, the *Daily Mail* published what it purported to be a letter from Zinoviev, president of the Communist International to the British Communist Party encouraging a range of seditious activities. It was claimed that the timing of publication had a major impact on the defeat of Labour at this election. Certainly the publication was intended to harm Labour but this has been used partly as an excuse for their defeat. The votes cast do not support this suggestion as a comparison of the 1923 and 1924 results clearly show. 'The Labour poll ...went up by more than one million, or 3 per cent of votes cast on a higher turnout, giving Labour more seats than they had held in 1922, and establishing their clear role as the Opposition.' (49)

Baldwin's incoming government lasted the full five year but in 1929 when the Conservatives increased their number of votes by over half a million they lost 159 seats! The Liberals gained over 2 million votes but only gained 19 seats whilst Labour gained nearly 3 million more votes and saw their number of seats almost doubled to 288. Some would suggest this was evidence of an electoral system which often distorts the political views of the population.

The second Labour Government was making good progress when, like many other governments around the world, it was adversely effected by the 'Wall Street Crash' of 1929. In attempting to cut back on public expenditure, Philip Snowden, in the manner of orthodox chancellors, introduced large cut-backs on public expenditure including unemployment benefits in an attempt to 'balance the books'. The Cabinet was split by such a move, many Labour MPs refusing to adopt a policy which disproportionately imposed hardship on the lower income groups; the very people many Labour MPs had been elected to help. This impasse brought about the mood of crisis in 1931 which led the *Eastbourne Gazette* to use their editorials to recommend Eastbourne citizens to vote for a National Government.

Summary of Government Changes 1922-1935:-

Year	Government	Prime Minister	
1922-23	Conservative	A. Bonar Law	
1923-24	Conservative	Stanley Baldwin	Went to country over Tariff Reform
1924	Labour with Liberal support	Ramsay MacDonald	Brought down by 'Campbell Case'/loan to USSR/ Zinoev Letter.
1924-29	Conservative	Stanley Baldwin	

1929-31	Labour	Ramsay MacDonald	Economy improving then 'Wall Street Crash' – public expenditure cuts including unemployment benefits. Treasury press to 'balance the books' split Cabinet.
1931-35	National	Ramsay MacDonald Lord Pres. Baldwin	General Election Result: Labour 52; National 556
1935-40	National	Stanley Baldwin	

Shortly afterwards the Conservative and Unionist Party in Eastbourne combined their AGM with an adoption meeting at the town hall and chose John Slater, who had been a close friend of Marjoribanks, as his successor.

In his acceptance speech he made his views clear. He was against unlimited free trade but:

> Vigorously in favour of speedy application of protective measures to our national trade...urging that we must try to build a ring round the British Empire and show the world what a league of nations there is within the Empire. (50)

Slater was only MP for three years. He died at the comparatively early age of 45 in February 1935. (51) Charles Taylor succeeded him at a by-election in March being returned unopposed at 25 years of age, making him the youngest member of Parliament at the time. (52) In the General Election following later in the same year he was again returned unopposed making this the third Parliamentary Election in a row when the Conservative Party had faced no opposition; a clear illustration of the strength of support for the Party within the town, as well as, conversely, the restricted appeal of the Labour Party within specific areas. Income and housing were a good guide to the voting patterns of the town as they are in many other places. At the risk of over simplifying; prosperous West, not so prosperous East. A fact accepted by the Labour Party whose financial circumstances made them realise that at times standing in a Parliamentary election in Eastbourne could be simply a waste of money. Taylor had attended Epsom Public School and Trinity College, Cambridge. Within a year of being elected he married Mrs Constance Ada Gibbons, an actress and dancer who had appeared in several British films. (53)

Taylor fought in the Second World War and became Managing Director at Cow and Gate, (Unigate) and later President of Grosvenor House (Park Lane) Ltd., Residential Hotels Association. He would remain as Eastbourne's MP for almost 30 years before being deselected by his local Party in 1974, who became concerned that the demands of his business interests were detracting from his Parliamentary duties; illustrated by his comparative decline in electoral support at General Elections from 39,278 votes in 1951 to 26,039 in 1966, and the combined votes of opposing candidates from

1964 onwards being greater in total than his own, in what was among one of the safest Conservative seats in the country.

Party Politics in the Town

The politics of the population of Eastbourne were in many respects similar to those of any other town. They were usually related to income, occupation, education, life experiences and the neighbourhood in which a person lived. There were of course always exceptions and some people chose to be associated with certain views even though they were against their own self interests. However it would not have been necessary to be an estate agent to make an intelligent guess as to the political sympathies of the majority of people when walking through an area, such as Meads or Seaside. This was only of relevance if adults chose to exercise their right to vote. As has been shown the Labour Party was always in a minority on the town council and during the period under consideration. The Conservative Party was the dominant force; particularly when the role of 'unelected' aldermen is considered. The elected councillors voted for aldermen replacements when one retired for some reason or died. Generally, but not always, voting was along political party lines which usually strengthened the dominant group on the Council, although there were examples of senior council members of a minority political party being elected aldermen in recognition of their long service.(E.g. Tommy Hasdell and Percy Wood, both outspoken Labour councillors.) Aldermen were abolished by the Local Government Act of 1972 which came into effect in 1974.

CLIVE GRIGGS

"Independent" Councillors in Local Elections

Local Council Elections were dominated by the return of candidates standing as 'Independent', a title which suggests they were not associated with any particular political philosophy. As a generalisation they were politically to the Right knowing full well that this reflected a large number of the town's inhabitants and election results illustrate quite plainly in this regard their judgement was sound. 'In the inter-war municipal politics of Eastbourne, the Liberal and Conservative parties did not play an open role. Instead the ruling councillors in Eastbourne claimed to be 'independents', although their 'independence' had its roots in old established Toryism and Liberalism. The inter-war council chamber in Eastbourne was controlled by this ostensibly non-party group of councillors who claimed to govern in the interests of all ratepayers. Both the *Eastbourne Gazette* and the *Eastbourne Chronicle* rarely gave party labels in their reporting of the municipal elections, with the exception of Labour party candidates, fuelling the myth of 'independence'. Yet the ruling group of councillors were often presented in the press and in their own speeches, as 'anti-Labour'. How far they were separate from, and therefore truly independent of the local Conservative and Liberal party organisations is questionable. Many of Eastbourne's Independent councillors of the period were, in both policy and speech, of a conservative persuasion'. (54)

Evidence supporting this view is to be found in the *Eastbourne Gazette* (55) which reported that 'the National Citizens' Union…have provided the bulk of the new (council) candidates in recent years.' It is clear that most of their membership consisted of conservative minded thinkers. Mr Weller Kent, the 'Independent' councillor in Meads in 1931 was chairman of the Eastbourne NCU and as mentioned earlier, Mr H.J. Temple, an active NCU member held the same office the year before. At Hampden Park in 1933 when Dr Porter retired from the Council, 'The National Citizens' Union were first in the field with Mr J.H. Walton, of Alton, Park Avenue'. (56) Yet he still described himself as Independent on the ballot paper and defeated A.J Marshall (Labour) and J.W. Woodnough Independent, who had nine years experience as a councillor and 'gained a reputation as an idealist and independent thinker.' (57) Col. F.S. Garwood, 'supported by the NCU' stood as an 'Independent' (58) as did Alderman R. Gidley Thornton when he won the local election at Hampden Park in 1923, yet he presided as chairman of the meeting at which Charles Taylor reported on his first year as an MP to the Eastbourne Division of the Conservative & Unionist Party. (59)

By contrast the Ratepayers Association had a policy of not running their own candidates, but lending support to those they considered suitable. A few examples will suffice to prove this generalisation. To begin with an extreme example, Meads Ward. Between 1919 and 1938 at annual council elections Independent candidates were elected unopposed every year with only one exception. In 1926, Miss W.G. Wilkinson stood for Labour and polled 34 votes whilst Miss M.H. Ramell, Independent, received 652 votes. Looking back on this result five years later when there was a council by-election in Meads the *Eastbourne Gazette* commented:

> In the past a contest at Meads has been considered scarcely a practical proposition, although there has

been no lack of opportunity in recent years. But the practice has almost invariably been to return a member unopposed, or, as when a Labour candidate had the temerity a year ago to seek election there, to return a well-known resident by such a thumping majority as to indicate in the plainest possible way that outside interference with the time-honoured plan would not be tolerated. (60)

Whilst the result was of no major importance in itself, it can be used both to illustrate some of the assumptions about the political and social values of most of the residents of Meads and the perception of Eastbourne in many other parts of the country. On two other occasions in the 1930s rival candidates contested the council seat

In Devonshire ward between 1931 and 1938 'Independents' were returned unopposed each year with the exception of 1934 when there were three candidates, all standing as Independents, in which the results were W.L.W. Bird (630 votes), C. Matthews (223) and R.W. Lomas-Smith (198). Another victory for an Independent candidate!! At Hampden Park between 1919 and 1926 Independents were returned unopposed most years with a few exceptions. In 1919 R.Alice (Independent) was challenged by Miss Mill Bolero (Labour); the result 288 votes to 88 in favour of the former candidate. Two Independents contested the 1920 Election. The last example chosen is Central ward. Between 1929 and 1938 Independent candidates were returned unopposed in every year with two exceptions; in 1933 both candidates standing were 'Independents'. H. Harvey polled 1,124 votes to E. Martyn Anderson's 472. It was not until the following year that a Labour candidate, H.R.

Hazleden challenged the Independent candidate, H.D. Swan. The result was Swan 679 votes to Hazelden's 333. Councillor Thornton who stood in Devonshire Ward successfully as an Independent in the local elections of 1933 and 1935 accepted the invitation to become chairman of the Eastbourne Conservatives in 1934; for some this might question the extent of his political neutrality, and he was not alone in this regard. For example, C.J. Knight stood as an Independent councillor for Hampden Park 1919-1946 and was town mayor 1925-26. 'In fact he was in Politics a Conservative.' (61) Summarising this period of the Council politically in the 1930s John Surtees stated, 'The Council was firmly Tory and the membership seldom changed, which gave a continuity and reduced the need to go vote chasing'. (62)

In 1928 the 'Equal Franchise Act' lowered the voting age for women to 21. It was not accompanied by a rapid change in long entrenched social attitudes towards women; this would still take many more years to evolve. Moreover there would be steady resistance in some areas, partly explained by many years of custom by some men to challenges from women for equal consideration in so many areas of life. These included education, earnings, their role at home and in the place of work. To take just two entirely disparate examples which indicate attitudes that would have been still quite prevalent among many men::

> Two men in the casual ward refused to work with women. 'I was willing to do any work except laundry work. I am not the kind of man who can work with women and I do not like doing women's work. They were both sentenced to 7 days hard labour. (63)

Bathing....Strong swimmers (Gentlemen only) can take a header from the Pier any morning between 6 and 9 a.m...Fee 6d; season ticket 9s.
Eastbourne & District Guide Book, Ward Lock, p.9. (1931-32)

Resistance to Woman as Mayor

Prejudice could be found in other areas of town life as well, however polite the views were expressed. In September 1934 the *Eastbourne Gazette* carried a report of the Selection Committee of the Town Council to nominate Councillor Miss Thornton as next year's Mayor. Before the ordinary monthly meeting...the Town Council met in committee and approved the selection of Miss Thornton. There were 'Piquant comments on the suitability or otherwise of women councillors to occupy the position of Mayor of Eastbourne.'

> Councillor Addison said he wished to put forward another name for the consideration of the Town Council. He hoped that his action would not be taken as in any way discrediting the wonderful ability of Councillor Miss Thornton....But there are some of us who feel that the Mayoralty should be carried out by a man and being one of those who think in that way, I am going to suggest the name of a member who is willing to take office if the town council think fit to elect him.. That member is Councillor Edgar Hill.
> Councillor Weller Kent, K.C., seconding, said that he, too, felt very much embarrassed in putting up anyone against Councillor Miss Thornton...But there are people outside the Town Council, as well as inside it, who feel that the first citizenship of the county borough

of Eastbourne is a man's job....He added that, we are facing a difficult year, for which a strong man was needed as Mayor...

He was very sorry that the Selection Committee had seen fit to put some of them into the position of having to oppose the nomination of Councillor Miss Thornton. He continued by saying that if Councillor Miss Thornton is elected Mayor I shall act in complete loyalty to her, but I confess that I would rather sit under Councillor Edgar Hill as Mayor.

The amendment was defeated. Seven members voted for it. The Commitee's recommendation that Councillor Miss Thornton should be nominated as next year's Mayor was then put, and 24 members voted in favour of it.

Economic Depression – early 1930s

Throughout much of the 1930s economic conditions were bad with widespread unemployment the cause of so much distress. Continued price squeezes caused further downward pressure on wages. Two alternative policies were advocated; reduce wages in order to cut costs and prices further or invest in infrastructure to reduce unemployment and allow wages and salaries to create demand for goods, thereby encouraging expenditure in order to reverse the downward spiral created by low demand. Such opposing policies would not just be a debate for the 1930s. The vociferous NCU and Ratepayers' Association kept up strong pressure on the town council to cut back on expenditure in order to freeze or reduce the rates. The large membership of the Eastbourne NCU has already been mentioned and their councillors working under the name of 'Independents', such as Weller Kent, were forceful in demanding reduced spending in all local authority departments.

Typical of the attacks on the Town Council were those launched in October 1931 on the twin questions of economy and salaries of officials. H.J. Temple led the attack by putting forward an amendment which would make all cuts immediate rather than suggestions for discussion. A lengthy discussion followed in which several members opposed the demand to cut expenditure. It took Alderman Soddy to explain why these simplistic demands failed to grasp the overall situation of the council and many people working in the town. Their expenditure on building houses created work in the building trade which employed many people in the town. The wages they received were spent in the community which created demand for goods which in turn helped to pay the income of other families. On completion of the houses income for the town would increase from rents. Moreover a large reduction in expenditure would mean 'a big influx of people on the poor rates.'

Tommy Hasdell, the long serving Labour councillor, challenged the approach of Weller Kent. Rejecting his amendment, 'He wished to remind (him) that all the rate payers did not live in the Meads....the Public Assistant Committee would have every regard for economy but if it was necessary to spend money on relief they would do it even if it meant putting a penny on the rates. He could take councillor Weller Kent to places in the east of the town, where he would not care for his dog to be kept. He was sure the decision of the Public Assistance Committee would have the sympathy of the Council when it was realised that cuts of five per cent might have the effect of taking a loaf of bread off the tables of the poorest people in the town.'

The possible savings of £29,000 on proposed schemes had been mentioned but the loan charges were on £2,500 and the schemes would provide a great deal of work, whereas in one year the Public Assistance Committee had paid out £6,000 without getting anything back....If all work was held up hundreds of working people would be effected. It was easy to suggest economies for other people, but he would like to see some people apply it to themselves. Councillor Temple's amendment was defeated. (64)

NCU claims of High Rates v. the Reality

The NCU frequently returned to the issue knowing that many of their supporters liked the idea of paying less in rates, believing in the claims made by their 'Independent' council representatives of wasteful expenditure and overpaid council employees being responsible for high council costs. In August 1932 the *Eastbourne Gazette* interviewed Councillor Soddy, who had a detailed knowledge of the finances of the Council. He worked steadily through the issues raised by the newspaper's reporter supporting his responses with numerous facts and figures. 'With regard to the constitution of the Finance Committee it is not correct to say that it is confined to the chairmen of the spending committees; three of its members are appointed by the Council – they may or not be chairmen of committees –and the committees each appoint a representative, not necessarily the chairman.' Such details might seem of little interest to most of the town's population but many of the assumptions made by critics really were from a position of little detailed knowledge of the system. Few would check the facts for themselves when criticisms of the council's organisation were made.

E.C. Knight, now an Alderman, who had been one of numerous 'Independent' councillors elected in the 1920s suggested an 'expert' should be appointed to examine council expenditure in order to suggest areas which could be recommended for financial cuts. Education had been mentioned as a possibility in the belief it had been too generous. Councillors Chatfield and Soddy wished to know the name of the 'expert' and what his fee might be. This information was refused and the proposal accordingly withdrawn. (65) The NCU kept pushing for the appointment of a government auditor claiming quite correctly that they 'represented a large body of influential ratepayers.'(66) There was no doubt that they represented a disproportionate number of higher income groups but in effect their main demand was a financial one; to pay lower rates and still hope to enjoy the same amenities provided by the well managed finances of the town.

Soddy poured scorn on many of the suggestions of the council's critics who believed that small committees should prune the Council's expenditure. 'If the members of that committee were to make any suggestions worthy of consideration they would first have to learn all that there was to be learnt about the work in all departments of the Corporation...I cannot escape the conclusion that it is a fair analogy to say that the danger would be as great as if one entrusted oneself to an operation to a person with no knowledge of anatomy.' He produced details of the Council's expenditure over the last 17 years pointing out that 'it will be seen how absurd it is for anyone to think that there has been a wild orgy of capital expenditure.' In addition comparisons were made for capital debt to allow the town to be compared to other seaside towns; Hastings (£1.1.4d), Bournemouth (15s11d), Brighton (19s9d), Blackpool (£2.8s.7d), Eastbourne(15s.5d). Finally he declared that 'while it was a very good thing that there should be a live interest in public affairs, it was desirable that criticism should be based on accurate knowledge of the facts....No good purpose is served by making things out to be worse than they are.' (67) Yet the exposition of the reality of financing local authority expenditure did not prevent some councillors constantly seeking a reduction in their rates and even suggesting where cuts should fall.

The *Eastbourne Chronicle* reiterated this general analysis two years later in an Editorial leading up to the Municipal elections of that year which provided an 'opportunity to protest against the growing, ill-natured practice of belittle (*sic*) the personnel and competency of the Town Council. From the sneering, deprecatory tone affected by many busy irresponsible critics, the ruling Authority might be merely incapable of administering the town's affairs, but be positively indifferent when not expressly hostile to the true interests of the ratepayers. The unfairness, not to say danger, of keeping alive and encouraging this tendency to scoff at and disparage the work of those charged with important official duties, is in the misleading effect it has upon the townspeople generally, an impression being created that the Council as constituted are unworthy of public confidence'. The newspaper supported thoughtful criticisms aimed at the Council's policies on certain issues for these could clearly be helpful but this was not always the case. It was the constant bickering by 'irreconcilable malcontents' which was of no benefit to anyone and the Council 'should be given credit for having as its invariable objective the real welfare of the borough'. (68)

The demands to cut back on other people's incomes was a familiar cry in the town. Given the scale of unemployment in most regions of the country working people found it difficult to resist these pressures. The occupational structure of the town had not changed fundamentally since the late Victorian period with the building trade still the major employer of male labour. Workers in the various aspects of construction work were vulnerable to the economic slumps of the time, the seasonal demands of a seaside town, which were in turn related to the weather. The effect of unemployment could be tragic upon some individuals; '..Albert C. of Longstone Road became depressed....invalided out of the army, suffering from asthma and bronchitis, and unable to obtain work on the Bourne Street Drainage scheme, he kissed his wife as he left home as usual to try to find work. Later in the day he was found with his throat cut! (69) Building companies were in no position to make demands as there were a number in the town and no shortage of employees.

By contrast, The Eastbourne Association of the NUT, were more outspoken in their objection to proposed Government cutbacks in the salaries of their members. The planned 'economy cut' to the salaries of teachers was to be around 20%.. A letter was sent to Mr Marjoribanks requesting him to use his influence in resisting the proposal. The Burnham scale was fixed as standards with the knowledge that they would be of greater value when prices fell and continued to do so for a number of years. 'During the War,' it was stated, 'when other members of the community were receiving very high wages, the teachers struggled on without any increase, trying to make their pre-war pittances meet the ever-increasing cost of living.' The average salary of teachers including heads was £233 per annum and now they were being faced with cuts of 20%. 'Teachers are citizens, and as such will be called upon to make sacrifices in common with the rest of the community. Why, then, should they be called upon to make a double sacrifice?'

The Mayor's Unemployment Fund

Unemployment in so much of the country was a cruel factor during the early 1930s; especially in areas of declining traditional heavy industry such as coal mining, iron and steel manufacturing, shipbuilding as well as textiles. Overall it never fell to less than I million down to 1940. These areas were comparatively isolated from the more prosperous Midland and Southern areas of the country which were attracting the new light industries during these years. The result was that whilst unemployment was widespread its scale varied enormously. There were some places which escaped the widespread loss of jobs experienced by the worst effected areas but few where there was no impact on the community. The seaside towns were among these more fortunate locations but this was naturally not of great consolation to those who faced the loss of their paid employment. In these towns the seasonal nature of their economies was largely responsible for fluctuations in available work. The holiday trade was reliant upon the weather as well as the incomes of urban families. Those involved in such work often found themselves in a precarious position as such events were outside their control. Most working class families did not have surplus money to save enough to go to a boarding house or small hotel for a short break. The spectre of unemployment or reduced working hours was always in the background. A day visit to a local area of interest or a seaside town during a bank holiday was more likely to be within the means of a family where there was a small surplus in the weekly income; usually an indication of a secure white collar job. As the economic depression continued those within the building trade probably suffered the most. It is to Eastbourne's credit that across most sections of the community there were genuine actions taken to help those who were made redundant.

One of the most successful undertakings in this direction was the Mayor's Unemployment Relief Fund. One example from within its programme took place on 18th April; a day long series of events aimed at raising money for those out of work. The scale of the event can be gauged from the fact that two committees numbering nearly 50 people representing 'all classes of residents, including civic dignitaries, the leisure classes, those renowned for achievements in all realms of the arts, the town's workers and the unemployed themselves, united in a tremendous effort to raise money for the Mayor's Unemployment Relief Fund.' The mayor, the town's MP John Slater and large numbers of the public were attracted by a day long programme which included music by the municipal orchestra (who took the opportunity to suggest the need for a new bandstand), a three hour vaudeville show at the Winter Gardens with all takings donated to the Fund, school choirs and dance groups. (70) This was not a one-off event. For example 500 wives and children of the unemployed were the guests of the Oswald Fitzgerald Conclave of Crusaders to a tea and entertainments, including a circus group, at the Town Hall the following January. Mr MacLachlan, chairman of the Unemployed Committee, with support from many others had raised more than £1,000 for the unemployed fund. There was sound evidence to show most of the town responded well in support of those who were out of work. A list of possible building schemes was forwarded by Mr H.R. Haselden (Chairman of the Unemployed Committee) and Mr Watkinson, to Colonel Gwynne who listened to their suggestions which included the erection of 57 houses at Churchdale, a new bandstand, an underground car park and a bus depot in Victoria Drive. In following discussions with the Chatsworth Estate it was agreed to allow the erection of 32 houses on the back land of Churchdale Road and 16 fronting the road.

Unity of opinion is unlikely with regard to social problems and whilst there was widespread genuine support for the Mayor's Relief Fund an unsigned article appeared in the *Eastbourne Gazette* (71) highly critical of moves to support the unemployed in the town. One of the suggestions to help had been the construction of a bathing pool which was seen as an added attraction for the town and an opportunity to provide work for those in the building trade. The writer disagreed with this approach. 'It should be considered only as a business proposal' as any other work undertaken by the Corporation. (72) Some construction work such as building sea walls, was highly specialised and should be put out to contract with the proviso already agreed that not less than 95% of local labour should be used' This seemed eminently sensible. However the whole tone of much of the article in its choice of words seemed hostile to the opportunity provided by promoting construction work for projects identified by the town as general amenities from which the holiday trade in particular could benefit. The writer believed the unemployed would exploit such a programme.

> ...the furious agitation now being conducted by the leaders of the unemployed can only mean that they realise that in the hands of a private contractor the tempo of the job will be too speedy for their liking, whereas, if carried out by administration, it could be "spun out" to use a popular phrase.
>
> There is another aspect of this important subject to which the attention of thoughtful "*Gazette*" readers must now be directed. About nine months from the beginning of the work the employment provided by the building of the bathing pool will come to an end, and then the position of the men engaged on the work will be precisely as it is today, for only the optimism of congenital idiocy could imagine that however great the recovery of business, there will be regular work in Eastbourne for the unskilled labour which for the past two or three years has made its daily peregrinations from the Employment Exchange to the public libraries, to the street corners, to the public gallery at the Police Court, or to the adjoining room in the Town Hall where the Public Assistance Committee goes about its thankless task.
>
> ....There is also a problem arising from...The importation of several hundreds of men and women from the

> mining and industrial areas, who have no hope of obtaining permanent employment in a town which has no industry beyond catering for holiday makers and a limited amount of building which can be done by Eastbourne's own skilled craftsmen.
>
> ...single men in the ranks of the unemployed ought to be told in their own interests, that they have not the remotest chance of finding permanent employment in Eastbourne and that their sensible course would be to pack their bags and leave the town before enforced idleness becomes an ingrained habit and the desire for work a lost motive. (73)

This critical nameless writer did not seem to recognise that with the exception of necessary maintenance all building projects are of a finite nature and those working in the building trade know that by its very nature the work entails constant moves to new projects, some of which will entail travelling to other areas which they hope will not be too far away. As for the advice to young single men in Eastbourne to move elsewhere, this was precisely the same advice being given to their contemporaries in the areas hit hardest by widespread unemployment resulting in considerable numbers moving South within the country, some of whom had had arrived in Eastbourne and other coastal towns. The anonymity of the article makes it difficult to make a judgement as to whether the strongly expressed views were based upon any personal experience of manual work, skilled or unskilled. Nor if the pronouncements concerning unemployment arose from the writer suffering from a similar lengthy period of being out of work.

It is to the credit of the town that help for the unemployed was maintained. Miss Thornton, the Mayor, explained to one hundred unemployed men at the Technical Institute the Winter programme of the Eastbourne Occupational Centre of which she was president, not designed to help them find jobs but to occupy their time 'which hangs heavily'. Under the supervision of Hugh Adam constructive work such as mending shoes for a small charge, or even free if they cannot afford payment, could be undertaken. This included repairs for the shoes for their family. Tickets were obtainable from six grocers who would charge lower prices in return. Free dinners were to be provided for members at the centre in turn. One penny per week was charged to attend the centre which was well used. (74) All considered this was a well organised relief system for the unemployed for the time and three years later the fund was still in operation providing 92 men with employment carrying out public work in the town dealing with the maintenance of roads and parks. (75)

A few weeks later a proposal to repeat the raising of a penny rate to provide another £3,500 to finance direct labour work for the unemployed was rejected. Some argued that a rate increase 'would press onerously on small traders, pensioners and people with small fixed incomes who already had great difficulty in making both ends meet.' (76) There was talk of a march of the unemployed to the Town Hall to 'rouse the Council to a sense of the urgency of the problem.' More to the point was that 'A terrible amount of money would have to be paid out in relief during the coming months and the town would get nothing in return. Councillor Wheeler was sympathetic to the situation of the unemployed pointing out the best way to help them was 'to put the men to work on schemes which must be done which is why he regretted that the Town Council had turned down the proposal to deal with the Upperton Road by direct labour.' (77) The proposal was defeated, only Morgan, Hasdell, Wood, Bass, Tidman and Watling voting in favour.

Stevenson and Cook (78) have argued that in some areas with comparatively low levels of unemployment, of which Eastbourne would be included, there was greater sympathy among many of those living in the town. Whilst there were voices such as the nameless NCT columnist who seemed indifferent to the plight of those who were unemployed in the town this was not true of many of the town's councillors, regardless of their political allegiances. Even then, where there was less support, it was largely once more a matter of resisting schemes which might call for financial help from ratepayers.

Workers' Voluntary temporary pay cut

The situation at the Eastbourne Borough Council's Bus Corporation provides a good example of their employees accepting the problems facing the Company during the worst of the depression and of most councillors recognising their cooperation by taking a voluntary reduction in their pay to help the financial system. The issue was raised in council during the first week of January 1934 when a proposal was put to restore the voluntary cuts in salaries and wages which they had experienced. Councillor Watling opposed the suggestion arguing that 'the restoration be deferred until time was more opportune.' Tommy Hasdell disagreed saying 'he was in favour of restoring all wages – but wanted to see it done with uniformity'. (79) Alderman Knight reminded the Council that the 'temporary voluntary reduction in their pay' had been to help the financial system. In return, when that improved, most of the councillors were in favour of the restoration of their salaries, but not all! The original one year agreement had been extended to two years. Allowance had been made in the estimates for their restoration'. Similar temporary policies taken elsewhere had already seen wages restored in Brighton, Bognor Regis, Tunbridge Wells and Worthing.

Councillor Addison claimed that the wage rates at Southdown's Bus Corporation were lower and that if the town's own bus company was sold off it would no longer be a drain on the rates. Hasdell pointed out that in fact 'the corporation had built up an undertaking with a capital of £100,000, which paid rates of wages of which they could be proud, and which had contributed nearly £40,000 to the relief of rates. The last thing to which he could ever agree was that the undertaking should ever be sold.' (80) The proposed amendments not to restore the voluntary temporary reduction in the bus crews' wages or sell off the town's bus company were both defeated with only Watling, Rush, Weller Kent and Addison voting in favour whilst Knight abstained. It had also been pointed out that many of the busmen had contributed many years of loyal service and deserved support in return. The Eastbourne Corporation Bus Company founded in 1903 claimed to be the oldest municipal bus service in the country. Having overwhelmingly rejected selling off the company in 1934 it was privatised 66 years later in 2008!

EASTBOURNE 1851-1951

Most places gain reputations which can be based upon some characteristic that may be deserved at a particular time and remain even if the original reason has been overtaken by other events. Eastbourne can deservedly be described in general as an elegant town. The power and control of the two largest landowners has been described earlier and their ability to plan the major areas of the town; in particular the lengthy promenade separated by lawns and gardens from a line of large Victorian hotels across the road. Their power to plan and control building has enabled the town to avoid some of the less attractive features in other seaside towns where there is an over abundance of seasonal goods for sale from various 'souvenirs' to ice creams and fast food outlets. This reputation of Eastbourne has some validity for examples can be found in the official reinforcement of bye-laws and occasional individual reactions to certain behaviour. In general they receive approval, although inevitably attitudes change over time and opinions as to what is accepted behaviour are never uniform. Like any other place there are areas which are not in the category of elegance to be found in the eastern part of the town because they were developed more cheaply to provide housing and service facilities for the majority of the less prosperous inhabitants. Indeed large numbers of the town's population were to be found living in the rows of Victorian and interwar terraced housing, with shopping facilities and other services further away from the more elegant planned town of the major landowners.

Local newspapers provide a good coverage of news and in doing so present a broad and reasonably accurate picture of life in the town covering a wide a range of human experiences. First a few examples from the Inter-War years:-

> .....a visitor staying at the Royal-Parade, went out for a bathe at five minutes to eight in the morning clad only in a bathing costume and a macintosh. She discarded and, not requiring a bathing machine, plunged into the sea. A policeman saw her and she appeared before the magistrates on Monday to answer a summons for bathing in the sea apart from a bathing machine during prohibited hours. She admitted the breach of the regulations but explained that she did not know she was doing wrong.
> Miss C. said she was told she must not bathe, exactly in the front of the house in which she was staying...The Chief Constable did not wish to press charges but explained, '...it was necessary to take steps to give publicity to the by-laws.' ..The Mayor dismissed the summons but made the defendant pay the cost of the summons.(81)

Times have changed – perhaps not altogether for the worse, but certainly in some respects it is necessary to check certain tendencies which if allowed to pass unnoticed, will do Eastbourne no good. Perhaps one ought not to be too susceptible at Bank Holiday time, but I could not help feeling on Sunday afternoon that a little gentle supervision on the Lawns would have done good.
There is a notice, I believe, warning visitors that games are not allowed, but in spite of this there were several men, coatless and even waistcoatless, who were engaged in a ball game with children. It would do no harm to warn these people that

the lawns are not the place for Sunday games, It would be a pity to offend them, but if they do not like a mild chiding for breaking the rules they must go elsewhere....etc.(82)

The Cult of the demi-nude – its effect on public morals

(What is the Church doing about it?)
The other morning when walking along Terminus road I passed a young woman – probably a visitor – whose garments, or rather lack of them, drew more than a passing glance from passers-by. She was a tall, good looking girl whose physical charms were apparent without the emphasis which she, by her manner of adornment, had put upon them. She wore a large shady hat; her back was bare to the waist; her neck was bare to the chest; her breast was emphasised by the drawing in of her upper garment; her eyebrows were pencilled half-way up her forehead; her lips were carmined; her arms were bare; so were her feet, except for a pair of low shoes... she smoked a cigarette, and she carried a toy dog. Frankly, she ought to have been arrested for indecent exposure directly she stepped into the public street.

A few days ago I went ...to the sea front...The beach was crowded with people – men, women and children – lying half naked on the shingle..women shorn of modesty; men who had no hesitation in exhibiting the greater part of their nakedness....Several of the men had divested themselves of the upper part of their bathing garment and exposed their torsos to the waist. Half nude men and women congregating together. When I saw two white girls with a coloured man I wondered if the public cult of the semi-nude could go any further!

.....I think that the Church has a great responsibility in this matter... We can all name religious teachers of the past who would not have tolerated such a state of affairs for a moment. Where is the priest or minister of the present day to be found who has the courage to declaim against this folly of the age?... some of them should go out into public places and observe these things for them-selves and determine upon a campaign against public indecency and determine also upon the restoration of that old-fashioned virtue called Modesty.' (83)

It is also easy to find reports covering issues, versions of which, would be found in most other towns The following are just a sample:

It was alleged against G.W. At the Police Court on Monday when he was charged with larceny of a woman's nightdress, that when arrested he was wearing the following articles of women's clothing: four nightdresses, two camisoles, two petticoats and three pairs of knickers. Det.Constab W. said he met G.W. on November 15 and noticed that his clothing appeared to be very bulky. When asked W. said, 'I have got the stuff, you have caught me red-handed.' The clothing was missing from...(84)

Thrashed with a Strap-Young Wife's Story of Husband's Cruelty

A young wife's allegation that her husband had thrashed her with a strap led the Mayor to ask her why she did not attempt to get away...she replied that she had her baby in her arms, her husband locked the door and took the key. When she screamed he stuffed one of the baby's garments in her mouth and threatened that if she screamed he would 'put her to sleep'. The woman had applied for an order for separation and maintenance against her husband...on the grounds of persistent cruelty and wilful neglect to maintain her....He pleaded guilty to both accusations.. There were many instances of cruelty culminating in a very violent thrashing on Jan 23 when he beat his wife with a strap. (85)

His arm was not around the Girl

The allegation by a constable that a defendant had his arm around a girl while he was driving a car along the front was denied at the police court...FGS, of Royal Parade pleaded guilty to having no driving licence ...but not guilty to summons alleging that he drove on Grand Parade without due care and attention. Police cons. D said that at 10.50 p.m. On Aug...he saw defendant's car coming towards him.. the driver took no notice of a horn being sounded and another driver had to swerve to avoid him. As the car passed the policeman noticed he had his arm around a girl sitting beside him. He denied he was going too fast and had to pull up. When asked for his licence it was found to have expired . He was fined 5 shillings for having no driving licence and £1 in the second case. (86)

References - Chapter 10

(1) Mellors & Hildegard
(2) *E.Gaz.* 25.5.1932

(3) op.cit. 11.1.1928
(4) ibid.
(5) op.cit. 9.6.1926
(6) v. Heath, A. (2013) *Life of George Ranken Askwith 1861-1942*
(7) Lineham, T. *British Fascism 1918-39*, p.45
(8) op.cit. pp.54-55
(9) ibid.
(10) *E.Gaz.* 29.9.1926
(11) op.cit. 13.10.1926
(12) ibid
(13) op.cit. 26.1.1927
(14) op.cit. 23.2.1927
(15) op.cit. 2.3.1927
(16) *Hansard.* 1.12.1922, bd. 157, cc 1254-5
(17) *E.Gaz.*30.6.1930
(18) op.cit. 21.1.1931
(19) op.cit. 20.3.1929
(20) op.cit. 25.5.1927
(21) op.cit. 20.3.1929
(22) op.cit. 10.4.1929
(23) op.cit. 14.10.1931
(24) op.cit 15.11.1933
(25) op.cit. 20.7.1927
(26) Thomas, H. (1965) *The Spanish Civil War*
(27) *E.Gaz.* 25.5.1932
(28) v. Tawney, R.H. (1922) *Secondary Education for All*
(29) *E.Gaz.* 24.2.1932
(30) op.cit. 31.8.1932
(31) op.cit. 17.6.1936
(32) op.cit. 4.12.1935
(33) op.cit. 15.6.1938
(34) op.cit. 31.10.1930
(35) 22.11.1930
(36) *E.Gaz.* 7.10.1931

(37) op.cit. 14.10.1931
(38) ibid.
(39) ibid.
(40) v. article on Arthur Henderson in Morgan, K.O. (1992) *Labour People; Hardie to Kinnock*, pp. 78-87
(41) *E.Gaz.* 21.10.1931
(42) op.cit. 28.4.1933
(43) op.cit. 14.10.1931
(44) op.cit. 6.4.1932
(45) ibid.
(46) Pelling, H. (1976) op.cit, p.57.
(47) Taylor, A.J.P. (1977) *English History 1914-1945*, pp.218-219.
(48) ibid., and Clark, A. op.cit. pp. 47-48
(49) Clarke, C. (1996) *Hope and Glory 1900-1990*, p.127
(50) *E.Gaz.* 13.4.1932
(51) op.cit. 20.2.1935
(52) op.cit. 13.3.1935.
(53) For details of Charles Taylor's career as Eastbourne's M.P. v. *E.Her.* 1.4.1989. For MrsTaylor (nee Shotter) (1911-1989) v.*E.Her.* 25.2.1989, p.2. She was the middle of three sisters, all professional dancers, who appeared in the West End. The eldest, Winifred (1904-1996), led the way, going on to appear in a number of films, including *Petticoat Fever*, a Hollywood production with Robert Montgomery and Myrna Loy (1936) and her last film *John and Julie* in 1955. Ada appeared in about seven films between 1932 and 1935 including *For the Love of Mike*, (1932), *Brides to Be* (1934) and *Off the Dole* (1935). v. also obituary *Eastbourne Herald* 25.2.1989, p.2.
(54) Davies, S. & Morley, B. (2006) Vol. 3. *op.cit.*
(55) *E.Gaz.* 14.10.1931
(56) op.cit. 11.10.1933
(57) ibid.
(58) *E.Gaz.* 19.2.1936

(59) op.cit. 25.3.1936
(60) op.cit. 15.4.1931
(61) *E.Gaz.* 8.2.1950 'Obituary'
(62) Surtees, J. (2002) *Eastbourne – A History*, p.95
(63) op.cit. 27.3.1925
(64) op.cit. 7.10.1931
(65) op.cit. 6.7.1932
(66) *E.Chron.* 2.9.1933
(67) op.cit. 10.8.1932. Fred Solly was born in poverty in Hastings. He joined the army at 17 years of age, was captured in France and sent to East Prussia to work in the mines for 2 years. He returned to Hastings in 1923, joined the Post Office, and four years later transferred to Eastbourne. He was a leading trade unionist for 50 years, a councillor for 20 years. v. Obituary *E.Gaz.* 23.5.1979
(68) op.cit. 28.9.1935
(69) *E.Gaz.* 6.3.1935
(70) op.cit 19.4.1933
(71) op.cit. 16.8.1933
(72) ibid.
(73) ibid.
(74) *E.Chron.* 19.10.1935
(75) *E.Gaz.* 26.10.1938
(76) ibid. 7.12.1938
(77) ibid.
(78) op.cit.
(79) *E.Gaz.* 3.1.1934
(80) ibid.
(81) *E.Gaz.* 22.9.1926
(82) op.cit. 5.8.1931
(83) 'Censor' *E.Gaz.*16.8.1933
(84) op.cit. 19.11.1930
(85) *E.Gaz.* 4.2.1931
(86) *E.Gaz.* 14.9.1932

CHAPTER 11

CONFLICTING POLITICAL IDEAS, LEFT AND RIGHT

Housing Plans

As a generalisation, as one moved from the west of the town towards the east, houses became smaller and roads narrower, as intended, and explained to the Devonshires, by their agent, George Wallis. Density of population increased so that by the Edwardian period there was considerable overcrowding in some areas. Front and back gardens were very small with the former in some roads no more than a metre in depth. There were also roads in which access to the front door was directly from the pavement. (e.g. Susans Road) Many back gardens only had space for a washing line and significant numbers had outside toilets. A considerable proportion of these Victorian houses were in need of replacement and the expanding population of the town meant that there was a shortage of decent affordable housing. During the year 1913-1914 the Medical Officer for Health in Eastbourne reported on the necessity of providing additional houses for the working classes in the town. The Council agreed to the purchase of two sites from the Duke of Devonshire; one at the Archery, the other at Victoria Drive. The two combined would provide sufficient space for about 236 dwellings at a total capital expenditure of over £60,000. (1) The outbreak of the 1914-1918 War prevented any construction taking place but the Council still purchased the land in order to begin building when the War was over. Hence in 1918-1919 the construction planned earlier got underway commencing with homes along Victoria Drive.

This was followed with land conveyed free of charge by Lord Hartington on the Crumbles in the East of the town for the erection of more homes for the working classes. By 1932 Councillor Higgs who was on the Housing Committee, was able to point out that the largest owner of working class property in the town was the Council with approximately 1,000 homes. However such was the demand that there were still many families on the waiting list living in conditions which could only be described as 'shocking'. To cater for these people would require approximately a further 1,300 residences; a formidable challenge for the Town Council. Housing would remain a problem for although the council did put building schemes into operation this programme was brought to a halt by World War 2 and needs increased still further by the bombing suffered during that War. This meant that by January 1947 there were 4,000 houses without fixed baths or bathrooms resulting in hundreds still using the local authority town baths. (2) Given all the problems of the shortage of building materials progress was still made. 'The Ministry of Health statistics showed that Eastbourne appeared second in the official list for the number of houses erected in the southern area of England up to the end of March with 122 in the course of construction in September 1947. This led Raymond Williams, the Borough Surveyor, to state modestly that "good progress is being made"'. (3)

Improvements in the Health of School Children 1908-1939

In 1894 Dr W.G. Willoughby was appointed Medical Officer of Health for Eastbourne and produced the first of what would be annual reports from 1908 onwards until his retirement in1939. His position enabled him to chart the changes in the health and welfare of the town's school population during this long period of service. In the early years he was frequently requested by teachers, parents and the authority to examine individual children, an undertaking which increased steadily until compulsory medical inspections were introduced in 1907. A Special School was introduced for 'backward children' after discovering that there were 50 children considered 'not fit to attend ordinary schools'. It needs to be remembered that at this time attendance at school was not compulsory until the Fisher Act of 1918. In 1912 a very unusual school was opened in Beach Road known locally as the 'Ringworm School'. This was a result of so many cases of highly contagious ringworm in the town which led to long absences from school. It was opened with 22 pupils and by 1913 had 95 children in attendance, the average length of stay being 158 days. Treatment and isolation proved effective so that by 1920 the school was closed for lack of cases. A pioneering 'Open Air' school was established in the same year using surplus army huts.

Admitting that there still remained much to be done Dr. Willoughby could record with confidence when he retired in 1939 that the obvious improvement in the health of the children was one he had been able to see take place during his many years in office. The evidence was clear: 'The average child, to-day, is heavier, taller, happier and better clothed, and the improvements continue from year to year.' (4) Such evidence led him to maintain that 'The soundest economy is the retention of good health'.

Blackshirts in Town

In April 1933 Eastbourne experienced the first appearance of the Blackshirts; one of several Fascist movements which had arisen during the interwar period. A reporter under the heading 'Fascists come to Eastbourne' (5) wrote an account of how 'Fascist "storm troopers" invaded Eastbourne on Easter Sunday – six earnest young men with an anti-Jewish complex and blackshirts'. They were selling the 'Fascist', the newspaper of the Imperial Fascist League. Their attempts to attract the attention of the holiday crowds consisted mainly of asking onlookers whether they were patriots, whether there were any Jews employed at their place of work and expressions of approval at 'Hitler's action…in persecuting the Jews.' They claimed there was an Eastbourne 'cell' or branch of the Imperial Fascist League. Six young men were clearly incapable of "invading" the town but this exaggeration was probably a combination of journalistic licence and surprise at the first public appearance of fascists in the town.

A few months later a more significant member of Mosley's political party 'expounded to a huge crowd at St Aubyn's slipway the principles of Fascism, to an audience so attentive there was not a single interruption'. (6) Mr G.S. Guesoult, 'an eloquent young man in a blackshirt', who was the national propaganda officer for Sir Oswald Moseley's (sic) Fascist organisation and Capt. F.E, McCormick, the head of the Eastbourne branch of the movement had organised the meeting. The *Gazette* reporter was informed that within its short existence the local branch had attracted more than 20 members.

Gueroult told his audience that 'Fascism was being ignored by the Press because individual papers represented national interests which they knew would disappear with the advent of the Fascist Corporate state. 'This was why Roosevelt's new policy was doomed to fail because he was attempting to put Fascist ideas into operation without the essential machinery of the corporate state'. He told the crowd that large Fascist parties were growing rapidly in Holland, France, Germany and Austria and that 'this country of ours is on the brink of disaster from which only a Fascist corporate state can save it. (7) Part of the solution he argued was 'to build industry into 15 big corporations which would be fully represented in a Parliament which had no parties with no politicians. Parliament would then be equipped to tackle the problems which went to the roots of our livelihood as a nation. He believed that in a very few years Britain would be Fascist, because it was the only way out of our difficulties'. At the end of his long wide ranging speech questions were invited 'but the audience failed to respond to the invitation and the meeting terminated.' Another meeting was scheduled for the following Friday but if it did take place it did not attract a similar level of attention for there was no mention of it in the *Eastbourne Chronicle* published the next day.

It was not until the following year that the activities of the Blackshirts gained further attention when they held a meeting at the Fountain, then in the centre of Seaside Road, a well known spot for speakers wishing to address a public gathering. By the time Mr Dunlop, the national organiser for the BUF arrived by car, dressed as the two members accompanying him in a black shirt, the group of people waiting had grown to a considerable number. He told the gathering, 'Whether we like it or not, Fascism must come to Britain because we were just beginning to feel the effects of the crisis....Sir Oswald Mosley, their leader, (8) had said that economic booms became shorter whilst corresponding periods of depression got longer...' Mr Dunlop told the audience that they all wore blackshirts because they wished to abolish the barriers of class...and so we can recognise friend from foe.' Their major aim was to bring about 'a corporate state and an intense sense of nationalism.' He said, '...they did not allow Jews to enter their movement in self-protection .... alien Jews who were definitely international in outlook would be sent back to their country of origin...and if they were harmful to the prestige of that nation then they would be sent to Palestine.' (9) A large indoor rally at Olympia on the 2nd June 1934 ended in widespread fighting as stewards set upon those who stood up to question the views expressed by Mosley. These tactics led Lord Rothermere to withdraw his support as did many other conservative minded people. The violence at the meeting gained considerable public attention so that when the BUF announced a meeting to take place just over a week later at the Eastbourne Town Hall a large audience was attracted to hear William Joyce promote their cause. (10)

There were 40 blackshirt stewards in attendance. The meeting was in complete contrast to that which had taken place at the fountain. There were 'Scenes of disorder unprecedented at a political meeting in Eastbourne during recent years' according to the *Eastbourne Gazette*. (11) Joyce had been interrupted at intervals during his speech and when answering made a strong attack on the Jews. This sparked off a demonstration at the back of the hall, some jeering and cheering from within the hall. One man stood on a chair and waving his walking stick protesting against the insults from Joyce calling on people to walk out of the meeting. Many did as several blackshirts bundled the interrupter out of the hall. From then onwards there were numerous raised voices, shouts of disagreement especially in response to the hostile comments from Joyce concerning Jewish people. He spoke of the 'antagonism of the Jews to the British Fascists and said that the Jews had tried to precipitate a war between England and Germany.' He did not anticipate persecution of the Jews for reasons of religion or ancestry yet he went on to make derogatory comments on Jewish people, and there were further signs of an uproar.

Joyce claimed the British people were crying out for a leader which prompted a member of the audience to ask 'Do you mean Mosley?' 'Wouldn't trust him for two minutes', shouted another man. 'You shut up,' said Joyce with annoyance. 'In Mosley we have the greatest leader this century has produced or will produce.' This brought a mixture of applause and laughter. 'I have never met a greater man than Mosley' declared Joyce. 'You're only young yet' came a shout from the audience. The whole event and explosive atmosphere of the meeting was out of character for Eastbourne but probably partly expected after the response to the meeting in Olympia during the same month. A considerable number of letters on Fascism appeared in the *Eastbourne Gazette* on July 7th and a lengthy open letter to Mosley the following month pointing to some of the early signs of dictatorship in Germany and Italy arguing that this system was not wanted in the U.K. (12) John Slater, after a long illness, made a speech to the local Conservatives at Hartington Hall condemning Fascism which 'he claimed was 'being sponsored by a man who has changed his coat so often that he was reduced to a shirt, and a foreign one at that!' (laughter). (13) Another letter just over a year later from Frederick Glyde argued that the Blackshirt movement in England was only three years old and critics should remember that when such ideas come from the Continent it is an Englishman's boast to 'improve any idea, so let us not fear that Fascism will come any other way than by constitutional means. (14)

Dunlop was back in Eastbourne promoting the cause of the BUF & National Socialists at the Seaside Recreation ground in the Summer of 1936, telling his small audience that the Government 'had reached no proper remedy for their troubles. They had experienced the supine direction – no one would call it leadership – of Mr Stanley Baldwin, whose Government after all the pledges and promises to the British people, deliberately committed this country to a policy which he afterwards admitted must mean war…'. (15) The speaker claimed,

'The markets of the industrial North had slumped because of goods coming in from foreign countries, not because the British people desired to buy foreign goods. These goods came solely because the City of London had invested money in foreign countries and received their interest in the shape of cheap goods sold in Britain.' He claimed that the old parties had failed whilst Fascism offered a definite plan in bringing hope for the British working man denying that 'it destroyed freedom'.

In November Mr Clemence Bruning, the administrative officer for South Eastern propaganda of the BUF, addressed a gathering at Seaside library, a meeting which was quiet and attentive but generally hostile to the ideas he promoted. ('Blackshirt Speaker given a Good Hearing'. (16) He started well when he suggested there was one bill...very close to the Government's heart. It was a Bill to raise the salaries of Ministers. (laughter) From then onwards he tried to explain the tactics of the BUF in London's East End in which parades and meetings frequently led to violence. There was much emphasis on Nationalism, the use of the Union flag and wholesale criticism of all other political parties. He asked whether there were any grounds for the Government's self satisfaction when millions of English people could not get enough food....and Mr Baldwin had had the impudence to tell them that there must always be a hard core of unemployment and that something like a million people must be denied the right to work and rely upon doles for food, clothing and shelter'. (17) Bruning's generalised statements concerning the difficulties facing a considerable proportion of working people were well recognised although by the mid-thirties unemployment was on the decline. More challenging for him to deal with were the stories now emerging from the activities of the new regimes in Italy and Germany upon which he heaped so much praise, such as the description of the experience of Labour camps described to a *Gazette* reporter a year earlier. By early 1939 there was a greater awareness of the results of Fascism on the Continent with meetings arranged by some organisations such as the Eastbourne Branch of the Independent Labour Party (I.L.P.) at which Fenner Brockway, their National Secretary, spoke at 'Red House', of their ideology and activities in Germany in particular. (18)

Rise of the European Dictators in the 1930s

Much of the world was in turmoil during the 1930s and this included countries in Europe too. Four major dictators arose between 1922 and 1936; Benito Mussolini, 1922 (Italy), Antonio Salazar, 1932 (Portugal), Adolph Hitler, 1933 (Germany) and Francisco Franco, 1936 (Spain). They were all ruthless. With the exception of Salazar, comments concerning aspects of their regimes appeared at times in Eastbourne local newspapers.

Controversial issues on both a national and international scale were raised in the local newspapers but understandably not on the scale covered by the national press. They might appear in the correspondence column, a report of an organisation in the town or an article devoted to the subject. For example in early February 1936 an article appeared in the *Eastbourne Gazette* supporting the invasion and occupation of Abyssinia (Ethiopia) by Mussolini's armed forces which had taken place in October, 1935. (19) In 1935 a talk by Gilbert

Pass with experience of international affairs was given to members of the Rotary Club in the town and reported in the *Eastbourne Gazette* (20) He explained how in 1889 attempts by Italy to invade Abyssinia were repulsed but their ambition not diminished. The African country applied to join the League of Nations but initially was rejected by Great Britain who argued they 'did not possess the right spirit of civilisation...'. Whilst criticising Italy for their aggressive attitude towards Abyssinia Mr Pass clearly did not hold the latter in much regard. '...it was not right to regard the Abyssinians as a collection of delightful people. They were extraordinarily barbarous and extremely unpleasant...There was a small Christian minority ...but the majority were Moslems or complete pagans....Italy had no business, under the League Covenant, to undertake warlike activities...but it seemed to him that Mussolini was going on and that only a miracle would stop war.' In October Italy invaded Albania.

The Rev W.M .Evans at a conference held by the Prophecy Investigation Society held at the Cavendish place chapel on Sunday evening discussed the 'Signs of the Times' and pointed to Italy stated that 'Mussolini was the most determined and ruthless man that had arisen in history. Besides presenting Fascism as a national ideal, he also emphasised the spiritual nature of that system of Government, which was attempting to oust Christianity from the allegiance of men. Many countries in Europe were fast becoming paganism. Mr Evans concluded; 'He believed that a last stand for Christianity would be made in this country.' (21)

General Carmona led a military coup in Portugal in 1926, became prime minister for life and then passed power over to Salazar who became a dictator in 1932. He supported Franco in the Spanish Civil War and whilst claiming neutrality acted as a conduit for German and Italian military equipment to pass through to Franco's forces. Whilst the prosperity of the wealthy in the country increased, by 1939 the country had become the poorest in Europe.

Adolf Hitler renamed a small political party in which he had become a leading member, the National Socialist German Workers' Party in 1923. Ten years later he became Chancellor and suspended the Constitution, closed down all opposition and promoted the Nazi Party to power. He expanded the country into a 'Greater Germany' by absorbing Austria and Sudatenland; the German speaking part of Czechoslovakia. (22)

Charles Taylor MP invited to Nazi Germany 1935

The radical changes which had taken place in Italy during the 1920s and Germany just over ten years later under the respective dictatorships of Benito Mussolini and Adolf Hitler, attracted widespread attention as certain aspects of the regimes were publicised, especially large scale building programmes and falling unemployment. In September 1935 Eastbourne's MP was an invited guest of the Nazi party and told of his experiences at length to a reporter of the *Eastbourne Chronicle*. (23)

> Leaving England at 5 p.m. on Saturday, Mr Taylor travelled by aeroplane to Amsterdam, thence by train to Nuremberg, arriving at 8.30 a.m. on Sunday. Producing a letter that had been given to him by the German Embassy in London, he was provided with

a room at the Grand Hotel, and henceforth was a guest of the Nazi Party. He arrived too late to see a mass demonstration of all the political organisations that had started at 7 o'clock. Regarding these organisations, Mr Taylor said, 'Hitler realised that he would probably not be able to get everybody enthusiastic about politics unless he had some other attraction....just as English people like to go and watch a football match, so everybody in Germany likes to march...with a band and banners...

'as a guest of the Nazi party he attended a meeting of the Reichstag sitting next to the ex-Kaiser's daughter, who translated to him the gist of the speeches made by Herr Hitler and other notabilities....(He) was one of about 60 guests at a dinner given by Herr von Ribbentrop, who is the most important Nazi leader dealing with foreign affairs. Several English people were present, including Lord and Lady Gage of Firle, Lord and Lady Rennell and Unity Mitford,, sister-in-law of Oswald Mosley, who sat with him.

He went to Congress Hall where ..the banners of the Nazi party from various districts were carried in by the S.S. Guard, consisting of 20,000 picked men in black uniforms, who are Hitler's personal guard, and whose main duty is to suppress Communism.... Hitler made a long speech and emphasised the Nazi party and their principles could not have been a success without the assistance of Christianity in drawing people together.

Giving his impressions of Hitler, Mr Taylor said:

"I do think he is a very, very great man ...He appeared when Germany was going through most terrible times...It was a case of Germany either turning Communist or following Hitler and becoming Nazi. Fortunately, I think for the world, and certainly for Germany, they followed Hitler, and the leaders of the Communist party are now in concentration camps....The Nazi party are working for all sections to make Germany a better place and a better country....I think there must be some terrific spirit in him...He must be super-enthusiastic. Incidentally, he does not smoke and does not drink.

I think people misunderstand the word "Socialist", because the Socialists as we under-stand them in this country are completely different. After all a Socialist only means a person who works for the good of the country, and I think we are rather apt to get a wrong idea of the meaning. In fact I don't see why I should not myself be called a National Socialist, because I am trying to work not for a few individuals but for the good of all, as the National party are. We are not working for a particular party. The Nazi party are working for all sections to make Germany a better place and a better country....I don't want to appear terribly pro-German, but I do think it is a wonderful thing Hitler has done – a marvellous thing, suited to the German mentality.

He described a concentration camp as being, "definitely a prison, in that it is surrounded by a wall, and the people inside are not allowed outside. I was told that the conditions are excellent. The occupants are not maltreated. They have good quarters. They are allowed to walk about. They do not have set tasks to do, but they have to run their own camp and do their own cooking – they have no servants. They are treated as political prisoners who would do harm if they were let out; therefore they are not let out.

On Wednesday he flew from Berlin to Amsterdam and after a brief stay went on by air to Croydon before motoring down to Eastbourne to a Red Cross Fete at Birling Manor he had promised to attend. 'But for this engagement he would have stayed a little longer in Germany to see a concentration camp. He hopes to do so at some future time.' This report covered some 36 column inches (90 centimetres) and at the very least it suggested the rather restricted programme of organised visits might partly explain the remarkable naivety of his comments.

In the same edition of the *Chronicle* a report appeared of a talk to the Rotary Club in Eastbourne by Mr S.M. Thorpe who had visited an 'agricultural club' in Germany where they were 'cordially received by the Commandant and allowed full liberty in exploring the camp buildings and studying the routine of the camp. He also provided a rather benign description of his experiences explaining that the camps were first voluntary but they were so popular they were organised on a national scheme and became compulsory. Now every young man had to spend six months in a camp with pick and shovel before moving on to military service.... there were similar camps for women but at the moment these were voluntary.' Rotarian R.E. Watkins had also recently returned from a visit to Germany and thanked the speaker adding that he had been told the shovels used were the same weight as the rifles! He had been impressed with the efficiency, thoroughness and cleanliness of everything.' (24)

By contrast three days later a lengthy and detailed article appeared in the *Eastbourne Gazette* (25) by a man who had spent six months in Heuberg camp in the province of Baden providing a completely different picture of life in Germany to a reporter from the newspaper, under the heading 'Horrors of the Nazi Concentration Camps.'

> The methods which Hitler uses with those who have the courage to oppose him were a feature of Nazi rule that apparently escaped Mr Charles Taylor, MP, during his recent visit to Germany. An interview followed from a man now living in England, who for six months was confined in Nazi concentration camps because of his political views. The ghastly brutality he saw and suffered is a terrible instance of what goes on in Germany today. "The concentration camps have one aim – to make prisoners break down mentally so that they blurt out everything about their political connections". Cruelty has been refined to a fine art in order to realise this aim. When they arrived at the camp '...they were made to run round the yard. As the prisoners passed the storm troopers kicked them with their boots and hit them with their rifles, their fists and with rubber truncheons....When a prisoner collapsed...a guard would run to him and kick and hit him until he pulled himself together or fainted. Later they were made to face the wall with their feet about a yard and a half apart and their noses against the wall with the full weight of the body pressing on the nose. Some men were kept in this position for an hour." More details followed of this form of treatment in stark contrast to the reports of the MP and rotary club guest speaker. ...Their heads were shaved

and they were made to wash in the yard. They were divided into three categories; the first two were made to undertake hard manual work; the third category were never safe from the guards who would set them special tasks such as cleaning a floor with a toothbrush. Their clothing for the time of year was inadequate.' More of this cruel treatment was described.

Taylor was concerned at the impression he had provided claiming 'he had not seen the proofs of the publication of the account he had given.' I reiterate that I was elected as a Conservative supporting the National Government and my principles have not changed in any way. In practically every political speech I have made I have denounced Socialism as one of the greatest dangers of our time'. That was true enough. However he never contradicted any specific part of his experience in Nazi Germany which appeared in the *Chronicle* reporter's account of their interview.

Bearing in mind that travel overseas for holidays or business was uncommon in Britain during these years, Taylor's account from his brief visit was unlikely to be challenged. Nevertheless he was taken to task for the picture he painted of mid 1930s Germany. 'A Democrat' wrote; 'I was sorry to read that our MP had allowed his reason to be overcome by the hysterical enthusiasm manufactured by the Nazi party and that he was apparently unable to resist the magnetism of Hitler's personality any better than the millions of Germans who have sunk their individualities in blind worship of the Fuhrer. (26) Taylor was still trying to distance himself from the favourable comments describing his visit to Germany at the election rally the following month when he addressed local Conservative supporters:

> 'I have been accused of being pro-German. (laughter) I have never heard of anything so ridiculous in my life. (applause)...I cannot protest too strongly, therefore, against what I can almost stigmatise as slander...' It was not being anti-German that had come through in the report which had appeared in the *Chronicle* in September but of being sympathetic to Hitler and the Nazi Party. At least this was how the newspaper's reporter had interpreted Taylor's opinion from the interview he had given on his return from Germany. The M.P. did not challenge any specific part of the report. A month later at a meeting of the Conservative Party in Willingdon memorial hall he was asked what he thought of Mussolini to which he replied: When men attain the position held by Mussolini or Hitler – whether good or bad does not enter into it – the fact remains that they have attained that position, and because they have attained it they must be counted as great. (applause) (27)

Little more was heard of the controversy locally at the time but later the issue was raised again at a talk given at the Eastbourne Conservative & Unionist Association (C.& .U.A.) by Professor V. Korostrovetz, a former diplomat who had been in the Russian Foreign Office during the times of Tzarist Russia. He was comparing the state of affairs in Russia and Germany. He condemned 'the Russian system of terror' and claimed the fight in Germany and Spain had done much to stem the westward flow of the system....emphasising.. that he acknowledged by implication..the aims and achievements of the Hitler movement for Germany. Questioned about the persecution of Jews in Germany he replied that 'the Jews were not treated as badly as many people thought...he gave instances of huge fortunes they had amassed in Germany and added ...they were merely agents of the Third International'. He told the audience 'Hitler is a very religious man. I have read his articles on God. He fights the church in Germany not as a religious but a political body.' He was then asked by the chairman whether the Spanish Government was definitely Communist and if Franco was a Fascist. Korostrovetz replied, 'The Government was Bolshevik and directed from Moscow. Franco was not a Fascist. He stood for God, country and property..' In fact the elected Spanish situation was far more complex than the Russian speaker had suggested with a large number of rival factions struggling for dominance. (28)

Within weeks the municipal elections were being held in Eastbourne. Councillors were returned unopposed in Upperton, Meads and Devonshire. In local elections, with the exception of those who openly stood for Labour, the notion of 'neutrality' was propounded within electoral wards and by the local newspapers, although it was difficult to sustain when one considers for example the contest at Old Town. The Labour candidate was A.J. Marshall, a member of the Labour Party, trade unionist and train driver on the Southern Railway. He was opposed by William James, a builder, who was openly supported by the Joint Committee of the Chamber of Commerce, the National Citizens' Union and Ratepayers' Association. These organisations were not without social and political opinions of their own!

Six months later at the AGM of the Eastbourne C. & U.A. warnings were given of the potential strength of the Labour Party in spite of the fact that the Conservative Parliamentary candidate had been returned unopposed in the Parliamentary election of 1932 and found himself in a similar situation in 1935. At a meeting of the ETC & L.P. in October in 1935, Labour adopted Mr J. Mason, a Worthing businessman with cycle shops in Seaside Road, Hove and Worthing, as their prospective Parliamentary candidate. He had served on the W. Sussex and Worthing Councils, had been chairman of the town's Electricity Committee, (29) and made a good impression in Eastbourne when he opened his campaign at a nearly full Town Hall. Yet by the time Charles Taylor opened his Parliamentary candidature in the election campaign at the same venue news was already filtering through that Mason had withdrawn from the contest. (30) No explanation had been offered but it was understood that Labour had been trying to get a replacement for him at short notice but to no effect. As the Liberal Party had decided not to stand Taylor was returned unopposed. The attention of Conservative supporters now turned to the local elections and the need for the use of professional canvassers in certain areas 'to concentrate on those parts of the division where Socialism is known to have a comparatively large following'. The audience were told, 'There was a great deal more Socialism in Eastbourne than many of them imagined. The committee knew the spots where it was rampant and they were fighting it in the only effective way by the employment of professional canvassers.' (31)

Alderman Thornton speaking in support of Taylor addressed the large numbers of Conservatives present in the audience; of whom approximately half were women, a reflection of their greater number than men in the town and the result of the 1928 Parliamentary Act which had given women over 21 years of age the Parliamentary vote. He pointed to the development of measures dealing with the health and social conditions of the people, including an impressive house-building programme. He praised the Tory candidate who was...'vigorous, had decided ability...and above all was a strong Conservative, being a firm upholder of the British constitution and religion and of everything that made the Empire great.' (loud applause) Questions were then taken from the audience, the first of which asked whether the Conservative party (would) secure better working conditions and pay for hotel employees, and whether steps might be taken to remove alien members of staffs? Taylor's reply was that he had sympathy for any demand on the part of workers for improved working conditions and any movement to that end would have his support. Beyond that he could not go, for he was not going to make any rash promises.' (32)

One interesting point he raised in relation to the success of Socialist candidates in the municipal elections was whether from a Conservative point of view, it was desirable to fight ward contests on party political lines. He had asked the Chairman his view, and Alderman Thornton said the practice had been for candidates supported by the Conservative party 'to appear as Independent.' This policy did not guarantee that they were without political opinions! The question for Taylor was whether the non-party barrier would need to be broken down in the future; others might see the issue as one of offering greater transparency as to the candidate's views.

The Spanish Civil War 1936-39 – and Eastbourne

Harry Turner, (1917-1988), a member of the Labour Party, who lived at Polegate, is one of only two known volunteers in the Eastbourne area it has been possible to trace from this period of time. With fellow Labour Party members Harry went to Spain at 18 years of age. Initially considered too young he fought as a member of the British Section of the Karl Marx Brigade. Support by the Roman Catholic Church for Franco led him to turn away from religious beliefs and organisations and he became an Agnostic. His daughter Joan suggests he thought the disunity on the Republican side led to frustration among many of the volunteers. He joined the British Army in the Second World War and fought in North Africa, Italy and with Tito's partisans in Yugoslavia. He died in 1988. Don Renton was the other volunteer for the International Brigade. He spoke of his experience of fighting with the Republicans in Spain to prevent Franco overthrowing the elected government in an address to a Labour Party rally at the 1945 General Election. (33)

Little Spain Shop – 5 Cornfield Road

Apart from a political dispute there was a religious aspect to the Spanish conflict as well. The Rev. Progreso Parrillia was a pastor of the Spanish Reform Church who attended a meeting called by the vicar Canon Warner at the Holy Trinity vicarage gardens in connection with the Spanish and Portuguese Church Aid Society. He said the Spanish people today are fighting for their liberty. 'You English know what liberty is, but we have never known that in Spain until about seven years ago. We lived for 4 years enjoying the full benefits of religious, political and social liberty, but one part of the Spanish people thought that was not the best for Spain and they started a rebellion... That is the issue in the Spanish Civil War...' He claimed that the Roman Catholic Church had been established in the eighth century and had since been the undisputed ruler of the country until six years ago. Every time the Spanish people had had an opportunity to express their wish it had been against the Church...Every time the Spanish people had risen it had been against the Roman Catholic Church.' Canon Warner in thanking the speaker asked the gathering to remember the Spanish Reformed Church in their prayers.

Shocked by the suffering and casualties of the War the National Joint Committee for Spanish Relief was established in Eastbourne. This organisation had linked up with Save the Children Fund, Service Council of the Society of Friends, Spanish Medical Aid and several others. They worked on a non-party, non-political and non-sectarian basis as the wide membership of those participating made clear. The President was the Mayor J. Wheeler; in support were Mr & Mrs Caffyn, Mr & Mrs Anderson, Dr & Mrs Churcher, and 23 other committee members, including a Canon and four Reverends. Numerous volunteers were willing to help and one notable enterprise was the opening of 'The Little Spain Shop' which took over the premises at 5 Cornfield Road for a week. The 'artistic' goods for sale included many gifted from different countries, including Spanish coloured china, Moroccan leather work, Russian dolls, china from Czecho-Slovakia and Hungary, and numerous games and puzzles. Appeals for money were made with information that threepence would buy a tin of milk to feed a starving baby, a shilling food for several children. Both the *Eastbourne Gazette* (34) and *Chronicle* (35) interviewed several of those involved in the project which was well supported in terms of people visiting the shop.

The *Eastbourne Chronicle* (36) interviewed Rev. A.W. Anderson and asked him about the cause his Committee were supporting. He explained that Miss Diana Forbes-Robertson had made a broadcast upon her recent return from Spain and given a touching account of the scenes she had witnessed: '..hungry little children waiting in long queues to receive a ration, of relief canteens closing for want of funds, of pinched faces and anxious eyes giving mute evidence of acute hardships and privations.' Anderson went on to tell of a member of the Society of Friends writing of some refugees he had visited. 'Conditions were beyond description. No soap had been seen for weeks, only one meal is given in the day. It consists of beans chick-peas or greens. We saw the ration for a family of four, It just filled the little plate we use for porridge...In addition the family get one pound of bread for a week...That, from a Quaker, is surely good evidence.' Members of the public were informed when visiting the shop they might be served by the Carnival Queen, Miss Patricia Prew, who supported the humanitarian work of the Committee. The shop's work was also helped by Mr Barratt Terry, a Conservative councillor, who had lent the Estate Hall to the Committee for its work. (He retired as Upperton councillor in 1950) During the week it was open 22 people gave their time to serve customers and after expenses had been met the enterprise raised £100, plus another £5 from collections. A tidy sum when weekly wages at the time were around £3 to £4 per week for many people.

One interesting hand written paper attached to material in the Eastbourne library of the time was a poem entitled 'In Stricken Spain?', by kind permission of Mr R. Barratt Terry:

> Can you hear the children cry
> Can you hear the mother sigh
>   In Stricken Spain?
>
> Hell's own angels whirl around
> Dead and Dying strew the ground
>   In Stricken Spain?
>
> Homeless, orphans, widows call
> 'Help us brothers or we fall'
>   In stricken Spain?
>
> Will you hear the children cry
> Will you head the mothers sigh
>   In stricken Spain?

As with all controversial issues there were those who supported Franco and his allies; (37) just as there was a considerable amount of political controversy and strong feelings in support of Communism or Fascism arising from the way in which these two strongly opposed political forces were perceived. Some support could be explained by the belief that the success of one was the best guarantee of defeat for the other. Strong praise for one system initially could be explained by relatively short visits but as time passed it became apparent that some of the initial euphoria needed to be re-assessed in the light of deeper knowledge.

Religious and Political Influences

Eastbourne was rich in the number and variety of societies and interest groups in the town. The political attracted a considerable amount of attention from local newspapers but accounts of other interest groups also received good coverage. Among these were notices of church events and those of other religious organisations. As a gross generalisation there was greater toleration of a variety of religious views and opinions in England than in many other countries. There was at least a nominal acceptance that the Church of England played a significant part on many formal occasions; prayers at official meetings, school assemblies, some colleges and official blessings at certain times. Leading figures in society were often practising members. To take just one example which was probably considered quite normal at the time. Alderman Thornton, who had been mayor, was born in Epsom (1868), his father, a clergyman of the Church of England. He was educated at Westminster and then Keble College, Oxford. He became head teacher at a Preparatory school in the town. 'In matters of religion he was a keen and practising Churchman, and for many years Vicar's Warden of St John's Church in the Meads, a councillor and leading member of the Conservative Party. This is not to suggest he was a typical resident but neither would it be considered uncharacteristic for someone of his background to hold such a prominent position in the town. This was true despite a considerable decline in church attendances during the inter-War period which had taken place for a number of reasons; a response to the slaughter of the 1914-1918 War and a weakening of the feeling that attendance at church was an expected part of weekly routine, which needed to be observed among some social groups. In spite of an increase in the population within the country the number of vicars had fallen by about 4,000. These trends were reflected in the Town Council's decision to relax Sunday Trading restrictions accepting that the Sabbath was no longer looked on in a 'Terribly Strict Way.' (38) Doubtless there was an element of pragmatism also here given that the town's main source of income came from visitors enjoying a holiday break with money saved for such an occasion.

Speakers from various organisations were critical of ideas which challenged some of the traditional religious beliefs taught in compulsory 'scripture' lessons in schools and the sermons preached in churches. A few examples must suffice to illustrate the strength and source of some of these views. In the Saffrons Rooms, Mr Watts, a well known religious author and journalist, delivered the first of six lectures promoted by the British Bible Union (BBU) concerning the anti-God movement pointed out that although the Communist Party in this country kept out of religious controversy they nevertheless ran Communist Sunday Schools for the instruction of the young. (39) The B.B.U. which stood for 'the Deity and infallibility of Our Lord Jesus Christ and the doctrines of the Evangelical Revival', were active in many areas working to counter what they perceived as an increase in anti-Christian ideas throughout the country.

A few months on they promoted a further six lectures, one of which dealt with 'The case against evolution theory' by Mr Douglas Dewar, supported by the Rev. G. Kirkby White and Archdeacon Maynard. In the same month the 'Holy Trinity Campaigners' together with 'Young Life Fellowship of All Souls' met to oppose 'Atheism in England'. The speaker, Mr White, criticised many school text books on biology and the practice of young teachers at an age when they had hardly begun to think for themselves adding that 'there were many books on this subject to-day which proved the complete truth of the Bible'. (*E.Gaz.* 25.1.1938) (40) In February Dr Norwood from City Temple opened a series of evangelical meetings in the town.

Views among religious groups were no more uniform than any others and controversy just as frequent. For example a statement which brought a wide range of critical responses was that of Bishop Walter Carey, chaplain of Eastbourne College, speaking at an Empire Day service, he was reported to have said he 'thanked God for Hitler because he had awakened the British Empire'. The editor of the *Eastbourne Gazette* wrote that, 'readers criticise the suggestion that Providence should be thanked for Hitler on the ground, for example, that the rape of Czecho-Slovakia, the overrunning of Austria, and the horrible persecution of the Jews, is far too terrible a price to pay for the awakening of the British Empire, even if it could not have been accomplished in some less terrible manner.'

Typical of the letters which flooded into the newspaper was one which asked 'Dare we thank God for a man who has so shamefully ill-treated and despoiled the Jews, in whose veins flows the same racial blood as that of our Lord and Master. Surely we cannot thank God for a man who preaches and practises the doctrine that might is right, and who, over and over again, has proved himself to be the big-stick bully of Europe, keeping all his neighbours in a constant state of suspense.' (41) There was no support among correspondents for the suggestion that the maintenance of any Empire was worth maintaining at the expense of such widespread brutality. Bishop Carey received no support for the opinions expressed in his sermon. He had completely misjudged the mood of the town's inhabitants.

WEA and Left Book Club

The Workers' Education Association (W.E.A.) founded in 1903 was a well organised society providing weekly classes and Summer schools for working people who had been required to leave school when very young in order to contribute to the low incomes of many families in rural and industrial areas. The raising of the school leaving age to fourteen years without exception in H.A.L. Fisher's 1918 Education Act improved results but still left many working people, especially women, with little opportunity to study the sciences and arts, as their more prosperous contemporaries had been able to do through leaving school later and often attending college for further study. The W.E.A. tried to offer ordinary working people the opportunity to make up for some of the areas of interest they had missed. (42)

One 'Day School' organised by the WEA in Eastbourne took place at the Towner Art Gallery where the speaker was Jomo Kenyatta, originally from Kenya but at the time studying in England. His talk was entitled 'Educated Native', which would appear strange to the ear in years to come. He was campaigning for the end to British colonialism which had taken place in his country with the establishment of the East African Protectorate in 1895 and colonisation in 1920. He described the composition of the inhabitants as 3 million Africans and about 20,000 Europeans, chiefly English. He told of the 30,000 Kenyans who had helped Britain in the 1914-1918 War and doubted whether they would do so in any similar forthcoming conflict. (43) In most towns there were well organised WEA classes often linked to nearby universities who often provided teachers for programmes lasting a term.

Another organisation which was more left wing than the W.E.A. was the Left Book Club founded in 1936 by Stafford Cripps, Victor Gollancz and John Strachey 'to revitalise and educate the British Left'. This book club started with 2,500 members and had reached 57,000 by 1939 playing 'an important role in the evolution of the country's book trade.' The books appeared as paperbacks in a distinct orange coloured cover and a range of well known authors wrote for them including G.D.H. Cole, George Orwell, Clement Attlee, Author Koestler, Clifford Odets, J.B.S. Haldane and Stephen Spender. They covered history, science, reporting and fiction, with a left-wing slant.

The Saffrons Rooms were also the meeting place for the Eastbourne branch of the Book Club. Their gatherings aimed to encourage the public to take an interest in world matters, and, ' through the club, acquire knowledge so essential to that interest.' The subject of the meeting chaired by Councillor Percy Wood, was the war in China, where the country was trying to cope with an invasion by Japanese troops in 1937. The chairman said, 'The meeting had been organised to give Eastbourne people the opportunity of expressing their horror of what was happening in the Far East....and that the things we see before us now and the happenings in Spain and Abyssinia are things which could occur shortly in this part of the world. Victor Gollancz who also attended the meeting welcomed people of any or no political party as different views helped the organisation to thrive. It was important for members to understand the issues 'so as to be able to see through propaganda.' (44)

In response to the success of the Left Book Club in Eastbourne an education branch had been formed within the town's Conservative Party 'with a strong committee under the chairmanship of Mr H. Court.' They had established a 'Right Book Club' in order 'to counteract the efforts of the Left Book Club.' The project was to be backed up with Speakers' and Canvassers' classes very shortly. It 'will distribute to its members a 'good healthy list of high moral quality and of essentially Christian ideal, especially that which portrays our traditional British character.' (45) However when they held a meeting in April their Organising Director in a speech he gave at Hartington Hall must have surprised some of the audience when he told them, 'Everyone in this country should realise that it is far more important to be a good Briton than to be a good Conservative, a good Liberal, or a good Labour supporter.' (46) He expressed his support for conscription and said he thought money power as well as man-power should be conscripted.

Trade Unionism in Eastbourne

Trade unionism was not strong in Eastbourne in the inter-War period primarily due to the lack of large scale industry. The town's main source of trade, namely tourism, with agriculture in the immediate area surrounding the town, meant that it's income was partly dependent upon the weather. While some people booked their annual holidays in hotels or boarding houses others waited to see how the weather would develop; a difficult assessment to make given the unpredictability of the British climate. Those catering for holiday makers had to accept that demand for their goods fluctuated from one season to another or even during the same season. Hence money earned from the renting of deckchairs, sales of ice cream, cold drinks, sun-hats, sun tan lotion – were all linked to the daily weather. And this in a period when weather forecasting was less sophisticated due to the level of knowledge in this field at the time.

Whilst there was never any doubt that Eastbourne was a conservative town both politically and socially there were also organisations and groups who challenged these views and who in turn found their ideas criticised. Apart from the Labour Party, trade unions became increasingly better organised and along with other groups played a significant role in promoting alternative ways of analysing society. Given the occupational structure of Eastbourne it was not easy for trade unionism to thrive. Work in department stores and other shops was reasonably consistent even if wages were very modest. However most of those employed in the large stores, such as Bobby's and Plummers, did not identify themselves with those in 'blue collar' occupations or 'unskilled work'. Membership of a trade union would not have been encouraged by their employers nor sought after by most working in such circumstances.

There was little in the way of large scale enterprises in the town and this together with the fragmented nature of the holiday trade did not encourage working people to join trade unions. Enrolling new members was always a challenge. Nevertheless there were unions in the town which worked hard to recruit members and improve working conditions during these years. Labour councillors were supportive of trade union organisations because most of them were active members of local unions. However it does not follow that councillors who stood as 'Independents' before World War 2 and were in general favourable to conservative thinking were unsympathetic to the trade unionists in the town. Just like the financing of the town's unemployed, in general, most councillors realised the problems facing local residents. Unions worked hard to get agreements covering working conditions although some employers ignored agreements reached regionally or nationally, displaying little interest in the working conditions of their employees.

For example a largely attended meeting was held at the Red House, in connection with the effort of the Amalgamated Union of Operative Bakers and Confectioners (ASOB&C) to obtain local observance of the agreement covering working conditions. 'Fred Smith, the General Secretary said it was regrettable that only three or four local employers were honouring the agreement. In many shops last week the employees were working from 60 to 70 hours without a penny for overtime, although the agreement entitled operatives to a 48 hour week. This meant that they should have been paid overtime for 12 to 22 hours' work, but they got nothing for those excessive hours.' (47) It was decided to inform the public which firms were honouring the agreement. There was high praise for trade unions by Mayor (Alderman) J. Wheeler, an old trade unionist himself, at a dinner and dance of the Journeymen Butchers' Federation (JBF) who referred to the 'bad old days' when membership of a trade union often led to a worker being victimised'. A great improvement in conditions had followed as the local branch had grown to nearly 50 members. The *Eastbourne Gazette* (48) covered the event under the heading 'High Praise for Trade Unions', reporting a speech by councillor Wood at the meeting who had stated, '..today trade unionism was not struggling for existence, but had become a part of our national life, and was welcomed not only by workers but also by good employers.' In some industries however, such as several of the hotels, wages and conditions were poor and one Saturday people were surprised to find 'local hooded hotel workers patrolling the streets of Eastbourne on a Saturday afternoon demonstrating their grievances, led by by Frank Watson, an assistant manager at a local hotel.' (49) They carried sandwich boards bearing slogans such as 'Hoteliers want employees but expect slaves' and 'How can a man keep a wife and family on 25 shillings a week?'

At the annual dinner of the Building Trade Operatives held at the E&DTU, Clapham House, Seaside, the guest of honour was the Mayor, Alderman A.E. Rush, and the principal speaker George Hicks, MP, President of the Union, who spoke of the difficult times facing them all.

> A stage in history has been reached when our ideals and standards of civilisation were challenged by dark and sinister forces. Democracy must revitalise itself

and realise the value and meaning of freedom of speech and action, for when these things were realised, democracy need have no fear of Fascism....there was a necessity for strengthening the Trade Union movement since it was essential to work through organisation and understanding and not to rely upon sentiment.

Referring to the local situation he said,' He knew the Mayor was as deeply concerned over the 2,000 unemployed in the town, and was as eager as anyone to place men in work instead of allowing them to slip downhill.' (50)

Percy Wood, Labour councillor, in his address to the members, greeted those he described as 'absent friends', the Trade Unionists in Germany who were suffering and fighting a battle, and to the journalist who had recently returned from Spain to send their greetings to the members of the International Brigade

In March a Deputation representing nearly 2,000 unemployed men who had tabled a list of demands for the alleviation of the hardships they were suffering were granted an audience with the Mayor, Alderman Rush, and Town Council, even though they had not strictly followed Standing Orders, nor submitted their application within the required time. The Mayor ignored the formalities on this occasion and agreed to listen to their requests, rather than delay the issues which their representatives wished to put before the Council Committee, whilst large numbers of the men observed from the Gallery. The leader of the deputation, Mr R.F. Barton, organiser of the National Unemployed Workers Movement in Eastbourne was introduced by councillor Percy Wood. He put forward a list of demands for the alleviation of the hardship many were suffering; free meals for necessitous children, free milk for nursing mothers, free use of the public baths for the unemployed and their families and free boots for out of work men who needed them. These requests were reasonable enough given the conditions they faced. For example most rented accommodation in which they were housed was without access to a bath and whilst the payment for public baths was reasonable for many people it was one more payment to find from their restricted incomes. Staying clean was a matter of both personal hygiene and public health. Mr Barton pointed out that when families were included it meant that 6,000 people were trying to live on the money paid at the Labour Exchange and 50% to 60% of this was paid to the landlord. Little children were walking about ill-nourished and unemployed men both under-clothed and underfed. A request was also made for the Council to proceed with the erection of 300 houses at Langney which would provide work and much needed accommodation. However the Council did not have the resources to fulfil all these requests. Neither were they legally permitted to meet all these demands however reasonable they might have seemed. (51)

Alderman E.T. Hill suggested that 'able-bodied young men who have no work should join the army'. A response which brought forward derisive laughter from the men in the gallery, which in turn led to the Mayor threatening to clear the chamber if there were any further interruptions. The problem for the Council was that they had neither the funds for such demands nor the legal right to provide money for such requests. Most councillors were sympathetic to working people when it was considered they were being treated unfairly.

However there were issues on which they could not agree on a matter of principle. One arose in which it was proposed the council should not purchase stationary from a company who would not allow their employees to join a trade union. Alderman Knight claimed they could not insist a company follow such a policy as it would be difficult for them to ascertain whether such a clause had been complied with. Initially Councillor Hill said the whole discussion was rather unfortunate because, 'The Labour Group knew that every member of the Town Council believed in the right of every man to join his union....The General Purposes Committee reported that having considered their own Clerk's report as to the legal position under the Trades Disputes and Unions Act, 1927, it meant that the Council should not concern itself with the question as to whether the employers of any firm gave their employees liberty to join a trade union. 'They could follow this principle themselves but in practical terms not insist all other employers adopt such a policy'.

In June the Typographical Association (T.A) held a conference at the Town Hall attended by 450 delegates with representatives from the master printers, the workers and the borough council. Labour councillors from the borough including Percy Wood and Lionel Turner were present as well as the Deputy Town Clerk (Mr E.P.J. Felix) and the Deputy Mayor, Alderman J. Wheeler. There were good relations in the town between printing companies and the T.A. and these were expressed by both sides. The main call from the delegates was to see the success of the Holidays with Pay Movements to provide working people with the right to have two weeks paid annual holiday which was still denied many people. They were forced to join saving clubs so that when their annual holiday came they hoped there was enough money to provide for the weeks in which they received no wage and in the hope there would be a surplus to provide some holiday spending money for their families. These were years when most blue collar workers struggled to achieve such a 'luxury'.

In March 1939 Charles Taylor told a meeting of the Junior Imperial League, an organisation founded in 1908 for young people correlating closely with the Conservative & Unionist Association, that, ' he did not think they need be worried about Eastbourne being bombed in the War because whoever the attackers might be they would not go to the trouble of carrying high explosive bombs for the purpose of bombing Eastbourne. They would use them for bombing stations and essential services in London and other cities.' In general this was true but in fact the town was to suffer considerable bombing for complex reasons as the study by George Humphrey has made clear. (52) No doubt part of Taylor's reply was to reassure the young audience he was addressing at the time. (53)

References - Chapter 11

(1) Forfargue, H. (1993) *Municipal Eastbourne 1883-1933*, p.8
(2) *E. Gaz.* 27.1.1947
(3) ibid. 10.9.1947
(4) ibid. 26.4.1939
(5) ibid. 19.4.1933
(6) ibid. 30.8.1933
(7) ibid.

(8) Sir Oswald Mosley (1896-1980) Served with the RFC and was invalided out after a crash. He married Cynthia, daughter of Lord Curzon and became Tory MP for Harrow, then an Independent. Disillutioned with the situation he joined the Labour Party in 1926 and became Chancellor of the Exchequer in 1929 but after 3 years when unemployment was still widespread, he formed the British Union of Fascists. (BUF) He adopted some of the Anti-Jewish views to be found on the Continent, especially in Nazi Germany. Violent clashes took place between his Blackshirts and those representing Jewish groups and organisations of the political Left, especially the fighting which took place at Cable Street and Olympia. The displays of violence led to the withdrawal of financial and political support to the Movement from Lord Rothermere and his *Daily Mail* newspaper. Mosley was interned during the 1939-45 War. Similarly William Morris, later Lord Nuffield, donated £50,000 to Mosley's Party whilst much later it was learned that Mussolini had provided £36,000 between 1933 and 1936.

(9) *E.Gaz.* 30.5.1934

(10) William Joyce (1906-1946) was propagandist for Mosley's BUF who spoke out strongly in support of his ideas. He had a 'strange' voice and this prevented him from being a very effective public speaker. He went to Germany and broadcast to Britain supporting the Fascist cause. Arrested in 1945, he was tried, found guilty and hanged. There was some questioning over the sentence because he was born in the USA, his father was from Ireland and a naturalised American.

(11) *E.Gaz.* 13.6.1934

(12) ibid. 22.8.1934

(13) ibid. 1.8.1934

(14) *E.Chron.* 19.10.1935

(15) 'Poor Audience for Fascism' *E.Gaz.*15.7.1936
(16) ibid. 18.11.1936
(17) ibid.
(18) ibid 11.1.1939
(19) ibid. 12.2.1936
(20) ibid. 28.9.1935
(21) ibid. 6.10.1937
(22) v. Shirer, W. (1960) *The Rise and Fall of the Third Reich*.
(23) *E.Chron.* 21.9.1935
(24) ibid.
(25) *E.Gaz.* 2.10.1935
(26) ibid. 25.9.1935
(27) *E.Chron.* 19.10.1935
(28) v. Morgan, K.O. (Ed) (1984) *The Oxford History of Britain*,p.16
(29) *E.Chron.* 26.10.1935
(30) ibid. 9.11.1935
(31) ibid.
(32) ibid.
(33) *E.Her.* 7.7.1945
(34) *E.Gaz.* 17.8.1936
(35) *E.Chron.* 13.8.1938 & 20.8.1938
(36) ibid.
(37) *E.Gaz.* 21.4.1937
(38) ibid. 7.7.1937
(39) *E.Gaz.* 13.10.1937
(40) ibid. 25.1.1938
(41) ibid.
(42) v. Ministry of Information; Centenary Essays on the WEA (2003) Roberts, S.K. (Ed.)
(43) Jomo Kenyatta (c.1889-1978) was arrested by the British in Kenya and exciled, elected President of the New Kenya African National Union, when it became an Independent Republic in 1964. He did not enjoy a completely unblemished reputation in his future role.

(44) *E.Gaz.* 10.11.1937
(45) ibid. 16.3.1938
(46) ibid. 26.4.1939
(47) ibid. 11.8.1937
(48) ibid. 2.2.1938
(49) ibid. 23.3.1938
(50) ibid. 18.1.1939
(51) ibid. 8.3.1939
(52) Humphrey, G. (1989) ' *Wartime Eastbourne; The Story of the Most Raided town in the South-East'*.
(53) *E. Gaz.* 15.3.1939

CHAPTER 12

HOPE FOR PEACE - PREPARE FOR WAR

Hopes for peace in Britain had been raised by Prime Minister Neville Chamberlain's visits to meet and come to terms with Adolph Hitler at Berchtesgaden, Bad Godesberg, and finally Munich in September 1938. (1) On his return to England he was greeted with praise and relief as he announced he had averted War. 'The Mayor and councillors of Eastbourne congratulated P.M. Chamberlain on efforts to secure peace which had been crowned with such happy results (2) and Charles Taylor addressing the local Conservative Association in their annual meeting at Hartington Hall, also praised Mr Chamberlain and the Government 'for the part it was playing in the preservation of peace'.

However the mood in the country changed quite rapidly as the response of Germany to Chamberlain's efforts for peace were revealed; Germany seized Austria and supported the actions of the 'German' Sudetens for 'independence' in western Bohemia. Anthony Eden resigned from the Foreign Office in protest at Chamberlain's conduct of foreign affairs. With memories of the 1914-1918 War still vivid in the minds of so many peole, Reverend Dick Sheppard, leading Pacifist, spoke to a meeting at the town hall which was so full that an overflow of 500 people were accommodated in the Saffrons Rooms. He told of similar experiences of packed sessions at which he had recently spoken at 16 cities in 3 weeks. (3)

In fact, for all the initial hopes for peace Chamberlain may have raised there was considerable activity in the town to suggest that just as economic and social factors in Britain inevitably had an influence upon ideas and policies in Eastbourne so too did foreign affairs. War rapidly seemed to becoming a distinct possibility. The *Eastbourne Gazette* ran a headline in March 1938, 'Make Eastbourne safe for yourself and your visitors', (4) followed by an account of progress being made. Badges were issued to the 473 citizens who had enrolled as Air Raid Precaution Wardens (ARP) at the town hall (5) and questions arose over the need for the provision of air raid shelters for the town which some claimed would cost £45,000. There was a growing need for more ARP wardens and a problem over the insufficient number of gas masks available for people in the town. Arrangements were also under way for the billeting of military personnel in the town. An amusing rumour arose that when women joined the ATS they would find that 'lipstick had been banned! A Council meeting considered introducing conscription to increase the number of ARP wardens but this was defeated as being counter productive. There had been complaints earlier that demands had led to some volunteers working excessive hours; a problem which declined as more volunteers came forward. Rumours were also circulating of some people 'food hoarding' to avoid facing possible future shortages. (6) The following month at a re-union dinner at a branch of the British Legion the matter of recruitment to the Territorial Army was addressed by Charles Taylor:

> '...I dont know why it is the young people do not seem to come forward in the numbers they should for the Territorials. There are tremendous gaps still in the Territorial Army and they are exceedingly hard to fill. I do not want to see compulsion; I do not like compulsion in any form. But if we cannot succeed in making this country safe from aggression voluntarily, then there is no doubt about it, we shall have to fall back on other means.' (7)

This was an issue to which he would return again in the Spring of 1939 at the annual meeting of the Hampden Park Conservative Association in an appeal to revive the languishing recruiting figures in Eastbourne which he described as 'one of the worst recruiting places in the country' although the age structure of the town may have been one possible reason for this result. This was in contrast to recruiting figures elsewhere which were showing considerable signs of improvement. Although he had far too little spare time himself he had nevertheless joined the Territorials with a view to preparing himself for any national emergency. (8)

Following a football match at the Saffrons Ground Lieutenant-General Sir George MacMunn held a recruiting rally addressing the crowd in the fading light appealing for volunteers to the Territorial Army and speaking to the women in the crowd. He said, "I would like the women of Eastbourne to help. I want the mothers to urge their sons to go and prevent war and so save the world. I should like to think that all you young ladies expect your boys to be serving..... Rule your boys and make them soldiers....conscription was the finest thing out for the young of this country. They would get six months of discipline, training and good food. They would come back looking stronger and happier than they were before.' No fewer than 37 young men enlisted after the parade and a further 20 at the R.E. Drill Hall. (9) At the end of the month information appeared in the local press concerning 'joining up' details. All young men came under the Government's compulsory military training measures; those born on or between the 4th June 4 1918, and 3rd June 1919, must register their names at the Labour Exchange in Seaside.

The BUF had increased its membership during the 1930s, especially in some deprived inner-city areas but never won a parliamentary seat. Marches of uniformed members inspired by fascist groups in Italy and Germany were resisted by those opposing the party's aims and violence expressed by the movement's followers. The Government passed the 1936 Public Order Act banning uniformed marches which had been considered to create a threatening atmosphere in BUF marches. Their support for the aggressive acts of the German and Italian Governments, especially as these regimes began to pose a threat to Britain, reduced further their influence within the country. However, they continued to attract followers, stood in some London borough elections and it is estimated, had a membership of several thousand until the outbreak of war in 1939.

Taylor – 1939 - I don't believe there is going to be a War

In spite of all this activity when Charles Taylor addressed a meeting of the Cavendish Ward of the Conservative

Party several weeks later, after some references to the forthcoming General Election and the assurance that they will meet the Labour candidate 'in a fair and sporting way' he turned to the issue which was increasingly occupying the minds of the population, namely, a possible forthcoming war, which seemed to be approaching ever closer into the public mind by the passage of the Military Training Bill going through Parliament. Yet Taylor told his audience, 'I look into the future with great hope and I don't believe there is going to be a war. We are now so well prepared that the possibility of Hitler entering into a war with us is getting more and more remote. You will be able to enjoy your holidays in peace this year and for many years to come'. (10) This was the second occasion within two months that Taylor had told an audience that they could look forward to a peaceful future. (11) Lord Beaverbrook made a similar announcement on the 1st September, the day Germany invaded Poland!

These reassuring views turned out to be wishful thinking as virtually all areas of the country were making rapid plans for dealing with the real threats of a devastating war even if 'normality' could still be found in certain areas. As late as August the *Eastbourne Gazette's* front page headline ran 'Eastbourne calm in face of the crisis – Holiday season goes on as usual while town prepares for civil defence.' Yet within the same article alluding to the town's precautions against possible attack, it was also stated, 'There is no sign of panic nor is there any need for panic...the protection of babies and the question of food reserves, the duties that will fall upon residents in the event of war' were all clearly outlined in the paper.

On the last Sunday in August a comparatively large demonstration of Communist Party branches from Sussex, including Eastbourne, Brighton, Haywards Heath, Hastings and Worthing marched from Seaside Recreational Ground led by the South West Working Class Band to the Sea Front where a large open air meeting was addressed at the top of St Aubyns road by Isobel Brown and Ernie Trory from Brighton. The banners carried depicted scenes of the struggle by Sussex people for their rights and liberties throughout the centuries; from 1264 onwards showing how Simon de Montfort defeated King Henry 111 at the Battle of Lewes resulting in the calling of Britain's first Parliament. (12)

There were numerous small signs that changes were afoot; whitewashed rings appeared around trees to help people see them more easily in the dimmed lighting now in use just as traffic lights were no longer so bright because only a lighted cross was visible to both pedestrians and road users. Home office leaflets to residents advised them how to screen their house lights; all moves suggesting that whatever hopes there might be for peace the country was preparing rapidly for War. As late as the 30th August the editorial in the *Eastbourne Gazette* wrote of how 'the dominant feeling among a considerable section of residents was that means would be discovered to avoid the catastrophe of a world war; although to be sure, when reasons for optimism were sought they were found to be based on a wishful estimate of the situation rather than upon reasoned grounds.' The newspaper's estimate of the outcome of events was accurate. Four days later on the 3rd September, Britain and France declared War on Germany.

CLIVE GRIGGS

Plans for evacuation to Eastbourne

Throughout 1939 planning had been going on within the country in preparation for a possible future war. Accounts of the suffering of refugees from Nazi Germany in the country were being described; in Eastbourne accounts of 'fifteen homeless men and women, exiled from such cities as Vienna, Frankfurt and Hamburg because of their Jewish origin,were being cared for by a committee of Eastbourne people. Broken in health and haunted by bitter memories of the treatment which they and received in Germany and the old Austria,...they came to England to take up work permitted to them by the Ministry of Labour.' (13) They were being cared for by the Eastbourne Committee for Refugees, many of them transmigrates hoping to go on to other countries, in particular, the USA.

It was accepted that the bombing of towns would be a major part of military offences against the country; partly as a means of destroying strategic industries directly and indirectly related to those producing vital goods in a war-time situation. The destruction of towns and their inhabitants would take place also as a means of breaking morale among the citizens of the country; a tactic the German military had employed relatively recently in the Spanish Civil War. The Government began to make preliminary plans for the evacuation of young children and their mothers to places deemed to be at less risk to the general population from aerial bombardment. Given that many residential areas surrounded factories, docks and vital communication networks meant that many civilian casualties were bound to occur. To minimise such probable outcomes plans were put in place for large scale evacuation from vulnerable cities to areas which were likely to be comparatively safe from large scale bombing.

The Government devised a massive scheme to evacuate thousands of children and their mothers or carers. Given the scale of the project it was a considerable success even though preliminary surveys did not work out quite as expected. For example, a survey of parents in London prior to the War suggested that the majority would choose to evacuate their children but in fact when the War did break out whilst many sent their children away, within a few months a large number had returned after a short time for a variety of reasons. The pattern among evacuated children remained mixed; some stayed in the place they moved to for most of the War; others returned home during periods when there was a comparative lull in bombing raids. This meant that there were schools in London which were half empty whilst those in areas to which evacuees had moved were overflowing; similarly where teachers had moved away with the school it meant they were no longer available for the pupils who had returned to the cities. One fact is quite outstanding; thousands of children went from vulnerable towns en masse on long journeys by public transport and in all the years evacuation was in operation there was not one child fatality. Those accompanying the children were housed voluntarily; the remainder, children of under school age, accompanied by their mothers or some other adult relative, compulsorily.

As might be expected the local newspapers received a deluge of correspondence on the subject; some emphasising the potential problems facing host families, others pointing to the need to help those living in London who would face the main onslaught of bombing raids. Extracts from a sample provide some indication of the different attitudes expressed:

> ...I am particularly opposed to this mad scheme being forced upon the country, entirely smashing the home life of the people, nearly as bad as an enemy occupation. The friction in households would soon lead to a revolution in this country while at war......they should make proper provision for them, either in camps or in many of the large empty houses which are in less vulnerable positions than Eastbourne and similar towns, and not to dump people into private houses where there is no accommodation for them, many of whom may be defectives and probably a greater number, undesirables. (14)

> I must say this is a most alarming prospect. Just fancy six or seven thousand children being free to roam the town mornings and afternoons! There would be no end to the mischief that they would get into, especially, if as I suspect, the London children would come from the slums....Our juvenile courts will be working overtime. (15)

Another similar letter from the Meads expressed concern that,

> children from slum areas could be billeted in homes with elderly residents whose servants would leave in such circumstances'. (16)

These were in fact minority views for a survey revealed that Eastbourne residents had already offered care 'to no fewer than 5,209 children with every possibility that accommodation would be found for as many as 6,000 children. The town hall described the response as magnificent. A reporter was told 'There have been a few exceptions, of course. That was to be expected, but the great majority of this townspeople have not only been willing but really anxious to co-operate with the task of providing a refuge for children who, in London, would be at the mercy of bombs'. (17) An analysis found that willingness to care for the children is not confined to any one part of the town. The response is the more gratifying because it has been general. (18) (*ibid.*)

By May the Ministry of Health issued a comprehensive memorandum on the Evacuation Scheme dealing with all aspects; transport, billeting, medical services and welfare work. 'The number of evacuees now allocated to Eastbourne is 17,000, of whom roughly half will be unaccompanied school children with their teachers and helpers, and the other half will be children under school age – accompanied by their mothers...' The move will take place over three days. Communal mid-day meals were to be provided to help those taking in evacuees. (19) An Evacuation Committee was established comprising Miss Hudson (Chair), Councillor Croft, Miss H. Campbell and Mrs Muddell. Accommodation was the first priority but the Ministry of Health would not give permission for finances to be provided for hostels to be equipped with the necessary resources. Furthermore they stated that the '...operation of plan lV is not governed by the number of children registered for evacuation.' (20)

Eastbourne had been scheduled as a safe place to which children and adults residing in vulnerable areas could be removed in times of danger. Plans had been carefully made for such a possibility as Mr Busby had outlined. They now swung into action. 'Many hundreds of volunteers assisted on Saturday in the big task of receiving hundreds of women and children – many of them babes in arms – who were brought to Eastbourne under the Government's vast evacuation scheme....the children were for the most part happy and extremely cheerful...mothers had to shoulder responsibilities such as the schoolchildren knew nothing about. Whilst organised by the town hall they relied upon the co-operation of so many groups; the police, the railway station staff and members of the Corporation staff at the Winter Gardens. The Air Defence Cadet Corps dealt with the large and complicated issue of the luggage containing hundreds of items from the trains on which the evacuees had travelled. An indication of the scale of the undertaking was to realise that nearly 1,500 mothers and over one thousand children had been placed in homes on the first day; evidence of a readiness to help mothers and their children from London where they were in grave danger from air raids. There would be more trains over the next two days and all the children were accommodated. The next task would be to place the evacuees in schools and in order to cope with the considerable influx of hundreds of extra children it was suggested that Eastbourne children would attend school in the morning and evacuees during the afternoon. (21) (For details concerning the arrival of evacuees v. *E. Herald* 2.9.1939; *E.Gaz*.6.9.1939) The mothers and children from London were in a comparatively safe situation for now! Unfortunately it would not last for long!

A Parliamentary Election was due in Eastbourne in 1939. Labour chose Mr E.D. Hunt to stand against the sitting Conservative MP, Charles Taylor. He was critical of the Government's conscription plans and claimed that certain items of expenditure were being forced upon ratepayers, such as the Bill for ARP, which should be paid for by the Treasury. This meeting held at the Trade Union Club in Seaside was introduced by Reg Groves, a prospective MP for Mid-Bucks. He told the meeting that, 'the Labour Movement was first and foremost the political expression of the organised working class...founded by a decision of the various trade unions to form a committee for the purpose of securing Parliamentary representation...' (22) Just over ten years later Groves would be back in Eastbourne standing himself as a Parliamentary candidate in the 1950 General Election where he would be facing Charles Taylor again. In 1939 Taylor's response to the election speeches of Hunt was that he looked forward to the future contest. In fact this would not take place. The Election was cancelled and the National Government remained in Office until a Coalition was formed in 1940.

Over the months to come there would be much discussion concerning evacuees. Many did come from some of the poorest parts of London and their appearance, poor health and behaviour were a shock to some residents who had no idea of the poverty suffered by a considerable number of families within their own country. To give just one example of how the town was able to help some of the children, Councillor A.L.D Skinner, the chairman of the Education Committee declared:

> It has been a great shock to many of us to realise that so many children in the great cities are living in

conditions of degrading filth. That is where
Eastbourne can make, and is making, a real contribution to the health of the country. Over 1,300
Londoners have attended the clinics and I think we
owe a great debt to those of the doctors who have
given yeoman service free of charge....the London
children would return home after the war much
better off than when they arrived. (23)

Within less than a week there was a newspaper report headed 'Evacuees are going home' allegedly due to the recent decision to ask parents to contribute towards the fee received by households that agreed to receive evacuees. 'But if approximately 300 children have gone home, more are expected to arrive next week. It has been anticipated that 250 would arrive...billeting authorities are anxious to receive applications from residents who are willing to provide homes for these newcomers, particularly in the Meads and Central districts.' (24)

Inevitably evacuation went smoothly in most families but there were difficulties in other households. Taking children from completely different areas of the country with the intention of providing a safe place away from areas of London which would be prime targets for German bombing raids would not always work smoothly. To allow for possible problems a Tribunal was established to which those taking in evacuees could appeal if they believed they had particular problems. This provided an opportunity for householders to present any difficulties they were facing in looking after evacuees, especially children of school age who were on their own.

Some of the reasons given to the Tribunal for wishing to have a child removed from a house included a home where they were all vegetarians and could not cope with providing meals containing meat, a practising Church of England family who wished to have one of four evacuees who was Roman Catholic moved to a Catholic household, a married nurse with four evacuees who pleaded she could not cope as she was sometimes on night duty and lacked the finances to look after them. One woman explained, 'I cannot tolerate their filthy, dirty ways and their disgusting language'; another complained, 'Their heads are dirty, and one of them had to have all her hair cut off before her head could be cleaned'. Not being a married woman she did not see 'why I should have to clean up other people's filth.' Some asked for the number of children they had to be reduced from 3 or 4 to 1 or 2, 'another with four boys asked for two to be removed as they were rough, untrained and needed a man's control.' In response to an appeal for doctors to be excused from the evacuation scheme because 'they have many extra burdens placed upon them' the Billeting Tribunal's response was 'every case will be dealt with on its merits'. (25)

By contrast evacuees were in no position to complain if they were not treated well by any host family, whilst their parents in London could be worried if they had concerns for their children billeted in a particular home, yet were reluctant to bring them back to face potential danger of bombing from German aircraft. There were constant reports of the poor behaviour of some evacuees but by contrast there were few letters praising the children because the majority settled in comfortably with their host families. In general, whilst not denying some of the real problems host families were faced with concerning individual children it does seem that there was a greater readiness to complain than to praise evacuees taken into local homes. Poor behaviour also makes for a more dramatic read than comments concerning the everyday behaviour of children with host families. Accepting 'strangers' into a household with different routines was not an easy situation for any of those involved with the scheme, especially when parts of it were compulsory. It was neither easy for host families nor children of infant and primary school age to cope with their new circumstances. In any event by April 1940, 'of the total number of children billeted with private residents in the safe areas approximately 50 per cent have returned to their homes.' (26) There was even a report that some host families had asked families in London to take their children back on the understanding they could return them if air raids increased. (27)

The complaints put before the Tribunal filled many columns of the local newspapers during the year following the first arrival of the evacuees. Occasionally a letter whilst not challenging the many complaints did ask for current circumstances to be considered.

> 'Many Eastbourne people have not yet realised that this country is at war...we are fighting for the restoration of the world's standard of honour, which can best be defined as a sense of duty...Eastbourne should be proud to have some share in the preservation of the young life of the nation from the horrors of aerial bombardment. At this time it is a small thing to ask residents to give some part of their time and their homes for this purpose, and I believe they will do so the more cheerfully when they remember the millions – some of

them the fathers of these same children – who will give up their lives to save us from Hitlerism.' (An occasional correspondent) (28)

In June 1940 the town's evacuees were back at Eastbourne railway station ready for another journey; this time to new war-time homes in Wales. A letter was received from the Ministry of Health to the Town Clerk thanking everyone for the care the evacuees billeted in the town had received for the last 8 months and for the rapid efficient preparation made for their journey to Wales. (29) The LCC also wrote to thank the town for the ten months of hospitality afforded to the children.

> As the children left, women who had looked after them since they came last September stood in tears at the station barrier and by the side of the railway line at Susans Road coach station. They were parting with boys and girls who, for all the difficulties and differences to which evacuation had given rise, meant almost as much to them as their own children. Never mind all the stories that have been told about Eastbourne not wanting the evacuees. The great majority of Eastbourne people had taken the children to their hearts as well as into their homes, and it is not being sentimental to say that many a family in the town will seem incomplete now with the evacuee boys and girls no longer sharing in the life of the household. (30)

The Salvation Army had also played an important role at their canteen in helping to feed the children between 3rd September 1939 and 20th July 1940 serving 10,262 dinners and 3,374 teas.

There can be little doubt that the habits and behaviour of some of the children from the poorest parts of

London were a shock to some host families who were trying to meet their needs and it is difficult to gain a clear picture as generalisations do not allow for the considerable differences between individual children. Three years later two young boys from the Eastbourne Youth Centre went to the area in London which had been the source of many of the evacuees to see for themselves the conditions in which people lived. They were clearly shocked by what they saw in some areas. They visited shelters for the homeless and wrote an interesting report on their findings. Men and women provided with beds in separate dormitories for men and women; among whom were those who 'cannot adapt themselves to the ordinary struggles of life and others who have gone down through drink'. Their conclusion was that 'urgent reconstruction of the area was necessary after the war'. (31) (*E.Gaz.* 13.1.1943) A recognition that the poor living conditions were a major factor in the squalor and poverty people faced daily within the area.

Eastbourne now was no longer the safe haven for children. The situation in France had changed drastically. Retreating before the German army British and Allied troops reached Dunkirk on the 21st May with the British Expeditionary Force (BEF) fighting a rearguard action. Evacuation from the beaches began on the 26th May; undertaken by almost 900 sea craft of every possible size and description in extremely difficult and dangerous conditions. The result was that 338,226 mainly British troops were rescued and almost a month later France surrendered. Eastbourne now stood facing German occupied territory across the Channel. It was no longer regarded as a 'safe' area in which to live. Some 3,000 children of the town would soon become evacuees themselves, some to Hertfordshire and Bedfordshire, others to small towns in Gloucestershire. (The West country evacuation was clearly a success for all concerned as within two years they were holding annual reunions at Cheltenham!) The seaside town was now facing the prospects of being near to a possible invasion spot for the German army. (In fact the town would experience a reprieve as Hitler decided to change direction and invade Eastern Europe instead!) In the Summer of 1940 the town made their evacuation plans according to the current situation they faced.

Parents awaited news from the new 'homes' of their evacuee children. Mr Gent, headteacher of Bedewell School wrote to the *Eastbourne Gazette* (32) to express his thanks to all those in the town who had provided spare clothing for many of the children 'who are poor'. A similar level of support had been provided to help the 'new arrivals, in the area, as had taken place one year earlier in Eastbourne. There were indeed poor families in Eastbourne but never approaching the number or scale of some of the children who had been sent to the town from deprived areas of London's East End. Understandably there were teething problems in the evacuation; among the group of 288 from Bourne School 4 returned home within a few days, largely as a result of home sickness, which brought the comment that, 'Let it be known that this is considered sheer weakness by the Bourne School and is not the stuff that true Britons are made of.'

Not everything ran smoothly in the evacuations to Hertfordshire. Some of the girls in Hitchin were faced with lengthy coach journeys of up to 9 miles to school which made for a long day. They found that they were not allowed to use the swimming pool made available to the boys and had greater restrictions placed upon their activities. Some host families complained that the Eastbourne children expected too much; regular baths in houses which did not possess such a facility! In general the move worked out satisfactorily given that most children prefer to remain in their home town if at all possible. It would be four years before all the Eastbourne evacuees returned home; about 35 children and mothers, around mid-December one day followed shortly afterwards by another group of 45 children and mothers. (33)

For some of these families returning from evacuation their immediate happiness to be back turned into a 'horrifying home coming'. This was not an exaggerated choice of word.' (34) Some found their homes had been broken into, the furniture torn, '..looting had been going on to a shameful extent in these deserted houses in all parts of the town'. The looters, who had carried out their work, unbeknown to local residents, had systematically taken whatever they could easily carry; bed linen, bedding, electric kettles and irons, cooking utensils – the very goods in short supply and most expensive. (35) There was not even an opportunity to light a fire in what had usually become a damp house after being empty for so long because the thieves had stolen the coal as well! It was not easy to imagine how some people could act in such a way when the whole country was working so hard to defend itself in a terrible war.

Evacuation by Sea

With the onset of war some comparatively wealthy parents sent their children from Britain by sea to

Australia, Canada and the USA. to escape the worst of the bombing raids by German aeroplanes. A similar opportunity for children from less prosperous families was introduced by the Government in 1940 known as CORB. Both the destinations and method of transportation, namely ocean liner, were the same. It was probably assumed that passenger liners would not be attacked by German U Boats and that child evacuees would therefore be safe. In September 1940 the *Eastbourne Gazette* (36) reported the sinking of an ocean liner bound for North America of which 300 boys and girls were among the passengers. They had undergone strenuous boat drill. The ship was struck by a torpedo and sank but not before the passengers had been transferred to life boats. The sea was so rough that most people suffered from seasickness but, 'In record time the entire party was landed at a Scottish port.' Those aboard the S.S. Benares about two weeks later were not so fortunate. The ocean liner was torpedoed resulting in considerable loss of life including 80 children who died mainly from exposure. This tragedy ended the programme of evacuation of children by sea during the War.

Air Raid Shelters for Schools

News related to every aspect of the War rapidly claimed the attention of the public. In November the *Eastbourne Gazette* drew attention to a report in the *Herald* describing measures taken in Brighton to protect school children in the event of an air raid:

> It was explained that by the construction of deep concrete lined and covered trenches in the school

playgrounds complete protection had been provided; and it was suggested that in view of what Brighton had done with the warm approval of its residents and with the assistance of a 50 per cent Government grant, Eastbourne might care to reconsider its plans.

However at the Eastbourne Town Council meeting it was explained that 'While certain Eastbourne schools such as the two grammar schools and some private schools had air raid protection, for elementary schools the Education Committee had proposed to rely 'on a dispersal plan by which, at the sound of the sirens children would be marched, in orderly fashion, to neighbouring private dwelling houses where they would have the same protection as the householders. We need scarcely observe that this amounts to no protection at all...'which led to some local organisations passing a resolution calling upon the Education Committee to follow Brighton's example and provide the school children of the town with properly constructed trenches.

Parents' meetings and signed petitions took up the theme; 800 parents signed two petitions urging trench shelters for children in the event of an air raid which they presented to Mayor A.E. Rush. Later in the day they were read to the town council but a full debate did not take place as it was decided it should be referred to the Education Committee, but not before Tommy Hasdell had stated 'he was loath to think the ARP authorities had not considered the protection of the children of the town.' (37) One meeting held over the issue took place at the Seaside Library under the auspices of the local Communist Party at which Dr Jordan, an engineer at Brighton Technical Institute, contrasted Brighton's scheme of concrete lined trench protection and Eastbourne's policy of dispersal which he condemned. He explained the method of constructing the covered trenches which afforded good protection for children and related how in Brighton too a mass deputation by the Parents' Association on the day the Brighton Council discussed the scheme had brought pressure to bear on their councillors. The Eastbourne local newspapers were praised for 'taking up this matter of adequate protection for school children'. A lady in the audience asked what would happen in an air raid if children went to a designated house only to find no one was at home at the time?

At the next meeting of the Eastbourne Town Council when school shelters were discussed several members expressed the view that 'the possibility of aerial bombing attack on Eastbourne is very remote...But having considered the matter from all angles, the committee decided to continue its dispersal policy whereby, in the event of an air raid, children will be sent to neighbouring houses for shelter and this decision was confirmed by the Town Council. (38) As for the assumption that the chances of bombing attacks on Eastbourne being 'remote', Humphrey's study of Wartime Eastbourne, by its very sub-title, namely 'The story of the most raided town in the south-east', shows how inaccurate that turned out to be.

References - Chapter 12

(1) Morgan, K.O. ibid
(2) *E.Gaz.* 1.6.1938
(3) *E.Chron.* 23.10.1937

(4) *E.Gaz.* 23.3.1938
(5) ibid. 29.6.1938
(6) ibid. 19.10.1938
(7) ibid. 23.11.1938
(8) ibid. 2.3.1939
(9) ibid. 3.5.1939
(10) ibid. 24.5.1939
(11) ibid. 15.3.1939
(12) ibid. 30.8.1939
(13) ibid. 22.2.1939
(14) ibid. 1.2.1939
(15) op.cit. 12.4.1939
(16) ibid. 25.1.1939
(17) ibid. 15.2.1939
(18) ibid.
(19) ibid.
(20) Eastbourne Borough Council mins – 3.5.1940
(21) v. *E.Her.* 2.9.1939; *E.Gaz.* 6.9.1939
(22) *E.Gaz.* 17.5.1939
(23) ibid. 25.10.1939
(24) ibid. 1.11.1939
(25) *EBC Mins.* 3.5.1940, pp.835-837
(26) *E.Gaz.* 10.4.1940
(27) ibid. 7.2.1940
(28) 'An occasional correspondent' op.cit. 11.10.1939
(29) E.B.C. Mins, p.1024,
(30) *E.Gaz.* 26.6.1940
(31) 'Report by Youth into conditions for children in areas of East London
(32) E.Gaz. 24.7.1940
(33) *E. Gaz.*12.12.1944
(34) ibid.
(35) ibid.
(36) *E..Gaz)* 11.9.19407
(37) *E.Gaz.* 6.12.1939
(38) ibid. 3.1.1940

Part 4
Early Post-War Years 1945-1951

CHAPTER 13

THE WAR AND IMMEDIATE AFTERMATH 1939-1945

When the German armies moved eastwards to attack the Soviet Union there was at least a temporary reprieve felt in the U.K., although there were still reports of major setbacks, such as the fall of Singapore in February 1942 after the Japanese had declared war on Britain and the USA in 1941. There was also the ill-conceived landing by largely Canadian troops at Dieppe who were repulsed with high casualties. Yet there were signs also of military success which helped to boost morale in Britain, such as the fall of Tobruk in June 1942 and El Alamein in October of the same year. The Soviet victory at Stalingrad at terrible loss of life in the bitter Winter of 1942-43 was a tremendous morale booster for those involved in the War against Germany and her allies. All of these actions seemed to lead some people to believe that the major threat of invasion might be fading. In Eastbourne as early as January 1942 there was a suggestion to set up a small Council Committee to consider possible post-War problems with several more groups to meet later as new issues arose. Councillor Caffyn criticised such a suggestion doubting the value of the proposal when there was no real idea of what future issues might arise. Accordingly the idea was abandoned.

There were numerous fund raising schemes put forward to support all efforts aimed at providing the necessary finances for the War. Flag days were part of the means used to appeal to the public. In January 1942 there was an appeal to raise funds for a warship to be named *HMS Eastbourne*. By the 1st April £606,956 had been collected. In February the Council gave its approval to a flag day for the National Air Raid Defence Fund. There can be no doubt that such projects were popular with the public who understandably were willing to give their support for all efforts to bring about an allied victory. An unannounced visit by the prime minister, Winston Churchill, to the town on the 8th April attracted enthusiastic crowds as news of his presence became known. He was undoubtedly a great morale booster to those living in the town, and indeed throughout Britain at the time.

Less than one month later the town suffered another air raid:

> It was five minutes to two on the afternoon of Monday, May 4, 1942, when suddenly nine Messerschmitt Me109 fighters, each carrying a 250kg bomb and firing its canon and machine-guns, swept low over the sea below the radar and raced across the town from the Holywell area, dropping their bombs in one of the most scattered attacks to date. The temporary lull (the town had been experiencing) was broken with a vengeance. St John's Church, Meads, was hit and gutted by fire. Other bombs struck houses in Willingdon Road; the railway station; Commmercial Road; the coal wharf

(now Sandell Perkins yard) behind Winter Road (now Winchcombe Road); the east wing of the Cavendish Hotel; the locomotive sheds; the main gas holder at the gasworks at the far end of Gasworks (now Finmere Road). Five people were killed and thirty-six were injured. (1)

Many more such raids on the town would follow. Just glancing through the local newspaper at random for 1943 provides evidence enough for their frequency; 10th March, 7th April, 5th June, lst and 15th September with plenty of dates in between, which are well documented and illustrated in Humphrey's study. To give some indication of the scale of bombing suffered by the town, from 1940 to October 1944, 'nearly 700 high explosive bombs had fallen on Eastbourne.' (2) A familiar cry in the streets by traffic wardens was, 'Put that light out!' when a combination of undrawn curtains and poor blackout material, or even a moment of forgetfulness, had led to a light shining from the house. Offenders might escape with a warning; others would find themselves before a magistrate charged with a light showing from their house. Some would offer an apology and hope to escape lightly only too aware magistrates were rarely willing to accept excuses. These could range from 'Sorry I forgot for just a moment' to other more elaborate explanations. On one occasion a police constable observing a light shining from a house, gained access by an unlocked door to turn the light off. The householder claimed he had not switched the light on and this must have been the result of an intruder! He was fined one pound. Later it was suggested that the light shining from one single 40 watt bulb could not be seen by aircraft flying overhead but it was much simpler to keep to a single rule for everybody than to cope with a variety of 'reasons'. It was also a way of promoting solidarity between people.

One Summer evening Major Charles Taylor, the local MP, accompanied by his wife, was driving from Aldershot where he was stationed, to their home about 6 miles away in Dogmersfield, when he was confronted by three Canadian soldiers waving to him to stop. It was not clear whether they were trying to get a lift but he stopped the car, got out and remonstrated with them pointing out how he had been forced to brake hard to avoid hitting any one of them. This led to Thompson, one of the three replying, 'We will show you where we come from' and taking off his coat he struck Taylor who called upon them not to be so foolish. With that the other two joined in and he was knocked to the ground, his face rubbed in the road, whilst Thompson then banged it on the road. His wife jumped out the car and tried to come to his rescue but was advised by one of them, by the name of Mackenzie, she should go for the the police! They were charged at Winchester Assizes. In support of their usual good character it was explained they had all volunteered for the Canadian Army in 1940 and come to England the following year. They claimed that drink was not an excuse but it was the explanation for their behaviour. It was accepted that whilst they were not drunk they had been effected by consuming too much alcohol. (3)

The 1944 Education Act

One problem which had bedevilled attempts to raise the standard of education in England for much of the

19th century was that there had been no official school leaving age and many children left at twelve years of age being required to work in order to supplement the family income. H.A.L. Fisher's 1918 Education Act introduced a common leaving age of 14 years for all children, (4) thereby removing the Exemption clauses which had been used in some areas to enable child labour to continue in some form, legally, well down until 1918.

The division in the world of employment could be characterised by some of the differing conditions experienced by the majority of working class people in that period of time. They received wages as opposed to salaries. Many of them had to clock on at work in the morning and off again at the end of the working day so that the exact time they had worked was recorded, penalties being given, such as the loss of a quarter of an hour's pay if they were more than two minutes late. Most did not receive paid holidays or payment if they were off work sick; hence the need to pay into savings clubs to cover such events. They did not receive occupational pensions. These general career patterns were closely related to the post eleven years education most children experienced.

The 1902 Education Act had provided a system of secondary schooling for children whose parents could afford the fees whilst a growing minority of children who were successful in an examination gained entrance to the schools by receiving a scholarship where parents lacked the financial means to pay. The Board of Education did not wish to provide free secondary schooling to all believing that 'a fee of a substantial amount is desirable, both in order to ensure the financial stability of the school and also to emphasize the fact that the education provided is of a superior kind, and consequently of a greater value to the scholars, than that in schools, which, although they go beyond the ordinary elementary curriculum, do not aim at the higher standard and fuller course of an efficient secondary school.' (5) In Eastbourne with its numerous private schools varying widely in their size, quality of staff and tuition, fees and the social background of the pupils, the 1902 Education Act provided an early opportunity for some children from lower income backgrounds to gain an education beyond the elementary. Until this time many believed that purchasing power in most circumstances should be the main criterion for the acquisition of a good education just as much as the purchase of any other 'product' in society.

H.W. Forvargue, who had been appointed town clerk in 1889 led the way in establishing what would become Eastbourne Municipal Secondary School for Boys at Grove Hall, Saffrons Road. The move turned out to be along the very principles of the 1902 Education Act; boys selected by a competitive examination, the majority of whom would be fee-payers with some free places available for those from low income families. (6) The school moved to the new Technical Institute and Library opened in 1904 and five years later the number of pupils had risen to 90, of whom 21 were on scholarships One problem with this site was although it contained good classrooms and occupied a central position in the town there were no adjacent playing fields for outdoor activities. This was largely solved when the school moved into Eversley Court in 1911, previously a private school known as Ascham House. Numbers continued to grow; 197 boys in 1917 and 235 a year later. One of the most successful pupils was Sydney Caffyn, the first winner of of a £60 scholarship who would go on to have a brilliant career in the school of mines before eventually returning to Eastbourne where he became a town councillor and governor of his old school. (7)

The Beveridge Report

This Summer marked the announcement that the hotels were full again, leading to the happiest Bank Holiday since France capitulated. People and government were now beginning to think seriously about post-War planning, especially concerning major social issues, such as education and medical treatment. For many people, especially after all the sacrifices made during the War, there could be no going back to the situation of the interwar period in which the services provided for working class people were in general inferior to those of higher income groups. In 1931 Max Nicolson published his 'National Plan for Britain' proposing among other things a planning council for each industry, co-ordination of transport, fuel and power, and a new town-planning act. (8) Before publication it was circulated to William Beveridge and G.D.H.Cole, as progressive intellectuals, Walter Elliot and Duff Cooper as reforming young Conservatives, John Strachey and Oswald Mosley as innovative on the Labour benches, Bevin and Citrine as progressive trade unionists, and Melchett and McColl as progressive industrialists. The article stimulated so much interest that its supporters decided to set up a research organisation to advance the principles of planning – namely 'Political and Economic Planning'.

They attracted a range of intellectuals who collected information and produced reports on 'several basic industries,...housing 1934, social services 1937 and location of industry 1939', which influenced thinking for the changes introduced later in the 1940s. The most dramatic and far seeing was the Beveridge Report published in 1942; an incredible event in that the study was over 600 pages long and 'within a month had sold 100,000 copies; eventually six times that number would be sold. 'It was distributed to British troops, snapped up in America, and dropped by Lancaster bombers over occupied Europe as propaganda.' (9) On the day it was published the BBC broadcast the findings in 22 languages. By contrast the Political Warfare Office was told by Brendan Bracken to give it no publicity and the War Secretary, Sir James Grigg, withdrew a pamphlet on the Report for the Army Bureau of Current Affairs. The Employers' Confederation argued that the cost of its implementation would increase the costs of production and undermine competitiveness. (10) Lord Sainsbury, President of the NUC&UA condemned the Report at once, stating that, 'it was "insecurity which was a great, if not the greatest, stimulus to effort."' (11)

Beveridge stated he wished 'to slay five giants – Want (i.e. poverty), Disease, Ignorance, Squalor and Idleness....he was lucky in his timing. After the bleakest of the war years, Britain's fate was on the turn.... Popular expectations were too high and memories of the thirties were too vivid' to believe that the general population would accept a return to the mass unemployment and widespread squalor resulting from government policies of those years. (12)

The Conservatives set up a Committee of MPs to look at the Report; Sir Archibald Grindley, Sir Herbert William, Dr. A.B. Herbert, Spencer Summers and Florence Horsburgh, a member from the Information Department at Central Office and a representative of an Industrial Assurance Company. They gave their report to Churchill in January 1943 concluding that universal unlimited benefits would "encourage malingering and laziness, and more fundamentally, that it was not, in any case, the duty of the State to guarantee subsistence income." Grindley stated his fears that "the plan for Social Security is first and foremost a method of redistributing income...it was the skills and vagaries of the market that ought to redistribute wealth...not the State." (13) However it was the mass unemployment of the 1930s when up to three million people were without paid employment which suggested that in social terms 'the market' was the mechanism by which distribution of income and wealth became so distorted and was a major cause of the social poverty experienced by so many families. This was the very stimulus which had led to the undertaking of the Report in the first place as Beveridge had declared:

> My plan is not a plan to develop social insurance; it is a plan to give freedom from want by securing to each citizen at all times...a minimum income sufficient for his subsistence needs and responsibilities .(14)

Churchill claimed it boosted morale and in a broadcast accepted 'a broadening field for state ownership and enterprise in "health, welfare, housing and education."' (15) It is worth remembering that when he was in a reforming Liberal Government he established the Trades Boards Act of 1909 for any industry in which wages were 'exceptionally low compared with that in other employments'. It was the first step in minimum wage legislation in the country. Over the next few years widespread debate of the issues was raised. Some defended the pre-war services at which some payment was required following medical treatment provided; others demanded medical care and secondary education to be available to all free at the point of delivery.

In January 1943, 89 Sussex trade union delegates met at the Labour Club in Brighton to discuss the Report. Mr. J. Park, the chairman of the Federation 'expressed himself as wholeheartedly in favour of the report and mentioned that one of the largest insurance offices in the country – the Co-operative Insurance Society - had endorsed it. Sussex workers were aroused at last and were determined to fight for social justice despite the politicians.' Mr Allen from ASLEF 'gave a brilliant exposition of the Report and detailed the attempts being made to sabotage it.....The TUC would take steps to ensure that if the Report was adopted; employers would not be permitted to exploit young widows to force down wages. Women were at last being treated as partners in industry'. Conference unanimously passed a resolution endorsing the Report and the action of the Secretary of State for War in preventing it from being officially discussed by soldiers was severely condemned ' (16)

Given Charles Taylor's seaside constituency it is understandable that the Catering Wages Bill in Parliament captured his immediate attention because of the issues involved concerning inspection of premises catering for seasonal visitors. The wages of employees were never high and because of the seasonal nature of the trade, inconsistent. On visiting the town during a week-end in March he explained to a reporter his reasons for opposing the Catering Wages Bill. He went on to discuss the Beveridge Report, declaring that a rumour was being spread that at a public meeting he had declared 'he was prepared to fight the report "tooth and nail". He claimed this was untrue, stating that there were a number of other issues which he regarded as deserving greater priority: '..the question of national security...in other matters consideration of war pensions and gratuities for members of the Forces should have priority over everything'. (17)

A three day debate on the Beveridge Report was initiated by Arthur Greenwood who called for it's immediate implementation but Sir John Anderson, the Chancellor, whilst accepting part of the Report argued that due to its complexity and cost of implementation it 'would have to wait in the queue and battle with alternative claims on government resources in the post-war world. (18) Fearing this might be a ploy to dismiss the findings of the Report the majority of 45 Tory left wing Reform MPs, tabled an amendment to make sure Anderson was not using delaying tactics whilst 121 MPs, mostly Labour, voted against the Government. (19) The Parliamentary Labour Party backed down accepting the Government would continue with plans to implement parts of the Report. A consequence of this guarded Government response however was a growing unpopularity with the Conservatives. By contrast the support by large numbers of Labour MPs 'gave Labourites a chance to coalesce around a concrete set of issues. The result was that individual party membership rose to 265,763 in 1944 and 487,047 in 1945 – a new record level.' (20)

During the 1939-1945 War, initially, there was a measure of agreement between the political parties and the doctors. These included medical cover from National Insurance for dependants of the wage earner, administrative integration of the local authority and voluntary hospitals and the broadening of the Emergency Medical Service (EMS) which had developed to cater for victims of air raids, unaccompanied evacuees and sick servicemen. What emerged by 1941 was a hospital system of nearly 450,000 beds whilst buildings and staff were financed by the state. The main objectives of health policy on which there seemed to be agreement were:

(1) A complete health service available to every member of the community.
(2) The health service to include the service of medical practitioners
(3) Such medical practitioners to be based in clinics
(4) A network of hospitals providing all forms of diagnosis, treatment, etc. (21)

All three major political parties set up series of committees to consider post-War planning; the Liberals in 1940, the Conservatives and Labour a year later. However there were already a number of well known academics also producing recommendations in numerous areas of public services including education, health and unemployment. To a great extent their ideas would be of greater influence when government bodies began to consider necessary post-War development. The aims which emerged were expressed clearly by Harold Laski and met with considerable sympathy from much of the population: 'The way to victory lies in producing the conviction now among the masses that there are to be no more distressed areas, no more vast armies of unemployed, no more slums, no vast denial of genuine equality of educational opportunity.' (22)

National Health Service

Keen discussions on any future health service were stimulated by the Public Relations Committee of the Eastbourne Division of the BMA who issued a questionnaire for discussion among the residents of the town at numerous meetings. Local doctors helped to explain some of the issues being proposed by various interests, bearing in mind that no firm proposals for a National Health Service had been agreed upon at the time. A majority of those completing the questionnaires tended to support an extension of the system in operation at the time, although as with all attempts to gain the views of the public, those who completed the forms distributed at meetings did not necessarily reflect the views of the majority of the town's population. (23) However, at a meeting held at Hampden Park where doctors attended to explain some of the issues raised, in general, those attending, 'expressed their keen interest in such a scheme as do most audiences who meet the doctors for discussion.' (24)

In the same month a lengthy article appeared in the *Gazette* (25) by 'Dunelm' expressing:-

> 'the need for creating a new consciousness towards the broad issue of the nation's health....In a word we need

to become physiologically aesthetic, keen to observe the laws of bodily health and mental poise...we have no right to boast of culture while there are children who suffer from rickets and are allowed to grow into a likeness of misshapen gnomes; while the bodies of men and women are wasted to the bone by malnutrition; while whole families are penned into boxes that are euphemistically called homes...squalor and dirt are still rampant in our midst, in spite of all measures taken by the legislature to preserve the public health.'

This call for changes to improve the general health of the nation was seen as fundamental if proposed new plans for medical treatment were to prove more fully effective. It was this kind of approach providing good treatment for all regardless of their financial situation which was sought by those attending the meeting presided over by Councillor P.G. Wood of the town's trades council. Dr P.W. Mathews and Dr Lucas Young also attended the meeting to help with questions from the audience. Percy Wood told the meeting, 'There is no doubt that we can do with a better medical service in this country. There is no doubt, too, that the doctors could do with a squarer deal.' Dr Mathews stated that with the present system panel patients received the same treatment as private patients. This was challenged by Mr Smyth who claimed, 'That did not include specialist or hospital treatment.' A fact conceded by Dr Mathews! (26)

Three years later discussions in the town were still ongoing with Mr. G.F. Bowes, chairman of the Princess Alice Hospital at a Press Conference declaring that, 'the voluntary system is a better system than any state-controlled system can ever be, because it preserves the personal element.' Yet looking to the future the need to expand hospital provision throughout the country was clear if advances in medical knowledge were to allow for more complex treatment to tackle conditions previously considered inoperable. The cost of necessary hospital treatment could well become beyond the means of average families to afford. The scale of fees at Princess Alice for example were 'patients 6 pence a day, fees waived for the poor and "well to do" 2 guineas a day'. (27) The continued reliance upon a voluntary hospital system was no longer perceived to be viable to meet growing future demands but this was not an issue which would be resolved without considerable resistance from certain sectors within the medical profession, especially the hospital consultants. There were questions as to whether a national system however efficient might lose feelings of identifying closely with the local community and this would depend to a great extent upon the organisation and structure of the system established.

When raising the issue of finance Mr Bowes accepted that, 'We recognise that the time is come when it is quite impossible with increased costs to maintain voluntary hospitals on a purely voluntary income. We realise that we must get State aid...' The financial reality of this statement was recognised in John Surtees study of the history of St Mary's. The National Health Service was inescapable because voluntary funding of health care had proved inadequate – the deficit of the Princess Alice Hospital had doubled during 1947, so as soon as there was the political will to create a service paid for by taxation and free at the point of use all the hospitals were absorbed into the NHS. (28)

There was much debate on the idea of a National Health Service with considerable support for the principle of free treatment at the time of delivery in a hospital, a doctor's surgery, a dental practice or audiology clinic. All of the town's hospital services were voluntary and their foundations Victorian; Princess Alice (1883), the Leaf Homeopathic (1888), whilst St Mary's was built as a cavalry barracks in 1794, transformed to a workhouse 1834-1919, before becoming a hospital in 1920. Downside (1889) dealt with infectious diseases and Gildredge (1885) became a Sanatorium. They were financed by subscriptions, local taxes, and money raised by flag days. In the late 1930s a donation of £30,000 was made but such a rare single generous gift could be no substitute for the regular guaranteed income which would be necessary in the future. Careful forward planning, ever increasing medical knowledge, more advanced training of staff to cope with the continuing changes in medicine would need regular guaranteed income for medical services. For example a flag day for the voluntary hospitals as late as August 1945 only raised £330 on the day with a further £30 to come. (29)

The British Medical Association (BMA) led by Dr Guy Dain and Dr Charles Hill were strongly opposed to any form of state control or a salaried system. They fought a rearguard action to prevent the establishment of the NHS, although there was considerable support for a free system. (30) The Conservative party opposed the NHS Bill at all three phases of its passage through Parliament, supported by newspapers sympathetic to its views. Gallop found 69% of the population thought the NHS a good thing whilst 13% were opposed. Bevan received advice from Lord Moran, Head of the Royal College of Physicians. In general young doctors were in favour as well as the 45 strong Tory Reform Group who realised how much the public wanted it. (31) Discussion on possible reforms to who and how medical care should be provided continued as did meetings to discuss the issues raised in many venues. In 1945 the Old Town Parents' Associate met at St George's Institute at which Mr W. Russell Rudall, Secretary of the Princess Alice Hospital gave a talk on the White Paper with special reference to the future of the voluntary hospitals. In time 'they would not be equal to the cost of providing the service…whilst their future was going to be affected…the Government's plans, it was agreed …were very good. It was to weld together the municipal and voluntary systems into a single comprehensive and first-class service available to everyone without any cost at the time although of course everybody would be paying for the service in rates, taxes and national health service contributions.' (32) On the 5th July 1948 the hospitals were taken over by the Ministry of Health following the National Health Service Act to be administered by Eastbourne Management Committee. Mr.G.F.Bowes from Princess Alice Hospital was appointed chairman.

Whilst he had been a fierce critic of a national health service he had recognised that the previous voluntary system would no longer be capable of coping with the growing future demands for hospital treatment. This was recognised most by those who were working in the front line of Eastbourne's hospital services and recognised the increasing needs of the town. Miss H.J. De Pinto, matron of Princess Alice and St Mary's Hospitals, when reviewing the past year's work of the Eastbourne Hospital Nurses' Training School at a prize-giving ceremony in August 1949, in acknowledging their thanks for the teaching given by doctors, ward sisters, departmental and night nurses to the training of new nurses, declared, 'Eastbourne needed a larger hospital, and building up to that future, they were contacting the student nurses who would be the teachers of the nurses of that hospital. ...We are never going to be complacent...we are going to keep on fighting for better services to the people of our town.' (33) It would be 27 years before the surgical and some other units moved to the new District General Hospital in Kings Drive which was formally opened the following year.

Conscientious Objectors

Those claiming to be conscientious objectors during the War had been required to go before a Tribunal in Brighton to gain recognition that the opinions they held were genuine. Many people had been hostile to their stance given that their own sons and husbands had been recruited into the armed services and the nature of the German regime the country was facing.

In June1940 a proposal to maintain the services of conscientious objectors by the Eastbourne Town Council was approved only to be reversed the following month. Alderman Knight stated they should 'Kick 'em out'. The Leader in the *Eastbourne Gazette* (34) informed its readers that 'the Town Council has done no more than come into line with popular opinion on the subject and has decided to dispense with the services of conscientious objectors. One reason given was that the town was involved in work associated with the War and therefore unsuited to them as employees. Five years later attitudes had changed. A Quaker and conscientious objector had been recommended for the post of assistant solicitor to the Corporation. There was a move to enforce a resolution passed in 1940 denying employment to 'proved conscientious objectors who refuse all forms of military service'. The resolution was soundly defeated and the appointment ratified. (35) A marked contrast to the attitudes held by so many in the 1914-1918 War and at the start of the Second World War.

Travels by Charles Taylor M.P.

Charles Taylor took the opportunity to travel abroad when possible. In September 1943 he undertook a good will mission to parts of 'The Empire' as a member of the 'Mother of Parliaments' to our brethren overseas. The phrasing suggests both he and many others were unaware that post-War, 'the Empire' would be facing an entirely different situation with increasing demands for independence, starting with the Indian sub-continent.

Two years later he was travelling in France with a colleague to observe the food situation in the country. It may seem that some of the observations he made were rather obvious. 'In Paris the people were almost starving...it was tragic.' Given that they had been under occupation by Nazi Germany for most years of the War this was not particularly surprising but rather a common condition of countries which had experienced a similar situation. He suggested improved transport organisation would help matters and whilst this was clearly the case, road conditions, available lorries and fuel were not matters easily provided in a country where such goods were in short supply. In some areas there was no shortage of food as he recorded on his way to Bordeaux when 'we had an excellent lunch at a reasonable price.'

(36) A couple of years earlier he had asked if junior officers could have an increase in pay to compensate for loss of field allowance, a plea which was rejected by Sir James Grigg, Secretary of State for War, who pointed out it had been an additional allowance and not part of their salary.

Homecoming of Eastbourne's Prisoners of War

Local newspapers provided frequent reports of British service personnel who had been prisoners of war of the Germans for long periods of time, some captured initially at Dunkirk. Many had been taken to the eastern areas of Germany. To take just two examples from the many recorded. News had just come through that Sergt Edwin, Percival Road, Hampden Park, missing on the Western Front, was a prisoner of war and was quite well. A past pupil of Hampden Park, he went to France on D-Day to serve with the Tanks. He had two other brothers in the services; one in the navy, the other in the air force. (37) A lengthier account of a soldier captured at Dunkirk and released by the advancing Russian Army told of Capt. A. Crook who was a regimental medical officer in the 2nd Warwick battalion and captured at Dunkirk. By coincidence he found himself a POW with three other medical officers from Eastbourne, Drs. Cuffey, Gilder and Henry Wilson, all in Eastern Germany. As the Russian army advanced and ferocious bombardments took place they were fortunate enough to have with them a Russian officer who was able to let the Russians know of the camp containing British POWs in order to avoid it being shelled. When they were rescued they were surprised to see Russian women combat soldiers. They praised the treatment they received and soon learned the word for 'Vodka'! Their journey home took them to the Black Sea port of Odessa, thence by sea through the Mediterranean to Malta and finally by plane to England. (38)

The war in Europe ended on the 7th May 1945 with the unconditional surrender of Germany at Reims and of Japan on the 14th August following the dropping of the two atomic bombs by the Americans at Hiroshima and Nagasaki on the 6th and 9th August respectively.

1945 – The Year of Elections

In 1945 there were two important elections; on the 26th July voting would take place for Parliamentary elections which had not been held since 1935 to be followed by Municipal elections which had awaited for a similar amount of time. Major Charles Taylor who had been returned unopposed in the 1935 election as Conservative MP for Eastbourne was to face a challenge for the first time as there were now three other candidates; Capt., Duncan Smith (Labour), Flight-Lieut., J.S. Gowland (Liberal) and W.R. Hipwell (Independent). Many people assumed that as Churchill's war-time leadership had made him such a genuinely popular prime minister the Conservative Party would comfortably win the 1945 General Election; indeed there were some people who wanted him to remain prime minister but have a Labour Government! He was the Tory Party's biggest asset. A fact which Taylor used in his campaigning as was made clear in a well-attended meeting at Polegate:

> I am absolutely confident of victory provided that all my supporters – all those who want to see Mr Churchill

at the head of the nation's affairs – go to the poll on
Thursday. Every vote for me is a vote for Mr Churchill,
and every vote for any of my opponents is a vote
against Mr Churchill. Major Taylor said ...he had
never made anything out of being an MP. His only
reason for going into Parliament was that he believed
in the Conservative cause which was the only cause
which could keep Great Britain great. (39)

The Central Bandstand provided a contrasting venue at which Captain Duncan Smith, the Labour candidate 'was given a close and attentive hearing at a crowded meeting' which 'numbered over a couple of thousand. 'He was introduced to the audience by Percy Wood. 'The Labour Party believed in free speech and had invited Major Taylor...to come onto their platform for 20 minutes.' Both parties had a 'gentlemen's agreement' which had insured that relations between them had been 'very clean and the election as far as both of them were concerned had been conducted in a commendable manner.'

It was pointed out that during the War a number of Labour politicians had served with Mr Churchill during the war with Germany...Mr Attlee was in charge for a time when Mr Churchill was engaged elsewhere... Apparently all these Labour leaders were trusted by Mr Churchill at that time. 'Can you tell me what has changed since then?' Councillor Wood questioned. I leave it to you to think for yourselves....The Labour Party had admired Mr Churchill as a man and a war strategist, but they now said that during the first few weeks he had lost stature by engaging in misrepresentations and scares which they thought were below the standard he set in the dark days of 1940.' (40)

In an editorial the *Eastbourne Gazette* (41) wrote that 'It must be obvious to any sensible reader that while we are strictly independent and impartial in recording political news, taking pains not to favour one party beyond another in the length and quality of reports we are not without our opinions.'

> However it would be folly to suggest 'we ought not to have anything to say on the most important topic of the day. For example, we hold that free enterprise with the absolute minimum of interference by the State is the political system best to the liberty loving British temperament....We are firmly convinced that socialism, carried to its logical conclusion – and this is an issue which few if any Socialist candidates are prepared to face – would be the negation of nearly everything that distinguishes man from the domestic animals whose lives are planned for them by the farmer from the moment of birth until they arrive at the abattoir...It will surprise nobody except the Socialists to find us on the side of Mr Winston Churchill.'

The results of the General Election nationally were a great surprise. 'Political pundits and Conservative leaders predicted a Conservative majority of up to 100 seats. The result, which was declared on 26 July to allow service votes to be collected, could hardly have been more different. The votes cast were Labour 11,967,746; Conservative 8,716,211; Liberals 2,177,938 and Liberal National 686,652. The Conservatives had suffered their greatest reverse since the Liberal landslide of 1906. Labour had won 166 seats from the Conservatives, and lost none of them. Labour had gained a total of 393 seats and 48.0 per cent of the poll, compared to 154 seats and 38.1 per cent in 1935...The Liberals held 12 seats and 9.0 per cent...the swing to Labour was 11.8 per cent..the turnout 72.7 per cent.' ((42) Eastbourne did not follow this trend for whilst the record breaking Conservative vote of over 31,000 votes for E. Marjoribanks in 1931 was down by over 13,000 votes, Charles Taylor still polled more votes at 18,173 than the other three candidates combined; Duncan Smith (Labour) 12,637, J.S. Gowland (Liberal) 2,797and Hipwell (Independent) 521, the latter two losing their deposits. Initially the results seemed to confirm that the town was one of the safest Tory Parliamentary seats in the country. In fact the *Eastbourne Gazette* suggested the results no longer supported this assumption because of the keenness of the Socialists, 'which is their biggest asset'. The result also gave evidence to the fact that the local newspapers, the *Eastbourne Gazette* and *Herald*, were well tuned to the political views of the majority of the town's electorate. A lengthy account of the results and speeches by the candidates appeared in the *Eastbourne Gazette* (43) including the longest by the 'Independent' candidate which rambled over a variety of issues attracting considerable barracking from the gathered crowd.

The *Eastbourne Herald's* Editorial (44) wrote 'Eastbourne's Verdict was "Right" and went on to state that it was their pleasant duty to congratulate the majority of electors in the Eastbourne Division upon their sound sense in selecting Major Charles Taylor to represent them in the House of Commons. By doing so they have not only expressed their conviction that Mr Winston Churchill should remain at the helm of the ship of State - a desire not destined to be fulfilled – but they have done themselves a good turn, inasmuch as they have chosen a Member who after ten strenuous years has unique knowledge of the special needs and problems of the Division. ..a word about the growth of the socialists in the constituency will not be out of place. With 12,637 votes, Captain Duncan Smith polled substantially more heavily than any preceding candidate. It was undoubtedly a remarkably fine effort...certainly a tribute to the effective way in which the Socialist machinery has been built up under the unremitting attention of councillors P.G. Wood and W.G. Bignell.... they will take justified encouragement from the increase in the Labour vote.'

When it came to the municipal elections in the Autumn the town was in for a shock. Polling day was fixed for 1st November and there were nine wards in the town. Thirty one candidates were putting up for 15 places on the Town Council. On the day before polling took place the *Eastbourne Gazette* produced another editorial explaining its 'political sympathies'. It divided the candidates into 'Socialists' and 'Moderates'. Having explained the responsibility of town councillors called upon to consider the expenditure of millions of pounds of public money it was important that they had a 'well defined mandate from the broad mass of the ratepayers...So far we have been dealing with considerations of the kind which would be reached by any sensible man who sat down and thought the matter out quietly.' There seems to have been no thought to the idea that 'sensible women' might also engage in such a process. The simple issue is whether the elector desires a socialistic form of government or whether he or she prefers a town council composed of members who are not pledged to political action but have promised to study the welfare of all classes. We have always been the first to admit that the Labour members of the Town Council are zealots and that according to their lights they are unremitting in their attention to their municipal duties. By contrast 'With non political Municipal Progressive candidates in every ward the ratepayers now have the opportunity of saying in the clearest possible terms that they prefer a Town Council which wastes no time in jockeying for political advantage...' (45)

The local paper could well illustrate that in their reporting of political meetings they were indeed objective but the views expressed concerning the organisations under which candidates were seeking office in the Municipal Elections made it abundantly clear where their political sympathies lie. To refer to Labour candidates as Zealots, does not indicate a neutral approach to competing candidates. Moreover, unlike Labour, all other candidates campaigned under labels not allied to a political party, (i.e. Independent or Progressive), although this did not mean they were neutral when deciding who they would support in the election. There was clearly a relationship with the area and the political views of the residents. e.g. Meads. In all areas local councillors face pressures from business and ratepayer interests which may be controversial and lead to decisions which favour one group of people over another. It is impossible to please all residents of a town. For example, schemes for 'redeveloping' areas often led to controversy. Councillors work to support the views within their wards but some decisions do not easily lend themselves exclusively to self interest. Such a case was raised when a proposal to acquire Lynchmere School for a new Poor Law institution led Alderman E.H. Hill to protest at the Town Council meeting in early October,

'..it is manifestly unfair to put such an institution right in the middle of what is a first-class residential district ...because there you have some of the highest assessments in the town.' This view was challenged by Labour councillor Percy Wood who declared, 'I think it is monstrous that people should stand here and talk about the relative values of property when they are dealing with human lives.' The Social Welfare Committee were trying to find adequate accommodation for elderly people in the town but this was not proving easy due to a lack of suitable sized buildings which could be adapted for this purpose. Prosperous residential areas were resisting the aim of adapting the old school to this end. The amendment to refer the matter back was carried, the issue summarised succinctly by the heading chosen by the *Eastbourne Gazette*, "Rights of Man versus Rights of Property"

In the event the Eastbourne Municipal elections brought considerable surprises suggesting that this time the local newspapers had not sensed the changes in political support within the town. The report of the *Eastbourne Herald* (46) told how the town went to the poll in the first municipal election since 1938, and the result was a victory for Labour, nine out of ten of the party candidates being returned at the top of the poll. Nineteen 'progressives' were put forward, eleven of them being successful. Five of these were returned unopposed in the Upperton and Meads wards. There were surprises as well known councillors were unsuccessful in the elections; Mr H. Harvey 'Progressive', Mr D.G. Honeysett and Mr E. Paxton both standing as 'Independents'. Electors were asked to return 15 of the 31 candidates putting up for seats on the Town Council. The results were:

CAVENDISH

George Rainey [L]	876
Edward Butler [L]	800

Edward Hyde [P]	482
Miss Jane Newman [P	477

CENTRAL

Robert Dodds [L]	520
Frank Swain [P]	265

Harry Harvey [P]	214

DEVONSHIRE

Miss G. Parker [P]	846
R.E. Richards [P]	781
H. Jowett [P]	754

E. Paxon (I)	504

HAMPDEN PARK

A.E. Davis [P]	1395
O.F. Richmond [P]	1388

R.T. Steven [P]	813
D.G. Honeysett [I]	754

OLD TOWN

G. Bass [L]	1747
S. Holden [L]	1542

Mrs E. Muddell [P]	856
Mr M. Lambert [P]	765

REDOUBT

William Bignell [L]	1287
Robert Shard [L]	1212

Albert Allchurn [P]	630

ROSELANDS

A.J. Marshall [L]	1484
W.F. Haffenden [L]	1425

N.S. Hemsley [P]	775
Mrs. E.M. Gurd [P]	681

UPPERTON & MEADS

All 5 returned unopposed, i.e. 3 Meads, 2 Upperton

All 5 candidates returned unopposed

[L] = Labour [P] = Progressive [I] = Independent

In general many people were fully aware of the political sympathies of the candidates but the practice of some implying they were somehow 'independent' of party politics became increasingly difficult to sustain. When it was announced that Frank Swain had won a seat at Central ward a voice from the crowd called out, 'Well done Frank, Good old Tories!' whilst at Devonshire when the results were announced someone in the crowd shouted out 'That will please the *Eastbourne Gazette*'. How far such sentiments were representative of the ward electorate is not easy to know but in terms of the results they were in line with the outcomes. At Roselands when Marshall, who had won his seat for Labour alongside Haffenden, addressed the waiting crowd, he said, 'Dont forget we have a few more seats now,' and went on to say, 'Perhaps Labour will get a square deal now.' He was referring to the fact that whilst Labour were almost equal in the number of representatives to other councillors, there were still an overwhelming number of 'Conservative minded' unelected aldermen so they could easily be outvoted on an issue. (47)

At Cavendish, where Labour had won both seats, George Rainey who had come top of the poll for Labour, thanked his supporters when the result was announced and 'was gratified that the electors had been fair-minded and taken no notice of the Press, especially the leading article that came out at the last minute'. Mr Bignell was Secretary of the Labour Party from 1940 to 1948 while serving as a councillor for Redoubt during the same years. He relinquished his seat on the Council and gave up the secretaryship in 1948. In May 1951 he stood unsuccessfully for Labour in Central Ward but became

Secretary once more in November 1951 when Mr G. Pryor, a railway employee moved to Dorking. (48)

1945 - The First Labour Government

Any government faced with the need to reconstruct the economy following the most devastating War in the 20th century and trying to move rapidly from production for war to a peacetime situation was bound to be faced with a multiplicity of problems; 'they faced a dauntingly immense task as (they) set out to reshape Britain at a time of post-war hardship, shortages and crisis which called for inordinate effort merely to keep up with events'. (49) Understandably, after a comparatively short time, people were impatient for the country to 'get back to normal', a phrase which became heard increasingly in numerous situations. One major difference between the UK and many other countries involved in the War was that Britain had not suffered the ravages of invasion and occupation. Nevertheless the problems facing the nation were still on an incredible scale.

Housing Shortage

Yet for all the problems facing the country substantial progress could gradually be seen. Among the many problems facing so many areas was a shortage of housing, partly a result of the destruction of living accommodation due to aerial bombardment, especially within urban areas. In Eastbourne '475 were totally destroyed, 1,000 seriously damaged and 10,000 slightly damaged.' (50) All manner of other buildings had also been affected; schools, hospitals and factories. The task facing the building industry was phenomenal especially as all manner of goods were in short supply. Meeting all the genuine needs was an impossible task because like most towns in the country there were those in which the facilities were comparatively poor, those which were war damaged and sometimes structurally unstable as well as demands for more new houses to meet the demands of the town's growing population. There was unanimous council support for raising council house rents by one shilling and ninepence per week; a move necessitated by the 'present inflationary spiral and the heavy cost for the maintenance of pre-War homes.' Councillor Broomfield questioned the logic of then spending £4,000 on a car park which would be free of charge when four thousand homes in Eastbourne lacked a fixed bath or bathroom. Such houses were largely built pre 1914-1918 War and were a feature of most British towns. Approximately 1,000 people in Eastbourne visited the municipal baths weekly, the first of which had been erected in 1902 and then extended by public demand in 1924.(51)

Understandably those awaiting housing were impatient for their demands to be met but in fact the town's house building programme was a good one given the circumstances they faced; '...let it be said without reservation that Ministry of Health statistics show that Eastbourne appeared second in the official list for the number of houses erected in the southern area of England up to the end of March, 1947'. (52) There were 122 houses under construction when this report was published in September of the same year. The Borough Surveyor, Mr R. Williams, commented modestly that 'good progress was being made'. This recognition of the town's successful building programme was reinforced by the Labour councillor Percy Wood who said, '... it was a fact that the building force in the town was greater to-day than ever before in its history. Notwithstanding the shortage of materials the whole of that building force had been employed.' (53) Yet with the need of so many people for new houses or fundamental repairs to their war damaged houses it was impossible to fulfil demand solely by traditional methods of building.

One way of helping in the shortage of houses was by the introduction of prefabricated single storey buildings constructed in sections within factories which were then assembled on site. For the time they were considered very modern, especially the kitchens, which included a refrigerator! (Still a rarity in most British homes in the 1940s.) Initially they were considered to be temporary accommodation and regarded by some as not quite a 'real house'. However many families became attached to them and by the time they had been renovated a few years later they had become 'permanent' features in parts of numerous towns. They had surrounding gardens and were to some extent similar to living in a bungalow. Councillor Percy Wood suggested 'Prefabs in the Meads' but it is difficult to know just how serious his suggestion was meant to be taken. (54)

A couple of years later Mr Parker contesting Roselands ward for the Conservatives supported the idea of the Council selling off their houses to those tenants who might wish to buy them. A.F. Marshall for Labour disapproved of the suggestion claiming that, 'at a time when there was a shortage of houses to live in...I can't see what good it is to own your own house if you already have security of tenure'. (55) His approach to housing like that of most people at the time was to regard houses and flats primarily as places in which families would live, rather than an investment which could increase in value, especially if they were in short supply. (This would be a major issue for dispute a generation later. v.(56)

A leading article in the *Eastbourne Gazette* (57) under the title 'Let's get on with it,' drew attention to the fact that of the town's housing allocation not one brick had yet been laid. Mr F.H. Busby, the Town Clerk, responded with a lengthy factual statement which the newspaper printed in full taking up the greater part of a page which is far too detailed to repeat here. (58) It was a master class demonstrating the difference between the understandable disappointment with the delay in house-building which had led to all kinds of disapproving comments among many people in the town, much of it based upon misinformed information, and the detailed facts which the Borough had to face. Busby first dealt with the accusation of delay at the start: the Council's officers are in constant touch with the Ministry on the subject and in fact, a discussion (between them) took place on 2nd August. The Council's housing allocation for the calendar year 1951...was 160 new dwellings. Of this number one fifth was the maximum which could be used for licences to erect new private houses and 32 such licences have in fact been issued

The allocation for new Council houses was therefore 128. The Chatsfield Estate, Hampden Park, will provide the sites for 126 of these 128 houses. The purchase of the land which forms this estate was completed in September 9, 1950. Part of the land was required for 70 houses from the 1950 programme. The erection of the

126 houses from the rick-road and Henfield-road are already complete....With regard to the carriageways... tenders were received 23rd February 1951, submitted to the Ministry 6th March, and approved by Ministry 23rd June. Contract documents were sent to contractors 28th June with work to commence 13th August although contracts have yet to be returned. One reason for some delay was the new specification for carriageways concerning recent heavy rainfall and change in specifications. There was considerably more detail included in the Town Clerk's Report but no doubts could be left concerning the Council's efficiency in dealing with the housing allocation with which they were faced. The average building cost of the 32 private houses was £2,611; that is £1,120 in excess of the average cost of the Council houses of the Chatsfield Estate as approved by the Ministry.

Food Rationing

Many items of food continued to be rationed maintaining the policy that it was better that all people were able to receive a fair supply of food and goods rather than a system where distribution was based solely on purchasing power, thereby allowing some families to buy any item because they had a higher income whilst others had to go without because they could not afford them. Having rationed essential food and goods during the war-time years when the people were united in working towards a common aim it was not difficult to maintain this attitude. This is not a sentimental view of the war years in the UK. There was a black market in operation organised by those always willing to exploit a situation where they can make money but in general people accepted rationing of key items and developed the habit of queuing to ensure people were served in turn; a custom which has continued to be a feature of British life.

Britain had to pay its way in the world again hence the priority given to exports. It was a great struggle and frustrating for people to see British goods on display in shop windows, such as items of furniture, with a label stating 'For Export Only'. However, gradually progress was made and items came 'off the ration' thereby making them available always subject to supply. Some, which had become only a memory in the minds of adults, became available in the shops, bananas for example, finally making a welcome reappearance after an absence of nearly six years. One of the most gratifying feature of immediate post-war Britain was full employment, especially for those with bitter memories of the 1930s when millions had been out of work, sometimes on the dole with the added humiliating treatment of some families who were refused aid whilst they still possessed items which could be sold for cash. These harsh conditions had never been a policy of the town council. Now such was demand that many jobs now required overtime working and with the growth of trade unions at many places of work negotiations with the management had led to extra hours at unsocial times earning higher rates of pay.

Equal Pay for Equal Work

Campaigns for women to have equal rights to men have a very long history. (v. Ch.7, 'Women still

Disenfranchised') The National Council of Women was founded in 1895 due to the poor working conditions of many women. By 1900 it had set up special committees to focus upon particular issues. One hundred and thirty delegates attended their annual meeting at Eastbourne in early 1934. (59) For much of the 20th century women were denied equal pay for the same work as men. At the Conference in Eastbourne of Weights and Measures Inspectors in September 1949 Mr T.G. Poppy, Controller of the Standards Department of the Board of Trade when regretting that a lady was not replying to his toast light heartedly quoted from the New Testament, (60) 'Let the woman learn in silence with all subjection.' The rest of the verse continues, 'But I suffer not a woman to teach, nor to usurp authority over the man, but to be in silence'. Whilst many rejected such Christian doctrine in Britain by the mid 20th century, it might still be quoted to justify inequalities in pay between men and women. Indeed, for all the laughter the quote had raised, Mr Poppy pointed out that if the apostle was alive today he would have approved of the British Weights and Measures service, which remained a fine example of a closed shop, for as far as he was aware there had never been a lady inspector of weights and measures, though he saw no reason why there should not be. (61)

In Eastbourne there was an advertisement in Local Government for an Assistant to the Housing Superintendent; the salary offered depended on whether a male or female was offered the post. Some employers put women to work in different sections of a business so that it could be argued they were not doing the same work. There were working men also who supported higher rates of pay for men arguing that they had to support a family, an argument to be found among some teachers when the National Schoolmasters Association broke away from the National Union of Teachers over the issue. In 1950 before an audience of more than 1,300 people – '"attractive" Miss Hamilton, speaking with "a strong Scots accent" at the Conference of the National Association of Local Government Officers (NALGO) was supporting a motion reaffirming the association's policy of equal pay, and urging the National Executive Council to take vigorous action in all appropriate quarters to secure the implementation of this policy'. (62); (Nb. This was clearly a time when journalists thought a description of how a woman speaker looked and sounded was relevant to what she was saying!) She pointed out that there were 60,000 women in the Association and the whole question boils down to whether you believe in equality for women. 'Apparently our own NEC do not. She told of a woman solicitor in Scotland who had to fight for 20 years to obtain recognition. ...There had to be a national campaign for equal pay, and already people up and down the country were realising this. The question was one that had gone beyond the village pump level, it had now assumed international importance.' Miss Taylor from the London County Council claimed the motion was treated 'as one of the less serious ones when brought before Conference...regarded as a sort of consolation...' (ibid). (63)

For years women performing the same duties as men were paid at a lower rate simply because they were women. After the Second World War women were able to win equal pay in the Civil Service and Teaching mainly through trade union activity although it was not fully implemented for several years. . The 1945 Education Act also ended the practice in some areas of women having to resign when they married!| (In 1970 the Labour Government passed the Equal Pay Act in order to remedy the situation by law.) The Burnham Committee had been established in 1919 to negotiate teachers' salary scales for various groups of teachers. Once agreement was reached local authorities were bound to pay civil servants and teachers equal pay. In 1970 the Labour Government passed the Equal Pay Act which became operative in 1976. (64)

Another aspect of better pay for women was to ensure that much of the work they did was fully valued and the proper status given to tasks carried out principally by women. This was part of a theme addressed by members of the Association of Domestic Teachers when they met for their annual conference in Eastbourne. Miss M. Pallister, author and broadcaster said, 'I can never understand when we talk about the professional women in the home, why home-making is not in itself a profession. To my mind, home-making is the profession of professions'. It needed a great deal of organisation and it was thought the lack of this was a great cause of unhappiness, stress and strain as could be witnessed only too readily in some households. One positive feature for increased future opportunities for women was the establishment of the National Health Service and the developments arising from the 1944 Education Act. Miss Elliot believed the enhanced role of women in society would enable them to make their contributions to international activity. 'I believe it is in that sphere in the next few years that women have to join together in their single-mindedness towards active peace in the world.' (65)

Within two years of the local elections in Eastbourne providing evidence of profound progress by the Labour Party the situation had reversed to the more familiar pattern of Conservative Party dominance but at least now labels such as 'Independent' and 'Progressive' had been discarded by several candidates who now openly proclaimed themselves as supporters of the Conservative Party. The *Eastbourne Gazette* (66) had unambiguously advised voters; '..if every anti-Socialist would take the trouble to vote, the march of the Labour Party towards a majority on the Town Council would be deservedly halted. Events on Saturday proved the accuracy of this prediction.' Five out of six contested seats went to the Conservatives: Cavendish(W. Benson Dare), Central (Frank Swain), Roselands (Mrs Llewellyn), Hampden Park (E. Paxon), and Old Town (H. Archer), the solitary Labour success was W. Bignell at Redoubt. The *Gazette* concluded that, 'The affairs of Eastbourne are safely in the hands of a Moderate majority, who may be relied upon, as past performance proves, to honour their election pledges and govern the town in an orderly sensible way.'

There was evidence within the town that Conservative Party wealth was still reflected in the rallies supported locally. For example in April 1949 the annual meeting of the Primrose League was held in the Albert Hall, attended by Winston Churchill with Anthony Eden the principal speaker. Alderman Miss Thornton helped to organise a party of 70 from the town to attend the event. The following month a rally was organised by the the Conservative Provincial S.E. Area which attracted an audience of about 700 people, including three Conservative politicians, Lennox Boyd, MP

Mid-Bedfordshire, R. Thompson, candidate for Croydon and Beverley Baxter MP. Miss Barbara Bell was seated as Britannia on the throne, trumpets played and flags of Europe were carried by young Tories. Martia Rawnsley, mezzo soprano from Glynde Opera House sang 'Land of Hope and Glory'. (67) By contrast to this display of splendour a thriving Co-operative Guild met at the Red House, headquarters of the ILP in Beamsley Road, to discuss their progress. (68)

Meanwhile George Bass, a Labour councillor of some 15 years working for Old Town ward with a good record of public service on numerous sub-committees dealing with issues facing those living in the ward, was facing competition from a new grouping calling themselves the Council Tenants Association (CTA), in addition to the local Conservative Party. Speaking at the Old Town ward meeting he said, 'I want to be as charitable as I possibly can but there is nothing they can do for the people in Council houses that we cannot do or or have not attempted to do all the time we have been on the Council'. (69) Percy Wood chairing the meeting pointed out some of the positive results Bass had gained for Eastbourne people by his work on the Old Age Pensions Committee and the Public Health Committee including the situation some elderly residents had faced. He had found that old age pensioners who became chargeable to St Mary's Hospital had their pension stopped by the Government after being patients for over three months. He thought that was very unfair and he suggested to the Ministry of Health that patients should retain their pensions so long as they contributed 8s 6d a week towards their maintenance, leaving them 1s 6d for stamps and other necessities.' (70) In fact the CTA was finding organisation more difficult than they had first envisaged. Only 23 turned up out of a membership of 500 to the meeting of the Old Town branch on the 11th April and when J. Brady, who hoped to stand as a councillor for Roselands, asked for nominations for officers none was forthcoming. Capt Needham of the CTA informed the meeting that he intended to stand for Old Town and would be opposing George Bass. (71)

May Day still brought out a 'fairly large crowd' for the traditional celebrations of the Labour Movement in the Recreation Ground at Seaside. Mr A.W. Lee, M.P. For West Ham, and relevant for Eastbourne, champion of the hotel workers, looking back on the present Government's record, claimed that they could truthfully say that 'never has there been a Government that has done so much for so many in so little a time.' a remark which was greeted with a chorus of "Hear, hears." They had implemented all their election pledges which had been set out in their pamphlet 'Let Us Face the Future'. (72)

References - Chapter 13

(1) Humphrey, G. (1989) *Wartime Eastbourne*, p.47
(2) *E.Gaz.* 18.10.1944
(3) *E.Gaz.* 21.7.1943
(4) Griggs, C. (1983) *The TUC and the Struggle for Education 1868-1925'* pp.50-65
(5) Banks, O. (1955) *Parity and Prestige in English Secondary Education*, p.61
(6) v. Blackburn, C.J. (1949) *Eastbourne Grammar School for Boys*
(7) ibid., p.12
(8) Addison, P. (1994) *The Road to 1945; British Politics and the Second World War*, pp.38-39

(9) Marr, A. (2007) *A History of Modern Britain*, p.63
(10) op.cit.,pp.292-293
(11) Salisbury, 'Post War Conservative Policy' Sept. 1942, Quoted in Clark, op.cit.,p.294
(12) Marr, A. ibid.
(13) ibid. p.292
(14) Clark, A. (1998) *The Tories; Conservatives and the Nation State 1922-1997*, p. 293
(15) op.cit. p.64
(16) *E.Gaz.* 27.1.1943
(17) ibid. 10.3.1943
(18) Clark,A. op.cit. p.298
(19) ibid.
(20) Thorpe, A. (1997) *A History of the British Labour Party*, p.106
(21) v. Addison, P. op.cit, pp. 178-214
(22) Laski, H.J. (1940) *Where do we go from Here?* p.88; v. also Addison, P. p.184
(23) *E.Gaz.* 22.9.1943
(24) ibid.
(25) *E.Gaz.* 15.9.1943
(26) op.cit. 22.9.1943
(27) Surtees, J. (1992) op.cit.
(28) op.cit. pp.87-88
(29) *E.Gaz.* 20.8.1945
(30) Eatwell, R. (1979) p.63
(31) Clark, A. op.cit. p.295
(32) *E.Gaz.* 28.2.1945
(33) ibid. 3.8.1949
(34) *E.Gaz.* 3.7.1940
(35) ibid. 9.5.1945
(36) ibid. 28.3.1945
(37) ibid 22.11.1944
(38) ibid. 4.4.1945
(39) ibid. 4.7.1945
(40) ibid

(41) ibid. 4.7.1945
(42) Eatwell, R., op.cit.pp.36-37
(43) *E.Gaz.* 8.7.1945
(44) *E.Her.* 28.7.1945, 'Editorial'
(45) *E.Gaz.* 31.10.1945
(46) *E.Her.* 3.11.1945
(47) *E.Her.* 3.11.1945
(48) *E.Gaz.* 28.11.1951
(49) Straus, G. *Tribune* 28.12.1945
(50) Humphrey, G. (1989) op.cit. pp.7-8
(51) v. Surtees, J., op.cit. p.24
(52) *E.Gaz.* 10.9.1947
(53) ibid. 9.6.1948
(54) ibid. 7.5.1947
(55) ibid. 4.5.1949
(56) Keegan, W. (1984) *Mrs Thatcher's Economic Experiment,* p.138; Seldon, A .(1998) *Major – A Political Life,* p.34 & 80.
(57) *E.Gaz.* 8.8.1951
(58) ibid. 15.8.1951
(59) ibid. 30.1.1934
(60) 1 *Timothy*, Ch.2, v.11
(61) E.Gaz 21.9.1949
(62) E.Gaz. 14.6.1950
(63) ibid.
(64) For further dertails v. Jones, J. & Morris, M. (1986) *A-Z of Trade Unionism and Industrial Relations,* pp.99-101
(65) *E.Gaz.* 26.5.1948
(66) *E.Gaz.* 12.11.1947
(67) *E.Gaz.* 25.5.1949
(68) ibid.
(69) ibid. 13.4.1949
(70) ibid.
(71) ibid.
(72) ibid. 4.5.1949

CHAPTER 14

THE POST WAR YEARS 1945-1951

Growth of Trade Unions

One major change throughout the country for several years following 1945 was the growth in trade union membership and a change in attitude among thousands of working people who had strong memories of the social conditions many had faced during the economic slump of the 1930s. They could also easily recall how harsh the policies towards ordinary people had been. This affected Eastbourne in two ways; an increase in organisation and trade union membership within the town as well as throughout the country, which in turn, attracted several trade union annual conferences. Government ministers also held meetings in Eastbourne as well as other organisations. This was a development which would gather apace, often focussed on the facilities of the Winter Gardens, a Victorian building which could seat over 2,000 people. It was the venue for Hugh Gaitskell as Minister of Fuel in October 1947 and the Brighton Equitable Co-operative Society's public conference on the National Health Service in December of that year.

This Conference Trade was seen as a key service which the town was in an ideal situation to exploit. Excluding the Isle of Wight, on average, in most years, Eastbourne was the sunniest place on the South Coast (e.g.1950 - Hours of sunshine: Eastbourne 1,841.6; Weymouth 1,820; Worthing 1,805) It had good rail connections with London and most parts of the South East, with relatively easy connections to major London rail termini for onward journeys to the remainder of the country. Initially they had to rely on the attractive planning and architecture of the town and the two main Victorian venues in which to hold conferences. Excluding major political organisations and parties the town gradually began to attract more conferences. This growing success was shown by the figures for January to October 1951 when 21 Conferences were booked for a total of 8,000 delegates, including one for the largest rotary districts with a total of 2,000 members and their wives. (1) This trade increased steadily as a sample from these years indicates:-

1948	Catering Section of NUGMW
	Association of Teachers of Domestic Subjects
1949	Conference of Weights & Measures Inspectors
1950	Health Congress – Royal Sanitary Institutions (c. 2,300 delegates)
	National Association of Local Government Officers
	Society of Civil Servants – Executive & Analogous Grades (400 delegates)
	Association of Teachers in Technical Institutions

Prestige in this area continued to grow when the International Three-Day Dollar Convention organised by the Dollar Exports Board opened at Eastbourne in February attended by 3 Ministers of State, the Canadian High Commissioner, Secretary of the TUC, with leading British and American industrialists. The principal speakers were Hugh Gaitskell, Chancellor of the Exchequer, and Walter Gifford, the American Ambassador. However, later this Dollar Convention was considered to be of little benefit to local trade as others had been. There were several complaints because some sections of the holiday trade gained little benefit from the Convention and its organisation as was usually the case. Apparently only ten hotels were chosen by the conference organisers themselves, coaches were arranged to move delegates to the annoyance of local taxi drivers, newspapers were delivered directly from London and 'visitors were entertained so royally at somebody's expense, and refreshed in an enormous marquee so that they had no time to visit the town centre.' The cost to the town was about £500 but they seem to have derived little benefit from the event. (2)

With this notable exception, the town's holiday trade was progressing well with enquiries up from 6,200 to a record 7,525. In spite of all the hard effort, like many other towns wishing to expand this industry, a hindrance was the dominance and restrictions of the traditional Summer season in seaside towns. As the Mayor, alderman Fred Taylor believed, 'I think I am speaking for every hotelier when I say that to bring conferences to Eastbourne in the off season is like jam on the bread to the trade.' (3) Hence the continued ambition for the the construction of the Congress Theatre which was still many years into the future and not opened until 1963.

There was a desire on the part of many trade unionists for the town to be able to provide work for their members throughout the year so that they may receive regular wages and income to avoid their dependence on the seasonal nature of the holiday and developing conference trade. A considerable number of people earning a regular income would be of real benefit to the town. The Trades Council had in mind a trading estate for light industries of about 3 factories employing between 250 to 300 people. They made it clear that they were not seeking a 'Birmingham on Sea' but the means by which significant numbers of people could gain regular employment. They were disappointed when the Ministry of Town and Country Planning refused to grant a licence for such a development. (4) Light industries did come to the town later which proved successful in terms of another source of employment and new facilities for light industry.

A dinner and social gathering inviting 200 people including members of the TGWU representing drivers, conductors on the Eastbourne Corporation bus service and their wives and friends to which John Atherton and Mr Cannon, general manager and deputy manager respectively had been invited, brought together all those working for the Eastbourne Corporation Bus Service. The good working relationship between management and staff was praised, probably made easier by the service being comparatively small so that it was easy to discuss problems which might arise in the everyday running of the service. The fact that Eastbourne Corporation Bus Service was the oldest in the world seemed to instil a sense of pride among those working for the corporation. However developments in the U.K.

bus industry in the mid-1980s were profoundly influenced by Government policy towards nationalised industries. The town's bus service was privatised in 1986. (5)

The NUGMWU was specifically relevant to Eastbourne. W. Haffenden, Chairman, pointed out that, 'Looking after visitors was the chief industry of Eastbourne, and it was very important that amicable arrangements should prevail between employers and employed so that visitors could take away happy and lasting impressions of their stay here. Unless the workers were contented the best results could not be expected from any industry. The Eastbourne Trades Council would do all it could to help the local organisation of catering workers. 'A leading speaker, Mr H. Crane, referred to the Catering Wages Boards which should be monitoring working conditions but were found to vary widely; the hours in some sections of the industry little short of fiendish.'

Political meetings were held quite regularly in the town and in an age before widespread ownership of televisions they were often well attended. The Conservative Party booked the Winter Gardens inviting people to attend a 'Brains Trust' event based upon the popular Radio programme of that name in the 1940s produced by Howard Thomas. Professor Joad made his reputation on this show often beginning his response to a question with the reply 'It depends what you mean by...' The Tory Party event did not have much in common with the radio programme other than the title. It was really a vehicle to bring a like-minded audience together. For example Colonel Sutton told those attending to consider whether 'a rejuvenated Conservative Party would be able to save the country from madness if the Socialists were returned to power, then tragedy would stare the country in the face.' Councillor Parker told the audience, 'Conservatives stand for England and we must have them back in power.' (6) A few months later on a warm sunny day Labour celebrated May Day at the Seaside Recreation Ground. Reg Groves made a speech which was heckled by a man in the crowd concerning the London dock strike to which he replied '... they went on strike for a principle, a principle which we all serve – that is, to help one another.' Much of the rally was of a social nature with an opportunity for people to chat whilst their children played games.

Areas of Government Success

By 1948 a large part of the legislative programme of the Government had been approved by Parliament and was being put into practice; in 1946 the repeal of the Trades Disputes Act of 1927, the National Health Service Act, the National Insurance Act, the nationalisation of coal and civil aviation, with gas, electricity and transport to follow in 1948. Moreover the balance of payments was now in surplus and one result of devaluation a year later was to strengthen exports further. A remarkable achievement when the conditions of immediate postwar Britain are considered. It really seemed as if the government which had done so much to improve the living conditions of the majority of the population in a comparatively short time through the expansion of the welfare state, would be able to continue with this progress at an increasing rate thereby fulfilling the high expectations of the majority of the electorate.

That this recovery did not continue at the same pace was primarily because the government chose to divert a disproportionate amount of investment to a programme of armaments. Following the American Government's decision to end collaboration on atomic weapons with Canada and Britain, Attlee decided the UK should produce its own nuclear bomb. The Cabinet was not consulted and the £100 million cost was hidden in the supply estimates. (7) There were always bound to be demands from various sections of society for extra funding and the UK was no different in this respect. There was external pressure from the American military complex and President Truman for Britain to support their foreign policies; usually reinforced by the British military leadership. There were also associated demands for resources to exercise some control over various parts of the British Empire seeking independence which were sometimes a source of conflict. Fortunately the early granting of independence to India and Pakistan in 1947 had avoided the most complex and potentially contentious area of dispute. More lay ahead. Within the Labour Government there was opposition to plans to increase the armament budget as it followed that cuts in expenditure would have to be made elsewhere and that clearly meant in areas of welfare expenditure. The policy led to fierce debates within the Labour Party and numerous leading members such as Aneuran Bevan, Barbara Castle, Tom Driberg, Ian Mikardo and Harold Wilson were all highly critical of the diversion of funds from social to military expenditure.

During World War 2 conscription had been in force from 1939 until 1945. It was re-introduced in 1947 for 18 months, extended to two years in response to the

Korean War, the extra 6 months being paid at the full rate of regular servicemen maintained until 1963. More than two million young men entered the forces, inevitably some from Eastbourne, a minority of them fighting in a variety of areas from Palestine to Africa, and the Far East; Korea being one of the hardest experiences; 'An estimated 395 conscripts were killed in action in the fifty plus engagements overseas during National Service, while a couple of dozen are said to have been killed in secret experiments using chemical weapons at Porton Down in Wiltshire.' (8)

'The original rearmament programme – drawn up by the British General Staff in co-operation with the Pentagon – would have increased the defence budget to £6,000 million. The Cabinet reduced that total to £4,700 million. But that figure was still £1,000 million more than the maximum which the Cabinet had agreed to the previous September as the largest burden the economy could bear. Harold Wilson – then President of the Board of Trade – had no doubt that such military spending could not be sustained for long. He was vindicated when Winston Churchill... came back to office in October 1951 and reduced Labour's defence budget.... when Labour left office defence expenditure soaked up 14% of national income and half of total government expenditure.' (9) To try and cope with the increase in defence expenditure Gaitskel had frozen NHS expenditure at £393 million, cutting hospital budgets and saving £20 million by charging for false teeth and spectacles.... although the saving on the NHS budget was less than half of one per cent of the total rearmament package. (10) Aneuran Bevan, Harold Wilson and John Freeman all resigned over the issue. As Bevan was to say,

'Rearmament should be approached with restraint, not with enthusiasm.'

From this time onwards Britain's expenditure on armaments would be out of proportion to its gross national product. The result meant that the numerous demands to invest in much of the economic and social structure of the country which had been neglected by the economic slump of the 1930s and the funding necessary to fight the Second World war were forced to take a backward place. To take but one example, the railway system, a product of the Victorian age, needed vast investment to rationalize routes, undertake a unified system of electrification and renovate stations, many of which were essentially Victorian buildings. Because the system had been one of individual private companies dominating regions the electrification which had taken place was one in which there was a third rail system introduced in the Southern Region from 1929 onwards whilst an overhead pantographic cable system was developed on the Midland Region from the 1950s onwards. The investment needed for the whole rail network was vast and more than half a century after the second World War had ended it was still incomplete, with plans for the Western Region to electrify its system not under way until a further 25 years later. This gives some indication of how the country's infrastructure was constantly held back by vast expenditure on armaments. Such choices were the result of a combination of pressures from economic, political, military and industrial sources of influence. How far they were the correct choices for the country then, and now, will always be a matter for debate and political opinion.

In spite of all this the country had made rapid progress primarily due to the introduction of Marshall Aid in 1948 to Britain, France, the Benelux countries and then Italy....It provided a huge injection of economic aid to these countries; 'Britain was a supreme beneficiary ...In all, twelve billion dollars was assigned to European economic recovery up to 1st January when Gaitskell, then the Chancellor, felt able to announce that Britain no longer needed its quota of Marshall Aid, so rapid had been its economic recovery'. (11)

1944 Education Act

The 1944 Education Act was a response to demands which had been building up during the inter-War years. To that extent it could be argued it was out of date by the time it was enacted but whilst at times of conflicting ideas, progress for those seeking change can be irritatingly slow, it can still be seen as progress. The two major products of the Act were the raising of the school leaving age to 15 years and the provision of secondary schooling for all children. (12) Prior to this date the majority of children went from a junior school at 11 years of age on to a senior school until they left at 14 years, most of them entering routine jobs in factories, warehouses, offices and retail. A small minority were able to enter into an apprenticeship to train as skilled workers becoming for example engineers, plumbers, carpenters or electricians. The wages were low whilst training, but once qualified, they were able to earn above the average income of workers termed as 'unskilled' or 'semi-skilled'.

A few upon leaving school would continue their studies at evening classes and gain qualifications by part-time study in order to make progress at their place of work but those who completed a course independently in this way needed a great deal of determination and effort. It was easier when employers provided them with some time during the week to attend day-time courses. Large numbers of people stayed in certain areas of employment for most of their working lives on the basic wage paid by their employer. There were no occupational pensions for most workers during these years and in many factories there was no pay for sickness, bank holidays or annual holidays. Hence many workers paid weekly into a club which provided some money if they became ill or to cover unpaid annual and bank holidays.

Entry to secondary schools for most children was by parents paying fees with a growing minority receiving some financial help from the school in question or a scholarship from the local authority. Even so only a minority of pupils, 545,000 by the late 1930s, received a secondary education. An even smaller number entered technical, commercial or art colleges at 13 years of age. This general description of schooling which applied to Eastbourne was true for most areas but there were always exceptions. For example many areas did not offer 13 plus colleges because their population was insufficient to justify such provision. In these cases it was often possible for students to travel daily to a larger town providing relevant courses. Whilst the 1944 Education Act recommended raising the school leaving age to 15 and providing secondary schooling for all, implementing this took some time because there were insufficient school facilities and teachers available. Moreover, the country was in the process of trying to recover from the most destructive war it had ever faced.

However progress was made; the rise in the school leaving age to 15 years for all children took place in 1947 whilst the recommendation to 16 in 1970 was implemented in September 1972.

In the Eastbourne area there were 'senior schools' where the majority of children went until they left school at 14 years of age, many in buildings which had originally been constructed as elementary schools, now changed to secondary modern schools where all pupils received a secondary education; such as Bedewell Central School/ St Philip's 1907 which later moved to Priory Road and was renamed Bishop Bell in 1958. Cavendish was a centrally located senior school opened in 1905 which became a secondary modern school and was relocated to the former girls' high school in Eldon Road in 1981-82. There was a boys' grammar school opened in 1899 followed by a separate girls grammar school in 1903. When Eastbourne adopted a comprehensive system in which children moved on at 16 years of age to a separate 6th form, the two schools would amalgamate and move to a common site on King's Drive to form a 6th form college.

The story of education in Eastbourne is complex and there is no space to deal with a detailed history here but suffice to say that among the numerous schools in the town during the first half of the 20th century, both private and 'local authority', many had their origins in the late 19th century, changed their names at different times and moved their premises on several occasions. (v. *Historic Schools in Eastbourne,* Eastbourne Public Library) There was a need for change to cope with a continuing decline in the rural school population and by contrast, the increasing urban school population. The proposed raising of the school leaving age increased the need for new secondary schools in the town even further. The rural problem could be seen in the district of Wealden bordering on Eastbourne; Jevington was unviable as a school by the interwar period, the last log book entry being recorded in 1926. Wilmington numbers of 'senior' pupils had also declined whilst Pevensey could not cope with an increase in numbers of older children. The answer was the construction of a purpose built secondary school in Willingdon in an area of growing population, to which older children were bused from rural areas daily. This secondary school was opened in 1953.

Eastbourne was faced with many demands for new buildings and repairs to those damaged by war-time bombing. Just prior to the outbreak of the Second World War a 'senior school' had been built in Broderick Road in 1939 to cater for the children on the 'new' Hampden Park estate and the Girls' Grammar School had moved into new premises in Eldon Road in November of that year. To fulfil the intentions of the new 1944 Education Act in providing secondary schooling for all children, many schools would have to be enlarged to cope with the extra numbers of pupils staying on at school. By 1947 all children were gaining the benefit of an extra year of schooling although widespread 'streaming' meant that only a minority were following national examination courses. With continued pressure for new buildings and repairs to those badly damaged during the War, older schools had to wait their turn, until the 1950s. They were forced to cope in old cramped buildings with few facilities. It was not until the mid 1950s that two new secondary schools were constructed to cope with a continuing increase in pupil numbers; namely Ratton (1956) and Bishop Bell (1958). These were years when the influence of the Educational Psychologist Cyril Burt were gaining ground. Alongside some of his like minded colleagues he argued that a person's academic ability could be measured fairly accurately around eleven years of age by tests designed to measure their intelligence, or 'intelligence quotient' as it became known. Initially it was believed that these tests would be fairer for all children because they would not reflect the quality of the school, the environment within the area in which the school was located or the education, occupation and social background of the parents. It was true that a number of working class children did gain entry to selective secondary schools due to their success in these examinations but follow up studies showed that a disproportionate number of them did not complete the five year course.

Many of the national issues concerning education were aired by delegates attending conferences held in the town and were therefore almost bound to encourage discussions locally. So too did annual speeches given by senior teaching staff to parents at the end of term. Education by the 'practitioners' was always less prescriptive than that by those from 'outside the system' who sometimes ran the risk of basing their ideas upon personal school experience which took place a generation earlier. Moreover whilst comparatively few can speak from the experience of being a train driver, nurse or factory worker, virtually everyone in the country once attended school. It is often difficult for some to realise that schools and colleges have to constantly adapt to new ideas and circumstances to meet the constant changes they face. Mr G. Boyden of the Boys' Grammar School (13) in an end of term speech to the pupils and staff said that when it came to standards;

> We need our minor aims and lesser goals, and they are all to the good if we do not lose sight of our greater purpose. And this is the total education of each individual and on this road certificates, prizes, achievements, accomplishments are encouraging milestones. No less, but certainly no more. (14)

The need to make space for a broad curriculum to emphasise the importance of the arts was made by Kenneth Holmes from the Leicester School of Art when he opened an exhibition of 450 drawings and paintings and 200 pieces of craft at the Towner Art Gallery from a wide range of local schools. At the same time he expressed the need to encourage music and dance 'as an antidote to the dullness of mechanisation and the drabness of so many lives, and for the right use of greater leisure in an increasingly complex world.' (15) (*ibid.*)

Post-War Shortage of Teachers

There was a shortage of qualified teachers in the years immediately following the end of the War as many young men and women who would have trained during those years had been members of the armed forces or in other national organisations such as the Land Army. In addition the demand for teachers had been increased by the requirement of the 1944 Education Act for all children to undergo a course of secondary education. In December 1943 Gilbert Flemming returned to the Board of Education to cope with this situation and a number of 'Emergency Teacher Training Colleges' running 13 month courses were established in several places such as Trent Park in Middlesex and Bognor Regis College in West Sussex. In Eastbourne, Mr J.C. Aspden, Chief Education Officer of the town, was very aware of the empty premises of many pre-War private boarding schools, which had been evacuated, many of which would not be returning to the town. The demand for such schooling had declined. Some did return, such as Eastbourne College, but others had collapsed financially for lack of pupils. Their buildings remained, some still occupied by various organisations from the War. Aspen would play a key role in bringing two teacher training colleges to the town.

Chelsea College of Physical Education, once the responsibility of Chelsea Polytechnic, had been evacuated to Borth, on the West Coast of Wales. It was assumed that the earlier link with the Polytechnic would be resumed after 1945. The Chelsea College of P.E. was anxious for this to take place in order to restore mutual contact between staff, the educational value of polytechnic functions for all students, a centralised administration and opportunities for experimentation. (17) In time it was recognised that a suitable site in the London area could not be found for the P.E. College. The Ministry of Education, anxious that the college should survive and the L.C.C., approached Eastbourne Education Committee where Aspden realised the opportunity this presented to the town. Numerous meetings throughout 1946-47 finalised the details but some delay was experienced whilst Admiralty personnel vacated Hillbrow and St Winnifreds, once private boarding schools, which together with Granville Crest were purchased for £52,919. Chelsea College of P.E. finally moved in after a further £64,179 had been spent on fittings. Eleven acres already obtained could be used for six full-sized hockey pitches and two cricket squares. The administration of the College was formally transferred from Chelsea Polytechnic (LCC) to the Eastbourne Local Education Authority on 1st April, 1947. (18) (*ibid*) By October 1948 the college was ready to receive students and the future of the college was assured.

A further opportunity now arose for the town from the Emergency Training Scheme for Teachers. On the 15th December 1942 E.C. Bray produced a memo on the *Supply of Teachers* indicating that there would be a problem in providing a sufficient number of trained teachers because many were still in the armed services or other organisations related to issues of war. Moreover, the proposed introduction of secondary education for all would bring further demands for teachers to cope with the extra year of schooling to be introduced after the War. They would not only include teachers who had been called up for the War but also those who would like to train as teachers. 'The LEAs were advised that the Board proposed to set up 20 to 30 additional colleges, each accommodating about 250 students to be provided by LEAs and funded centrally. Selected LEAs were to be encouraged to earmark suitable buildings, ...with a view to the future need of permanent provision and select and prepare tutors who would ultimately staff the centres.' (19) Already there were plans to expand the programme to a further 50 colleges, each catering for 200 students and when fully operational providing accommodation for about 10,000 trainees

(8,000 men and 2,000 women) each year; the colleges to be organised by LEAs acting as agents for the Board. The intensive course of 12 calender months did raise a few questions as to whether it would be long enough given earlier two year courses but it soon became apparent that the experiences gained by many during the War years, in the armed forces or other services, would more than make up for the shortage of time they would be given to train as teachers.

The practical problem facing some LEAs was a matter of finding suitable buildings which would have space for classrooms and accommodation. Eastbourne would take advantage once more of the pre-War boarding school facilities of private schools which were no longer financially viable. Aspen was able to offer the facilities of Robert Dodd as a possible site for a college to the Ministry of Education who had been pleased to accept, although at the outset, as with many of the Emergency Colleges, there was no understanding that they would last more than a year or two.

In February 1948 a farewell meeting was held for the first batch of student teachers who had undertaken a thirteen month course in teacher training at Eastbourne Training College which was housed in Robert Dodd in the Meads area of the town. Over 200 hundred students had enrolled when the course started in 1947; 189 completed the course one year later, during which time, some decided, for a variety of reasons, it was not a career they wished to pursue. Significant numbers of those who had qualified were mature students with various previous work experiences which sometimes gave them considerable initial respect among the children they were to teach.

Mr M.L. Jacks, Director of the Department of Education at Oxford University gave the address at the final assembly. He praised the range of activities and societies the students had developed in such a short time at the college. He told them:

> Now they were going out into the world, not to make large fortunes, but to educate the young and try to bring them up as good men and women.... (We) were coming to look upon education as, what he might call, one of the key industries of the times with the teacher one of the key members in modern civilisation.....(one of the biggest challenges...is the problem of providing secondary education for 100% of the children in this country.) A new humanism was coming into education and the schools. In the new Education Act for the first time we had the child at the centre and the system trying to fit itself to the child. He believed that was a tremendous change and made an enormous difference to our whole educational outlook. (20)

Within months of the planned Emergency Teachers Training College closure, plans were afoot for a new Training College for Women under the principalship of Miss P.E. Ward, (formerly principal of Oakley Training College at Cheltenham) together with ten colleagues. They had only 16 weeks to formulate a contract to acquire adequate buildings, equipment and funding as the college was scheduled to open in September 1949. All the expenditure would be reimbursable by the Ministry of Education but it was important to receive tenders for the work as soon as possible. Initially a quotation from a London based company for £11,185 was considered for the complete refurnishing of Boston House but when the full Education Committee met on the 28^h June the amount of this order was reduced to £6,819. Disagreements arose from those 'protesting against orders being placed outside the town without any local competition, and Councillors Swain, Parker and Wood argued that local firms should be able to submit tenders for the work.' (21)

The college for women following a two year teacher training course opened on time in 1949 and proved such a success that the Senate of London University resolved it should continue as a Constituent College of the Institute of Education. From the start the college received the support of the town councillors, including Alderman Caffyn, who was one of the college governors. Sir Maurice Gwyer, ex-Chancellor of Delhi University, spoke of the importance of doctors and teachers in any society making the observation that 'doctors are concerned with sick bodies; teachers with those who are healthy and their business is to develop mind and build up character.' (22)

Meanwhile further along the coast a smaller town was able to exploit the same situation they found themselves in when another proposed teacher training college was looking for premises. The Board of Education wished to site the new colleges in urban areas with a considerable population and Beddington near Croydon was suggested as a possibility for one of the new emergency teacher training colleges. The newly appointed principal, Roy Macklin, visited the area but rejected it because, like Eastbourne, there were empty private boarding school premises available at Bognor Regis, in what had been, St Michaels School. These buildings had been previously owned by the Woodard Corporation, a Church of England educational establishment which occupied this 18th century crescent of very large houses originally built by the Earl of Hotham in the hope of persuading George 1V to spend some of his time in this area along the coast from Brighton. Hence it was known as Hotham Terrace. There were four buildings within extensive parkland which offered an ideal place for a residential college, although considerable renovation was needed. The citing of the college at a Sussex coastal town owed its location to the same reason as Eastbourne's post-War Teacher Training Colleges; the availability of empty boarding school facilities. These 'temporary Emergency Colleges' would all be absorbed into universities in later years. The three mentioned here, Chelsea, Eastbourne and Bognor Regis, would all provide a basis for steady expansion over the following years and develop a wide range of courses in addition to teacher training.(23)

Nursery Facilities

At the other end of the age range a decision was made by the Eastbourne Town Council to acquire premises for a children's residential nursery by acquiring Thornwick, Selwyn Road. There would need to be considerable work on the site including the cost of 'extending, adapting, equipping, and furnishing the premises as a nursery for 21 children at a cost of £13,670 plus a further £4,549 annually. There were so many strands to education in general, many of which were interrelated, that various aspects were always seeking to gain the attention of society because of the specific needs of different children; a matter which came under lengthy discussion by Superintendents of School Attendance Departments at a three day conference at the Winter Gardens. In this complicated and taxing area of work, Mr S. Brogden, the new President of the Association stated, 'he was still awaiting evidence that the work was being done better than, or in some cases, even as well as under their guidance'. (24)

More difficult for the Council to decide upon was the question of acquiring and maintaining a residential nursery for children under five years of age who were in the Council's care. At the time they were accommodated at 120-122 Green Street but these premises were now considered unsuitable for a nursery although they could be adequate for older children. The Medical Officer had reported that facilities were inadequate for the health and welfare of the children under five. The Highlands Nursing Home in Carew Road was proposed and by six votes to two it was decided to go ahead with this proposal providing the future use of Green Street premises could be decided. However doubts were raised when the proposed costs were considered. The purchase price was £10,350; the annual upkeep would be £5,022. Based on 21 children it would work out at £4.12s.2d. per week per child. One problem was that the Council had been told by the Inspector of the Home Office that the present children's home was 'inadequate, unsuitable and obsolete'. The Council had a duty to them. They were children deprived of the care of their parents,...the need for this home was urgent'. It was the running costs which worried the councillors if they went ahead with the scheme; £340 for a matron, £190 for her assistant and a nursery teacher at £350.

General Election 1950

The Constituency had been enlarged by 1950, now comprising Eastbourne, Bexhill and the following parishes in the rural district of Hailsham; East Dean, Friston, Jevington, Willingdon, Pevensey, Hooe, Ninfield and Wartling. The size of the electorate had increased from 44,124 in 1945 to 69,932 in 1950. The General Election was scheduled to take place on the 28th February. First came the adoption of candidates with Charles Taylor selected again for the Conservative Party. He was the favourite having polled 18,173 in 1945 to Labour's 12,367 votes. Not surprising given the location of his constituency in 1948 he had become President of the Residential Hotels and later Vice Chairman of the Council of British Hotels. *(WikiPedia's* entry for Taylor later would describe him as an 'English Business man and Conservative politician') He became Managing Director of Cow and Gate, later Unigate, and President of Grosvenor House (Park Lane) Ltd. He received a knighthood in 1954 and several other honorary awards)

Speaking in Eastbourne at the Business and Professional Women's Club in 1950 he declared, 'The two world wars proved for all time the case for the emancipation of women, who did men's jobs extremely well.' However he expressed some worries about aspects of the Welfare State: '...he hoped the women would advise the youngsters that self reliance and the serving of others were more pleasant than what was obtained from a more beneficent state.' This was in line with Conservative Party policy. The Liberal candidate chosen first was Major Turner Bridger but he had to withdraw due to ill health. His replacement was Lt.Col. C.L.H.

Douglas-Bate. Born in Ladysmith, he had served with the Royal Fusiliers, commissioned in 1916 and retired in 1926 only to be recalled to the army in 1939, finally retiring in 1946. (25) He believed 'The Services should be brought into one big defence force, and he was not able to give conscription his full support. He thought that young men should be released for production and the export drive....Old age pensions and unemployment and sick benefits should be raised and all contributions under the present National Insurance Act abolished.' (26)

Reg Groves was the Labour candidate and his background contrasted considerably with his political rivals. His parents were poor and confined to a one room dingy apartment so when they had a second child he went to live with his grandparents in Essex. He left school at fourteen years of age and gained experience of a variety of jobs; messenger, engineer, journalist, editor of a weekly journal and author of several books on social and political history. In 1937 he became Labour candidate for Aylesbury, Bucks, where the Labour vote was around 4,000 in the 1930s. He worked to increase it to 7,000 in 1938 and 16,000 in 1945. Eastbourne would present him with a major challenge. (27)

The Conservative and Labour candidates faced a considerable programme of meetings; the Liberal candidate less so:-

February:-

- 4th Lottbridge Arms then Hampden Park (Open Air) [Cons]
- 6th Little Common (Cons), Town Hall (Lab)
- 7th St Andrews (Cons), Winter Gardens (All Parties)

8th Stone Cross (Cons), then Pevensey Bay (Cons)
9th Boreham Street (Cons) then Wartling, (Cons) - Hampden Park (Lab)
10th Eldon Road (Lab),then Willingdon (Lab)
14th Winter Gardens (Cons), Polegate Recreation (Lab)
15th Winter Gardens (Lib)
17th Meads Parish Hall (Cons)
20th Seaside Library (Lab)
22nd Winter Gardens (Cons)

23rd – Polling Day

The local newspapers contained reports of all the meetings during these days and some attracted large audiences for few people possessed television sets enabling them to hear political arguments when sitting in their living room in 1950. There were certain features common to all the speakers; they had nothing complementary to say about any aspect of the policies of their rivals and they seemed to imply that they had the solutions to most of the problems facing the town and the country. Indoor meetings were more likely to be attended by those supportive or sympathetic to the ideas of the Party who organised the event; outdoor meetings usually provided a venue where there were opportunities for some vocal disagreements to be voiced within the audience to points made by the principal speaker. One Saturday lunch time at Hampden Park, Taylor faced a considerable amount of heckling from some members in the crowd 'but he appeared to enjoy the experience and was never at a loss for words.' (28) Reg Groves experienced 'some laughter and dissent' from some ladies at a meeting held in the Winter

Gardens. Some meetings attracted those who were in general agreement with the speaker and it could be partly a matter of telling most of them what they wanted to hear. The main exception to this was the meeting arranged by the Eastbourne Business and Professional Women's Club at the Winter Gardens presided over by Miss E. Hilton. The three candidates were invited to address them. Mr Groves believed that a major achievement of 'Five years of Labour government had seen an extension and expansion of the social services.' Mr Douglas-Bate claimed '...although the other political parties professed Liberal principles in some form or other only the Liberal Party could carry them through...it was the champion of democratic principles, tolerance, independence and responsibility.'

It is not possible to summarise the many claims and counter-claim of the candidates, less still of their followers. There were occasions speakers faced supporters with questions which were not possible to treat in a logical manner. Taylor was asked about 'the increase in gangsterism during the Socialist Government...as a result of the punishments they are dealing out as anything like sufficient...' In agreeing with her in part of his reply he suggested, 'I feel we want a little bit more religion in State schools.' In fact religious education was a compulsory part of the curriculum in all local authority schools as was morning assembly, which included an act of 'collective worship'. Mr Taylor was not to know this from personal experience as he had been educated privately. At a Labour meeting a Miss Pallister stated, 'She was one of those who felt that long ago they should have brought their politics into the House of God...' Fortunately in most areas religion was not a divisive issue.

Questions were sometimes asked mischievously by those fully aware of the likely response to try to wrong-foot their rivals. For example the Conservative agent told a *Gazette* reporter that his Party did not intend holding any political meetings on the Sabbath....the Liberals were in agreement with this policy. (29) There was clearly a hope of embarrassing Labour on this issue but they replied that Sunday meetings were something of a tradition in the Labour Movement. This 'tradition' derived from the reality of the past conditions of working class people who worked a six day week, often comprising hard manual labour, with Sunday their only day to relax. In the same vein Mr Hamilton Fyfe challenged Charles Taylor 'to debate the issues of the election in circumstances mutually agreeable before the end of the campaign.' Taylor replied, 'The issues at this election are so tremendously important, that it is simply not possible to carry on an academic debate on Socialism with every Tom, Dick or Hamilton.' (30)

In June 1951, just as there was sometimes humour in political pronouncements, so too one can find feigned pity for opponents such as that of Lord Burghley at a Conservative Party Meeting at the Winter Gardens commenting on the Labour Government: 'These men (the Government) have been trying to do their best – let us give them credit for it – but it is not good enough. They are not men enough for the job'. [Applause] (31) Reg Groves, by contrast, thought Labour's programme had brought real benefits to many of the population: 'The Labour government had set British industry and trade on the road to recovery and had legislated, carried on and developed the social services as well, including a national health service'. (32) The latter would prove to be one of the most significant achievements of any modern government and remain popular among most of the public whatever their political views might be.

At political meetings, statements of principle could be made knowing there was little chance of them being put to the test. At a meeting of the Conservatives at Meads Parish Hall councillor Eric Edgerton who was presiding said, 'Those who don't vote will definitely deserve Socialism' whilst his fellow councillor Leonard Parker claimed,' Universal franchise carries a fearful responsibility. I would rather see you vote the other way than not vote at all!' On the 18th February at a Conservative Party meeting of nearly one thousand people at the town hall held under the chairmanship of Alderman Caffyn with the principal speaker being Sir Alan Herbert, (1890-1971) the English humorist, playwright and law activist. He wrote for *Punch* magazine and had been an MP representing Oxford University since 1935 at a time when there were 12 university places for MPs. (a system abolished in 1948 alongside business and graduate votes for Parliamentary elections.) He was one of the speakers. (33) He had stood for the University under the title of 'Independent' but as he would make clear at this gathering he was strongly in favour of the Conservative cause now and in the past. . He told the audience, '.. he had been at a similar gathering in 1945 and spoke in support of Charles Taylor then and was glad to return and give a helping hand. He proclaimed his own determination to vote for the Conservative candidate in his own constituency of South Hammersmith....Even if I thought the Labour Government were right in all they did, he said, I would still vote against them because of their disgusting arrogance.' (34) It seems unclear how a person with such clearly expressed political preferences could stand as an 'Independent' MP for Oxford, or any other constituency.

The final result in Eastbourne was an overwhelming victory for Charles Taylor who polled 35,425 votes, with Groves for Labour receiving 18,304 votes and C.H.D. Bate 5,766 votes for the Liberal Party. As can be seen, Taylor's overall vote was greater than the Labour and Liberal vote combined. It indicated the immediate post-War popularity of the Conservatives and the early decline nationally of the Liberal Party for some years to come. Whilst the agreement between all political parties to forgo general elections during the Second World War for both practical reasons and those of maintaining national unity at such a time, given the social composition of the town the Liberal Party vote must have been worrying to their supporters; a proportion of whom voted for them because they were not either of the other two parties Almost an expression of political neutrality! After 1929 when they polled 7,182 votes, less than half of the Conservatives and approximately 1,000 less than Labour, they did not stand again in the town until 1945. By this time their vote had slumped to 2,797, which compared most unfavourably with the Conservatives 18,173 and Labour's 12,637. They improved on their number of votes in 1950 to 5,766 but this was a smaller proportion of a larger electorate in which the Conservatives polled more than six times that number and Labour more than three times. They did not put up a candidate at the General Election the following year!

Recognising their lack of electoral success at Eastbourne a Liberal Local District Association was formed in the town linked to Bexhill in March under the chairmanship of Mr W. Billeness, with proposals to put forward candidates for the forthcoming local elections in May with Central and Cavendish wards as their target. In the event their ambitions were not realised for a list of all the candidates standing for election on the 11th May, including those unopposed, were all listed as either Conservative or Labour with the exception of Mr Tomsett, who had been Labour but stood this time as an Independent. (35) Open support for the Labour Movement within certain areas of the town continued to be expressed by the traditional May Day celebrations in 1950 at the Recreation Grounds in Seaside, as witnessed by the attendance of about 350 people on a glorious sunny day. Councillor Rainey drew attention to the need for more council housing for working class families. Once that need had been fulfilled the town could then get on with building for private house demands. (36)

Charles Taylor's involvement nationally with the hotel industry was recognised as giving him a useful position to champion the town's major form of income. Some hotels and restaurants had good reputations and considerable prestige but salaries were not high. In such establishments trade union membership would be unknown. Few local inhabitants booked accommodation frequently in the town's hotels but they were often regular diners in their restaurants, either with a few friends, a social event such as a wedding or as part of a local organisation which had booked a meeting and meal for those attending. This limited the local demand in a way which did not apply to the associated entertainment industry where residents in the town and surrounding areas were just as likely to be interested in a show as visitors. Looking back to the 1930s it was clear that the stars of that era added to the attractions of the town for visitors as well as the local population. Among those who had appeared at local theatres were Fay Compton (1894-1978); stage actress who also appeared in films; Cicely Courtledge (1893-1980) stage/music hall actress married to Jack Hulbert (1892-1978); as well as the popular American actor and famous singer Paul Robeson (1898-1976), who sang at the Winter Gardens, which was also the venue for the Municipal Orchestra. The new bandstand was opened on the promenade in 1935 and by this decade there were about a dozen cinemas in the town with the familiar long queues of a Saturday evening.

By their very nature the hotel and entertainments industry were partly reliant upon the weather and general prosperity in the country. As has been mentioned the Trades Council wished to gain regular employment for men and women and were extremely disappointed when the Ministry of Town and Council Planning refused to grant a licence for the creation of a small trading estate. (37) A positive note was struck by Vic Feather, the Assistant Secretary of the TUC when he visited members of the EDTC at their annual dinner in November 1950. He pointed out that 'Seaside resorts would depend more and more on the weekly wage earner; there were now 20 million people who were getting holidays with pay. Eastbourne should give every encouragement to members of the great trade unions to visit them.' (38) Encouraging though this was as a source of income for the town it was nevertheless almost certain that most people would visit the town during the Summer months to fit in with the annual holidays of their employees at this time due to the need to fit in with school holidays and in the hope, not always realised, that these would be the warmest, if not necessarily the sunniest, weeks of the year.

During the same month the writer, Mr William Offord, chairman of the Sussex District Advisory Committee of the London and South-Eastern Regional Board for Industry, warned Eastbourne, Brighton and Hastings that they can, as pleasure resorts, 'earn only a small part of the income needed to support their populations and he suggested that the three towns must concentrate more on manufacturing industries to ensure their future'. In replying the Town Clerk, Mr Busby, pointed out that he regarded the hotels as 'Eastbourne's principal industry.' Moreover, 'Eastbourne has always been famous as a residential town, a place to which persons can come to live when they retire, knowing they will have an exceedingly pleasant place in which to spend their retirement. Nor should the large number of educational establishments in the town be overlooked'. In terms of the pre-War schools this was no longer true but the growing number of post-18 years students in colleges had by now taken their places, literally occupying the very buildings once used by the large number of private school pupils. It was also true that many of the retired who moved to the town were on restricted incomes and limited in their spending power. (39)

For many it seemed the pre-War image of the town no longer seemed sufficient by itself to carry on providing the jobs necessary to allow Eastbourne, as well as their neighbouring towns, to establish the necessary source of well-paid work which could only come by developing further industrial development. It was for this reason that there was pressure for alternative sources of investment to supplement areas of work primarily related to the 'holiday' trade. Such a positive move in this direction was the Dental Estimates Board which took over the buildings of the Amalgamated Approved Society retaining significant numbers of the original staff and recruiting within the town many more. Planning permission was necessary for construction of comparatively small units and gradually these began to gain approval, such as the Hampden Park Trading Estate, with more similar developments in the years following.

The Building Trade

Unemployment was the scourge of the building trade for much of the first half of the 20th century as demands for work were clearly related to cycles of economic boom and slump. Within this trade some outside work was particularly affected by adverse weather conditions, such as bricklaying, whereas painting could sometimes continue for interior work. However painting also faced seasonal problems as the following published letter illustrated:

> In soliciting the assistance of householders and hotels, etc., to put as much interior painting work as possible in hand this forthcoming winter we take this opportunity of conveying our thanks for the consideration given to our request in recent years gone by. Much of the unemployment in the painting trade during Winter months can be eliminated by an

intelligent anticipation of the requirements of the various departments....The work can be done equally well during the Winter months and the employment created will help to reduce the already heavy list of unemployed and the consequent drain of the unemployment fund.' J. Gibson, Secretary. (40)

During the years from around 1923 to 1931 with fluctuating patterns of economic demand many manual workers had faced hard and sometimes dangerous conditions, especially those engaged in heavy industry. There was an absence of safety measures, partly because equipment such as hard hats and steel capped boots were unavailable. In some places, where jobs were scarce, those who spoke up against poor conditions were likely to be in danger of losing their jobs. Working conditions for many did not begin to improve until the post-1945 years.

One building worker who was very aware of the precarious nature of the building trade in the town was Henry Haizelden (1884-1950) who was born locally and became an active member of the Labour Movement, including the National Society of Painters and the District Trades Council of which he was secretary for many years, resigning on medical advice in 1946. He was also a member of the Food Control and Co-operative Social Welfare Committees. In the local elections of 1933 and 1934 he stood unsuccessfully as a Labour candidate for Central Ward. He was typical of those people who freely devote many hours of their time and energy to an organisation which they believe will be of benefit to many other people. (He was presented with a Trade Union Gold Medal for 'long and devoted' service and there is a plaque acknowledging this work in the Trades Union Club in Seaside Road.)

He had been pleased to see the building trade enjoy comparative prosperity during the immediate post-War reconstruction boom. Yet within a short time of his death painters were faced with a deteriorating employment situation. By the late Autumn of 1950 'more than 40 were out of work – the highest figure for September since the War. Increased prices and the War in Korea are among the main factors contributing to the present slump.' (41) There were over 600 painters in the town, more than double the pre-War number, according to Mr Philcox, Secretary of the Eastbourne Branch of the National Society of Painters. The work needed for renovating the War damage in the town and its environment was all but complete, thereby contributing to the rise in unemployment. Increases in the cost of materials had affected small private contractors in particular who could no longer afford to pay their employees during 'waiting periods'. The Eastbourne Trades Council at a meeting with the Local Employment Committee were endeavouring to get an increased grant for jobs in which painters were chiefly concerned, as they believed this trade was the worst affected. Mr Philcox, stated that with the increased post War number of painters they were 'heavily over manned.'

The Union recognised the situation readily enough and the predicament it caused for without detracting from the skills and experience of painters, many believed that for small jobs around the home they could undertake the work themselves, for even if their attempts were not as satisfactory the total outlay would be cheaper. By contrast, few would attempt brick work, rewiring their house or large scale carpentry alterations. To that extent painters were more vulnerable than some other skilled workers within the building industry.

At a local Employment Committee there was some resentment expressed at the employment of Polish carpenters who it was feared might work for cheaper wages. A hostel would be required to supply necessary accommodation for them but there were doubts as to whether the numbers involved would make such a proposal realistic. Significant numbers of Polish workers had arrived in London during the early 1940s, having escaped from the German invasion and many joined the British military services. A considerable number remained in the country and after the War gained work with companies such as London Transport. Because of their wartime experience they did not attract resentment but clearly in Eastbourne with its precarious job markets there was always the fear that extra available workers might lead to reductions in wages. (42) (There would be considerable debate concerning the recruitment of non-native born British people in future years!)

Local requests for Council Funding

There was always pressure upon the Town Council to finance a wide range of projects but whilst the resources of towns were limited and relied heavily upon Government grants, interest groups varied in their capacity to persuade councils to support different schemes. To take but two examples. Given this was the period of the development of nuclear weapons, councillor W. Benson Dare proposed digging a nuclear shelter for the town's inhabitants under the Downs. It was rejected as completely uneconomical in terms of costs and impractical in attempts to evacuate the population to the site. By contrast the town's newly appointed Senior Librarian, Mr K. Harrison, drew attention to the library stock of books pointing out that many were in poor condition, and improvement was needed in their services to children and hospitals. He explained that recommended expenditure for libraries was 2 shillings per head but Eastbourne only provided eleven pence per head. He also condemned the system of a half day closure during the week. Dealing with library finances was likely to prove less costly and more practical than the provision of a nuclear shelter under the Downs! Some Conservative councillors put forward a resolution to ban the *Daily Worker,* which councillor Parker described as 'a filthy Communist rag'. He did not think it right that it should be subsidised by the ratepayers. Four Labour councillors, Rainey, A.J. Marshall, Mrs. E. Lee and G. Bass protested suggesting such action was not a matter of trying to suppress Communism but abolishing one of the selection of national newspapers provided by the library. However these were the years of the 'Cold War' when freedom of expression was under great pressure throughout most of the world. The newspaper was accordingly withdrawn.

There were a couple of meetings of Conservative groups within two weeks of the beginning of 1951. The first took place at the Winter Gardens where a group of Young Conservatives held a week-end Conference which contained a surprise for many. An ex-Army current affairs lecturer who had served in the War and travelled extensively cast himself as 'Socialist' to put forward as he claimed 'the strongest possible arguments in favour of the return of an enlightened Socialist Government as opposed to "Tory Plutocracy"'. (43) In promoting some of the policies of the Labour Government he was met with some laughter and cat-calls. It was all light-hearted and gave the audience ample opportunity to respond accordingly. For example when he advanced a plea for 'control of the water supply' he was met with the question, 'What about beer?' By his novel approach at least he held the attention of the young audience. The following month the Eastbourne and Bexhill Conservative Association held a meeting at the Claremont Hotel to discuss the May local elections. (44) In Central Ward Mrs Broomfield had been successful and joined her husband as another Conservative representative for the ward. This prompted some correspondence in the *Eastbourne Gazette* questioning how far a husband and wife with similar political allegiances could be be considered as truly representative of the people living in the ward.

The local Labour Party were also making preparations for the same elections. Inevitably in these years, many people had only returned comparatively recently from military service in World War 2. Among these people were Mr R. Dodds, who had served with the Queen's Royal Regiment and within two weeks of his release in 1945 had been elected councillor for Labour in Central Ward and was now a candidate for Roseland. Mr Frank Pope, who had served over four years during World War 1 and another six years with REME in World War 2, was standing for Labour in Cavendish ward. Dodds had been secretary of the AUBTW, a governor of the Technical, Arts and Commercial School; Pope had worked for the Corporation buses and was now Secretary of the EDTC. Dodds had won Central ward for Labour in 1945 but lost to D.H. Broomfield, the Conservative candidate in 1949. Percy Wood, chairman of the Eastbourne Labour Party would be standing in the forthcoming by-election for Central due to the resignation of Mr M. Borton whilst S. Holden would contest Redoubt for Labour. Both locally and nationally the town was full of political activity and interest.

Local Elections 1951

The May local elections produced a familiar pattern in three of the wards where candidates for the Conservative Party were returned unopposed; Mr J. Howlett of the Pier Hotel for Devonshire, Mr. C. Baker, already established in Meads and Major General H. Scott for Upperton. The remaining wards were contested between the Conservative (Con) and Labour (Lab) Parties: (45)

Cavendish – Mr. W. Benson-Dare (Con)	Central – Mr. G. Pryor (Lab)
Mr. F. Pope (Lab)	Mr. F. Swain (Con)
Hampden Park – Mr. H. Mepham (Lab)	Old Town – Mr. H. Archer – (Con)
Mr. E. Paxon (Con)	Mr. P. Wood (Lab)
Redoubt Mrs. E. Fordham (Con)	Roselands Mr. R. Dodds (Lab) - Mrs. F. Llewellyn (Con)
Mr. S. Holden (Lab)	

Mrs Fordham and Mr Holden had contested the Redoubt Ward before in the 1948 by-election with a remarkable result; each had received 1,263 votes! Following a recount Mrs Fordham was returned on a casting vote. Three of the Labour candidates had been former members of the Town Council; Percy Wood had been the leader of the Labour group on the Council for many years before he was defeated in a ward election by Bernard Raven. Both Mr R. Dodds and Mr. S. Holden had earlier Council experience. The political composition of the Council before this local election was Conservative 31, Labour 4 and Independent 1. The domination of Conservative members of the Council in the immediate post-War years was a result of the system by which long-standing councillors could be appointed aldermen. As a majority of most long serving councillors were Conservative, even if they had stood under other titles, the Conservatives were able to maintain a council majority. Hence the 1945 local elections at which Labour won the majority of contested council seats meant that they still did not have control of Eastbourne Council.

The General Election of 1951 was held some 20 months after that of 1950 which the Labour Party had only won by five seats. It was not really the ideal timing but partly a result of King George Vl's concern about his planned tour to Australia and New Zealand at a time when the Government's majority was so small. The Conservatives were way ahead in the polls and the Monarch would have been aware of this situation.

Christopher Attlee, nephew of the Prime Minister, was the Labour candidate. In a meeting held by the Labour Party at Hampden Park Hall in July 1951 he declared, 'I think we have pretty obviously brought the Korean War to an end.' He thought the agreement of the North Koreans and Chinese Communists spokesmen to cease-fire talks in a no man's land town just south of the 38th Parallel was very promising.

The General Election of 1951

In October 1951 Christopher Attlee was able to call upon his uncle, the Prime Minister, to visit Eastbourne and provide support for his candidature. Attlee duly obliged, although he knew that there was little chance in a Parliamentary election at the time of overcoming one of the safest Conservative seats in the country. Some 3,500 people provided a 'mixed reception' in the floral hall at the Winter Gardens at which the P.M. faced a noisy reception. Socialists mainly occupying the front positions cheered loudly whilst those favouring the Tories who took up positions at the sides and rear, booed. Whilst there were many interruptions and interjections in general good humour prevailed. Seventeen year old Mavis Harman Secretary of the Gosport League of Youth who had spoken at the recent Scarborough Conference was applauded enthusiastically by all the audience. (46)

In one early speech mention was made of the Conservatives' promise to build houses which led one of the audience to shout out, 'Yes, workhouses'. By the time the P.M. spoke the audience had overflowed into the foyer and on to the stairs. Attlee's experience as a soldier in the 1914-18 War and the time he spent in the East End of London where he witnessed widespread poverty shaped his political ideas and made him a passionate advocate for providing decent housing, schools and working conditions for ordinary people. These experiences together with those of being a member of the War-time Cabinet were behind his drive to provide good living conditions for all the people in the country. The first ever majority Labour Governments were founded upon such ideas. In a detailed address to the audience, including his replies to comments from those opposed to these activities and policies, he explained their policies.

When he mentioned his time in the War-Time coalition under Mr Churchill a cry of 'Good Old ~Winston' came from the hall, to which he responded by reminding the audience, 'Mr Churchill was rejected by the Conservatives and made Prime Minister by the Labour Party. (Cheers) He told of the 'many sessions when Mr Churchill attacked the pre-War Conservative Government and the members of the Government attacked Mr Churchill.' He went on to speak of the virtues of rationing during the war 'by which means, despite the prevailing difficulties the people were better fed than in times of peace. The general standard of nutrition in this country went up in consequence. That was all to the credit of the government, but he asked, was it not discreditable that under other Governments before that there should have been masses of people suffering from malnutrition. He told of how war-time Government policy organised every aspect of life in the country. Rationing meant that the general clothing of the people was better than it was before the war, when many people had too many clothes and too much food and suggested rationing was as good for them as it was for others.'

What was abundantly demonstrated during the war was that the Government saw that all the citizens were properly fed and properly clothed. That was a new thing. It seemed to us that if it was a good thing to do in war-time, it was also a good thing to do in peace-time.... the result of (these) policies carried on during the past 6 years was that on the evidence of every observer, babies and children in this country were finer than ever before.' Chris Attlee in his speech as the local candidate claimed that he had experienced unemployment for two years before the economy picked up as threats of war with Germany increased. He claimed that under the Labour Governments, 'British coal is the cheapest in Europe and more than one million houses had been built and they were building at the rate of 200,000 per year.' Another constituency he visited was Eastbourne, not because Labour stood the slightest chance of winning there but because Tom's son, Chris Attlee, was the candidate. Writing to Tom he told of how,

'We had some 3,500 in the audience with a large proportion of Tories. Chris made his points clearly and economically. Vi drove me down from Manchester via Chequers doing just under 400 miles for the day without being fatigued. We have had a remarkable tour, immense crowds and great enthusiasm, but what it will all mean in votes I can't tell. Vi always gets a great ovation and received floral tributes everywhere.'

George Vl had plans for visiting the Commonwealth countries and Attlee agreed to hold the Election before the King left the country, which was probably a tactical error in political terms. He informed the King on the 5th September that he would ask for dissolution the first week in October whilst Election Day would be fixed for 25th October. In the event illness prevented the

Monarch from travelling and he died a few months later on the 6th February as a result of coronary thrombosis. This together with the lung cancer he had contracted was a result of his addiction to tobacco for he was a heavy smoker. The result of the 1951 General Election was that whilst Labour were successful in gaining the most votes, indeed polling more than the Conservatives and Liberals combined, they 'lost' the election! Labour increased its vote, receiving, 48.8 per cent of the popular vote against 48 per cent for the Conservatives. But once again, thousands of working class votes piled up in already strong traditional Labour seats. (In two other General Elections in the 20th century the party which won the popular vote did not gain the most seats; 1929 and 1974; a result of the lack of proportional representation in the voting system)

General Election Results 1951

	Votes	% share of votes	seats
Conservative	13,700,000	48.00	321
Labour	13,900,000	48.80	295
Liberal	700,000	2.6	6

Andrew Marr has claimed that, "In private the King expressed fiercely right-wing views, falling into rages or 'gnashes' at the pronouncements of socialist ministers' but whether this had anything to do with his request it is impossible to know. (48) By contrast, Francis Beckett suggests the King had a good relationship with the P.M., who was in any case ex.Haileybury public school and had been a British army officer at Gallipoli during the

First World War. He also suggests that it was Attlee who expressed concern at the small Parliamentary majority when the Monarch planned to visit Commonwealth countries. (49)

Conclusion

Any attempt to write a 'conclusion' to sum up a town or place is likely to run into difficulties. A physical description would state that Eastbourne it is a coastal resort lying to the east of the South Downs which provide some protection from the prevailing south west winds. The planned buildings and gardens along the sea front present a splendid view which always proves attractive to both visitors and inhabitants of the town. Like most towns, social differences can be observed from variations in the style and size of housing within the town, its location and density of population. In 1851 the census recorded a population of less than 3,500 people which had expanded to just over 35,000 forty years later and 60,000 by 1940, only to plunge to 10,000 as widespread evacuation was undertaken within months of the outbreak of the 1939-45 War. With the coming of peace the population began to recover but even by 1951 at 567,801 it was still fewer than it had been in 1921. (50) Yet whilst one can accurately describe it as a traditional, even conservative town, it has undergone social changes like any other place. Moreover these social changes are still taking place thereby rendering stereotypes as of less value today than they ever were. This study provides some evidence for the validity of this conclusion.

References - Chapter 14

(1) *E.Gaz.* 24.1.1951
(2) ibid. 7.3.1951
(3) ibid. 10.5.1950
(4) ibid. 16.5.1950
(5) Spencer, D. (1993) *Eastbourne Bus Story*, p.111
(6) *E.Gaz.* 14.12.1949
(7) Eatwell, R. (1979) *op.cit*.p.90; Hennesey, P. (1992) *Never Again*, O'Morgan, K. (1948) *Labour in Power 1945-51*. pp. 280-283. OUP Hattersley, R. (1997) *Fifty Years On; a Prejudiced History of Britain Since the War*, pp.50-51
(8) Marr, A. op.cit. p.116
(9) Hattersley, R. (1997) op.cit. p.50
(10) Thorpe,A. (1997) ibid. p.133
(11) Morgan, K.O. (1984) *Labour in Power 1945-51*, pp.271-272
(12) McCulloch, G. (1994) *Educational Reconstruction; the 1944 Education Act and the Twenty-First Century*, pp.98-99
(13) *E.Gaz.* 7.2.1951
(14) ibid. 22.3.1950 & 14.2.1951
(15) ibid.
(16) Webb, I. (1999) *The Challenge of Change in Physical Education*, pp.63-64
(17) ibid.
(18) ibid. Considerable changes would take place in future years.
(19) Smith, B. (2014) *Doors of Opportunity*, p.14, Univ of Chichester
(20) *E.Gaz.* 11.5.1949
(21) ibid. 6.7.1949
(22) ibid. 4.7.1951
(23) Kilburn, V. (1996) *Bognor Regis College - A Chronicle of the First 50 Years*

(24) *E.Gaz.* 6.6.1951
(25) *E.Gaz.*8.2.1950
(26) ibid.
(27) ibid. 15.2.1950
(28) ibid. 8.2.1950
(29) *E.Gaz.* 1.2.1950
(30) ibid. 15.2.1950. Hamilton Fyfe (1880-1951) was twice a Labour candidate in Parliamentary elections in Sevenoaks (1929) and Yeovil (1931); he had been a barrister and war correspondent for the *Daily Mirror* and *Daily Herald* during the 1914-1918 War with British and allied armies in Eastern and Southern Europe.
(31) ibid. *E.Gaz.* 15.2.1950
(32) ibid.
(33) Butler, D. & Butler, G. (2000) *20th Century Political Facts 1900-2000,*p.258
(34) *E.Gaz* 22.2.1950
(35) ibid. 26.4.1950
(36) ibid. 10.5.1950
(37) ibid. 16.5.1950
(38) ibid. 15.11.1950
(39) ibid. 21.6.1950
(40) ibid. 7.10.1931
(41) ibid. 11.10.1950
(42) ibid. 9.7.1947
(43) ibid. 10.1.1951
(44) ibid. 21.2.1951
(45) ibid. 9.5.1951
(46) ibid. 17.10.1951
(47) Coxall, B. & Robins, L. (1998) *British Politics since the War*
(48) Marr, A. (2007) *A History of Modern Britain,* p.48
(49) Beckett, F. (2000) *Clem Attlee,* pp.290-292
(50) Surtees, J. (2002) op.cit. p.114

APPENDIX 1

RESULTS OF PARLIAMENTARY ELECTIONS FOR EASTBOURNE : 1885-1951

1885	**Capt. E. Field** (Unionist) [3,561] WGA Wallis (Liberal)[3,497]
1886	**Rear Admiral E. Field** (Unionist) [3,760] Col .J.C. Brown (Liberal) [2,501]
1892	**Rear Admiral E.Field** (Unionist) [4,037] Capt. T.S. Brand (Liberal) [3,674]
1895	**Rear Admiral E. Field** (Unionist) [4,139] Capt. T.S. Brand (Liberal)[4,079]
1900	**Sir L. Lindsay-Hogg** (Conservative) [4,948] Rear Admiral T.S. Brand (Liberal) [4,245]
1906	**H.G. Beaumont** (Liberal) [5,933] Sir L. Lindsay-Hogg (Conservative) [5,303]
1910	**R.S. Gwynne** (Conservative)[7,533] H. Morison (Liberal) [5,249]
1918	**R.S. Gwynne** (Conservative)[11,357] T.B. Hasdell (Labour) [4,641]
1922	**R.S. Gwynne** (Conservative) [14,601] Ald. E. Duke (Liberal) [9,550]
1923	**R.S. Gwynne** (Conservative) [13,276] Thomas Wiles (Liberal) [11,386]
1924	**Sir George Lloyd** (Conservative) [17,583] Capt. J.J. Davies (Liberal) [4,168] Ald. D.J. Davis (Labour) [4,138]

1925	[By-Election]
	Ald. Sir Reginald Hall (Conservative) [12,741]
	H. Johnstone (Liberal) [5,386]
	Lt.Col. B. Williams (Labour) [3,696]
1929	**E. Marjoribanks** (Conservative) [18,157]
	C. Burt (Liberal) [7,812]
	R.S. Chatfield (Labour) [8,204]
	P.E. Hurst (Independent) [2,277]
1931	**E. Marjoribanks** (Conservative) [31,240]
	A.J.Marshall (Labour) [5,379]
1932	**John Slater** (Conservative)
	[Returned unopposed]
1935	[By-Election]
	C.S.Taylor (Conservative)
	[Returned unopposed Twice in 1935!]
1945	**C.S.Taylor** (Conservative) [18,173]
	Duncan Smith (Labour) [12,637]
	J.S. Gowland (Liberal) [2,797]
	W.R. Hipwell (Independent) [524]
1950	**C.S. Taylor** (Conservative) [35,425]
	R. Groves (Labour) [18,304]
	C.H.D.Bate (Liberal) [5,766]
1951	**C.S.Taylor** (Conservative) [39,278]
	C.S.B. Attlee (Labour) [19,217]

APPENDIX 2

Alphabetical List of Councillors and Aldermen (1945)

	Councillor	Alderman (*)
Ashcroft, Harry	1941-1945	
Avard, Albert	1925-1950	1933
Barratt-Terry, Richard	1936-1950	
Bass, George	1934-1952	
Benson-Dare, Walter	1938-1946	
Bignell, William	1944-1948	
Butler, Edward	1945-1947	
Caffyn, Sir Sidney	1937-1974	1944
Croft, Reginald	1936-1964	1943
Davis, Albert	1944-1956	1952
Dingle, Hugh	1941-1948	
Dodd, Sir Robert	1941-1950	
Dodds, Robert	1944-1949	
Haffenden, William	1945-1947	
Hill, Edgar	1930-1952	1938
Hodgson, Herbert	1919-1949	1938
Holden, Stephen	1945-1947	
Hudson, Alice	1919-1952	
Jowett, Herbert	1940-1949	
Marshall, Alfred	1939-1967	1955
Martin, Ernest	1925-1959	1938

Morgan, Horace	1922-1946	
Morgan – Jones, Gerald	1940-1947	
Parker, Gladys	1943-1966	1952
Rainey, George	1945-1955	1964
Richards, Randolph	1938-1952	1949
Richmond, Oswald	1945-1947	
Rush, Arthur	1932-1955	1938
Shard, Robert	1941-1950	
Swain, Frank	1945-1954	
Taylor, Frederick	1945-1964	1950
Thornton, Ellen	1920-1962	1935

(Alfred Marshall was elected in 1913 but joined the British Army and was sent to France)

[Aldermen were abolished in 1974]

Source: Aspen, J.C. (1977) *Municipal History of Eastbourne 1938-1974* Appendix B, pp.265-269.

APPENDIX 3

RESULTS OF LABOUR CANDIDATES STANDING IN EASTBOURNE BOROUGH ELECTIONS 1913-1938

Allen, J.A.	ROSELANDS 1933 (*)
Baldwin, G.F.	ROSELANDS 1923 (-), 1930 (*)
Barnes, H.	CAVENDISH 1937 (*)
Burrows W.W.	ROSELANDS 1919 (*)
Bodero, Miss	HAMPDEN PARK 1919 (-)
Chatfield, R.S.	REDOUBT 1927 (*)
Evans, M.T.	ROSELANDS 1913 (-)
Fitzgerald, G.J.	REDOUBT 1928 (-), HAMPDEN PARK 1930 (-)
Hasdell, Tommy	REDOUBT 1929 (*), 1932 (-), 1935(*), (1938) (*)
Hazeldon, H.R.	CAVENDISH 1924 (-)
	REDOUBT 1933 (-)
	CENTRAL 1934 (-)
Honeysett, D.G.	CAVENDISH 1925 (-)
	ROSELANDS 1935 (-)
Huggett, F.J.	ST MARYS 1913 (*)
Kenyon, Miss	REDOUBT 1930 (*)
Lawrence, C.	ROSELANDS 1922 (*)
	ROSELANDS 1925 (-), 1926 (-)

Marshall, A.S.	CAVENDISH 1913 (*) 1920 (-)
	ROSELANDS 1921 (*) 1924 (*) 1927 (-)
	HAMPDEN PARK 1933 (-)
	REDOUBT 1934 (*)
Packham, J.W.	CAVENDISH 1923 (*) 1926 (-)
Pitcher, J.A.E.	ROSELANDS 1928 (-) 1929 (-)
Prosser, E.T.	REDOUBT 1931 (-)
Richardson, F.	CAVENDISH 1938 (-)
Tomsett, S.R.	ROSELANDS 1937 (*)
Underwood, W.H.F.	UPPERTON 1926 (-)
Uphill, F.	CAVENDISH 1921 (-) 1922 (-)
Walshe, J.P.	ROSELANDS 1936 (*)
Waters, E.C.	ROSELANDS 1931 (-)
Wilkinson, W.G.	CAVENDISH 1919 (-)
	HAMPDEN PARK 1926 (-)
Woods, P.G.	ROSELANDS 1934 (*)

(*) = WON
(-) = LOST

APPENDIX 4

EASTBOURNE TRADE UNION & LABOUR ORGANISATIONS FOUNDED NATIONALLY

1878	Amalgamated Society of House Decorators & Painters (ASHDP)	1872
1888	Eastbourne & District Teacheres' Association (NUET)	1870
1890	Society of Operative Stonemasons (SOS)	1832
1890	Amalgamated Society of Railway Servants (ASRS)	1872
1891	Operative Bricklayers Society (OBS)	
c1891	Amalgamated Society of Carpenters & Joiners (ASCJ) Meetings Wadey's Hotel 33 Terminus Rd, Alternate Mondays 8 pm. Sec: Mr G. Barnes, 82 Tideswell Rd	1860
1897	Ditto	
1901	Ditto Sec Mr W. Buchan, 75 Longney Rd (1902 –25 Cavendish Place)	
1904	Ditto Meet @ 5 Elms Buildings alternate Mondays 8 pm	
1906	Amal.Soc. Carpenters & Joiners, Prince of Wales Hotel, alternate Mondays.	

Sec: Mr. T. Evans, 9 Willowfield Sq.
Eastbourne Bath Chairman's Assoc.
Pres: Lindsay Hogg Esq.M.P.
Sec: James Phillips, 8 Birching St.
Meetings Presbyterian School
Room, Blackwater Rd.,Last Wed each
month.

1907	Amal. Soc. Carpenters & Joiners (v. 1906)	
1908	Ditto	
1909	Amal. Soc. Carpenters (v. 1906)	
	Operative Bricklayers Soc. Sec: W. Hobbs, 343 Seaside, [London 1818] Meet Windsor Tavern, Sat evenings	1829
1910	Amal. Soc. Carpenters. (v.1906)	
	Operative Bricklayers Soc. (v.1909)	
	Amal. Soc. Of Tailors, Terminus Hotel. Sats. 8pm., Sec: W. Field, 30 Tideswell Rd.,	
1911	Amal. Soc. Carpenters (v.1906)	
	Amal. Soc. Tailors, (v. 1909) [London/Manchester 1860s]	
	As United Garment Workers=	1915
	Operative Bricklayers Soc. (v.1909)	
1912	Amal. Soc. Carpenters (v.1906)	
	Operative Bricklayers Soc. (v.1909)	
1913	Amal. Soc. Carpenters (v.1906)	
	Amal. Soc. Tailors, Sec: J. Clarke. Meet Lion Inn, Sats 8 pm.	
	Operative Soc. Bricklayers (v. 1909)	
1914	Amal. Soc. Carpenters – Meets Labour Exchange, Seaside:	
	Sec: Mr M.T. Evans	
	Operative Bricklayers Soc. (v.1909)	

1915	Amal. Soc. Carpenters (.v. 1914)
	Amal. Soc.. of Tailors, Sec:W.Field
1916	Amal. Soc. Carpenters – Sec: W.H. Smith, 87 Langney R.
1917	Amal. Soc. Carpenters – Sec: Albert Leeves, 53 Cavendish Aven.
	Meet Prince of Wales, Seaside Rd.
	Operative Bricklayers Soc. – Sec.Mr Wood
1918.19	Amal. Soc. Carpenters & Joiners
	Amal. Soc. Tailors
1918	Workers' Union – Sec. Mr T. Hasdell, 1898
	1 Linden Terrace, Green St.
	Meetings – Employment Exchange, Seaside.

Eastbourne & District Labour Club, 112-114 South Street
(Open 6 – 10.30 pm each evening: 2.30 – 10.30 pm Wed/Sat)

 President: Mr A. Dillowy
 Vice Pres: Councillor T.B. Hasdell, JP.
 Sec: Mr S.C. Ball
 Asst. Sec: Mr H.C. Boniface

Headquarters of:-

 Eastbourne Trades & Labour Council
 Eastbourne Labour Party [Founded as Lab Representation Committee 1900] – Labour Party= 1906
 Independent Labour Party – local 1893
 branch
 National Assoc. Discharged Soldiers & Sailors
 Journeymen Butchers Federation
 Assoc. Soc. Carpenters & Joiners

	Amal. Soc. Of Operative House & Shop Painters	
	Amal. Soc. Of Engineers (AEU)	1851
	Amal. Soc. Of Locomotive Engineers & Firemen (ASLEF)	
	Amal. Soc. Tailors & Tailoresses	
	National Union of Railwaymen (NUR)	1913
	ASRS – 1871, NUR=	
	Railway Clerks Assoc. (RCA)	1897
	Workers' Union – 4 branches	
	Typographical Society	
	National Union of Coal Porters	
	National Union of Shop Assistants, Warehousemen & Clerks	1891
	Amal. Union of Operative Bakers, Confectioners & Allied Workers	1861
	Postmen's Federation	
1920	Amal. Soc. Carpenters (v.1917)	
	Amal. Soc. Tailors – Sec: Mr W. Pitfield, St Neots, 114 South St.	
	Operative Bricklayers Soc. – Sec: Mr Wood	
1923	Amalgamated Society of Woodworkers (ASW)	1921
	(Trades & Labour Club 114 South Street)	
	(Sec: L.J. Gutsell – 45 Gore Park Rd)	
	Amal. Soc. Tailors, Tailoresses & Allied Workers (Trades & Labour Club –	
	South St – Sec: W. Pitfield – 10 Dudley Rd)	
	Eastbourne Typographical Association – Labour Club – Sec:H.G.C. Hitch	

1924   Amal. Soc. Woodworkers (ASW)
         (v.1923)
Amal. Soc. Tailors & Tailoresses – Sec: J.O. Gallagher, 81 Pevensey Rd.
         Eastbourne Typographical Assoc.
         (v.1923)
         Amalgamated Union of Building Trade 1921
         Workers,
         Trades & Labour Hall, South St.
         Sec: Mr Charles M. Reed, 203 Seaside
1925   Amal. Soc. Woodworkers
         Amal. Soc. Tailors & Tailoresses
         Eastbourne Typographical Soc.
         Amal. Union Building Trade Workers
         Eastbourne & District Trades Council
         & Labour Party, 112-114 South St.
         Sec: John Pitcher
1926   Amal. Soc. Woodworkers –
         Sec:A.T.White, 15 Clarence Rd.
         Amal. Soc. Tailors & Tailoresses – Sec:
         Walter W. Field, 31 Ashford Sq
         Eastbourne Typo. Soc. – Sec: H.G.C.
         Flitch
         Amal. Union of Building Trade
         Workers
         – Sec: Mr Charles Reed, 203 Seaside
1927   Amal. Soc. Woodworkers – Sec: A. T.
         White, 15 Clarence Rd.
         Amal. Soc. Tailors & Tailoresses – Sec:
         Walter W. Field, 31 Ashford Sq
         Amal. Union of Building Trade
         Workers – Sec: Charles M. Reed, 203
         Seaside

1928	Amal. Soc. Woodworkers – Sec: A.T.White, 15 Clarence Rd
	Amal. Soc.. Tailors & Tailoresses – Sec:Walter W. Field, 31 Ashford Sq
	Amal. Union of Building Trade Workers – Sec: Charles Reed, 203 Seaside
1929	Amal. Soc. Woodworkers – Sec: A.T. White, 15 Clarence Rd
	Amal. Soc. Tailors & Tailoresses – Sec: Walter W. Field, 31 Asford Sq
	Amal. Soc. Building Trade workers – Sec: Charles Reed, 203 Seaside
1930	Amal. Soc. Woodworkers – Sec: A.T. White, 15 Clarence Rd
	Amal. Soc. Tailors & Tailoresses – Sec: James Gallogh, 81 Pevensey Rd
	Amal Union Building Trade Workers – Sec:Charles Reed, 203 Seaside

APPENDIX 5

Terms of Agreement for the Reinstatement of Eastbourne Corporation Bus Staff. (1926)

(1) All the men who have been working on the omnibuses during the strike who are eligible and competent and who desire to remain in the Corporation service, shall be retained. The committee believe the number to be about 20.

(2) Those employees who went out on strike to be taken back to work at once. This does not extend to persons, (if any) who have been guilty of violence or intimidation even if they have been reinstated. Any cases of men alleged to have been guilty of violence or intimidation to be notified within one week of the date of the settlement and each man will be afforded an opportunity of having an advocate to present his case to the Emergency Committee.

(3) The Committee is willing to take on all the men who are to be re-instated as they agree as far as may be necessary to work short time up to not later than July 1, 1926. If, however, at the end of the summer service some of the re-instated men have to be discharged the order of discharge shall be according to length of service and efficiency.

(4) The men re-instated shall be re-instated in their old positions and grades, and be entitled to any benefits that are due or may become due in respect of previous service, that is to say men are not to be affected by reason of their having been out on strike. This has always been the intention of the committee acting on the advice of the manager.

(5) There is to be no victimisation of the men retained under paragraph 1, or of the employees who have been already re-instated.

(6) The undertaking given in Clause 3 of the settlement by the Trade Unions with the railway companies to apply.

The settlement was signed on behalf of the Emergency Committee by the Mayor, Alderman R.G. Thornton, Alderman Sir Charles Harding, Alderman G.B. Soddy, Councillor J.W. Woodnough, Councillor A. Avard, and Councellor W.E. Wood.(Chairman of the Motor Bus Committee). The signatories on behalf of the men were: Councillor T.B. Hasdell (district organiser) and Messrs. E.G. Ashdown,

BIBLIOGRAPHY

Addison, P. (1994) *The Road to 1945; British Politics and the Second World War.* Pimlico

Allom, V.M. (1967) *ExOriente Salus; A Centenary History of Eastbourne College*

Arch, J. (1966) *The Autobiography of Joseph Arch* MacGibbon & Kee (1st pub. 1888)

Aspen, J.C. (1977) *Municipal History of Eastbourne 1938-1974*

Attlee, V.M. (1995) *With a Quiet Conscience; Thomas Simon Attlee 1880-1960*

Bagwell, P.S. (1963) *The Railwaymen; A History of the National Union of Railwaymen,* Allen & Unwin

Barnard, H.C. (1961) *A History of Education,* University of London Press

Ball, F.C. (1973) *One of the Damned* Lawrence & Wishart

Banks, O. (1955) *Parity & Prestige in English Education*t, RKP.

Beckett, F. (2007) *Clem Attlee; a Biography,* Politico

Benson, J. (1989) *The Working Class in Britain 1850-1939* Longman

Berry, P. & Gordon, K. (1996) *Around Eastbourne* Sutton Publishing Ltd.

Betts, R. (1998) 'A new type of elementary teacher': George Collins 1839-1891' *History of Education,* Vol.27, No.1

Birch, L. (Ed) (1968) *The History of the TUC 1868-1968,* TUC Pub.

Blackburn, C.J. (1949) *Eastbourne Grammar School 1899-1949*

Blake, R. (1985) *The Conservative Party from Peel to Thatcher* Fontana

Borough of Eastbourne *Council Minutes 1899-1900*

Brivati, B. & Heffernan, R. [Eds.](2000) *The Labour Party: A Centenary History*, Macmillan.

Brown, W.H. (1938) *Brighton's Co-operative Advance* Co-op Union

Budgen, W. (1912) *Old Eastbourne* Frederick Sherlock Ltd.

Butler, D. & Butler, G. (2000) *Twentieth-Century British Political Facts 1900-2000*.MacMillan Press

Caffyn, J. (1998) *Sussex Schools in the 18th Century; Schooling Provision, Schoolteachers and Scholars* Sussex Record Society

Cannadine, D. (1980) *Lords and Landlords; the Aristocrcacy and the Towns 1774-1967* Leicester Univ Press

Chambers, G. (1910) *Eastbourne Memories of the Victorian Period 1845-1902* Sumfield

Clark, A. (1998) *The Tories; Conservatives and the Nation State 1922-1997*, Phoenix

Clark, D. (1985) *Victor Grayson; Labour's Lost Leader* Quartet Books

Clarke, P. (1996) *Hope and Glory; Britain 1900-1990*, Penguin Books

Coxall, W. (1992) 'Bridging the experience gap in the early 1900s: the literary relationship between H.G. Wells and George Meek' *Literature and History* 3rd Series, Autumn

Coxall, B. & Griggs, C. (1996) *George Meek – Labouring Man; Protégé of H.G. Wells*, New Millennium,

Crook, R. (2015) *Eastbourne in Detail*, DG&P, Aves Press Ltd.

Davies, A.J. (1992) *To Build a New Jerusalem*, Michael Joseph

Davies, S. & Morley, B. (2006) *County Borough Elections in England & Wales 1919-1938; A Comparative Analysis, Vol.3, Chester-East Ham.* Aldershot-Ashgate

Davison, L.M. (1990) *'Rural Education in the Late Victorian Era; School Attendance in the E. Riding of Yorkshire 1881-1903'* History of Education, No.45

Durr, A. (1979) 'Sussex Trade Unions 1890-95' *Sussex History* 1.8

Durr, A. (1982) *The Socialist Revival and Sussex*

Eastbourne's Historic Street Furniture, (1984) Eastbourne Local History Society

Eatwell, R. (1979) *The 1945-1951 Labour Governments* Batsford

Elliston. R. (1999) *Eastbourne's Great War 1914-1918,* S & B Publications

Enser, A. (1976) *A Brief History of Eastbourne* Eastbourne Historical Society

Fagan, H. (1975) 'Engels in Eastbourne' *Visual History* No.1, August 1975

Fagan, H. (1976) 'Engels in Eastbourne' *Eastbourne Gazette* 24.4.1976

Foot, M. (1996) *H.G., The History of Mr Wells* Black Swan

Ford, B. (Ed)(1992) *Early 20th Century Britain,* Cambridge Cultural Studies

Fovargue, H. (1933) *Municipal Eastbourne 1883-1933*

Francatelli, C.E. (1852) *A Plain Cookery Book for the Working Classes*

Goldstrom, J.M. (1966-67) *Richard Whately and Political Economy in School Text Books 1833-1880.* Irish Historical Studies Vol. XV

Griggs, C. (1993) 'George Meek the ragged trousered Robert Tressell of Eastbourne' *Labour History Review* Vol.58, No.1, Spring

Griggs, C. (1991) 'The National Union of Teachers in the Eastbourne Area 1874-1916; A Tale of Tact and Pragmatism' *History of Education* Vol.20, No.4

Griggs, C. *The Rise, Fall and Rise Again of Selective Secondary Schooling, in* Cole, M. [Ed] (1989) The Social Contexts of Schooling,Falmer Press

Griggs, C. (1983) *The Trades Union Congress and the Struggle for Education 1868-1925* Falmer Press

Griggs, C. (2002) *The TUC and Education Reform 1926-1970* Woburn Press

Griggs, C. & Wall, D. (1984) 'Eastbourne and the school board era that never was, 1870-1902' *History of Education* Vol.34, No.4

Grossmith, G. & W. (1892) *Diary of a Nobody*

Groves, R. (1975) *The Strange Case of Victor Grayson* Pluto Press

Hailsham, Q. (1990) *A Sparrow's Flight – Memoirs* Fontana

Hammond, J.L. & Hammond, B. (1948 eds) *The Village labourer Vol 2* Guild books

Hannington, W.A.L. (1937) *The Problem of the Depressed Areas*, Victor Gollancz

Hattersley, R. (2006) *The Edwardians* Abacus

Historic Schools in Eastbourne, Eastbourne Public Library reference section, (n.d.)

Hobsbawm, E.J. & Rude, G. (1973) *Captain Swing* Penguin

Hobsbawm, E. (1948) *Labour's Turning Point; 1880-1900*, Lawrence & Wishart

Hobsbawm, E. (1964) *Labouring Men,* Weidenfeld

Hofstader, R, Miller, W, & Aaron, D. (1967 ed) *The United States; The History of a Republic*, Prentice Hall

Hopkins, E. (1979) *A Social History of the English Working Classes 1815-1945* Edward Arnold

Horn, P. (1971) *Joseph Arch 1826-1919; The Farm Workers' Leader* Roundwood Press

Horn, P. (1974) *The Victorian Country Child* Roundwood Press

Humphrey, G. (1989) *Wartime Eastbourne; The story of the most raided town in the south-east.* Beckett Features

Hunt, E.H. (1981) *British Labour History, 1815-1914*, Weidenfeld & Nicolson

Hutt, A. (1962) *British Tyrade Unionism; A short History 1800-1962*, Gollancz

Jackson, B. & Marsden, D. (1952) *Education and the Working Class*, Penguin

Jenkins, R. (1996) *Gladstone* Papermac

Keegan, W. (1984) *Mrs Thatcher's Economic Experiment* Allen Lane

Kilburn, V. (1996) *Bognor Regis College – A Chronicle of the First Fifty Years 1946-1996*

King, C. (1891) *Marching with Music* (Eye-witness account by Bandsman Walter Guy of Salvation rmy Riots of 1891) Eastbourne Public Library - EAS 287.96 (1963)

Kramer, A. (2007) *Sussex Women* Snake River Press

Kynaston, D. (2008) *Austerity Britain 1945-51* Bloomsbury

Lane, T. (1974) *The Union Makes Us Strong*, Arrow

Laybourn, K. (1992) *A History of British Trade Unionism* Sutton Pub.Ltd.

Leslie, K. & Short, B. [Eds](1999) *An Historical Atlas of Sussex* Phillimore

Linehan, T. (2000) *British Fascism 1918-39; Parties, Ideology and Culture* Manchester U.P.

Marr, A. (2007) *A History of Modern Britain* Pan Book.

Mathews, M. (2006) *Captain Swing in Sussex and Kent; Rural Rebellion in 1830* The Hastings Press

McCulloch, G. (1994) *Educational Reconstruction; The 1944 Education Act and the Twenty-First Century* Woburn Press

McKibbin, R. (1974) *The Evolution of the Labour Party 1910-1924* Clarendon Press, Oxford

MacLure, S. (1965) *Educational Documents; England & Wales; 1816 to the Present Day,* Methuen

Meek, G.E. (1910) *George Meek, Bath Chair-Man* Constable & Co.

Mitchell, V. & Smith, K. (1986) *South Coast Railways; Eastbourne to Hastings* Middleton Press

Morgan, K.O. (1984) *Labour in Power 1945-1951* Oxford University Press

Morgan, K.O. (1992) *Labour People; Hardie to Kinnock* Oxford U.P.

Morgan, K.O [Ed.](1984) *The Oxford History of Britain* Oxford U.P.

Morton, A.L. & Tate, G. (1989ed) *A People's History of England* Lawrence & Wishart

Neville, G. (1982) *Religion and Society in Eastbourne 1735-1920,* Eastbourne Historical Society

Pedley, R. (1962) *The Comprehensive School,* Penguin

Pelling, H. (1976) *A Short History of the Labour Party,* Penguin

Pugh, M. (1994) *State and Society; British Political and Social History,1870-1992,* Edward Arnold

Pugh, P. (1987) *Grand Hotel-Eastbourne,* Grand Hotel

Richardson, S. *Political Worlds of Women; Gender and Politics in 19th Century Britain*

Richardson, W. (n.d.) *The People's Business; A History of the Brighton Co-operative Society* Brighton Co-operative Society

Robert, S.K. (Ed)(2003) *Centenury Essays on the WEA,* Pluto Press

Seldon, A. [Ed.] (1996) *How Tory Governments Fail; The Tory Party in Power since 1783,* Fontana

Seldon, A. (1998) *Major – A Political Life* Phoenix

Simon, B. (1965) *Education and the Labour Movement 1870-1920* Lawrence & Wishart

Simon, B. (1960) *Studies in the History of Education 1780-1870* Lawrence & WishartSmith, B. (2014) *Doors of Opportunity,*Univ. Of Chichester.

Spears, H. (1981) *Eight Town Walks in Eastbourne,* Eastbourne CivicSociety

Spencer, D. (1992) *Eastbourne Bus Story,* Middleton Press

Stevens, L. (1987) *A Short History of Eastbourne* Eastbourne Local History Society Publication

Stevenson, J. & Cook, C. (1994) *Britain in the Depression: Society and Politics, 1929-1939*

Surtees, J. (1992) *Barracks, Workhouse and Hospital; St Mary's, Eastbourne 1794-1990* Eastbourne Local History Society Publication

Surtees, J. (2002) *Eastbourne – A History* Phillimore

Surtees, J. (1994) *The Princess Alice Hospital and other Eastbourne Hospitals*, Eastbourne Local History Society

Thomas, H. (1965) *The Spanish Civil War* Penguin

Thorpe, A. (1997) *A History of the British Labour Party* Macmillan

Taylor, A.J.P. (1977) *English History 1914-1945*. Book Club Associates

Todd, A. (1967) *Beyond the Blaze: A Biography of Davies Gilbert* D. Bradford Bar

Tressell, R. [i.e. Robert Noonan] (1914, 1967 & 1981) *The Ragged Trousered Philanthropists*, Grant Richards, etc.

Vigar, J. (n.d.) *The Lost Villages of Sussex* The Dovecote Press

Vine, W. (1978) *Old Willingdon* Webb & Reed

Webb, I.M. (1999) *The Challenge of Change in Physical Education* Falmer Press

Williams, F. (1945 *Fifty Years March; The Rise of the Labour Party* Odhams Press

Theses

Thomas, I. (2010) *Confronting the Challenge of Socialism; the British Empire Union and the National Citizens' Union 1917-1927* M.Phil., Univ. Wales

Webb, I.M. (1977) *The History of Chelsea College of Physical Education with Special Reference to Curriculum Development 1898-1977* Ph.D. Univ. of Leicester

Video

Marching to Music (2012) Director: Jonathan Wilde, Riot Film Group

Journals:
Eastbourne Chronicle
Eastbourne & District Advertiser
Eastbourne Gazette
Eastbourne Herald

Name Index

Adam, Charles 50
Adam, Hugh 334
Alexander, Mrs 48
Allcock, F.W. 201
Allen, Frederick 75,80, 81, 215
Allice, R. 320
Anderson, E. Martyn 320
Anderson, A.W. 367
Anderson, Sir John 421
Arch, Joseph 8,53
Archer, H. 449
Askwith, George 286
Aspen, J.C. 469, 471
Austen, Jane, 15
Atherton, John 457
Attlee, Christopher 493
Attlee, Clement 374, 493
Atlee, James 59
Avard, A 265, 293
Aveling, Edward 142

Babbage, Charles 22
Baker, C 492
Balfour, Arthur, J. 40, 41
Baldwin, Stanley 249, 252, 253, 256, 267,312, 313, 352, 253.
Ball, S.C. 233

Banks, Joseph 18
Bancroft, Eleanor 144
Baring, Maurice 183
Barlow, Montague 290
Barton, R.F. 379
Bass, George 335,450, 451, 490
Bate, C.H.D. 479, 482
Bathuurst, W.A. 90
Beaumont, H. xv, 170, 303
Beaverbrook, William Maxwell 254, 299, 390
Beckley, Sydney 221
Bell, Andrew 65
Bell, Barbara 456
Bell, Richard 170
Belloc, Hilaire 183
Benson, Dane, W. 449,489
Bevan, Aneuran 460,461
Bernstein, Edward 142
Beveridge, William 417
Bevin, Ernest 136, 251, 417
Bird, W.L.W. 320
Blatchford, Robert 138, 139, 229
Bolero, M. 320
Booth, Charles 57
Borton, M. 492

Bowes, G.E. 424, 425, 427
Bowles, Henry 183, 185, 285
Boyd-Carpenter, Archibald 297
Boyden, G. 468
Bracken, Brendan 418
Brady, J. 451
Brand, Admiral 75
Bray, E.C. 470
Briggs, Fielden 200
Brockway, Fenner 354
Brodie, Alexander 46, 66, 67, 77
Brodie, Emma 49
Brodie, William 49
Brogden, S. 475
Broomfield, D.H. 491
Brown, Isabel 391
Bruning, Clemence 353
Burke, Thomas 36
Burn, Charles 287
Burns, John 136, 142
Burt, Cyril 305
Busby, F.H. 395, 443, 485
Byron, Lord & Lady xix

Cade, J. 6
Caffyn, Sidney 303, 367, 411, 417, 473, 481
Callaghan, Alfred 238, 240
Campbell-Bannerman, H 285
Campbell, H. Miss 301
Campbell, John Ross 312
Cameron, Gordon 194
Campion, Sydney 188
Cancellor, G.W. 186
Carey, Walter 371–2

Carter, Frank 200
Castle, Barbara 460
Cavendish, S.A.H. 17, 30, 61
Chadwick, Robert Burton 286
Chadwick, Edwin xix, xx
Chamberlain, Joseph 36, 40
Chamberlain, Neville 250, 386, 387
Chambers, George, F 76, 93, 130, 191, 205, 284
Chatfield, R.S. 265, 276–278, 305, 308–9
Champion, H.H. 137
Chaucer, Geoffrey 6
Churchill, Randolph 183
Churchill, Winston 249, 255, 289, 412, 419, 434, 449, 461
Cole, G.D.H. 374
Collins, G. 119
Compton, Elizabeth 12, 29–30
Compton, Fay 484
Connell, Jim 137
Cook, Arthur 251
Cooper, Duff 417
Court, H. 375
Courtledge, C. 484
Cramp, T.C. 235, 259, 267
Crane, H. 458
Cremer, W.R. 55
Cripps, Stafford 374
Crisford, Carlos 50
Crook, A. 430
Cruttenden, Edward 171

Davenport, H.D. 86
Davidson, J.C.C. 254
Davy, Humphrey 18
Dawson, Geoffrey 297
Delves, G. 176
De Pinto, H.J. 427
Devonshires;
 4th Duke p.29; 5th 29; 6th, 30, 493, 497; 7th, 12, 30, 31, 36, 46, 73, 74, 76; 8th 35–6, 39, 41, 73, 89.
Dewhurst, Wynford 291
Dickens, Charles xxiii, 13
Diggle, J.R. 80, 85
Dodds, Robert 491, 493
Douglas, Bate, C.L.H. 477
Driberg, Tom 460
Du Cross, Harvey 170

Eden, Anthony 386
Edgerton, Eric 470
Elliot, Walter 417
Engels, Frederic 57, 138, 142–3
Evans, Maurice 195, 200–202
Evans, W.M. 355

Faber, Walter 297
Farnswork, C.R. 259
Feather, Vic 484
Ferdinand, Franz 219
Field, E. 75
Fitzgerald, Charles 183
Flemming, Gilbert 468
Fletcher, J.B. 85
Forbes-Robertson, D. 368
Fordham, E. 492

Forster, William 68
Forvargue, H.W. 268, 416
Franco, Francisco 354
Fraser, James 54, 299
Freeman, John 461
Freeman-Thomas, Freeman 170
Fry, Elizabeth xix

Gaitskell, Hugh 461, 463
Gallagher, Willie 229
Galsworthy, John 15
Garwood, F.S. 319
Gaskell, Elizabeth 15
George 1V 474
George V 253
George, Lloyd 188, 239, 248–9, 255
Gilbert, Carew 28–9
Gilbert, (Giddy) Davies 12, 16–19, 21–25 74–5, 83, 89,
Gilbert, Mary 12, 22–7
Gladstone, William Ewart 36, 169
Gollancz, Victor 374–5
Gorst, John 284
Glennell, John 193
Gowland, J.S. 431, 434
Graham, Richard 124
Gray, Ernest 120
Grayon, Victor 179, 184, 188, 286
Greenwood, Arthur 421
Gregory, Arthur 188
Grindley, Archibald 419
Groves, Reg 397, 459, 477–480, 482

Guesoult, G.S. 399
Gwyer, Maurice 473
Gwynne, R. xv, 183–186, 226, 238, 240–1, 254, 285, 293, 303.

Haffenden, W.F. 439, 458
Haldane, J.B.S 374
Hall, Reginald 262, 288, 292 303–4
Hamilton, George 44
Hankey, Maurice 259
Hardie, Keir 137, 142, 170, 184, 228–9, 286
Harman, Mavis 493
Harvey, Harry 320, 437
Hasdell, T. 231, 233–6, 240–1, 263, 265, 269, 273, 306, 335–6, 273, 294, 306, 335–336, 406
Haster, J. 273
Hastings, Patrick 312
Hawkins, Christopher 19
Hazleden, Henry 487
Henderson, Arthur 228–9, 307
Herbert, A. 419, 481
Hill, Charles 426
Hill, E.T. 436
Hipwell, W.R. 431, 434
Hitler, Adolph 354, 356–7, 386, 388, 390
Hodgson, H.J. 277, 293
Hogg, Lindsay 170
Hogg, Quinton 310
Holbrook, A. 290
Holden, S. 492–3
Holmes, Kenneth 468

Holyoake, George xix
Honeysett, B.G. 259, 262, 267, 437
Hopley, Thomas 97
Horsburgh, Florence 419
Howard, Blanche 30
Howlett, J.Huggett, F.J. 213, 492
Hudson, Alison 302
Huggett, F.J. 198
Hulbert, Jack 484
Humphrey, George 382
Hunt, E.D. 397
Hurst, P.E. 305
Hyndman, H.M. 136, 139

Irwin, J.J. 72

Jacks, M.L. 472
James, William 363
Jeeson, P. 259
Jewell, Charles 238
Johnson, T.W. 233
Johnstone, Duncan 183, 285
Jones, Hesketh 88
Joyce, William 351

Keay, T. 122, 196
Kent, Weller 293, 301–2, 319, 324
Kenyatta, Jomo 373
Keynes, John Maynard 250
Kille, H.J. 233–4
King, William xix
Knight, C.J. 273, 321, 326, 336, 381, 427
Koestler, Arthur 374
Korostrovetz, V. 362–3

Lampson, Olive, B. 288
Lancaster, Joseph 64–5
Lane, A.H. 287
Langham, J.R. 73, 86
Lansbury, George 136, 189, 214, 228–9, 252
Laski, H. 422
Law, B. 254
Lawrence, T.E. 304
Leaf, William 33
Lee, A.W. 451
Lee, E. 490
Lessner, Frederick 142
Lindle, Alfred 137
Lloyd, George 303–4
Lomas-Smith, R.W. 320
London, Jack 57

Macaulay, Thomas 119
Macklin, Roy 473
MacDonald, Ramsay 138, 177–8, 180–1, 229, 252, 310, 312
MacLachlan, Lachlan 293, 331
MacNamara, J.J. 120
McLaren, Andrew 289–90
Magginess, R.S.Mallon, J 210, 216
Mann, Tom 136, 142
Marjory-Banks, Edward 299–300, 303, 305, 308–310, 328
Marlowe, Thomas 253
Martin, E.C.Mason, J. 294
Marx, Eleanor, 142–3
Marx, Karl 142
Mathews, Charles 296, 320

Meek, George xxii, 8, 34, 53, 109–111, 141, 144–145, 159, 160–1, 165, 171, 173–4, 176, 178, 180, 221, 225
Meek, Joe 162
Mikardo, I. 460
Mitford, Percy 284
Morant, Robert 39
More, Hannah 64
Morris, William 136, 142
Morrison, William Epps 51
Mosley, Oswald 349–50, 417

Newman, G. 308
Nicolson, Max 19, 417
Noonan, Robert 34, 57, 113, 155
Novello, Ivor 484

Odets, Cifford 374
Offord, William 485
Orwell, G [v. Blair] 99, 374
Ottley, Bickersteth 75
Owen, Robert xix, xx, 65

Paine, Tom 19
Parker, Leonard 470, 481
Parker, Thomas 8
Parnell, Charles, Stewart 35
Parillia, Progresso 367
Paxton, E.437, 449
Pay, E.J. 171, 173
Peters, E.C.P. 234
Phillips, Marion 235
Pickard, Benjamin 55
Pitcher, J 264
Pitfield, W. 194
Pitman, Thomas 45, 75, 120

Pocock, Roger 294
Pollitt, Harry 252
Pope, Frank 491
Poppy, T.G. 446
Pownall, F.G. 144
Prior, James 200–1
Pryor, G 440

Quirk, George 141, 148, 188, 206–7

Raikes, Robert 64
Rainey, George 439, 490
Ramell, M.H. 319
Rawnsley, Martin 456
Raven, Bernard 493
Renton, Don 366
Ridsdale, Edward 170
Roberts, H. 234
Robertson, Alexander 308
Robeson, Paul 484
Rosa, Grace Catherina 28
Rowe, T.B. 199
Rowntree, Seebohn 57
Rudfall, W. Russell 427
Rush, A.E. 336, 379, 406
Ryder, Alfred 98, 158
Ryder, Thomas 98

Salazar, Antonio 354
Schreiner, Frederick 94
Scott, H 492
Shaw, George, Bernard 138, 252
Sheperd, Dick 387
Shinwell, Emanuel 288
Simon, John 252
Skinner, Ald 397
Slater, John 284, 303, 313

Smart, Russell 141
Smiles, Samuel 20
Smith, Duncan 431–2, 434–5
Smith, Fred 377
Smith, W.H. 260
Snowden, Anthony 138, 312, 314
Snowden, Philip 250, 313
Soddy, Frederick 265, 324, 326
Spencer, David 269
Spender, Stephen 374
Stanley, Lynch 81
Stephen, Uriah 167
Strachey, John 374, 417
Summers, Spencer 419
Surtees, John xxi
Swain, Frank 439, 449, 473

Talbot, Edmund 170
Taylor, Charles xv, 293, 303, 316, 319, 356–7, 361, 364–5, 382, 386–8, 390, 397, 414, 427, 431–2, 434, 479–80,
Taylor, Fred 456
Temple, Fred 288, 292, 295
Terry, Barratt 369
Terry, Richardson 325
Thomas, Howard 458
Thompson, J 233
Thorne, Will 136, 228–9
Thornton, E.M. (Miss) 302, 322–3, 365
Thornton, G. Ridley 265, 273, 319, 321–3, 370
Thorpe, S.M. 359
Tillett, Ben 137

Tressell, Robert
  [v. R. Noonan]
Trevithick, Lionel 18
Trory, Ernie 391
Truman, Harry, S. 460
Turner, Harry 366
Turner, Lionel 381

Uphill, Frank 296

Villiers, Ernest 170
Vine, George 163
Vrooman, Walter 34

Wallace, W.R. 289
Wallis, George 13, 31–2, 36–7, 345
Walton, J.H. 319
Ward, P.E. 472
Warner, S.M. 292
Warwick, Daisy 136, 252
Watkins, R.E. 359
Watt, James 18
Webb, Beatrice 39, 138
Webb, Sydney 138, 249
Welch, Joseph 118, 121–2, 197, 199
Wellesley, Victoria 46
Wells, Herbert George 58, 138, 179, 182
Whelpton, George 47
Whately, Richardson 24
Wheatley, John 311, 377
Wheeler, J. 334, 367, 381
Whelpton, George 47
Whitbread, Samuel 20, 63
Wilkes, Vaughan 296
Wilkinson, W.G. 319
Williams, Raymond 347
William, Herbert 419
Williams, R 441
Willoughby, W G. 347–8
Wilson, Harold 460–1
Wood, Percy 232, 261, 335, 374, 379, 424, 432, 437, 442, 456, 473, 492–3
Wood, W.E. 272
Woolnough, J W 265, 274, 276, 278, 293, 319

Yolland, Colonel 116
Young, J 171–3, 179
Young, Lucas 424
Yoxall, James 120

Zinoviev, Grigorly 312

Subject Index

Acts of Parliament:
  (1832) Reform Act, 22
  (1833) Ten Hours Act, 143
  (1842) Mines Act, 143
  (1844) Factory Act, 143
  (1867) Reform Act, xvi, 143
  (1870) Education Act, 121, 124
  (1918) Representation of the People Act, 234
  (1928) Equal Franchise Act, 321, 365
  (1946) National Health Service, 459
  Nationalisation of Coal, 249, 459
  Nationalisation of Civil Aviation, 459
  National Insurance Act, 459
  (1924) John Wheatley Housing Act, 312
  (1875) Mutiny Act, 312
  (1919) Royal Commission – Coal Mining, 249
Alcohol – Conflicts of Interest, 33–5, 51, 188, 234
Australia, 4

Bathing Huts, 156
(1942) Beveridge Report, 417–419, 421
Building Trade, 111, 114, 155, 486–7
Brighton, 3, 12, 105, 122, 130, 181, 194

Captain Swing, 6, 8
Catering Wages Board, 458
Cavendish Estate, 31
Child Labour, 62
Coastguard Cottages 11
Conferences:
  ATTI (1950), 455
  NALGO (1950), 455
  NUGMW – Catering (1948), 455
  Co-operative Society, 2
  Weights & Measures Inspectors (1949) 455
Holiday Trade, 456, 485
Trading Estate, 457
Winter Gardens, 494
Youth Movements, 56–7

Dental Estimates Board, 486

Eastbourne Town Council, 268

Trading Estate Eastbourne
Council Expenditure,
1932:
  Workers' Voluntary
  temporary Pay Cut,
  Eastbourne Secondary
  School Building
  Programme:
    Broderick Road, (1939), 466
    Willingdon (1953) 466
  Education: Parliamentary Acts:
    (1870) Forster, 68, 121
    (1902) Cockerton, xxv, 415
    (1918) Fisher, 347, 415
    (1944) Butler, 414, 463–6
Madras System, 65, 67
NSPCK, 65
Nursery Facilities, 237
Robert Raikes Sunday Schools, 64

Flag Days:
  (1926) General Strike, 273–4
  World War 2, 412
Food Rationing, 444–5
Franchise – Extension, 208, 214, 234, 238
Freemasonry, 272, 283
Free Trade, 40, 315
Freedom Association, 294

General Election:
  (1906)   170–1
  (1910))   186
  (1918))   241, 284
  (1931))   305, 310–1, 314
  (1932))   364
  (1935))   364
  (1950))   476, 482
  (1951))   493–4, 497
Local Elections:
  (1883)   191
  (1913)   196–7
  (1933)   308

General Strike, 248, 254
  Effects in Eastbourne, xxiv
  Emergency Council Committee, 265–269
  Lord Mayor's Fund, xxv
  Meeting at Labour Party H.Q., 259
  Recreation Ground Rally xxv
Germany, 225, 239–40, 352, 354, 379, 386, 390
Gilbert Estate, 12

Hastings, 3, 12, 105, 113, 130, 194
Health:
  Eastbourne hospitals taken over by Ministry of Heealth, 346
  Improvements in Health – Children, pp.347–8
Hotel & Caterers' Association:
  The Grand, 159, 182, 262
  Queens, 160

House of Commons, 189
House of Lords, 16, 294
Housing:
  Eastbourne Housing Programme - Shortages1930's, 440, 444
  John Wheatley Housing Act, 312

Jack Cade Rebellion 1450, 6

Labour:
  8 Hour Day, 237
  Equal Pay: 154, 208, 35, 445–8
  Labour Club, 138, 257, 264
  Labour Movement, 89, 128, 137–8, 170, 196, 257, 264
Leaf Hall, 33–4, 172
League of Nations, 236, 238, 355
Liberal Party, 150–1, 293
(1958) Local Government Act, 6

(1948) Marshall Aid, 463
May Day, 451, 458, 483
Ministry of Health, 237, 451, 458, 483
Mortality Rate – Eastbourne, 132–3
(1882) Municipal Corporation Act, 6

National Health Service: 237–8, 422–8, 448, 459, 461, 480

National Union of Unemployed Workers, 379
Nationalisation, 237
NSPCC, 127
NSPCK, 71–2
Newspapers:
  British Gazette – 255, 259
  Clarion – 150, 169, 171, 177, 181
  The Courier – 144
  Daily Express – 253
  Daily Mail – 253, 299, 313
  Eastbourne Chronicle – 87, 89, 191, 196, 201, 204–5, 218, 241, 259, 261–2, 318, 327, 350
  Eastbourne Gazette -164, 175, 186, 200, 256, 260, 276, 290, 296–299, 305–6, 311, 314, 318, 325, 352, 354–5, 391, 435, 449.
  Eastbourne Herald – 189, 457
  Justice – 137, 169, 171, 181
  Labour Leader - 171
  Morning Post - 297
  New Statesman - 255
  The Schoolmaster - 118
  Sunday Chronicle - 138
  Sussex Advertiser - 26
  The Times - 297

Old Age Pensioners, 237
'Old Town', 11

Parish Relief, xx
Paupers, 23
  (1381) Peasants Revolt, 5
  (1348) Plague, 5
Poor Law, 20–1
Political Ideas:
  Bolshevism, 309, 232, 312
  Fascism, 258, 287, 297, 348–9, 352–3, 355, 389
  Pacifism, 387
  Proportional Representation, 232
  Social Democratic Federation, 136, 181
  Socialism, 136, 161
Political Associations/ Pressure Groups:
  Ancient Order of Shepherds, 283
  Clarions, 138, 140, 176
  Conservative & Unionist Club, 169, 282–5, 292, 362
  Constitutional Club, 283
  Eastbourne & District Trades Council, 193–4, 207, 257, 283, 308, 324–8, 457,
  Economic League, 283, 294, 304
  Empire Crusade, 286
  Fabian Society, 138, 170
  Independent Labour Party, 180, 193, 388
  League of Frontiersmen, 294
  Left Book Club, 373–4

National Citizens' Union, 251, 283, 286–95, 298, 301, 318–9, 323, 325–6, 363
(1872) National Society for Womens' Suffrage, 214
Noble Order of Crusaders, 286–8, 297
Primrose League, 183–5, 188, 216, 239, 272, 283–4, 293
Ratepayers' Association, 153–4, 293, 319, 323, 363
Right Book Club, 375
S.E. Federation of Socialist Societies, 171, 173–4, 176, 178, 180
Trades Union Congress, 250–1, 255–6, 263
Womens' Suffrage, 190, 213
Workers' Educational Association (WEA) 373–4
Places of Worship:
  All Saints 45
  Norway Mission & St George, 49
  St John's 45
  St Saviours, & Wesleyan Methodists 45, 58, 76
  St Marys, All Souls & Holy Trinity xxi, 44–7, 63, 66, 69, 223, 297–8,

Holy Trinity, 45, 47,
  69–70, 297
Primitive Methodist, Our
  Lady of Ransom,
  49–50, 53, 194
Primitive Baptists, 52, 58
Salvation Army, 50-1,
  192, 274, 402
Christ Church, 59, 69, 71,
  88
Society of Friends
  (Quakers) 50, 64, 223

Railways:
London, Brighton &
  South Coast Railway,
  11, 115–7, 129
Rearmament, 461–3
Religion:
Church of England, 46,
  53–4, 67, 74–7, 79,
  82, 84, 89, 92, 370
Opposition to School
  Boards, 73
Religious Beliefs, 371–373
Rented Pews, 45
Resistance to Women
  Mayors, 322–3

Schools:
Attendance Committee,
  122–4
Corporal Punishment,
  95–7, 127
Elementary Schools, 93, 95
Fee-paying, 93–5, 98–9, 416
Literacy, 62
School Boards, 5, 61–2

Sea Houses, 11
Sporting Clubs:
  cricket, 159
  golf, 159
  soccer, 158
  tennis, 158

Teachers:
  328–9
  Equal pay, 129
  Post 1945 shortages, 469
  Training colleges:
    Bognor Regis, 469
    Eastbourne, 471, 474
    Chelsea College, 469–70
Theatres:
  Devonshire Park, 13, 110,
    127
  Hippodrome, 189–90
  Winter Gardens, 13, 484
Trade Unions/Associations:
  5, 375–82, 454
  Amalgamated Soc. of
    Carpenters & Joiners,
    112
  Amal. Soc. Of House
    Painters/Decorators,
    43, 257, 488
  Amal. Soc. of Railway
    Servants, 115–7, 170
  Amal. Union of
    Confectioners, 377
  Associated Soc. of
    Locomotive Engineers
    & Firemen, (ASLEF),
    257
  National Federation of
    Women Teachers, 154

National Union of
  Mineworkers, 253–4,
  256, 371
National Union of
  Railwaymen, 129, 257
National Union of
  Teachers, 117–8,
  120–1, 125, 127,
  129, 154, 328–9
National Union of Vehicle
  Builders, 303
Operative Bricklayers
  Society, 112
Railway Clerks
  Association, 257
Society of Operative
  Stonemasons', 112
Strikes:
  General Strike (1926),
    xxv, 248, 270–84,
  Rhymney, 272
Transport:
  Bathchairs, 108–11
  coastal shipping, 11
  Electric trams, 130
  omnibus system, 267–70
    (Voluntary pay cut,
    335–6

Unemployment, 115,
  328–32, 335

Villages:
  Alciston, 4, 63
  East Dean, 4, 63, 67
  Ferring, 46
  Folkington, 4, 63
  Friston, 63
  Hankham, 4
  Heathfield, 63
  Jevington, 4, 58, 67
  Polegate, 115
  Westham, 4, 63
  Willingdon, xxvi, 4, 58,
    67, 122, 163
  Wilmington, 4

Working Class, 187, 190,
  192–3, 234
Workhouses, 34
Wars:
  (1870–71) Franco-Prussian,
    219
  Boer Wars, 139, 294
  (1914–18) World War 1,
    139, 214, 219, 226,
    228, 232, 236, 247–8,
    251, 294, 313, 386,
    498
  (1936–39) Spanish Civil
    War 10–12, 356,
    366–70, 375
  (1939–45) World War 2,
    346, 411, 422, 460,
    498
  Air raids, xxiv, 412–3,
    440
    Air raid shelters, 405–7
  ARP/ARW, 387
  British Legion, 388
  Evacuation:
    To Eastbourne, xxv,
      392–400
    From Eastbourne, xxv,
      401–5, 498
  Territorial Army, 388